· SC

PHILOSOPHY AND GEOGRAPHY III

PHILOSOPHIES OF PLACE

Philosophy and Geography   *A Peer Reviewed Journal*

Sponsored by the Society for Philosophy and Geography

Editors:

Andrew Light, Departments of Philosophy and Environmental Studies,
State University of New York, Binghamton,
Jonathan M. Smith, Department of Geography, Texas A & M University

Assistant Editor: David Roberts, University of Alberta

Associate Editors: Yoko Arisaka, University of San Francisco; Jean-Marc
Besse, Collège International de Philosophie à Paris; Edward Dimendberg,
University of Michigan; Thomas Heyd, University of Victoria; Eric Katz,
New Jersey Institute of Technology; Jonathan Maskit, Denison Univer-
sity; Don Mitchel, Syracuse University; Rupert Read, University of East
Anglia; Richard Schein, University of Kentucky; Joanne Sharp, University
of Glasgow

Volume I: *Space, Place, and Environmental Ethics*

Volume II: *The Production of Public Space*

Volume III: *Philosophies of Place*

Volume IV: *Aesthetics of Everyday Life,* Forthcoming, December 1999

Volume V: *Moral and Political Dimensions of Urbanism* (submission
deadline: September 15, 1999)

See page 307 for submission guidelines.

PHILOSOPHY AND GEOGRAPHY III

PHILOSOPHIES OF PLACE

Edited by
ANDREW LIGHT
and
JONATHAN M. SMITH

ROWMAN & LITTLEFIELD PUBLISHERS, INC.
Lanham • Boulder • New York • Oxford

ACABOO

20.9.99

ROWMAN & LITTLEFIELD PUBLISHERS, INC.

Published in the United States of America
by Rowman & Littlefield Publishers, Inc.
4720 Boston Way, Lanham, Maryland 20706

12 Hid's Copse Road
Cumnor Hill, Oxford OX2 9JJ, England

ISSN 1090-3771

ISBN 0-8476-9094-6 (cloth : alk. paper)
ISBN 0-8476-9095-4 (pbk. : alk. paper)

Printed in the United States of America

♾ ™ The paper used in this publication meets the minimum requirements of
American National Standard for Information Sciences—Permanence of Paper
for Printed Library Materials, ANSI Z39.48–1984.

Contents

4. Afterword

List of Illustrations

Acknowledgments

The present volume was supported by The University of Montana Foundation Excellence Fund. We are very grateful to President George M. Dennison and James A. Flightner, Dean of the College of Arts and Sciences, of The University of Montana, for their exceptional support of this publication. We would like to thank the Department of Philosophy at The University of Montana, the Geography Department at Texas A&M University, and the Department of Philosophy at the State University of New York at Binghamton, especially Tony Preus and John Arthur who have worked exceptionally hard to make a new home for the journal at Binghamton. At Rowman & Littlefield we thank Maureen MacGrogan, Robin Adler, and Jon Sisk for their continued work on this annual. A special thanks to David Roberts, now of the Philosophy Department at the University of Alberta for continuing his stellar work as Editorial Assistant. His efforts have once again been crucial in the completion of this volume.

As always, we are grateful to our referees who provided comments on the numerous manuscripts that were submitted to this issue. In addition to our Associate Editors, and many members of the Editorial Board, we wish to thank the following scholars for serving as manuscript referees: Allen Carlson, Matthew Gandy, Jeff Gritzner, Tom Huff, Roger King, Eugene McCann, Dorit Naaman, Mary Ann Tétreault, Paul Thompson, Zev Trachtenberg, Gail Presby, Dan Williamson, and Michael Zimmerman.

Introduction:
Philosophies and Geographies
of Place

Jonathan M. Smith, Andrew Light, and David Roberts

As with the two previous volumes of *Philosophy and Geography*, we have drawn together here a collection of papers on a topic that is receiving increased attention from philosophers, geographers, and many others in the humanities and social sciences.[1] While our prior editions of this peer-reviewed annual have focused on particular social issues concerning the environment (volume I) and public space (volume II), here we have taken a step back to consider the ontological and moral components of the location of these phenomena and others: place itself. But what is a place?

A place has two aspects that make it upon first inspection appear fundamentally unsuited to philosophical analysis. It is, first, heterogeneous—an assemblage of elements thrown together by diverse and sometimes contrary forces. Second, it is concrete, specific, and difficult to generalize. Immanuel Kant recognized the first aspect when he identified a distinct "geographical description of nature" that takes account of things "according to the places that include them on the earth," and that he contrasted with "a system of nature" based on concepts and "*logical* classification."[2] G. K. Chesterton recognized the second aspect when he wrote that "a place is not an abstraction, but an actuality." It has an identity in the strict but simple sense that it is itself, and not, or at least not entirely, a type, kind, or specimen.[3]

Beginning in the 1950s, geographers struggled to eliminate these difficulties by treating places not as actualities but as abstractions. Walter Christaller's central place theory reduced places to a range of types defined by economic function, and it described ideal spatial patterns of these types, such as might appear in a world altogether simpler and more orderly than our own.[4] William Bunge reduced places to spatial relations expressed as relative distance, and urged geographers to abandon carto-

1

graphic representation for the greater precision and abstraction of descriptive mathematics.[5] This spatial science reduced every place to a specimen, a thing essentially similar to all other places of its type. It was, and remains, undoubtedly useful to many geographical theorists, but for others this reduction of places to their theoretical essence was and is deeply troubling.[6] By 1972 the president of the Association of American Geographers warned members that "if one 'cleans up,' so to speak, complex problems by abstraction, oversimplification, and unambiguous categorization when the problems are inherently 'dirty' in their complexity, then humanity may be done a considerable disservice."[7]

Spatial science could not accept or appreciate what theologian Reinhold Niebuhr called the "profound arbitrariness of the givenness of things."[8] It recognized the apparent arbitrariness of places, to be sure, but then did its best to clear this away and reveal their deeper order. For Niebuhr, arbitrariness is not a nuisance, though, nor an impediment to understanding; it is, rather, evidence of the central role of freedom and creativity in an underdetermined world. Geographer Doreen Massey describes it as the "happenstance juxtapositions that occur in place" and often give rise to unique emergent qualities.[9] Places are properly depicted as human places—the creations and habitations of human beings—only insofar as they are revealed as settings in which humans can act.[10]

Geographers today are reluctant to apply the stiff brush and strong soap of abstraction to the dirty complexity of places. They have not abandoned theory but since the mid-1970s have worked to devise theories suited to places rather than places suited to theory. In many cases these theories have emphasized the subjective or intersubjective construction of places through imagination or discourse, sometimes to a degree that verges on mentalism. J. Nicholas Entrikin has followed a more promising tack, proposing that an adequate view of place can be had only from "a position that is between the objective pole of scientific theorizing and the subjective pole of empathetic understanding."[11]

This return to the experienced actualities of place has caused many geographers to seek the company and counsel of philosophers. As attention shifted from the economic efficiency of places to the social justice of places, some geographers found themselves involved in questions of moral and political philosophy. At the same time, a growing interest in individual experience and the structure of feeling lead others to grapple with phenomenology. Martin Heidegger's concept of dwelling, with its apparent relevance to problems of environmental degradation and psychological alienation, was particularly attractive.[12]

This intellectual movement coincided with a surge of popular interest in place. Environmentalists were sounding the alarm over destruction of natural places, unique and irreplaceable habitats that were being transformed into mass-produced commodities and monotonous, reputedly soulless, housing tracts.[13] Others looked to place for a secure anchor to stabilize personal identities at a time when traditional social roles were collapsing.[14] When one has lost any clear sense of who one is, it is consoling to know precisely where one is.

These antimodern reactions were powerfully reinforced by trends in postmodern consumerism. Place was caught up in the wave of connoisseurship that swept over America in the 1980s and 1990s—the same wave that brought us gourmet coffee, microbreweries, and the improbable revival of cigars. Places reflect, heighten, and prolong moods.[15] Places permit or prevent desired and undesired social interaction. Places carry clear and widely recognized connotations of social status. Increasingly sophisticated consumers demanded places that did all of these things in increasingly various and subtle ways, and marketers and developers provided what consumers demanded, a stunning array of carefully contrived places.[16] This is why every new restaurant is dripping with personality, and every new housing development is stiff with character.[17] This is why, according to geographer Paul Knox, the most striking characteristic of new places in the postmodern city is their remorseless stylishness.[18]

This volume is made timely by these trends in intellectual and popular life, and by the need to apprehend clearly the nature and significance of place in an age of accelerating time-space compression. The "miracle of the annihilation of space," which the New York *Tribune* first reported in 1844, has deeply altered the meaning of place, but it has not diminished the significance of place.[19] The ever-accelerating flow of goods, people, and information that we call globalization testifies to the fact that places remain different in ways that matter deeply. We might even say that humans have chosen to annihilate space because they recognize the value of place.

Philosophies of Place

The Christian Bible presents a philosophy of place in which every thing and person has a proper place, although few if any of them are presently in that place. It might be described as a theory of displacement.[20] In the fifth century B.C. Hippocrates presented an alternative philosophy of place. His naturalistic exposition of human disease and diversity, *Airs, Waters, and Places*, argues that humans are creatures of the places they inhabit.[21] The first philosophy of place prizes freedom and movement, necessities for the exile who would find his way home. The second philosophy of place prizes rootedness and local knowledge, necessities for the autochthon who would tighten his grip on home.

These are the two great themes in western thinking about place.[22] With time the first took secular form, and the heavenly home to which men aspired became an earthly place somewhere in the future. The second followed a long, complex, and occasionally bizarre career, and in time provided the intellectual foundation of environmentalism. Environmental historians like Donald Worcester and sociologists like William Julius Wilson are intellectual heirs of Hippocrates.[23]

These two philosophies of place are not necessarily incompatible; in fact, they combined to form a third philosophy of place, one which maintains that "to immerse oneself in what one most deeply feels is a proven route to the universal."[24] This was developed by Romantics who believed that transcendental understanding could be gained through private meditations on the particularities of people, things and places. It caused Romantic writers and painters to emphasize the singularity of their subjects, to attend to detail and to emphasize peculiarity.[25] It lead Henry David Thoreau to believe that a full and sufficient understanding of the universe could be had within walking distance of Concord, Massachusetts.

Making Places

Philosophies of place are intimately bound to practices of place making. The paradigm of all places is the sacred place, which Mircea Eliade described as "a break in the homogeneity of space."[26] Yi-fu Tuan echoes Eliade when he describes the universal human impulse to "transform space into home or world."[27] David Harvey takes a very similar position when he describes "the process of place formation" as one of "carving out 'permanences' from the flow of process creating space."[28]

Places are carved out of ambient space by several interconnected processes.[29] Of these, the simplest is the act of marking the place, as when Wallace Stevens placed his jar on a Tennessee hill and brought order to the sprawling wilderness. The act of marking is often followed by the act of naming, and the act of naming by the act of narration. As Paul Carter argued, "by the act of place-naming, space is transformed symbolically into place, that is, a space with a history."[30] Story tellers and authors make a place by giving a location significance and identity, by humanizing topography with history. This is why Henry Glassie contends that "history is intrinsic to the idea of place."[31]

The carving out of places is also accomplished through intentional reorganization of the physical world. This building is, as Heidegger noted, an inescapable consequence of human dwelling, since one's presence in a place almost always involves one in altering and rearranging that place to one degree or another.[32] Clearing sticks and stones from a spot on the forest floor where one wishes to sit is a minor expression of the same place-making impulse that leads humans to construct cities. This reorganized physical world is properly called a landscape, which J. B. Jackson defined as "a space or collection of spaces made by a group of people who modify the natural environment to survive, to create order, and to produce a just and lasting society."[33]

Humans make places to suit themselves, and often to suit others like themselves. This is not to say that power to make place is allocated equally, or even that those with the power to make places succeed in making exactly the places they would have liked to make. Place making is always hemmed by constraints imposed by nature, finance, and the law, and it is always debased by the necessity for compromises between multiple goals. But insofar as any individual or group succeeds in making a place, it will be a place that enables the individual to be himself or herself, or the group to be itself. This is why the making of places is ultimately part of the shaping of people.[34]

Changing Places

Places continuously change. Great crossroads and emporia of the past, such as Timbuktu and Merv, have shrunk to relative insignificance, while parvenu metropolises, such as Los Angeles and Buenos Aires, have grown in only a century or two to centers of enormous size and influence. Places change beyond recognition in a lifetime. Small towns evacuate, industrial centers collapse into smoldering heaps of brickdust, surviving residents surrender to a new local mood of despondency.[35] Cornfields are paved, mirrored glass towers rise amidst pine trees, natives and new arrivals imbibe a new local mood of euphoria.

These changes are familiar enough to anyone with even a passing interest in places. The processes behind these changes are complex, and largely beyond the theme of this volume, but they have one aspect that is of immediate relevance.[36] Places today are commodities in an international market, and they must to an unprecedented degree sell themselves as tourist destinations, industrial sites, or bundles of amenities suited to this or that class of prospective resident. The increased importance of global-scale processes has brought about a corresponding increase in the importance of place. Populations, ideas, investments, goods, weapons, and pollution move more or less freely across increasingly porous international boundaries; with the buffer of the state reduced, individual localities are more and more exposed to the vagaries of these global flows.[37] This globalization has prompted every place to adopt elaborate strategies to capture the flows it finds attractive (capital, tourists) and escape those it finds distasteful (refugees, nuclear wastes).[38]

Misgivings

The modern mind is attracted to the concept of place, and yet misgives when it considers the concept with any care. It cannot help but to notice that place is always exclusive, and the modern mind likes to imagine itself opposed to exclusion in any form. The placeness of a place is a subjective or intersubjective creation, and therefore apparent only to the individual or group members who create it. Each one of us has experienced the disappointment of excitedly introducing a friend to a favorite place, and then sensing the incomprehension at the heart of their feigned pleasure. Each one of us has stood amidst an exulting and admiring crowd, and looked without emotion upon what was for us an insipid and uninspiring scene.

The placeness of a place is also a legal and social creation, the product of rules and conventions that set territory aside and reserve it as the exclusive domain of certain types of human behavior and certain types of human beings. Violators, as they say, will be prosecuted, peacefully if possible, violently if necessary. Indeed, the threat of violence stands behind every place. Whether dealt out by individuals, gang members, vigilantes, the police, or some more or less official armed force, violence is the existential ground of place. People fight over places. In fact, nearly all fighting is fighting over places, over who will possess them, and over which peoples and behaviors will be permitted in them.

Place is difficult to theorize because of its confused and intractable qualities. It also arouses suspicion because it is undeniably associated with exclusion and xenophobia. Nevertheless, place remains an incorrigible philosophical problem, if only because it so fundamentally structures human experience. It is deeply human to make places, and to think in terms of places. Indeed, there seems good reason to believe, along with many of the contributors to this volume, that place is a satisfying, humane, and responsible way by which to approach larger questions of environmental prudence and social justice.

Contents of the Volume

The contents of this volume are divided into three sections, each approaching some of the themes above, but divided into questions of meaning, ethics, and economic, political and technological consequences of the notion of place. The essays range from specific analyses of particular places to more general treatments of theoretical concerns involving the idea of place. A final afterward by Holmes Rolston on broader notions of the Earth itself as a place closes the volume.

The authors in the first part of the volume explore the connection between place and meaning; these papers range from a general treatment of the subjective components of place to three very specific studies of particular places. For all of these authors, our lives take on meaning through our interaction with our environment, and that interaction characteristically occurs in a specific place. Indeed, the nature of places—geographical and cultural features—plays a prominent role in the formation of our identities, both as individuals and as groups. Places both take on the meanings of the lives lived in them and modify those meanings in a dialectical relationship.

Opening the volume is Jeff Malpas's "Finding Place: Spatiality, Locality, and Subjectivity." Here, Malpas undertakes a historical evaluation of the notion of place as such. A coherent account of place is lacking, despite the notion's ubiquity in contemporary thought. Rejecting the idea that place should be left to its intuitive, "everyday" vagueness, Malpas contends that an account of place as such is necessary if the notion is to play a prominent theoretical role in contemporary philosophy. The first part of Malpas's essay is historical. Beginning with Plato and Aristotle, and proceeding through fifth century theologians, fifteenth and sixteenth century Renaissance thinkers, early twentieth century scientific writers (particularly Einstein), and contemporary theorists such as Foucault and Lefebvre, Malpas traces the way that space has increasingly been identified as a featureless container, a void, an inert receptacle for objects. This conception of space leads to a subsidiary, derivative role for place; place, on this account, is simply a location, a set of coordinates, within abstract space. Some contemporary writers have attempted to distance themselves from this notion by stressing the affective aspects of place. However, simply conjoining place-as-location with emotional responsiveness does nothing to enhance our understanding of place as such.

In the latter half of his essay, Malpas sketches an account of place that distinguishes it clearly from space and gives it the prominence it deserves given its ubiquity in contemporary thought. This account is traceable, somewhat indirectly, to Heidegger. The key to this account is found in a revelation of subjectivity as part of the scope of place. Rather than viewing place as an outcome of our subjective appropriation of space, Malpas urges, we should view place as a *precondition* for the very possibility of subjectivity. On this account, place is primary; it is "a structure within which and with respect to subjectivity is itself established." This account, if true, has several implications. First, it demonstrates that no objective conception of space will yield an understanding of human beings in the world. Second, it urges on us a method of philosophy that is a "matter of coming to understand things through their interconnection rather than their reduction, through recognition of their complexity rather than their simplification." Malpas concludes by asserting that a coherent and inclusive account of place is of more than simply ecological import; it is a matter of finding and understanding ourselves.

Next, in "In Its Place: Site and Meaning in Richard Serra's Public Sculpture," James Dickinson investigates the role of place in the aesthetic, social, and cultural constitution of the art object, focusing on the "site-specific" art of Richard Serra. Dickinson traces the history of site-specific art from its roots in antiquity to its contemporary expression in minimalist critiques of modern art. He closely analyzes the minimalist critique and shows how Serra's ideas about site specificity and public sculpture emerge from a dialogue with that critique. In the final section Dickinson provides an extended analysis of *Tilted Arc,* a public sculpture commissioned from Serra for the New York City Federal Plaza in 1981. Dickinson shows how *Tilted Arc* is a direct expression of Serra's ideas about site-specificity, including the ways that it can transform both a specific site, aesthetically, and a viewing subject, phenomenologically. The arc serves as an "anti-environment," drawing the viewer's attention to the dialogue between sculpture and site. The essay concludes by discussing the history of controversy that has surrounded *Tilted Arc,* culminating in its removal in 1985. The controversy reveals the tension between an elite of abstract artists and a public weaned on anthropomorphic, historical public sculpture and more conventional identifications of place.

Next, in "Sites of Symbolic Density: A Relativistic Approach to Experienced Space," Katya Mandoki attempts a conceptual mapping of the experience of place onto Einsteinian relativistic space for the purpose of a detailed analysis of Mexico City. Einstein prompted a sea change in physics with his proposal that space and time are part of one four-dimensional continuum. This space-time fabric is not homogenous; rather, the presence of higher or lower densities of matter produces warps of varying size in the fabric. Mandoki contends that this idea maps intuitively onto the way that we have experienced space, private and public, throughout history. Certain things or events of significance produce warps in experienced space; that is to say, they become symbolically dense and thus produce a kind of cultural gravity. Examples of symbolically dense sites range from Mecca to Jerusalem to Mount Moriah to Graceland. What is called for, then, is a kind of symbolic cartography that maps these sites and explores their histories. Bachelard and Baudrillard have both attempted symbolic topoanalyses of the private sphere, showing how domestic space is organized around centers of significance from the hearth centuries ago to the television today. This proclivity for arranging spaces around centers of symbolic significance, says Mandoki, "attests to a human tendency against a homogenous, neutral, and flat space."

The same is true of public spaces. Mandoki demonstrates this fact at length through an historical analysis of the central square in Mexico City, the Zócalo. The square is built over the very spot where the Aztecs built their capital city, México-Tenochtitlán. Mandoki traces the accrual of layers of meaning upon this site, beginning with its mythological significance to the Aztecs, through its imperial significance to Moctezuma, its colonial significance to Cortés, and finally its significance for the battling powers of the past two centuries in Mexico. She shows that geographical and economic considerations do not reveal any compelling reason why the center of power in Mexico should again and again be located on this particular site; to explain that fact, one has to take into account its symbolic density, the gravity of its accrued significance. In her concluding sections, Mandoki asserts that symbolically dense sites become laden with power; thus, the colonialization of such sites is often a crucial step in the adoption of authority. This hints at the fact that not all such sites are worthy of celebration.

From New York and Mexico, we then travel to Israel. In "Transformations in the Myth of the Inner Valleys as a Zionist Place," Izhak Schnell traces the development of the myths surrounding the *Emek*, the inner valleys of Zionist settlement. Through a study of memoirs, poetry, and literature of the period, Schnell traces the way that the *Emek* has been represented in terms of space and its relationship to human beings. The paper begins with a short discussion of method. Schnell explicates and defends a hermeneutic methodology, claiming that art bears a representational relationship to reality and that it can capture qualities of the way the external world is socially constructed. These works of art are interpreted within a broader theoretical framework and read as token representations of that framework. Schnell elucidates five stages in the artistic representation of the *Emek*. The first characterizes the valleys as a land of milk and honey that would comply willingly with Zionist settlement. This characterization was common among diaspora Jews who had not yet made, or were just beginning, their settlement journey. The second stage characterizes the valleys as a wasteland, and was born of the settler's day-to-day experiences in taming a hostile environment. This stage was a result of harsh living conditions and a sense of isolation. The third stage depicts a hostile nature that must be overcome and tamed through determination and sacrifice. The fourth stage arose from those who were raised in the valley, and in the shadow of its myth. The final stage relegates the valley to the periphery and focuses on the failings of the society of Zionist settlers. Schnell concludes his paper with a brief theoretical reflection on the dialectic relationship between human beings and their environment, that is, the particular places where they find themselves. This dialectic is ubiquitous, Schnell asserts, and develops in discernible stages represented in works of art.

The authors in the second section, "Place and Ethics," explore ways that places urge moral obligations upon us and ways that we can properly respond—individually and culturally—to those obligations. The increasing attention in contemporary thought to notions of place bespeaks, among other things, a felt need to articulate values that have been lost or underemphasized in modern ethical and political thought. Places, and their specific histories and features, are worthy of our moral attention. Attachment to and respect for a particular place is more, our authors contend, than a "sentimental" or merely emotional affectation. Rather, a sense of rootedness in a place is an important part of what it means to be human, and that sense deserves an explicit and prominent place in moral deliberation.

In the first paper, "Democracy and Sense of Place Values in Environmental Policy," philosopher Bryan Norton and geographer Bruce Hannon address a thorny question of central importance to environmentalists: can a democratic society impose the necessary restrictions on natural resource use? Part of the key to their answer involves an articulation of sense of place values. The authors begin by contrasting two sorts of environmental policy making. Top-down approaches emphasize central control and decision making, while bottom-up approaches attempt to protect local prerogative. The two approaches contrast most importantly in their methodology, the way that they aggregate interests and values. The top-down approach urges an emphasis on those values that are aggregable across space. That is to say, centralized policy making is most likely to take into account those values that can be applied evenly to all places alike. Naturally, the principal value that lends itself to this sort of quantification and all-purpose application is economic value—market prices recorded as dollar value. However, claim the authors, the economic value theory used by top down policy makers systematically overlooks place-relative values, or as they term them, "sense of place values." If some environmental values are importantly place relative, then an approach to policy making that necessarily accepts only values aggregable across space will be deficient for developing appropriate environmental policy. The authors contend that sense of place values are (1) conditionally transferable, (2) local, (3) culturally constitutive, (4) pervasive, and (5) partially measurable. Each of these characterizations is explicated and defended.

Only a bottom-up approach, one based, to the extent possible, on local control, can accommodate these place-relative values. The reason for this is that these values are so context-dependent that they lose their character when aggregated across multiple communities. A bottom-up approach will be "multiscalar," or scale-sensitive. It will rest the burden of proof on centralized controllers to show why, in any given case, central control should trump local control. This should be true even of national or international environmental problems. The authors conclude by gesturing at some of the ways that a bottom-up approach could be realized in today's policy and planning, asserting that doing so would amount to an about-face in the trend towards centralization. The advantage is that bottom-up planning is more robustly democratic, thus answering with a hearty "yes" the question that begins the essay.

Next, in "From the Inside Out: The Farm as Place," Ian Howard turns to an analysis of a particular locus of environmental problems, namely, the farm. Howard argues that a sense of place can serve as a way of addressing environmental problems at the farm level. He begins by characterizing these environmental problems as problems of design. Namely, do we design farms for production and profit solely, or do sustainability and human flourishing play a part in the design process as well? Howard claims that sense of place, a sense of connectedness to a landscape, can foster sustainable farming practices. Sense of place suggests an insider's rather than an outsider's view. An outsider's view characterizes farms in terms of yields, energy inputs and outputs, hydrological effects, etc., whereas an insider's view characterizes farms in terms of the historical and affective ties that it has to a community. Howard ties the notions of place and of the insider's view to four objectives of farming: improvement in productivity and environmental health; beautification, and by extension the nurture of wild habitats; promotion or inculcation of moral character; and engagement with living processes and the places in which they flourish. Howard explains how a sense of place can encourage and advance each of these objectives, thus lending implicit support to Norton's emphasis on local control. The essay concludes with a general justification of the notion of sense of place in farming. Too often, it has been assumed that ethical dimensions related to farming must hinge on attitudes that are universal and disinterested. Indeed, the ecological approach to farming often falls into these traps, assuming that farming principles must be derived from universal, overarching ecological principles. However, this attitude tends to drive a wedge between farmer and farm and encourage the outsider's view that has led to current ecological problems. Instead, Howard urges, we should focus on and encourage the sense of intimacy between farmer and farm. We should center the producer more firmly in the context of place, in the producing landscape.

The opening suggestion of David Glidden's "Commonplaces," and the theme throughout, is that philosophers ought to be wary of their discipline's long tradition of generality at the expense of local particularity.

Too often this rush to the general, the universal, has been undertaken at the expense of marginalized victims. Glidden suggests another path to wisdom, one that he traces to the roots of ancient philosophy, manifested in one form in Aristotle's notion of *epigoge*. This is a rough-and-ready form of knowledge that seeks first to adequately picture the way that nature presents itself. Epicurus called it *metabasis tou homoiou*, or traversing common ground, "where salient similarities trigger associations connecting particulars together, without requiring the forceful linkage of a more rigorous abstraction which would strip away the separately defining identities of individual cases and localities." Glidden compares this way of knowing with that of the anti-dogmatic Greek physicians, who were content to record those patterns of life that lead to health and to sickness, and to treat symptoms with what had been shown to work, rather than proceeding from an overarching dogma about the nature of health. Something similar, Glidden says, is needed today in our thinking about places and communities.

Glidden applies this narrative approach to two examples. The first is the North Beach community in San Francisco, a place that has for the better part of a century been an Italian enclave but which is now increasingly encroached upon by Chinatown. The stories that Glidden tells about his time in North Beach emphasize the peaceful diversity of the area, the way in which diverse cultures have kept their identity while living amenably together. The second narrative is from Mammoth Lake in Mono County, California. Glidden tells the story of how various factions in the community were instructed at a town meeting to draw their vision of the future of the community rather than verbally describing it. By avoiding rhetoric and argument and focusing on *seeing* the best community in their minds, these factions discovered that they shared many more commonplace values and goals than they had thought. Glidden concludes by saying that these visions of pre-theoretical commonplaces, which are often brought to the fore by the kind of picturing done by travelers and novelists, can serve as a rudimentary basis on which to communicate with one another about the strengths and possibilities of the places we hold dear and the communities that inhabit them.

The authors in section three, "Changing Places: Political, Technological, and Economic," explore the ways that contemporary places are changing (or can change) and the ways that groups and identities are transformed as a result. In our contemporary world of globalization, which makes it easy and frequently obligatory for us to travel great distances, places rarely remain static. Places are transformed by technological developments, by the actions of governments, and by global market forces. New technology often allows us to transcend particular places. Governments, at the local and national level, are increasingly called on to regulate use and access to particular places. And global market forces have often meant the demise of traditional place-centered lifestyles as the division between good and bad jobs and living spaces grows and the segregation of the rich from the poor sends the former into sprawling suburbs and the latter into squalid and deserted inner cities.

The section begins with an empirical discussion of the problems involved in preserving place-bound ways of life against political and economic considerations. In "Can a Sense of Place Be Preserved?" David Wasserman, Mick Womersley, and Sara Gottlieb focus on the particular challenges raised in Calvert County, Maryland, a rural county bordering the Chesapeake Bay on the edge of Washington D.C.'s rapidly expanding suburban frontier. The authors began their study by gathering together four focus groups—middle- and upper-class suburbanite newcomers, old-time white residents, African-Americans, and watermen—and discussing with them their sense of place, their feelings about suburbanization, and their connections to the natural features of the county.

Because place-attachment is formed through a history of human interaction with natural features of the landscape, it is often subject to retrospective revision. It is also political, in the sense of privileging one or more groups. Retrospective revision was evident in the way that the old-time residents, who had once identified with one small area of the county or other, now, in response to the encroachment of outsiders, identified with the county as a whole. It was also evident in the way that both old-timers and watermen had sharpened and exaggerated their sense of past social cohesion in the face of an influx of newcomers, too numerous to be enculturated or educated about the place. The political dimensions of place-attachment can be seen in the somewhat less developed place-attachment evident in the African-American population of the county. Their attachment to natural features seemed to be occluded by considerations of race, and their memories of the "old times" were far less sentimental and utopian than those of their white neighbors. Also, the authors found place-attachment to be closely associated with the built environment, as old buildings gained new respect from residents and the urban landscape became more homogenous.

In the final section of the essay, the authors discuss the future of place. The authors suggest that, like community, place is not disappearing as a value so much as changing. One significant change, dealt with extensively later in this section by Philip Brey, is the decreasing importance of idiosyncratic natural features for the development of residents' place-attachment. The newcomers to Calvert County expressed an appreciation for the natural beauty of their new home, but their appreciation was generic and passive—"Platonic" in both senses of the word. It did not pick out specific features, nor did it involve any desire for or appreciation of hands-on interaction with the natural environment. Thus, their sense of place tended to be more associated with the built environment and less visceral than that of the watermen.

Nevertheless, much of the impetus toward natural preservation comes from newcomers. They tend to view nature as a pastoral abstract, and the "hands-off" attitude of their preservationism is in contrast to the messy and ambiguous hands-on relationship to the land of the watermen. Still, the watermen have not provided a more robust alternative. How can ways of life that are in close contact with nature be preserved? The authors conclude by discussing several recent alternatives, from bioregionalism to "smart growth," and point out their dangers and tensions in relation to the fishing culture of Calvert County.

In "New Meanings of Place: The Place of the Poor and the Loss of Place as a Center of Mediation," Lea Caragata discusses two important functions of urban places: as a space for association and mediation and as a ground for self-representation by its inhabitants. Globalization has spurred profound changes in the way we view cities and the way we think about place. Some inhabitants have been enabled by globalization to transcend place, while others are excluded from this opportunity. Cities, and especially city centers, have traditionally served as a place where groupings of diverse kinds of people come together and engage in discourse about shared and diverging social goals and interests. These centers of mediation have been crucial in resolving conflicting needs. However, globalization has led to segregation, both of work places and of living spaces. Those who have been privileged by this process increasingly view social mediation as unnecessary and undesirable. This attitude is legitimized by the increasing tendency to view the poor as responsible for their own plight. Thus, there are fewer and fewer shared spaces and opportunities for chance interaction.

Public spaces have therefore become bifurcated. On the one hand, the middle class increasingly views the public parts of cities as a jungle, a dangerous wilderness populated by various predators. On the other hand, there are those spaces that the middle class "reclaims," expelling the poor or disadvantaged, creating a segregated and privileged space that might still go by the name of a "public" park. As this process accelerates, it reinforces itself, and citizens forget the power of truly public spaces. Spaces for alternative or resistant life practices fade.

Next, in "Space-Shaping Technologies and the Geographical Disembedding of Place," Philip Brey defends what he calls the "geographical disembedding thesis," which asserts that geographical features play a decreasing role in the constitution of a place's identity due to the increasing prevalence of space-shaping technologies. Places, for Brey, have become geographically disembedded, cut loose from the idiosyncratic geographies that once largely constituted their identities. Brey discusses, in turn, four kinds of space-shaping technologies. The first are time-space compression technologies. These decrease distances between places in time-space, a theoretical construct that includes the time to travel between places, the cost of traveling, and the availability of travel. The second are time-space distancing technologies. These are technologies that enable the expansion of social fabrics and mechanisms such that a social order may be held in place even when its constituents are separated by vast physical space. The third are space blending technologies, a subset of space-time compression technologies that, rather than simply reducing relative distance, eliminate it and thereby free social relationships entirely from their dependence on geographical place. The fourth kind of technology discussed is computer technology. Brey offers an extended defense of the thesis that cyberspace can meaningfully be thought of as a place and that many activities are being relocated to that place.

Brey concludes by endorsing the trend in geography of conceiving of space, place, and distance pragmatically, in relation to human activity. Only with this kind of conception will we be able to make sense of current trends whereby distances between places are decreased or eliminated and places themselves become increasingly independent of the geographical features that once constituted their identity.

Finally, in "Something Wild? Deleuze and Guattari and the Impossibility of Wilderness," Jonathan Maskit poses a series of metaphysical questions related to the place of wilderness. Our intuitive notion of wilderness is that of an unnamed, unknown, mysterious Other to culture; however, Maskit points out that our attachment to wilderness springs from our feelings for particular places, and to the extent that we interact with these places and develop feelings for them, they are named, known, and bounded. Thus, Maskit urges his readers to rethink what they mean by wilderness, and to focus on a more broad conception of wildness. Maskit turns to the work of Deleuze and Guattari, specifically their notion of "smooth" and "striated" spaces to further this argument. The smooth/striated distinction lines up (loosely) with that between "earth" and "territory." Smooth space is that in which free movement is possible; it is uncharted, aesthetic, expressive, filled with becomings rather than Being. Striated space is that which has been codified, gridded, mapped, reduced to language; it is the space of the State. Maskit emphasizes that this is not a metaphysical dualism in the tradition of "nature vs. culture;" there is no pure case of either space, and all spaces are in a continual process of being smoothed or striated. If we think of wilderness as a purely smooth space, we must acknowledge first that no such space has ever existed and second that no such space is possible. In this sense, wilderness is impossible.

Wildness, however, is possible. Spaces can be more or less smooth. Thus, Maskit calls for a reconception of wilderness as primarily wild—characterized as "historically smooth space." This notion is admittedly fuzzy and ambiguous, and tied to normativity, but in its ambiguity it fits the world, where real spaces are always in process, always temporal and historical. Viewing smoothing and striation as historical processes raises some interesting problems. First, why should we value smooth spaces over striated ones? A second and more practical problem for contemporary ecologists, particularly those involved in ecological restoration, is the following: can a process sponsored and carried out by the State be anything but a process of striation? "One need only look at what has become of Yosemite Valley, Yellowstone, and the Grand Canyon for evidence of State striation in the name of protection."

In our final section, Holmes Rolston III takes a step back to offer a brief "apologia" for a view of the world as a place. In "Down to Earth: Persons in Place in Natural History," Rolston argues that Earth itself is as far as we know unique among planets in being a "storied place." On Earth there is a natural history, and within that a biological history, and within that a cultural history, and within that a host of individual biographies. The logic of these stories, and of humans' place within them, is narrative. There is no theoretical argument or framework that can present these histories as conclusions following inevitably from certain premises; the best any scientist or philosopher can do is to "begin to sketch nesting sets of marvelous tales."

While human beings are natural creatures, we are more than that as well. The development of culture, which speeds the transmission of information from generation to generation, provides humans with "an exodus from mere nature." The dialectic of nature and culture is our "home territory." However, Rolston notes, this should not be taken as a justification of human domination over nature. Rather than "looking down on" "lower" creatures, we ought to "look out over" and to "look out for" other orders of life. We are both immanent and transcendent; the former roots us in our natural, local "residence," the latter allows us to experience, value, and protect the whole. This amounts to a new argument for an older idea: "stewardship over creation."

While humans are Earth's only species of moral agents, Rolston claims that the time has come for ethics to gain further transcendence, to move from interhuman ethics to a global ethics. Importantly, this is done from a particular culture, a particular place—that is, from immanence—but it moves always towards transcendence, towards valuation of Earth as the source of value and values.

Common among all the papers in this volume is the claim that focusing on place invites us to move from the general to the specific, from the abstract to the particular, in all humanistic endeavors. As the papers suggest, our sense of self, home, community, nation, and history is tied into our sense of place. We are, in a certain sense, constantly in dialogue with where we are as an inextricable part of who we are.

Notes

1. Andrew Light and Jonathan M. Smith, eds., *Philosophy and Geography I: Space, Place, and Environmental Ethics* (Lanham, Md.: Rowman & Littlefield Publishers, 1997); Andrew Light and Jonathan M. Smith, eds., *Philosophy and Geography II: The Production of Public Space* (Lanham, Md.: Rowman & Littlefield Publishers, 1998).

2. George Kish, ed., *A Source Book in Geography* (Cambridge, Mass.: Harvard University Press, 1978), 399–400.

3. G. K. Chesterton, *The Common Man* (New York: Sheed and Ward, 1950), 217.

4. Walter Christaller, *Central Places in Southern Germany*, trans. C. W. Baskin (Englewood Cliffs, N.J.: Prentice-Hall, 1966).

5. William Bunge, *Theoretical Geography*, Lund Studies in Geography, Series C1, 2nd ed. (Lund: C.W.K. Gleerup, 1966).

6. Nicholas Entrikin has recently warned that social reductionism seems to have replaced spatial reductionism. J. Nicholas Entrikin, "Place and Region 2," *Progress in Human Geography* 20 (1996): 215–221.

7. Norton Ginsburg, "From Colonialism to National Development: Geographical Perspectives on Patterns and Policies," *Annals of the Association of American Geographers* 63 (1973): 1–21.

8. Reinhold Niebuhr, *Beyond Tragedy: Essays on the Christian Interpretation of History* (New York: Charles Scribner's Sons, 1937), 8.

9. Doreen Massey, "Questions of Locality," *Geography* 78 (1993): 142–149.

10. Antony Flew, *Thinking about Social Thinking*, 2nd ed. (Amherst, N.Y.: Prometheus Books, 1995), 111–33.

11. J. Nicholas Entrikin, *The Betweenness of Place: Towards a Geography of Modernity* (Baltimore: Johns Hopkins University Press, 1991): 133–34.

12. The most recent work in this theme is Anne Buttimer, *Geography and the Human Spirit* (Baltimore: Johns Hopkins University Press, 1993).

13. James Howard Kunstler, *The Geography of Nowhere: the Rise and Decline of America's Man-Made Landscape* (New York: Simon & Schuster, 1993).

14. Richard Sennett, "Something in the City: the Spectre of Uselessness and the Search for a Place in the World," *The Times Literary Supplement* no. 4825 (Sept. 22, 1995): 13–15.

15. J. M. Howarth, "Nature's Moods," *British Journal of Aesthetics* 35 (1995): 108–120.

16. Joel Garreau, *Edge City: Life on the New Frontier* (New York: Doubleday, 1988), 222.

17. For a discussion of themed environments, see Mark Gottdiener, *The Them-*

ing of America (Boulder, Co.: Westview Press, 1997). For a discussion of neotraditional design as a means to create a sense of place, see Andres Duany and Elizabeth Plater-Zyberk, "The Second Coming of the American Small Town," *Wilson Quarterly* (Winter 1992): 19–50.

18. Paul Knox, "The Restless Urban Landscape: Economic and Sociocultural Change and the Transformation of Washington DC," *Annals of the Association of American Geographers* 81, 2 (1991): 181–209.

19. Robert W. Desmond, *The Information Process: World News Reporting to the Twentieth Century* (Iowa City: University of Iowa Press, 1978), 103–4.

20. Jonathan M. Smith, "Ramifications of Region and Senses of Place," in *Concepts in Human Geography*, eds. Carville Earle, Kent Matthewson, and Martin Kenzer (Lanham, Md.: Rowman & Littlefield, 1996).

21. Hippocrates, "Airs, Waters, and Places, " in *Hippocrates*, vol. 1, trans. by W. H. S. Jones (Cambridge, Mass.: Harvard University Press, 1957), 71–137.

22. Stephen Daniels, "Place and the Geographical Imagination." *Geography* 77 (1992): 310–322.

23. Donald Worster, "Transformations of the Earth: Toward an Agroecological Perspective in History," *The Journal of American History* 76 (1990): 1087–1106. William Julius Wilson, *When Work Disappears: The World of the New Urban Poor* (New York: Random House, 1996).

24. D. W. Meinig, "Geography as an Art," *Transactions of the Institute of British Geographers* n.s. 8 (1983): 314–328.

25. Timothy F. Mitchell, "Bound by Time and Place: the Art of Caspar David Friedrich," *Arts Magazine* 61 (1986): 48–53.

26. Mircea Eliade, *The Sacred and the Profane: The Nature of Religion*, trans. Willard R. Trask (New York: Harcourt Brace Jovanovich, 1959), 37.

27. Yi-fu Tuan, "A View of Geography," *Geographical Review* 81 (1991): 99–107.

28. David Harvey, *Justice, Nature, and the Geography of Difference* (Oxford: Blackwell, 1996), 261.

29. Harvey, *Justice, Nature*, 78–9.

30. Paul Carter, *The Road to Botany Bay: An Exploration of Landscape and History* (New York: Alfred A. Knopf, 1988), xxiv.

31. Henry Glassie, *Passing the Time in Ballymenone* (Philadelphia: University of Pennsylvania Press, 1982), 665.

32. Martin Heidegger, *Poetry, Language, Thought*, trans. Albert Hofstadter (New York: Harper & Row, 1971), 145–161.

33. J. B. Jackson, "In Search of the Proto-Landscape," in *Landscape in America*, ed. George F. Thompson (Austin: University of Texas Press, 1995), 43.

34. Robert Sack, "The Power of Place and Space," *Geographical Review* 83 (1993): 326–329.

35. Peirce Lewis, "Small Town in Pennsylvania," *Annals of the Association of American Geographers* 62 (1972): 323–351.

36. Peter Hall, "Modeling the Post-Industrial City," *Futures* 29 4/5 (1997): 311–322.

37. Dani Rodrik, "Sense and Nonsense in the Globalization Debate," *Foreign*

Policy 107 (Summer 1997): 19–37; Peter Evans, "The Eclipse of the State? Reflections on Stateness in an Era of Globalization," *World Politics* 50 (October 1997): 62–87.

38. David Harvey, *The Condition of Postmodernity* (London: Blackwell, 1989).

Finding Place:
Spatiality, Locality, and Subjectivity

Jeff Malpas

I.

Notions of place and locale are ubiquitous in contemporary thought and writing. In the work of architects and artists, geographers and historians, sociologists and philosophers, feminists and environmentalists, topographical notions recur again and again, both as theoretical tools and descriptors. Yet, for all its ubiquity, seldom does one find any investigation of the concept of *place* itself, of what place is that distinguishes it from space, of how it stands in relation to time, of what the elements are that make up a place and what marks one place from another. What is often lacking is, one might say, a topography of place as such. Even a work such as Edward Casey's *The Fate of Place*,[1] while it offers an extremely detailed and valuable philosophical history of the concept, provides relatively little in the way of an elucidation of what place itself might be. For the most part, Doreen Massey's comments about the use of the notion of space apply equally to place: "Many authors rely heavily on the terms 'space'/'spatial', and each assumes that their meaning is clear and uncontested. Yet in fact the meaning which different authors assume (and therefore—in the case of metaphorical usage—the import of the metaphor) varies greatly. Buried in these unacknowledged disagreements is a debate which never surfaces; and it never surfaces because everyone assumes we already know what these terms mean."[2]

There are a number of possible and perhaps obvious reasons for the lack of any close analysis of topographic notions. Place, one might suppose, is already a concept with which we are familiar and the ideas associated with it are readily grasped. And as its familiarity could be seen to derive from its common and everyday use, so too may that very 'everydayness' be taken to indicate that the concept must remain a fairly loose and open-textured notion that will resist any attempt at closer analysis.

21

Yet, if this is part of the reason why so little attention is given to understanding the nature of place, then it would also seem to suggest real limits on the usefulness of place as a theoretical notion—although it may also suggest that many critiques of place are equally attacks on a target that can never be properly located. Another, and perhaps more significant, factor that may underlie the relative lack of attention given to the investigation of place, at least in some quarters, is a suspicion of the universalizing tendencies that might be thought to accompany any such investigation. From this perspective what is important is recognition of and attentiveness to the particularities of different regions and places rather than any attempt to arrive at some overarching concept of place as such. Such a unitary concept could only serve, so it might be supposed, to blind us to the more important differences that derive from race, gender, class and so forth. But trying to better understand what place itself might be need not blind us to difference—indeed it may help us to better understand the very nature of difference inasmuch as such difference may derive from the influence of place and locale. Moreover, arriving at some understanding of the structure of place—albeit a structure always instantiated in diverse ways—is also crucial if place is to have any theoretical significance at all. To reject the attempt to arrive at any sort of conceptual clarification in regard to place is effectively to reject its usefulness as a concept—moreover to reject all such clarification is to reject the very attempt to understand.

Lack of clarity about what place might be is not peculiar to contemporary discussion, but is indeed characteristic of much of the philosophical history of place within which place has often been only poorly distinguished from space. Indeed, place has most often been considered only within the context of an inquiry into nature and in a way that has typically resulted, especially in post-Cartesian thought, in the treatment of place as simply *derivative* of space. What then is place as such, and what philosophical significance might it have? In the following pages I wish to sketch out an answer to this question—an answer that will traverse some of the ground covered in more detail by Casey's work, but which will also look a little further afield.[3] I would emphasize, however, that it will indeed be no more than a sketch that is offered, since anything more would require more time and space, indeed, a different place, than is at my disposal here.[4]

II.

In a well-known passage, Michel Foucault identifies twentieth-century thought as characterized by its preoccupation with space—a preoccupation from which, of course, he was not himself immune. Foucault writes:

The great obsession of the nineteenth century was, as we know, history: with its themes of development and of suspension, of crisis and cycle, themes of the ever-accumulating past, with its great preponderance of dead men and the menacing glaciation of the world. The nineteenth century found its essential mythological resources in the second principle of thermodynamics. The present epoch will perhaps be above all the epoch of space. We are in the epoch of simultaneity: we are in the epoch of juxtaposition, the epoch of the near and far, of the side-by-side, of the dispersed. We are at a moment, I believe, when our experience of the world is less that of a long life developing through time than that of a network that connects points and that intersects with its own skein.[5]

Here Foucault seems to treat the idea of the spatial as inclusive of the concept of place or locale that also seems such a widespread motif in contemporary discussion. That both spatial and topographic notions are indeed self-consciously deployed in much twentieth-century thought, in a way that seems characteristic of this century, is not something with which I wish to take issue here. But Foucault's comments are notable in that they seem to imply an indifference to the variety of notions that Foucault includes under the heading of the spatial—"simultaneity . . . juxtaposition . . . near and far . . . side-by-side . . . dispersed." Similarly, Foucault appears simply to ignore the distinction between the notion of the purely spatial that is associated with ideas of pure simultaneity or extension and the concept of the topographic that is associated with place. Foucault is not alone in this—even Henri Lefebvre, who upbraids Foucault for his lack of attention to the problem of clarifying the spatial concepts he deploys, often seems just as oblivious to the differences at stake here.[6]

Of course the lack of clear differentiation between spatial and topographic concepts in Foucault, Lefebvre and others is only a reflection of a widespread tendency to mix such notions together. We think of places as locations within space, of places as giving a space or "room"; we think in turn of space as defined by the places that are located within it and so on. Yet it is also evident that places are not mere points within a space. The existence of a homogenous and undifferentiated realm of extension is not sufficient to make for the existence of any place. For that we need more than just extension, and, while a place may give room or space within it, the space we find within a place is quite different from the space that consists in nothing but a continuous and open expanse.

A crucial first step in making any move towards establishing the concept of place must be to distinguish it more clearly in relation to the idea of space. In fact if we look to the etymology of the English terms *place* and *space* we can see at least two quite different sets of ideas that are associated with these notions. On the one hand, the English *space*, like

the French *espace*, derives from the Latin *spatium*, and before that from
the Greek *stadion*, denoting a measure of length. *Place*, on the other hand,
comes from the Latin *platea* meaning a "broad way" or "open space"
which comes in turn from the Greek *plateia*, also meaning "broad way"—
the Greek term is in fact echoed in the name of the "broad-shouldered"
Plato. Other Latin-based languages include terms referring to place that
have a similar derivation, and are also closely related to the English 'place':
in German, *Platz;* in French, *place*; and in Italian, *piazza*.[7] One can see
how the notion of a broad and open space remains an important element
in these terms. Even the English word still carries something of this sense,
clearer in its German, French and Italian counterparts, of an open but
well-defined area—most often the square or marketplace within a town.
In most languages the term for *place* carries some connotation of such an
open, bounded region and as such is clearly distinct from the concept of
space as precisely the homogenous and extended realm, amenable to a
purely mathematical understanding, within which such "places" may
themselves be situated.

Place and space are thus distinct, if related, notions and are often recognized as such. Yet even where such recognition is explicit, it is also common to find that place is nevertheless regarded as a notion essentially
subsidiary to the notion of space—where space is narrowly understood
in terms of measurable and homogenous extension. Thus Einstein, in his
foreword to Jammer's *Concepts of Space*, distinguishes place from space.
He does so, however, in a manner that portrays place as merely a more
primitive way of understanding something that is much better grasped
through a concept of space—and specifically through a concept of space
tied to extension and a certain form of containment. Einstein writes:

> Now as to the concept of space, it seems that this was preceded by the psy-
> chologically simpler concept of place. Place is first of all a (small) portion of
> the earth's surface identified by a name. The thing whose "place" is being
> specified is a "material object" or body. Simple analysis shows "place" also
> to be a group of material objects.[8]

This primitive notion of place gives rise, according to Einstein, to a conception of space that is tied to locality—a concept of place that is dependent on objects or groups of objects. The idea of place or locality is thus
taken to be one way of understanding space, "space as positional quality
of the world of material objects," in contrast to another concept of space,
which Einstein takes to be the "logically more daring concept" (although
a concept itself eventually superseded by more recent views), as "container of all material objects."[9] Jammer also seems to allude to a concept
of place in his discussion of early concepts of space. Yet once again place

seems to be treated as little more than a primitive way of understanding space: "To the primitive mind, 'space' was merely an accidental set of concrete orientations, a more or less ordered multitude of local directions, each associated with certain emotional reminiscences. This primitive 'space,' as experienced and unconsciously formed by the individual, may have been coordinated with a 'space' common to the group, the family or the tribe."[10]

The emphasis, in Jammer and Einstein, on the concept of place as tied, first, to notions of locality and particularity and, second, to certain qualitative associations or characteristics (albeit characteristics arising from "emotional reminiscence") obviously picks up on some important and central features of the concept. Such ideas contain hints of the direction that must be taken by any attempt to investigate the notion of place more fully. Yet neither Einstein nor Jammer give serious consideration to the possibility of a legitimate and significant way of understanding place, or indeed space, that is other than as associated with notions of physical extension or location. And both treat place as essentially a derivative and secondary concept.

Of course, Einstein and Jammer might wish to bring to our attention here the fact that their concern is with space and place as objective concepts of physical theory, and not, they might say, with place as a subjective feature of our experience. Yet this is already to presuppose a particular way of understanding place and reflects a more general tendency to take space as paradigmatically a concept of physics, to treat place as secondary to it, and to view any other concept of place or space as purely a psychological phenomenon. Thus even ancient discussions of place, undertaken through investigations of the notions of *chora* and *topos*, and medieval discussions of the same topic that center on the concept of *locus* (the derivation of the English "location") are readily assimilated, as they are by Jammer, to the history of the concept of space, narrowly understood as a concept of natural philosophy or physics, rather than seen as part of any "history" of place or space in a broader sense. There is a real question, however, whether the primary sense of space or of place is that to be found in the particular instantiation of these concepts within physical theory or, indeed, whether the only other framework within which they may be approached is that of the "psychological." Certainly for thinkers near to the beginning of Western philosophy, thinkers such as Plato and Aristotle in particular, spatial and topographic notions were neither wholly distinct from one another nor did the idea of space as simply measurable extension provide the primary framework within which such notions were understood. Significantly, however, one can discern, even in Plato and Aristotle, the possibility of a contrast between different notions of space and place and indications of how a notion of space as pure extension might develop.

In the *Physics,* Aristotle takes up the notion of *topos* as a concept central to metaphysical inquiry. After criticizing a number of alternative accounts of the nature of the concept (as form, matter and extension), he arrives at his own characterization of the notion as "the first unchangeable limit of that which surrounds."[11] The place or *topos* of a thing is thus understood to be the inner surface of the body within which that thing is enclosed so that the place of a rosebud contained within a glass paperweight is the inner surface of the glass that surrounds the rosebud.[12] The implication is that to be in place is always to be contained within an enclosing body and Aristotle states this explicitly: "a body is in place" he says "if, and only if, there is a body outside it which surrounds it."[13]

However peculiar Aristotle's emphasis on the idea of place, or *topos,* as a *surface*—the inner surface of an enclosing body—may seem, it is easy enough to understand why this might be an attractive notion. Aristotle's interest is in being able to use the notion of place to explain that fundamental kind of change that is locomotion or change of place. His interest, then, would seem primarily to lie in the concept of *topos* as location. Rejecting the notion of void, and so accepting that every body must be enclosed within some other body, it seems that an obvious way to define a particular body's location is by reference to the body that encloses it. So the location of any particular body is dependent on the next closest body that encloses it—the boundary between the two bodies thereby limiting both the enclosing body and the body enclosed while also defining the *place* of the latter (the place of the former being dependent on yet another enclosing body). As Henry Mendell points out, this Aristotelian conception of place has a respectable pedigree. It is a view adumbrated in a passage in Plato's *Parmenides* and also in Gorgias' *On Not Being.*[14]

Yet even in ancient times the Aristotelian view of space or place as the inner surface of an enclosing body was not the only extant view on the matter. An alternative, which Aristotle seems himself to have held at one time,[15] was to understand space or place as more or less equivalent to the volume or dimension of the thing enclosed. Thus, to use the example briefly referred to before, on such an account the place of the rosebud within the paperweight would be coextensive with the rosebud itself, and not with the inner limit of the glass that encloses it.

This view of space/place as *dimensionality* is one that appears explicitly in Plato, in a famous but difficult discussion in the *Timaeus.* The topic at issue there is the manner in which things come into being and in which one thing can change into something else. This process of becoming requires, according to Plato, three elements: "that which becomes; that in which it becomes; and the model in whose likeness that which becomes is born."[16] That which becomes Plato compares with a child; that which is the model for that which becomes he likens to a father; and that in which becoming takes place—into which it is received—he compares to a mother.[17] This "mother" of becoming, which Plato also refers to as the Receptacle or nurse[18] of becoming, is the place in which the qualities of the thing that comes into being appear. Since the Receptacle cannot contribute any quality to that which comes to be within it, so it cannot have any qualities of its own, and "must not be called earth or air or fire or water, nor any of their compounds or components"; but is instead of "a nature invisible and characterless, all-receiving, partaking in some very puzzling way of the intelligible and very hard to apprehend."[19] The Receptacle is, in fact, identical with space or place (the Greek term used by Plato is *chora*) which is "everlasting; not admitting of destruction" and provides "a situation for all things that come into being."[20]

Aristotle refers specifically, in his *Physics*, to this Platonic account of space or place, writing that

> if we regard the place as the interval of the magnitude, it is the matter. For this is different from the magnitude: it is what is contained and defined by the form, as by a bounding plane. Matter or the indeterminate is of this nature; when the boundary and attributes of a sphere are abstracted, nothing but the matter is left. This is why Plato in the *Timaeus* says matter and space are the same; for the "participant" [i.e., receptacle] and space are identical.[21]

The Receptacle is indeterminate, it has no qualities of its own, but is that space or place that receives qualities and so provides the necessary "room" or space in which things can come to be. It is thus that the Platonic conception of space or place must be seen as quite distinct from that which Aristotle sets out in the *Physics*. Rather than being the inner surface of a containing body, space/place is the extended and open realm within which a contained body is held or "received."

Notwithstanding the differences between, what I will call for convenience, the "Platonic" and "Aristotelian" accounts of space or place (although the Platonic account is also to be found in Aristotle's *Categories*), both accounts seem to presuppose a connection between some notion of containment and the idea of space or place—on the Aristotelian account place is defined by reference to a containing body while on the Platonic account it is defined by reference to a body or quality that is contained. The idea of containment seems, in fact, to be central to any thinking about space and place and is crucial—especially as it gives rise to a notion of space as extension—to the historical development of those concepts.

There is another feature that is common to both the Aristotelian and Platonic accounts, but which disappears as the concepts of place and space develop further—namely, a view that ties place or space (and of course in the Platonic and Aristotelian context we cannot clearly separate these notions) to the things located within it. For Aristotle there can be no place or space without an enclosing body; for Plato the idea of space or place is understood always in relation to that which is received within it. This reflects, perhaps, the Greek tendency to understand place and space always in relation to particulars rather than in any more abstract way. It may also be seen to provide some support for Heidegger's otherwise somewhat ambiguous claim (given the difficulty in establishing exactly how either place or *topos* should be understood) that "The Greeks had no word for 'space' . . . for they experienced the spatial on the basis not of extension but of place (topos)."[22] One of the important shifts in the history of place and of space is the move toward a more abstract conceptualization of these notions in ways that separate them from the particular things located in them, and, in the case of space, from particular locations.

Within the history of these conceptual shifts, the Platonic idea of space or place as tied to dimension, even though it emphasizes the particular over the abstract, seems to stand in a more direct line of descent to modern ideas of space than does the Aristotelian conception. It is this, presumably, that leads Max Jammer to claim that the Platonic account of *topos* to be found in Aristotle's *Categories,* of which Plato's account in the *Timaeus* is a predecessor, is an account of space, while the later Aristotelian account in the *Physics* is an account of place.[23] So while Heidegger can maintain that the Greek experience of space or place was properly on the basis of the topographic—the located particular—he can nevertheless also hold that "the transformation of the barely apprehended essence of place (*topos*) and of *chora* into a 'space' defined by extension was initiated by the Platonic philosophy, i.e. in the interpretation of being as *idea*."[24] On Heidegger's reading it is Plato who inaugurates the understanding of space and of place as measurable extension.

Yet, even without reference to Plato one can see how there is already, in the very idea of space or place as a matter of containment, a tendency toward a conception of space as extension. After briefly discussing the "psychologically simpler" concept of place that is tied to the idea of the location of some object or set of objects, Einstein offers an alternative way of thinking about space. He writes:

> Into a certain box we can place a definite number of grains of rice or of cherries, etc. It is here a question of a property of the material object "box," which property must be considered "real" in the same sense as the box itself. One can call this property the "space" of the box. There may be other boxes which in this sense have an equally large "space." This concept "space" thus

achieves a meaning which is freed from any connection with a particular material object. In this way by a natural extension of "box space" one can arrive at the concept of an independent (absolute) space, unlimited in extent, in which all material objects are contained.[25]

Here it is quite clear, not only the way in which the notion of space at issue arises out of a concept of containment, but also the way it enables an explicit move to a more abstract conception of space that will enable a further move to a concept of absolute space of the sort advanced, finally, by Newton. The move to a more abstract concept is something for which the "psychologically simpler" notion of place seems rather less well adapted, since that notion is tied more directly to the particular. This is so even in Einstein's characterization of place, which treats place as just "position," according to which place is tied to a particular portion of the earth's surface or to a particular object or group of objects. Indeed, the development of an abstract concept of position or location seems to itself depend on the idea of an independent or absolute space that arises out of the idea of space as a containing region. Only within an extended and homogenous space is it possible to treat locations as mere points that differ from one another only insofar as they are represented by different coordinate values. Thus the idea of space as the region of containment gives rise to the notion of space as a system of simple locations and in turn to a transformed conception of place as mere location.

Einstein and Jammer both find elements of this modern concept of space in the work of ancient thinkers. And I have already noted the way in which a concept of space or place as extension is present in both Plato and Aristotle. But the idea that is central in enabling the development of the modern concept is an idea found, not in Plato or Aristotle, but in the atomists: the idea of void (*kenon*). It is this idea that John Philoponus, writing in the sixth century, explicitly treats as identical with the concept of space. Thus he writes of "a space [*chora*] which according to its own definition [*logos*] is void, although it is always filled with body"[26] characterizing it further as "a certain interval [*distêma*, *spatium* in the Latin translation], measurable in three directions, different from the bodies which occupy it, and incorporeal in its very nature. Place consists of the dimensions alone and is empty of every body. In fact, vacuum [*kenon*] and place [*topos*] are essentially the same thing."[27]

Although other ancient thinkers also took place or space to be equivalent to a notion of quantifiable extension, Philoponus is unusual in his explicit treatment of space as identical with void. Indeed, it was not until the Renaissance that this idea came into its own. Amongst fifteenth- and sixteenth-century thinkers such as Gianfrancesco Pico and Giordano Bruno the development of a new idea of space went hand in hand with a rethinking and, in many cases, the rejection of the concepts of Aristotelian physics. Thus we find Pico writing of place as a *void,* in a manner Aristotle could not have countenanced, albeit a void that in fact is always filled: "thus place is empty, empty *(vacuum)* assuredly of any body, but still never existing as a vacuum alone of itself."[28] This conception of void or vacuum reappears in Bruno, who employs a notion of space as an infinite and empty realm in which all things are located: "There is a single general space," he writes, "a single vast immensity which we may freely call VOID."[29] This new conception of space could be seen as enormously liberating: just as it offered the idea of a realm of unfettered and unlimited movement, so it could also be seen as expressive of a new and exciting sense of intellectual freedom.

The shift toward this conception of space as sheer extension, and the accompanying tendency for place to be subsumed under the concept of space, reaches a particularly developed form in Descartes for whom space and place are scarcely distinguishable concepts. In his *Principles of Philosophy,* in a passage in which he draws upon the scholastic distinction between external and internal place (a contrast that can be understood in terms of the difference between the location of a body and the extension of that body),[30] Descartes writes:

> There is no real distinction between space [l'éspace], or internal place [le lieu], and the corporeal substance contained in it; the only difference lies in the way in which we are accustomed to conceive of them. For in reality the extension in length, breadth and depth which constitutes a space is exactly the same as that which constitutes a body . . . The terms "place" and "space," then, do not signify anything different from the body which is said to be in a place; they merely refer to its size, shape and position relative to other bodies . . . The difference between the terms "place" and "space" is that the former designates more explicitly the position, as opposed to the size or shape, while it is the size or shape that we are concentrating on when we talk of space. For we often say that one thing leaves a given place and another thing arrives there, even though the second thing is not strictly of the same size and shape; but in this case we do not say it occupies the same space. By contrast, when something alters its position, we always say the place is changed, despite the fact that the size and shape remain unaltered.[31]

Here one can clearly see how Descartes is able to deploy the notion of place, understood primarily in terms of the notion of containment, as the basis on which to develop a concept of space as extension. In the idea of containment is given, not only the idea of that which bounds the body contained ("outer place"), but also the idea of that open expanse which is established within those bounds ("inner place"). Thus a pitcher containing water can be understood as holding the water it contains in a place that is defined by the inner surface of the pitcher itself, but the area enclosed by that containing surface can also be understood as constituting a place or, perhaps better, a space. Place becomes merely the position of the contained body in relation to other bodies. Within this Cartesian account place and space are thus related concepts that refer to features of *bodies*—to their position and extension respectively—and within this account it is clearly space as extension that is the more significant notion.

The philosophical history of space and place is thus a history in which the concept of space as extension is steadily refined, but in the course of which refinement the idea of place as location is gradually lost or, at least, loses its theoretical significance. Part of the difficulty, then, that surrounds the use of place as a theoretical or philosophically significant concept in contemporary discussion is precisely that the notion has come to be subsumed under the concept of space as extension. This way of treating place as merely a variant of space results in the disappearance of much that is important about the notion of place as such. The idea of place as an open but bounded realm that has a character of its own is hard to give sense to on such an account. Places become interchangeable positions differentiated only by the objects that are located within them.

III.

In the history of philosophy we can thus chart a clear shift—a shift given a particularly detailed account in Edward Casey's work—toward a separating out of concepts of space and place from a primary notion of location that both contains and grounds to a concept of space as measurable extension and of place as mere location specifiable within such a spatial framework. And even though modern cosmological physics no longer understands space in the terms developed by Descartes and Newton, still the idea of space as tied to physical extension has not disappeared and, indeed, the Cartesian-Newtonian idea of space as 'container of material objects' remains perhaps the dominant conception of space within much everyday thought. Moreover, in the absence of any explicit examination of the concepts as such, the frequent deployment of spatial and topographic concepts in so much contemporary theory—whether in discussions of globalisation, ecological regionalism or whatever—really amounts just to the deployment of the Cartesian-Newtonian conception of space as physical extension and, derivative from that, of place as simple location.

Indeed, even the attempt to rehabilitate a concept of place by treating it as a specifically human appropriation of physical space—a tendency that can be discerned within much recent writing especially in environmentalism, but also in geographical and sociological theory—remains within the very same framework that was evident in Einstein and Jammer's treatment of space and place. So place is treated, even if only implicitly, as derivative of space or else, if the attempt is made to rehabilitate the concept as involving more than just this, it is so only to the extent that place incorporates some subjective, emotional or affective component. And this latter approach merely conjoins the idea of a part of objective physical space with the notion of some subjective emotional or affective quality or set of qualities, and so continues to treat place as derivative of these more basic ideas and provides no explication of place as a concept in its own right. On such an approach, the connection between any particular space and the emotional qualities associated with it could turn out to be completely contingent and there is no reason to suppose that it is the experience of specifically *topographic* or even *spatial* qualities that are actually at issue in such an experience of place.[32] The association of some set of felt qualities with a particular space need be no more than a result of the triggering of certain responses—perhaps in a completely accidental fashion—by some combination of physical (and, for this reason alone, spatially located) features in the immediate environment. Consequently, it is not place as such that is important here, but just the idea of emotional responsiveness—a responsiveness that need not itself be grounded in any concept of place or locality at all.

It is notable that this way of approaching the question of place seems to be at least implicit even in the work of many writers who seek explicitly to direct attention to place as a significant theoretical notion. Thus Yi-fu Tuan, an important and pioneering figure within environmentalist discussions of place who is otherwise remarkably sensitive to many of the issues at stake, often tends to treat place in a way that is suggestive of the concept as a purely subjectivist construct. Thus much of Tuan's work is explicitly written from "The perspective of experience" as the subtitle of his *Space and Place*[33] has it and experience is characterized by Tuan as "a cover-all term for the various modes through which a person knows or constructs a reality."[34] Elsewhere he characterizes his overall project in terms of the study of "environmental perception, attitudes, and values."[35] There is a certain equivocation in Tuan's work, common in much writing on place, between place or space as that which gives rise to experience on the one hand and space or place as experiential construct on the other. And this equivocation is indicative of some of the obscurity that seems to attend on the concept of place almost wherever it appears. Such equivocation aside, however, it does seem that Tuan tends toward an account of place in terms of the subjective human response to environment and so toward an account quite consistent, indeed continuous, with the approach already encountered in Jammer and Einstein.

Of course, since human responses to the environment are many and varied and since the environment has a role to play in almost all of experience, so too is the account of place similarly dispersed. This is so not just in Tuan's work—although it is perhaps a particular feature of those discussions that identify themselves as concerned with a "humanistic" approach to the issues[36]—but in the discussion of space and place throughout much of the literature irrespective of field. The proliferation of material in relation to place leads J. Nicholas Entrikin to refer to the "sometimes competing, and occasionally confusing, claims that have been made and continue to be made about the study of place and region" and he adds that "One of the reasons for this confusion may be that it is beyond our intellectual reach to attain a theoretical understanding of place and region that covers the range of phenomena to which these concepts refer."[37] The dispersed character of so many accounts of place across so many disciplines, so many different writers and with respect to such a variety of material and theme, provides both an impetus toward the attempt to develop some more integrated approach to place, while also, as Entrikin's warning makes clear, making any such attempt quite problematic. Yet, if place is indeed to be taken up as a concept in its own right, rather than as a convenient catchall for what otherwise appears to be only a loosely connected set of ideas and problems, then the development of some more integrated account is indeed essential. Only within the framework of such an account would it be possible to give any content to the idea that the set of problems and ideas to be found in discussions of place are indeed significantly related.

The appearance of place as a central, if problematic, concept is clearest in discussions that touch on aspects of human existence and experience. In this respect the emphasis on place as experiential or as tied to the human response to the environment, while it actually curtails the possibility of giving an adequate account of place as such, is nevertheless instructive. It is not, however, that the crucial point about the connection between place and experience is that place is something only encountered *in* experience, rather it is that place *is integral to the very structure and possibility of experience*. Such a way of thinking about place appears, though, as Edward Casey suggests,[38] in a somewhat indirect fashion, in the work of Martin Heidegger.

In *Being and Time* Heidegger treats human beings, or more properly *Dasein*, as essentially characterized in terms of their "being-in" the world. This leads Heidegger to distinguish the sense of being-in that is proper to human being from the being-in that is associated with the sense of physical containment that is part of the modern conception of space identified by Einstein and Jammer and that Heidegger himself characterizes as 'Cartesian'.[39] Failure to make such a distinction would, it seems, commit

Heidegger to understanding the relation between the world and *Dasein* as essentially no different from the relation between, for instance, a matchbox and the matches contained within it. It would also seem to entail a view of *Dasein* as existing in a way essentially no different from the way in which matchbox, matches or any other physical objects exist. Such a view Heidegger rejects as inadequate to any proper understanding of *Dasein* as such. It is inadequate, on Heidegger's account, because it makes problematic the very possibility of a relation between Dasein and its world (or the things within that world)—that this is indeed so is clearly evident, according to Heidegger, in the rise of relativistic and sceptical modes of thought.

In this latter respect the "objectivism" Heidegger associates with the Cartesian view of spatiality is seen as necessarily tied to "subjectivism"[40]—and this would seem, in fact, to mirror the connection we already seem to obtain between the view of space as primarily a feature of the physical universe and of place, or "meaningful space," as a human, and therefore subjective, construct. In distinguishing the spatiality of *Dasein* from the spatiality of objects, Heidegger thus asserts the impossibility of any purely objective treatment of *Dasein* that would treat Dasein as no more than an object among other objects while also rejecting any subjectivist understanding of Dasein in its relation to the world. Indeed, given the idea that Dasein is properly understood as already inclusive of the world, one can see how Heidegger could later comment that: *"Dasein* names that which should first be experienced, and then properly thought of, as Place [*Ort*]."[41]

Heidegger provides an important example of the way in which the concept of place may be seen as significant in the understanding of human being and so of human thought and experience. Indeed, something like the Heideggerian thinking of Dasein *as* place is what motivates my own inquiries here. So far, as the idea of experience is concerned (the idea central to the work of writers such as Tuan), it seems that understanding the structure and possibility of experience—in particular the sort of experience that is exemplified in the human—is inseparable from an understanding and appreciation of the concept of place. Understanding this is more than a matter of grasping the idea of mere spatiotemporal location. Such location is part of the concept of place, but it does not exhaust that concept. Indeed, as employed here and as already suggested by the inquiry into the etymology of the term, the idea of place is the idea of an open and yet bounded realm that has a character of its own—a character that can sometimes be expressed in the giving of a name to such a place— and that is structured in terms of the interconnection between the elements that are found within it. Moreover, as in Heidegger, such a realm is not constituted as a purely objective structure. In other words, it is not a structure that can be understood in terms simply of a system of interchangeable locations associated with objects. Neither, however, is it purely subjective, since the sort of realm at issue here is not dependent on the existence of subjects, but is rather a structure within and with respect to which subjectivity is itself established. Place is not founded *on* subjectivity but that *on which* the notion of subjectivity is founded. Thus one does not first have a subject who apprehends certain features of the world in terms of the idea of place; instead the structure of subjectivity is given in and through the structure of place.

Understanding human being in the world, with all its associated structures, is thus a matter of coming to understand a form of being-in, and so a form of spatiality, that is other than that associated with space as measurable extension. And although this point is brought out in a particularly important (although problematic) fashion in Heidegger's work, we do not need to look to Heidegger alone in order to see the way in which the problem of understanding human being, and more particularly, of understanding concepts such as knowledge, self, experience and so forth, is inseparable from the problem of understanding the possibility and nature of place. Human being is precisely a form of being-in that involves oriented, bounded location. To attempt to understand human being using only the resources given through an objective and "leveled-out" understanding of space as extension is to fail to understand the nature of the being at issue. No purely objective space can ever be sufficient to enable the development of the concept of the sort of place that is part of the structure of human being since such an objective space contains no topography of the sort required. If we tend to forget this it is only because we think of objective space always from a point of view that treats it from a perspective that is itself placed.

That the problem of place has a philosophical significance that goes beyond mere questions of spatiality alone is evident from consideration of a number of problems within contemporary philosophy. In fact the rise of notions of place and space in twentieth-century thought, something Foucault and others have noted, is itself merely indicative of the centrality of these questions to the philosophical inquiry into the human. Most often such questions have arisen in areas of ethics, particularly environmental ethics, in political discussion, and in considerations of identity. But the problem of place names a quite ubiquitous issue that can also be seen in contemporary philosophical discussions within even the so-called analytic tradition—the discussion of the nature of mental content provides a good example of this. While externalist theories of content—theories that take the content of a thought to be determined by objects and events in the world external to the body of the thinker—can be seen to fit with an emphasis on spatiality and locality, such theories face a

problem in determining just which features of an individual's environment should be taken to be the relevant external determinants of a particular creature's mental states. Only if we have a conception of the space in
which a creature is embedded as having a certain topography that marks
particular features as salient can we make any externalist view of content
plausible.[42] This is merely an illustration of one way in which a concept
of place might be seen to be indispensable to any inquiry into the nature
of thought or agency. Indeed, there is reason to think that only if we can
understand creatures as embedded in a world can we understand them
as in any way capable of thought—whether believing, desiring, hoping,
calculating, fearing, meaning or whatever—or indeed of purposive action.
Only a creature that is oriented and located can relate to objects and to
the world. Consequently, the unavailability of a notion of spatiality other
than that of measurable extension, and the relegation of place, if recognized at all, to the status of a subjective or experiential concept can only
make the inquiry into thought and agency problematic and obscure. The
problem of place is not a marginal problem concerning merely the way in
which spatiality alone is to be understood, but is fundamental to epistemological, anthropological and psychological inquiry—even, indeed, to
problems of ethics and politics. For in all these instances what must be
articulated is the structure of a particular region that is not the structure
of an extended, measurable domain, but rather the structure of an open
space of activity that is also bounded, focused and oriented—the structure
of place.[43]

IV.

If we take the turn to place seriously, then what emerges is the possibility
of thinking of subjectivity—and of thought and experience—as essentially
a function of place or locale. Thus we should not think of the relation
between human beings and their world as a relation in which human beings impose meaning onto an otherwise objective, physical structure. Understanding the possibility of human being—or meaning—is just a matter
of understanding how place as such is possible. Understanding human
being and understanding place are one and the same. Yet it is not just that
human subjectivity is tied to the structure of place. The manner in which
places are themselves structured, and the way in which that structure constrains the investigation and delineation of places, provides an important
model for the inquiry into subjectivity.

The concept of place is characteristically the concept of an open region,
in which things reside and in which relations between things can be established. The idea of place as it operates in talk of a place or square within a

town provides a neat example of this. But such a place is itself constituted through the interrelation of the elements within it. The town square thus provides a bounded, oriented space within which the affairs of the town are brought into focus, in which particular buildings and activities take on a certain character and identity, in which individual persons are able to take on the role of citizens; but the character of the place is itself dependent on what is brought to focus within it. If we look to the larger region of the town as a whole the character of the many particular places within the town is similarly dependent on the interrelation of places within the region as a whole and the same is also true of entire landscapes. Thus, if one is to delineate the structure of a place or region, then what is required is to exhibit the structure of the region as a whole as it is constituted through the interplay of the various elements within it. Indeed, this idea is neatly exemplified in the actual practice of map-mapping and particularly in the traditional techniques of the topographical surveyor.

Topographical surveying is, according to an old British Government textbook on the subject, "the science, artfully executed, of measuring the physical features of the earth and the art, scientifically controlled, of delineating them."[44] While the advent of aerial surveying and, more recently, satellite mapping techniques have wrought great changes in the actual practice of surveying not only over the last one hundred years, even the last forty, the basic principles for the surveyor on the ground have nevertheless remained much the same. In the centuries prior to the twentieth, surveyors relied principally on theodolite and chain, on a good eye and hand, and a strong pair of legs. For the surveyor equipped only with such basic equipment, then or now, and faced with a hitherto unmapped region, the task is to map out that region from within the region itself. Only by measurement of distance and angle, by repeated triangulation and traverse, can a picture of the topography of the region be built up. For such a surveyor there is nowhere outside of the region itself from which an accurate topographical picture can be obtained. It is thus precisely through the surveyor's active involvement with the landscape that an accurate mapping is made. A purely topographical understanding of a landscape does not, furthermore, look to some deeper topography that underlies the topography made evident through our active engagement within it. There is no such deeper topography to be found. The lie of the land is indeed given—almost literally—*on* its surface rather than being hidden *beneath* it.

If place is indeed taken to be a notion central to the understanding of human subjectivity, or to the possibility of thought, experience or action, then the structure of place itself, and the manner in which that structure is delineated, should perhaps also be a guide to the manner in which any inquiry into subjectivity ought also to proceed. In that case, it will not be a matter of reducing subjectivity to some more primitive substratum—of finding something beneath the surface of the human—but rather of understanding how subjectivity is structured through its being interrelated with other elements and through the interrelation of the elements within it. It will be a matter of coming to understand things through their interconnection rather than their reduction, through recognition of their complexity rather than their simplification. Such a mode of proceeding has a philosophical precedent, if only implicitly, in Heidegger, but it is also strongly reminiscent of Wittgenstein. Thus he writes of his method of approach in the *Philosophical Investigations* that

> The philosophical remarks in this book are, as it were, a number of sketches of landscapes which were made in the course of these long and involved journeyings. The same or almost the same points were always being approached afresh from different directions, and new sketches made. Very many of these were badly drawn or uncharacteristic marked by all the defects of a weak draftsman. And when they were rejected a number of tolerable ones were left, which now had to be arranged and sometimes cut down, so that if you looked at them, you could get a picture of the landscape.[45]

If philosophy is indeed seen to be essentially preoccupied with place, then perhaps the only approach adequate to the philosophical task will be one that is itself thoroughly "topographical."

V.

If we accept that the ubiquity of spatial and topographic concepts in contemporary thought is not just a matter of intellectual fashion, but also reflects something more, then the obvious answer is that the ubiquity of place reflects the central significance of place in any understanding of human being and experience. Yet just what significance is to be attached to place in this respect depends crucially on how place is understood. If we remain, even if only implicitly, within the framework established by the Cartesian-Newtonian model of space and place, then we are forced to accept a conception of place as either just a modification of space—a 'location' within an extended spatial realm or a region within such a realm—or as a modification of space to which attaches some emotional reminiscence or feeling. Perhaps such reminiscence or feeling might be considered an important aspect of human experience and perhaps it could be explained, within the parameters of such an account, by reference to biological or evolutionary considerations. Yet to adopt such an approach is effectively to strip place of any real significance in its own right while also creating serious difficulties for the attempt to arrive at an adequate understanding of human being or experience—treating place as a matter of subjective feeling does indeed assume an account of human being rather than provide one. Finding place is thus a matter of finding ourselves, and to find ourselves we need first to rethink the question of the nature and significance of place.

Notes

1. Edward Casey, *The Fate of Place* (Berkeley: University of California Press, 1996). In his *Getting Back into Place* (Bloomington: Indiana University Press, 1994), Casey does attempt to more directly address questions concerning the significance and structure of place (see also the discussion of place in Casey's *Remembering* [Bloomington: Indiana University Press, 1989] and in some of the essays in his *Spirit and Soul* [Dallas: Spring Publications, 1991]). Yet Casey's approach in this earlier work, though valuable, remains much more phenomenological in its orientation than the sort of analysis that I propose here. For all that, Casey is one of the very few authors—and there are indeed only a handful if that—who have attempted to address the issue of place directly.

2. Doreen Massey, "Politics and Space/Time," in *Place and the Politics of Identity*, ed. Michael Keith and Steve Pile (London: Routledge, 1993), 141–2; see also Neil Smith and Cindi Katz, "Grounding Metaphor: Towards a Spatialized Politics," in Keith and Pile, *Place and the Politics of Identity*, 67–83. Massey's concerns are not merely with theoretical clarity or rigor; she also sees certain uses of the notions of space and spatiality as depriving those notions of any political content and this she views as problematic.

3. Of course, since my interest is in the concept of place as such, I will not, for the most part, be discussing the more specific uses to which concepts of space and place have been put in particular theoretical contexts or in the work of particular theorists. Moreover, as my investigation is primarily conceptual, so I will not be drawing on empirical studies that may be thought to shed light on the human relation to place. Indeed, in the absence of any clearer conceptualization of what place might be, it must remain unclear exactly how to interpret any empirical evidence that might otherwise be thought to be relevant here.

4. I do, however, attempt to develop an answer to this question in much more detail in my *Place and Experience: A Philosophical Topography* (Cambridge, Mass.: Cambridge University Press, forthcoming, 1999).

5. Michel Foucault, "Of Other Spaces," *Diacritics* 16 (1986), 22.

6. See Henri Lefebvre, *The Production of Space*, trans. Donald Nicholson-Smith (Oxford: Blackwell, 1991).

7. Lefebvre, *The Production of Space*, 3–4.

8. Albert Einstein, "Foreword" in Max Jammer, *Concepts of Space*, 2nd ed. (Cambridge, Mass.: Harvard University Press, 1970), xiii.

9. Einstein, "Foreword," xiii.

10. Jammer, *Concepts of Space*, 7–8.

11. Aristotle, *Physics* IV, 5, 212a20 (all translations are taken from *Aristotle's*

Physics Books III and IV, trans. Edward Hussey [Oxford: Clarendon Press, 1983]). Elsewhere Aristotle presents the same idea in slightly different form. Place is "the limit of the surrounding body, at which it is in contact with that which is surrounded" (212a36).

12. See the development of this example in Henry Mendell, "Topoi on Topos: the Development of Aristotle's Concept of Place," *Phronesis* 32 (1987): 209–210. There are some difficulties with interpreting Aristotle's concept of place is this way. In particular it gives rise to the difficulty how an object can be understood to remain stationary when it is situated within a flowing medium—as, for instance, a ship that is moored in a river with the current moving around it. This is a difficulty Aristotle himself addresses (see *Physics* 212a8–19) seeming to identify the place of the boat with the unmoving banks and bed of the river rather than the water that travels past them. For more discussion of this and other problems in Aristotle see Richard Sorabji, *Matter, Space and Motion* (Ithaca, N.Y.: Cornell University Press, 1988).

13. Consequently the world does not have a place, since "there is nothing besides the universe [*to pan*] and the sum of things, nothing which is outside the universe; and this is why everything is in the world [*ouranos*]. (For the world is (perhaps) the universe). The place [of changeable body] is not the world but a part of the world," *Physics* IV, 212a31.

14. See Henry Mendell, "Topoi on Topos," 206–207; see *Parmenides*, 138A2-B6, and Gorgias, *On Not Being*, DK 82 B3, p.280.17–25 = Sextus, Adv. Mth. VII 69–70.

15. In *Categories* 6, Aristotle seems to assume a view of *topos* as extension—see Henry Mendell, "Topoi on Topos," esp. 208–210. The presence of this alternative view is noted, as Mendell acknowledges, by H. R. King, "Aristotle's Theory of Topos," *Classical Quarterly* 44 (1950), 76–96, esp. 87–88, and by J. L. Ackrill, *Aristotle's Categories and De Interpretatione* (Oxford: Clarendon Press, 1963), 93.

16. *Timaeus* 50c (trans., from F. M. Cornford, *Plato's Cosmology* [London: Routledge and Kegan Paul, 1937], 185).

17. *Timaeus,* 50d.

18. *Timaeus,* 49a.

19. *Timaeus,* 51a–51b (trans. Cornford).

20. *Timaeus,* 52b. Plato adds that space is "itself apprehended without the senses by a sort of bastard reasoning" (trans. Cornford). See also the discussion at 52d–53b of which the role of the Receptacle in separating out the various qualities with which it is filled through a process understood analogously to the winnowing of grain.

21. *Physics*, IV, 2.209b6–13. Here matter is being understood as pure mathematical extension, not as anything more than this—it is not, for instance, the material from which something is constituted (see Mendell, "Topoi on Topos," 213 and 213–214n19). Although Plato does himself draw an analogy between the Receptacle and gold that may be moulded and remoulded into many different things (*Timaeus* 50a-50b), he also indicates that this analogy is to some extent misleading.

22. Heidegger, *An Introduction to Metaphysics*, trans. Ralph Manheim (New Haven: Yale University Press, 1957), 66.

23. See Jammer, *The Concept of Space*, 17.

24. Heidegger, *An Introduction to Metaphysics*, 66.

25. Einstein, "Foreword," xiii. The modern conception of absolute space that Einstein discusses here is, of course, one that has undergone certain important revisions within contemporary physics. See Einstein's brief comments on this in "Foreword," xv, and also his discussion in Albert Einstein, "The Problem of Space, Ether and the Field in Physics," *Ideas and Opinions* (1956), 276–285.

26. Philoponus in Physica 557, 8–585, 4, in *Commentaria in Aristotelem Graeca*, ed. H. Diels (Berlin: H. Vitelli, 1887–8); quoted in David Sedley. "Philoponus' Conception of Space," in Richard Sorabji, ed., *Philoponus and the Rejection of Aristotleian Science* (London: Duckworth, 1987), 140.

27. Philoponus in *Physica* 567, lines 30–3, ed. H. Vitelli, in *Commentaria in Aristotelem Graeca*, ed. H. Diels (Berlin: 1882–1909); quoted in David Sedley. "Philoponus' Conception," 140.

28. "Spatium itaque locus est, ex sese corpore quidem vacuum, sed nunquam tamen re ipsa vacuum, sicuti materia aliud est quam forma, nunquam tanem sine forma", Gianfrancesco Pico, *Opera quae extant omnia . . .* Basel 1601, 768 (*Examen Vanitatis* VI, 4); quoted in Charles Schmitt, "Philoponus' Commentary on Aristotle's Physics in the 16th Century," in Sorabji, *Philoponus*, 219.

29. Bruno, *On the infinite universe and worlds*, trans. Dorothea Waley Singer in *Giordano Bruno* (New York: Schuman, 1950), 363. Casey points out that for all that Bruno and others like him seem to have been so taken up by this conception of space, they also retained a conception of place as distinct from space. Only later does place seem to become completely subsumed under space as extension, see *The Fate of Place*, 123–124.

30. The distinction of internal from external place can be found originally in Duns Scotus. For Scotus place is a matter of the relation between containing and contained body. Internal place is that which is internal to the containing body while external place is that which is external to the contained body. For Scotus these are both notions of *place* rather than space and the Latin terms he uses are *loci* and *ubi*. See Duns Scoti, Doctoris Subtilitis, Ordinis Minorum, Quaestiones in librum IV Sententiarum, dist. X, quaest. II: Utrum idem corpus possit esse localiter simul in diversis locis? (VIII, 513); see also the discussion in Pierre Duhem, *Medieval Cosmology*, ed. and trans. Roger Ariew (Chicago: University of Chicago Press, 1985), 183. Scotus' distinction may have its origins in Simplicius, although some form of the distinction between extension and location can be traced back to earlier sources such as Aristotle.

31. René Descartes, *Principles of Philosophy* II:10 and 14; *Oeuvres de Descartes*, ed. Ch. Adam and P. Tannery (rev. ed., Paris: Vrin/CNRS, 1964–76), 45 and 47–48; translation from *The Philosophical Writings of Descartes*, Vol. I, trans. John Cottingham, Robert Stoothoff and Dugald Murdoch (Cambridge: Cambridge University Press, 1985), 227 and 229.

32. See, for instance, Yi-fu Tuan, *Topophilia* (New York: Columbia University Press, 1974), 113. "The fact that images are taken from the environment does not,

of course, mean that the environment has   . need we
believe that certain environments have the irre   philic feelings. Environment may not be the direct cause   po   ivironment
provides the sensory stimuli, which as perceived i.nages   o our joys
and ideals."

33. Yi-fu Tuan, *Space and Place: The Perspective of Ex   *inneapolis:
University of Minnesota Press, 1977).

34. Tuan, *Space and Place*, 8.

35. Tuan, *Topophilia*, 245. In this work Tuan is quite explicit about the nature
of his work as an essay in environment psychology. He also makes clear that he
is well aware of the disparity in the materials and themes with which he is concerned and acknowledges that there is no "single all-embracing concept" that
guides his work (see Tuan, *Topophilia*, 2–3).

36. Tuan characterises his work as part of such an approach and lists a number
of publications as evidence of "a growing interest in the study of 'place' from a
variety of humanistic perspectives" (*Space and Place*, 7 n.3).

37. J. Nicholas Entrikin, *The Betweenness of Place* (Baltimore: Johns Hopkins
University Press, 1991), 14. Entrikin immediately goes on to suggest that "A more
modest, but not insignificant, goal is a better understanding of the narrative-like
qualities that give structure to our attempts to capture the peculiar connections
between people and places." It is noteworthy that Entrikin explicitly takes up
some of the issues relating to the conception of place as a purely mental or subjective construct and is explicitly concerned to encompass both 'objective' and 'subjective' aspects of place in his account (see *The Betweenness of Place*, 6–26), but
he attempts to do this by an appeal to the concept of narrative that he takes to
somehow occupy a position 'between' subjective and objective (see Entrikin, *The
Betweenness of Place*, 132–134). In fact Entrikin appears to retain a view of place
as an essentially subjective structure.

38. In *The Fate of Place* Casey titles the chapter that deals with the Heideggerian appropriation of place 'Proceeding to Place by Indirection'—see Casey, *The
Fate of Place*, 284, and more generally 243–284.

39. See Martin Heidegger, *Being and Time*, H54; I also discuss this issue in my
Heidegger's Topology of Being, chapter 3, in preparation.

40. See Charles Guignon, *Heidegger and the Problem of Knowledge* (Indianapolis: Hackett Publishing, 1983) for a detailed analysis of Heidegger's position in
relation to the traditional problems of epistemology.

41. *Gesamtausgabe, Wegmarken*, 202.

42. For more on this point see my "Unity, Locality and Agency: Bilgrami on
Belief and Meaning," *Philosophy and Phenomenological Research*, forthcoming.

43. I attempt a more detailed account of this structure in *Place and Experience:
A Philosophical Topography*.

44. *Textbook of Topographical Surveying* (London: Her Majesty's Stationery
Office, 1965, 4th ed.), 1.

45. *Philosophical Investigations*, trans. G. E. M. Anscombe (Oxford: Basil
Blackwell, 1976), ix. Elsewhere he writes that: "I am trying to conduct you on
tours in a certain country. I will try to show that the philosophical difficulties

which arise in mathematics as elsewhere arise because we find ourselves in a strange town and do not know our way about. So we must learn the topography by going from one place in the town to another, and from there to another, and so on. And one must do this so often that one knows one's way, either immediately or pretty soon after looking around a bit, wherever one may be set down" (*Wittgenstein's Lectures on the Philosophy of Mathematics: Cambridge 1939*, ed. Cora Diamond [Hassocks: Harvester, 1976], 44).

In Its Place:
Site and Meaning in
Richard Serra's Public Sculpture

James Dickinson

Since the 1960s, the art object has extended dramatically beyond painting and pedestal sculpture to include a vast, almost inconceivably heterogeneous array of made, found, and imagined objects. With the erosion of modernist parameters and definitions, art no longer is required to be aesthetically pleasing, unique, handmade, portable, or even permanently realized in a physical form. Artists are as likely to wield a bulldozer as a brush, to plan as to do, to write as to paint, to peruse industrial products catalogs and engineers' stress tables as to study old masters' brush strokes or the work of contemporaries. Today one can be a significant artist without being able to draw, without ever handling paintbrush or chisel, without hanging anything on a wall.

One feature of this new art stands out: No longer confined to studio, gallery, and museum, art is now found in many real-world places and landscapes. Hillsides and valleys, lakes, strip mines, volcanic craters, farmers' fields, public plazas, waste dumps, freeway embankments, and deserts are now or have been the site of significant artistic activity. As one commentator puts it, "art is escaping its confinement to private sensibility. It is descending into the streets once more and reclaiming its place in the public realm."[1] For an important class of postmodern art objects, site or place has become a constituent moment not only of the object but of the aesthetic experience as well.

In this paper I investigate the role of place in the aesthetic, social, and cultural constitution of the art object. I focus on contemporary site-specific art, which I explore through a critical examination of Richard Serra's public sculpture.

First I identify four main types of open-space art emerging from the American avant-garde of the 1960s and consider the distinctive problems

45

faced by this new art with respect to recruitment of audiences for its often ephemeral and geographically remote works. Then I trace the meaning of site specificity from its origins in antiquity to its more recent applications in postmodern art, investigating in some detail how Serra's ideas about site specificity and public sculpture emerge from his dialogue with the minimalist critique of modern art. This discussion lays the groundwork for a detailed analysis of Serra's controversial sculpture *Tilted Arc* (1981–1989), a site-specific work commissioned for the Federal Plaza in New York. Here I argue that the work's formal properties derive directly from Serra's concept of site specificity, and from his intent to use sculpture to transform the Federal Plaza site aesthetically and to reconstruct the viewing subject phenomenologically. Finally, I discuss the reception of *Tilted Arc*, noting that the heterogeneity of its audience, coupled with changing attitudes toward public art, doomed it to bureaucratic hostility and public indifference. I conclude that despite the untimely removal of *Tilted Arc*, site-specific art still has the potential to offer a powerful and sustained philosophical and aesthetic critique of contemporary culture.

A Typology of Open-Space Art

Site-specific public art emerged from the new landscape art that appeared in the United States in the late 1960s, when artists such as Michael Heizer, Robert Smithson, Dennis Oppenheim, Robert Morris, Walter De Maria, Nancy Holt, and others began to create large-scale works in spaces and landscapes far removed geographically and socially from studio, gallery, and museum. Influenced by abstraction, minimalism, and conceptual art and by philosophical movements such as phenomenology, these artists—no longer content with pictorial depictions of landscape—set about exploring the aesthetic potential of various real-world places, creating the new genre *open-space art*. By directly engaging and manipulating the landscape, open-space artists created an alternative art system, a new configuration of conceptualization, realization, and presentation of the art object that differed radically from the configuration characteristic of modernist art. Therefore, open-space art is one of the most important, most lasting achievements of the American avant-garde.[2]

Four main types of open-space art can be identified. First, *land projects or earthworks* are typically large-scale physical modifications of often remote real-world sites. Here the landscape may (1) be engaged directly, as in monumental earth-shaping projects such as Heizer's *Double Negative* and *Effigy Tumuli*, or Smithson's *Spiral Jetty* and *Amarillo Ramp*; (2) involve complex interactions with light or the weather, as with De Maria's *Lightning Field* or James Turrell's *Roden Crater* project; (3) incorporate manmade materials into the landscape, as with Heizer's *Complex One* or Serra's *Shift*; or (4) derive aesthetic effect from alignment with celestial bodies, as with Holt's *Sun Tunnels* or Morris's *Observatory*.[3] Consumed through direct visual experience and physical locomotion, these works offer a powerful experience for the audience, which it is hoped will lead the viewer to rethink the relationship between self and environment.

With *ephemeral landscape*, however, the modified landscape exists for only a short time, disappearing either because the artist deliberately removes the work from the site or because it is eroded by natural processes such as seasonal change or weather. In situ presentation of the work to viewer or audience is brief; therefore its physical existence elides rapidly into documentation and media representations. In the absence of the "original," audiences must reconstruct the work from available media traces found in books, photographs, videos, essays, and the like. The monumental wrapping projects of the Christos, in which buildings or other structures are covered or the landscape is otherwise marked and divided with synthetic fabric, are quintessential ephemeral landscapes. So are Dennis Oppenheim's early conceptual works in which lines of information were inscribed on landscapes, thus exposing hidden systems of knowledge and information underlying contemporary civilization.[4]

Dialectical landscape is a distinctive form of open-space art associated with Robert Smithson. Here a physical but otherwise undertheorized or absent landscape ("site") is brought to cultural awareness through a complex documentation ("nonsite") displayed in a museum or gallery. By presenting information about forbidding zones and landscapes such as geological systems, strip mines, or decaying industrial towns in the form of mineral samples, maps, writings, and photographs, Smithson hoped not only to bring entropy under intellectual control but also to stimulate the viewer's interest in the real-world sites to which the nonsites referred. In this way Smithson, unlike many of his contemporaries, retained a significant role for museum and gallery space in presenting the postmodern art object.[5]

Finally, *urban site-specific sculpture* introduces large-scale, abstract artworks inspired by the aesthetic of remote land projects and earthworks into public sites in the socially complex and politically charged environment of the city. Although the aim is to remake public space and to extend the audience for open-space art, artists who are commissioned to produce artworks for public places often face the challenge of an indifferent public, which encounters and interacts with the artwork while pursuing mundane work and leisure activities. Richard Serra's austere public sculptures reveal the genre's capacity for both aesthetic rigor and intense controversy. In particular, his site-specific works are sculptural objects that function as an intermediary between the architectural and physical (the real, visible) components of place and the sociopolitical (the ideal, invisible) components. The ensuing dialogue between work and site aims both to reveal the physicality of the site to the viewing subject and to enhance awareness of the fundamental relation between self and place.[6]

Open-space art is a highly charged movement on several accounts. First, it emerged from a critique of the gallery system and the conventional art object. Its creators wished to challenge the corrosive effects of commodification by making art that resisted circulation in the marketplace and hence transformation into exchange value.[7] Gallery space, some argued, exerted a powerful, even determining influence on the art object. According to O'Doherty, the architecture of the gallery formed a "white cube" which "imposed a way of seeing . . . that was, in many ways, stricter than Renaissance perspective." It created a frame that overwhelmingly favored two-dimensional painting and pedestal sculpture, an illusion-based aesthetic much criticized by Donald Judd in his seminal essays on the minimalist art object.[8]

Also important was a new generation's rediscovery of the subversive power of Marcel Duchamp's Readymade—an ordinary object such as a snow shovel, a bicycle wheel, or a bottle rack selected by the artist and subsequently turned into a work of art through designation and reversal; this process involved collaboration with the audience. Logically, if the art object was to be drawn from everyday life, then the spaces of everyday life were the places where art could (indeed, should) be found. Responding to the "ethical imperative of site," open-space artists explored the role of ordinary space in the constitution of the art object, creating a startling array of outdoor artworks in many real-world places.[9]

By moving outdoors artists were able to work on a monumental scale and so to put into practice radical new ideas about the art object and the viewing subject. These ideas were drawn from Wittgenstein's analysis of language and French phenomenology, philosophical doctrines to which many were attracted at the time.[10] Robert Morris, for example, was influenced by the existential phenomenology of Merleau-Ponty, which stressed perception as a function of the body's relation to the world. Morris argued that large-scale sculpture placed in the landscape could transform the optically oriented, passive, attenuated self—the product of conventional gallery viewing—into an active subject and a world-transforming agent. According to Morris, perception is an unconscious but highly structured cultural and biological variable that presupposes a meaningful relation of the body to the world. Because viewing a monumental land project or earthwork in situ involves physical movement that continually alters the relation of body to world, the new landscape art allows the subject to directly experience basic perceptual meanings. In effect, physical locomotion "stretches" the art consumption process through time, extending it far beyond the retinal glance characteristic of viewing static paintings in the gallery. Thus, orchestrating interaction of body and world, landscape art not only reveals itself to be the product of the artist's own action and behavior, but also shows that the world is temporal as well as spatial, that existence is process, and that action or praxis continually constructs the world in which we live.[11]

Achievement of these philosophically inspired goals, however, was compromised by the new art's involvement in the "dematerialization of the art object."[12] "Dematerialization"—the disappearance of the art object as a solid, palpable thing—may be a formal property of the work or a consequence of contingent factors. On one hand, because the ephemeral landscape is deliberately dismantled by the artist or demolished or erased by some anticipated natural force or process, direct physical experience of the work in situ is necessarily limited. Consequently the work itself, should it continue to exist at all, is replaced by "abstract" representations such as the original plans or a photographic record. Future knowledge of the work is thus a function of economic, technical, and social factors which generate and structure these representations and which organize their dissemination as media within the culture.

On the other hand, the work of art may be absent not because it has disappeared physically but because of its remote, inaccessible location. Many existing land projects, because of remoteness or inaccessibility, are known to art audiences primarily as representations rather than as direct experience—as photographs in books and catalogs, or as the subject of travelers' accounts and critical essays. For some commentators, this mediated form of knowledge—knowing a work indirectly through media and documentation—is not necessarily inferior to that gained by direct visual experience and physical contact. As Sayre writes with respect to Smithson's iconic earthworks, "Most of us have never seen any of the five 'actual' Smithson earthworks. We know them through their reproduction in art books and magazines. This is the extent of our knowledge . . . (but) it is not necessarily a lesser knowledge."[13]

A strong, even compelling case might be made for the superiority of mediated forms of engagement between work and audience in ephemeral landscape. It is less convincing, however, with respect to phenomenologically inspired open-space artworks that seek to transform the viewing subject by altering perception and behavior. Mediated forms of knowledge of such works are necessarily inferior to those acquired by direct physical and visual contact. Serra hopes to address this limitation of open-space art with his urban site-specific sculpture.

Figure 3.1.   *Amarillo Ramp* by Robert Smithson. 1973. Earthwork. Estate of Robert Smithson. Courtesy of John Weber Gallery, New York.

Serra and the Return to the City

By introducing large-scale, abstract, site-specific art into the city, Serra intends not only to continue the aesthetic challenge to the commodity form but also to rediscover and reengage the broad audience that had been lost with the "escape" of art to remote and exotic places. "There is one condition I want," he declared, namely "a density of traffic flow."[14] In this regard, "confrontation with urban and industrial reality" creates "more interesting conditions and nuances"; it provides a unique opportunity to remake art as a critical dialogue between art and context, between sculpture and place, and to highlight the relation between self and environment for as large and as democratic an audience as possible.[15]

Serra's sculpture amplifies public art's inherent capacity to create controversy. For one thing, Serra's work is resolutely abstract. It is not intended to retrieve the audience for art by reproducing the representational work usually found in public spaces: generals on horseback, archbishops delivering sermons, soldiers planting flags. In addition, Serra favors a particularly charmless material, Cor-Ten steel, which is notorious for its brutal physicality and its peeling, rusty surfaces. Moreover, the strong lateral or horizontal thrust of his large-scale works often interferes with planners' and administrators' ideas about the way public space should be used: for passive enjoyment, strolling, sitting, eating, and watching. It also contradicts their criteria for evaluating public art: to create a sense of joy, stimulate play, promote communication, and provide comfort and amenity.[16] Thus Serra has alienated not only a public used to narrative art—historical or civic lessons in three dimensions—but also many professionals concerned with the management of public space.

Urban sites first explored by Serra were functionally as remote as the desert sites they were designed to replace. *To Encircle Base Plate Hexagram* (1970) was located on a dead-end Bronx street to which few midtown art cognoscenti, much less the general public, were prepared to venture. Perhaps the local audience for *Base Plate Hexagram* lacked sufficient social and political clout to register its reaction on the cultural seismograph, but other works by Serra have more than made up for this. *Twain* (1974–1982), sited in downtown St. Louis (the self-styled "sculpture city"), came under fire when a local politician claimed that it represented a "gap between *regular* people—my constituents and the overwhelming majority—and the elitist art community." *Terminal* (1977), located in Bockum, Germany, became embroiled in the city council elections of 1979. Right-wingers claimed that its brutal aesthetic and lack of conventional charm were an insult to a community that made its living by steel. In the words of a CDU press release, *Terminal* "looks like a clumsy, undifferentiated, half-finished ingot. . . . No steelworker can point to it positively with pride."[17] Zweite claims that apart from *Fulcrum* (1986) at London's Liverpool Street Station, there is possibly "no public sculpture by Serra . . . which has not been defaced, misused or even fouled."[18] Not surprisingly, then, many of Serra's commissioned works have never been built because of "opposition from architects and city officials."[19] Long before the installation of *Tilted Arc* in New York, Serra was known as a controversial, challenging artist.

Site Specificity and Minimalism

Site specificity—the idea of making art that is inextricably related to place—is quite old, but ancient applications differ considerably from current uses. In premodern civilizations, according to Herbert Read, art—especially sculpture—was generally subordinated to architecture; hence place was asserted over space. Thus "the Egyptian sculptor had no desire to isolate the human figure in space, to dissociate it from its niche or socket, for to do so would have served no rational purpose." Although freestanding sculpture originated with the Greeks, each figure still had its own place. Therefore sculpture "remained either bound to architecture . . . or anchored in some way to the earth."[20]

Traditional meanings of site specificity continued to inform the Gothic period. Art works of that period, although influenced by the Greek ideal of humanism, "remained, as sculpture, completely subordinated to architecture."[21] Indeed, the detached work of art did not appear until the Renaissance, when artists began "studying art objects for their own sake and not as a fraction of a greater architectural assembly."[22] As Read summarized developments, "One cannot emphasize too strongly that the *objet d'art*, as transportable and movable in space, is foreign to the Greek and Gothic civilizations; it is a peculiarly modern conception, the expression of a new change of human attitude."[23]

Contemporary conceptions of site specificity derive from the minimalist critique of modernism rather than from any attempt to return to the aesthetic imperatives of the ancient world. Minimalism was part of the radical rethinking of the art object that began in the early 1960s, challenging modern art's privileging of traditional forms and materials, its restricted view of the audience, and its complicity with the detached work of art and the commodity form. As part of this critique, minimalism came to favor sculpture over painting, plain objects over surface illusion, and abstraction over representation.[24]

The minimalists claimed that three-dimensional objects devoid of inflected surfaces, expressionist meaning, representational references, or even internal "formal" structure possessed enormous but previously unrecognized aesthetic power. Donald Judd ascribed such power to "specific objects," a new class of art objects he identified as appearing in the 1960s.[25] Artists soon demonstrated that this power was greatly enhanced by the careful deployment of these sculptural objects in space. Indeed, objects of appropriate scale, material, and form could assert themselves against context, and thus could establish conditions encouraging a dialogue between work (object) and site (context).

The idea that purely aesthetic objects could decode real space was first advanced by Carl Andre. His early sculptures revealed properties of space rather than exploring (as was conventional) the structure of anthropomorphic form or the expressionist possibilities of a worked surface. Andre, however, was unable to advance a full critique of the commodity form, the avowed purpose of the new art. Although Andre considered the "form of each piece is largely determined by the space for which it is initially constructed," he conceived this space in generic rather than specific terms: "I don't think spaces are that singular. I think there are generic classes of spaces . . . so it's not really a problem where the work is going to be in particular. It's only a problem of generic spaces: is it going to be the size of Grand Central Station or is it going to be the size of a small room?"[26]

Lever (1966) and *Equivalent* (1966), two of Andre's seminal early works, tell the story. Although innovative—even shocking—in their uncompromising way of redefining sculpture as a cut into space rather than a cut into material (as traditionally conceived), these works still could be moved easily from one (generic) site to another. Thus they could be reconstituted time and again without loss of aesthetic (or intellectual) effect. Consequently these minimalist classics, like the modernist pieces they were designed to critique, could circulate in the marketplace, embody exchange value, and thus function as commodities. Serra later described how this restricted notion of space functioned to reproduce the commodity form:

> One of the biggest limitations of Minimalism, ironically, is its relation to context. The work was originally made in and for a loft space, which was then imitated by the galleries of the 1970s and 80s, to be reproduced again by the new museums of the 1990s where it is perfected and neutralised into a well-lighted white shoebox. Simultaneous in the rarefaction of the context the Minimalist object turned into a high-tech, mass-produced commodity. Now the container and the contained can both go into circulation. The Minimalist's notion of site specificity was always limited to the room, the perfect white cube.

Placed in the landscape or in urban sites, minimalist sculptures thus are invariably reduced to "homeless objects."[27] As such, they could not possibly revitalize public sculpture. Andre's "failure" here (if we can call it that) therefore indicates a more general failure of minimalist sculpture: its inability "to produce a fully materialist critique of modernist idealism."[28]

Eager to overcome this perceived weakness of minimalism, Serra set about investigating the properties of particular places, of this or that space, by using the architecture of galleries to cast works on site. Thus, for example, he made *Splashing* (1968) by flinging molten lead at the intersection of a gallery floor and wall; in *Casting* (1969) he developed this idea by dragging out successive lead casts formed by the architecture of the room to create a series of metal ridges across the gallery floor. In contrast to Andre's sculptures, *Splashing* and *Casting* could not circulate, embody exchange value (except as scrap metal), or be conventionally owned or collected.

In these early sculptures, however, Serra put almost total emphasis on place, and relatively little on the aesthetic qualities of the sculptural object. As Douglas Crimp pointed out, the outcome of *Splashing* "was not really an object at all; it had no definable shape or mass; it created no legible image." Indeed, lacking aesthetic value, it was hard to imagine the work's "continued existence in the world of art objects."[29] Usually the focus of attention, the art object in this case appears as an anti-art object, a (material) afterthought to the intellectual discovery of architectural space, which produced a largely one-sided articulation of the relation between place and object. From a phenomenological point of view, such aesthetically impoverished objects could not form or sustain an artistic environment in which the viewing subject might be renewed.

To develop a site-specific sculpture capable of reconstituting both site and subject, the artists had to mobilize those aesthetic forms and materials that enabled the sculptural object to enter into an effective, sustained dialogue with place. In his mature work, Serra thus moved beyond a simple declaration of art *as* place to a careful consideration of art's *relation to* place. From this latter perspective, the sculptural object cannot be conceived of as an individual thing. Instead it must be grasped in its relational aspects, as a genuine dialectic of work and site. According to Serra, "The specificity of site-oriented works mean that they are conceived for, dependent upon and inseparable from their location. Scale, size and placement of the sculptural elements result from an analysis of the particular environmental components of a given context." "Environmental components" include not only topographical and architectural features but also less visible social, political, even ideological properties. For Serra, site-specific works "invariably manifest a judgment about the larger social and political context of which they are a part": only as a dialectic of the real and the ideal, the visible and the hidden, the physical and the social, can they "reveal the content of their sites critically."[30]

Figure 3.2.   *Equivalent I-VIII* by Carl Andre. 1966. Sand-lime brick/firebrick. Installed Tibor de Nagy Gallery, New York. Courtesy of Paula Cooper Gallery, New York.

Figure 3.3. *Casting* by Richard Serra. 1969. Lead. Installed Whitney Museum of American Art, New York. Photograph by Peter Moore. Courtesy of Richard Serra.

No longer a mere afterthought to place, the sculptural object sustains an aesthetic zone or "anti-environment," a new element or addition to site made possible by the careful design and placement of the object as well as its material properties. For Serra, the successful remaking of sculpture as site-specific art hinges on this capacity of the art object to make and shape its own aesthetic space:

> I think that sculpture, if it has any potential at all, has the potential to create its own space, and to work in contradiction to the places and spaces where

it is created. I am interested in work where the artist is a maker of an "anti-environment" which takes its own place or makes its own situation, or divides or declares its own area.[31]

The "anti-environment" creates the possibility not only of transforming the site aesthetically but also of altering the viewing subject's perception and behavior. This process is grounded in sculpture's capacity to stimulate critical rethinking of the relation between self and place and to expose the hidden forces that shape everyday life. In Serra's view, site specificity does not stress "qualities inherent in the sculpture"; rather, it demands "a behavioral reorientation to the context of which it is a part, thereby bringing into focus new connections within the entire sociological frame."[32] Systematic control of movement and visual perception thus promises to generate in the audience a new awareness of the relationship between self and place, in that "a new behavioral and perceptual orientation to site demands a new critical adjustment to one's experience of place."[33]

Reconstitution of both site and audience depends crucially on elevating the sculptural object's status from its minimalist origins. For Serra, site-specific works are necessarily abstract so that the object (sculpture) contrasts sharply with the context (place) and "the language of one (can be used) to criticize the language of the other." Abstract form also counters the "constraints of context" so that "the work cannot be read as an affirmation of questionable ideologies or political power." Consequently Serra's works "never decorate, illustrate or depict a site."[34]

The minimalist doctrine of "object sculpture" favored aesthetic manipulation of mass-produced industrial materials such as brick, glass, plastic, or steel. These homogeneous and anonymous materials, distinctive precisely because social meaning had not yet been built into them, allowed for the creation of uniform, smooth sculptural surfaces devoid of signs of artistic intervention. As Krauss has pointed out, such materials allowed object sculpture to replace the notion of the art object's inner life with the idea of "simple externality"; therefore "the minimalist sculptors, both in their choice of material and their method of assembling them, were intent to deny the interiority of the sculptured form."[35] Likewise, Serra's preferred sculptural material—immense plates, ingots, and rounds of Cor-Ten and raw steel—allow him to move away from decoding interior, psychological space and to reveal the properties of public or cultural space.

The Case of *Tilted Arc*

Tilted Arc is Serra's most controversial and certainly his best-known work to date, an important summation of his ideas about abstract form, elemental materials, and site specificity. Because it clearly illustrates the aesthetic and philosophical goals of the new urban site-specific public sculpture as well as revealing the particular hazards faced by open-space art in the crowded and highly differentiated metropolis, I consider the sculpture's genesis, aspirations, and ultimate demise in some detail.[36]

Tilted Arc is part of a sculptural series by Serra dedicated to exploring the aesthetic properties of steel curves. Beginning with *St. John's Rotary Arc* (1980) and continuing more recently with *Running Arcs* (1992), the magnificent *Intersection II* (1993), and *Torqued Ellipses* (1997), the series includes museum, gallery, and public space installations that express site specificity through a horizontal rather than a vertical extension of form. In particular, *Tilted Arc* expresses Serra's "aesthetic rigorism, which excluded all qualities of charm and appeal, all narrative elements."[37]

Tilted Arc was the outcome of a General Services Administration (GSA) Art-in-Architecture commission awarded to Serra in 1979 to devise an artwork for the Federal Plaza in New York. Serra proposed a site-specific work in the form of an abstract 120-foot curved sweep of Cor-Ten steel, which was to be embedded permanently in the plaza. His design, after slight modification, was approved by the GSA in 1980, and the work was fabricated and installed in 1981. In 1984, however, several Federal Plaza officials, including Judge Edward Re and GSA regional administrator William Diamond, launched an aggressive campaign against *Tilted Arc* which led to a quasilegal hearing in 1985 on "relocating" the work. Serra filed several lawsuits to protect his work, but the sculpture was removed from the plaza on the night of March 15, 1989. Because Serra claimed *Tilted Arc* was created for one site, it could not be installed elsewhere; hence "removal of the work . . . amounted to its destruction."[38] Serra withdrew his authorship, and *Tilted Arc* now languishes in a Brooklyn warehouse.

What made *Tilted Arc* so controversial? To answer this question, we first must know how the aesthetic properties and overall form of *Tilted Arc* related to Serra's concept of site specificity, his ideas about sculptural space, and his artistic vision for Federal Plaza. We also need to know about conceptions of public art, especially in New York, and how these have changed over time. Finally, we must know about the audience for this challenging and difficult public artwork.

Tilted Arc as Sculpture

The depositions and statements given by Serra in various lawsuits and public hearings reveal *Tilted Arc* as a precisely conceived attempt to transform a complex architectural and sociopolitical site with an entirely abstract work of art.[39] Its formal sculptural properties derived from Serra's careful consideration of the specific features of the Federal Plaza site. This ill-planned and ill-defined government complex comprises an underutilized public plaza framed by two incompatible and opposing architectures, the Federal Courthouse and the Jacob Javits Building. The plaza itself is a relatively featureless place: in Serra's words, "an open, windy, desolate area basically used for transit" where the surrounding buildings are "as uncharacteristic as the plaza itself" and "new and old federal architectures are set off against each other." Not surprisingly, this architectural ensemble, like dozens of other, similar government complexes, is "a foremost mediocrity."[40]

Serra hoped to transform this sterile site by devising a sculpture that would have three effects. First, the sculpture was designed to "structure the plaza, and create directions, accentuating existing pedestrian traffic patterns." Second, by linking the two sides of the enclave, the work was to form a bridge between the two federal architectures. Third and most important, Serra wanted the physical presence of the work itself to create a distinct "sculptural space within the plaza which could be experienced by those crossing the plaza on their way into and out of buildings."[41] In other words, Serra's plan was to create a unique sculptural object that would transform its site aesthetically by becoming an integral part of that site. Moreover, it would alter the perception and behavior of the people using it.

To realize these ideas, Serra planned a sculpture devoid of narrative elements, a horizontal steel "wall" 120 feet long and 12 feet high. The sculpture would orchestrate locomotion because its length would force pedestrians to walk around it and its height would prevent them from seeing over it. Careful placement would maximize the work's physical and material presence by controlling interaction with light. As Serra explained,

> The sculpture was laid out not only to direct the passage of the people but also to mirror the passage of the sun, so that there would be no shadows from the sculpture on the plaza at midday, which maximizes the effect of the sculpture at the time when most people are on the plaza.

Serra conceived this horizontal wall as a sweeping curve or arc that would not only connect the disparate architectural elements of the site but also would "carry the eye past the confines of the plaza." Thus it would permit a variety of perceptual orientations that would allow the plaza to be "continuously redrawn."[42]

The curve's principal function, however, was to form a sculptural space or "anti-environment" where the site would be revealed to the viewing subject. This concern explained both the brutal, dense materiality of *Til-*

ted Arc, and its marked tilt. To "answer the hardness of the stone and the flat extension of the plaza," Serra felt that *Tilted Arc* had to be capable of exerting sufficient contained weight and mass, an effect best achieved by a combination of large size and Cor-Ten steel. Thus, as a blank, continuous, uninflected facade, the arc would assert itself against place by "substantiating the absolute difference between the physical characteristic of site and sculpture." Serra saw the dialogue between work and site as emerging on the basis of this "absolute difference." Altering the viewer's perception in a coherent way, however, depended not only on this assertion of object against place but also on the creation of a significant sculptural space within the plaza. By carefully tilting the wall of the arc to one side, Serra hoped to create a "definite interval and volume between it and the architecture." The fundamental dialogue between work and site was to occur within this space.[43]

The "tilt" assumed by the arc is that of an angled cylinder rather than a resting cone. This distinction is crucial to the site-specific character of the work and the coherent structuring of perception. A cone is essentially a freestanding structure that sits on the ground. In principle, at least, it can be lifted and relocated at will; thus it suggests an object potentially independent of place. A cone therefore does not indicate site specificity.

In contrast, a cylinder creates a tilted surface only when it is held at an angle, away from its natural point of rest or balance. Such a tilt, however, can be sustained only if the cylinder is embedded in the ground. Thus, in contrast to the cone, a tilted cylinder suggests a fundamental grounding of object in place. For Serra this property is expressed by the fact that *Tilted Arc* "had to be anchored into the steel and concrete substructure of the Federal Plaza."[44] In this way the sculpture's essential form confirmed site specificity.

The tilt also had implications for structuring the viewing subject's perception. A cone draws the eye upward, but only to dissipate a sense of space as the eye reaches the vanishing point at the tip of the cone; perceptually, then, a cone shape cancels the object in relation to its place or location. Therefore, unable to grasp, order, and control space, a cone cannot form the basis of a significant site-specific sculpture.

In contrast, the curved surface of a tilted cylinder gives the sculptural object distinct convex and concave sides. The convex side creates an "infinite plane" that draws in the whole of the plaza as the eye traces out the volume of space encompassed by this plane; this surface expands and unites the overall space of the site. The concave side holds, defines, and controls the space of the plaza by gripping and holding the viewer in a finite, visually contained space; it enhances awareness of self in relation to place.

The viewing subject accesses these contrasting perceptual experiences by moving physically around the sculpture, thus making *Tilted Arc* "the sum of successive perceptions revealed only to the moving observer."[45]

> Two discrete sculptural volumes, concave and convex, are opened to the walking viewer. . . . On the concave side the sweep of the arc creates an amphitheatre-like condition. This . . . has a silent amplitude which magnifies your awareness of yourself and the sculptural field of the space. The concavity of the topological curve allows you to understand the sweep of the entire plaza; however, upon walking around the convexity at the ends, the curve appears to be infinite.[46]

The manipulation of perception by orchestrating physical locomotion around an apparently useless object is the aesthetic core of *Tilted Arc*. This suggests that an active viewer is a necessary component of the work. From Serra's point of view, the idea was not to create a work that would cause people to "stop and stare," but rather one that would form "a behavioral space in which the viewer interacts with the sculpture in its context." Therefore, *Tilted Arc* aimed to offer the pedestrians of Federal Plaza as significant a perceptual experience as might be gained, perhaps, by the intrepid traveler to *Amarillo Ramp*, *Spiral Jetty*, or *Double Negative*. Most important, *Tilted Arc* was not designed to promote or reinforce the bureaucratic sensibilities that governed Federal Plaza. On the contrary, it was "constructed so as to engage the public in a dialogue that would perceptually and conceptually enhance its relation to the entire plaza." By establishing "new meanings among things . . . space becomes the sum of successive perceptions of place (and) the viewer becomes the subject."[47]

The Demise of *Tilted Arc*

Far from being incomprehensible and hostile, *Tilted Arc* was a carefully thought-out work designed to achieve particular aesthetic and phenomenological effects. Donald Judd called it "visible civilization," whose very existence manifested "thought against thoughtlessness."[48] Because the sculpture lacked conventional charm, however, Serra's refined conceptualization and high aesthetic purpose were insufficient to save *Tilted Arc* from the "thoughtlessness" that ultimately engulfed it. How did this sorry state of affairs come to pass in a city that prides itself as the home of abstract expressionism and the world center of art?

Attitudes toward public art in New York have not favored abstract, difficult, or controversial art. Abstraction may have been valued by the elite—financial as well as artistic—but it has never been embraced as an aesthetic to guide public art or by average citizens, the likely users of

Figure 3.4a.   *Tilted Arc* by Richard Serra. 1981. Cor-Ten steel. Installed Federal
Plaza, New York. Destroyed 1989. Photographed by Anna Chauvet.
Courtesy of Richard Serra

Figure 3.4b.   *Tilted Arc* by Richard Serra. 1981. Cor-Ten Steel. Installed Federal Plaza, New York. Destroyed 1989. Courtesy of Gagosian Gallery, New York.

Federal Plaza. This tension between elite and popular conceptions of art was exacerbated by a top-down commissioning process for public art, instituted in the 1960s and responsible for the *Tilted Arc* commission. Indeed, open-space art located in the complex urban environment "has a much greater visual and psychological impact and touches a great many more people than does art in the traditional museum context."[49]

Surveys suggest that most users of urban parks and plazas are clerical workers from nearby offices. Their most frequent activities in these places

Figure 3.4c. *Tilted Arc* by Richard Serra. 1981. Cor-Ten Steel. Installed Federal Plaza, New York. Destroyed 1989. Courtesy of Richard Serra.

include relaxing (sitting, watching, and listening), eating, and walking. As modifications and improvements to public space, people prefer more seats, tables, and umbrellas, more concerts and events, and more flowers and greenery.[50] Appeals to users of public space at any point would more than likely exclude the possibility of "Tilted Arc." Thus, locating a work by one of America's most radical artists in as prominent and busy a place as the Federal Plaza was bound to create controversy.

Tilted Arc also fell victim to a seachange in the political economy of capitalism. By the mid-1980s the liberal capitalism that had sponsored public investment in the arts, championing abstraction and the avant-garde, had given way to a faceless corporate capitalism that feared all but the most conventional forms of artistic and cultural expression. To cultural bureaucrats, the radicalism and the anticommodity stance of works such as *Tilted Arc* stood as a constant reminder that art constitutes a barrier to the universalization of capitalism, a critique of the existing order, and a mode of activism and liberation. Even with the decline of meaningful political opposition in the United States, artists still managed to create entirely useless objects that celebrated cancellation of the commodity form and opposed the passivity and alienation on which the system depended.

Public space management in New York, beginning with Olmstead, has favored a conception of public spaces as reserved principally for recreation and leisure, not for the display of contemporary art works. In this tradition, art generally has been excluded from public sites such as parks and plazas on various grounds: that these areas were developed with tax money from the average citizen, not from the elite who typically promoted contemporary art; that art introduced a potentially discordant note into essentially architectural sites; and that because current art vogues might not last, the public could be left with aesthetically obsolete works as time passed. Treated as a means to promote social cohesion and construct historical memory rather than to engage in aesthetic experimentation and education, the existing public art tends to be highly representational. It celebrates and commemorates universal, common experiences for the broadest of publics. This conservative tradition has been relatively strong in New York; as a result, "experimental public art was not part of the urban scene in Manhattan as it had been in Philadelphia or Chicago."[51]

The situation changed somewhat in the 1950s and 1960s when the New York elite, especially liberal capitalists such as the Rockefellers, began to see art—that is modern art—as intimately connected to the financial and political power now centered on the city, and thus as directly associated with the triumphs of postwar American capitalism. Nelson Rockefeller, for example, held that the art of the late 1940s and early 1950s directly manifested the values of American individualism; indeed, for him, abstract expressionism was the ultimate cultural defense against international communism from abroad and creeping bureaucracy and regimentation at home. Thus it was perfectly appropriate for the elite to embrace the avant-garde; as Rockefeller put it, "modern forms of artistic expression were the only area left in democracy where there was true freedom and where there were 'no holds barred.' "[52]

This view justified something considerably more adventurous for the public sphere than the bland aesthetic conservatism promoted by New York's public servants. Increased government support for the arts was necessary, especially if the public was to be exposed to modern, abstract

art and convinced of its superiority to representational and commemora-
tive work. As Rockefeller saw it, official promotion of the arts was tied
closely to good government: "The arts are indeed a critical measure of
'quality of life'. [They] offer us the rare opportunity to further something
that is positive—the expansion of the human capacity and the pursuit of
happiness—which is after all not only the central element of the arts, but
of good government as well." As governor of New York, Rockefeller
forged practical links between the art world and government by institut-
ing a number of state programs to promote the arts. These programs became important models for later federal involvement in the arts. In this
regard, it is ironic that Rockefeller "helped create the political and economic climate in New York that ultimately brought Serra's *Tilted Arc* to
One Federal Plaza."[53]

The crisis in public art and the decay of Rockefeller's liberal-capitalist
vision culminated in the *Tilted Arc* controversy. The sculpture was highly
minimalist and abstract, a form likely to meet indifference or hostility in
a public fed for decades on a diet of highly representational public art.
Furthermore, *Tilted Arc* had been commissioned in a largely top-down
way; the public had had no input into the design, and the panel that selected and reviewed commissions consisted of Serra's peers in the art
world. Finally, *Tilted Arc* was to be seen not only by people who had
chosen to enter a traditional art space or to travel to some remote site, but
also by crowds of ordinary workers hurrying to and from alienating jobs.

The attack on *Tilted Arc* marked the end of Rockefeller's vision of a
link between modern art, American individualism, and good government.
With the return of Republicans to office at many levels in the early 1980s,
government no longer saw any connection between the avant-garde and
the viability of the ruling ideology. In the reactionary world of trickle-
down economics and corporate capitalism, abstraction itself was regarded
increasingly as a highly dangerous art form likely to fuel a new individualism, which threatened to undermine the creeping authoritarianism of a
now-global corporate system. As a harbinger of things to come, Reagan's
1980 election platform called for a radical cutback in funding for the arts.
Indeed, as Serra ruefully noted later, "The governmental decree to remove
and thereby destroy *Tilted Arc* is the direct outcome of a cynical Republican cultural policy that supports art only as a commodity."[54] In general
terms, then, attacks on *Tilted Arc* coincided with (indeed, ushered in) a
new and conservative phase in government's relation to the arts. In this
phase, any link between art, good government, and the quality of life, was
rejected. Moreover, liberal art policies and adventurous aesthetic forms
were viewed as symptoms of a profound national malaise.

The audience for *Tilted Arc* had three distinct components. One component consisted of the art cognoscenti: individuals typically well in-

formed about the difficulties of abstract and minimalist art, peers of Serra, and consequently generally supportive of *Tilted Arc*. Many spoke positively and eloquently about the work at the various hearings held to determine its fate. Members of a second group, the local population living near Federal Plaza, were likely to have some visual knowledge of the work but did not necessarily interact with it daily. With some exposure to abstract art, this group might be considered reasonably supportive.[55]

The third and largest component, however, consisted of the office and government workers in the Federal Plaza complex; although compelled to interact daily with the sculpture, this group was likely to have the least knowledge of, and exposure to, abstract modern art. Cynically manipulated by a handful of fanatics, workers at Federal Plaza were encouraged to sign petitions calling for the removal of *Tilted Arc*, or to speak against it at public hearings. Yet it is not certain that a majority of these workers, or indeed those who made or submitted statements to the various hearings, opposed *Tilted Arc*.[56] No steps were taken by the commissioning agency or by any local arts or community organization to help the public read the work, despite its obvious "difficulty."[57]

Criticism of *Tilted Arc* has not been limited to conservative political circles. Many liberal commentators disagree with Serra's notion of public art and his idea of site specificity; they detect an authoritarian, antidemocratic streak not only in the work itself but also in avant-garde and orthodox left politics generally. Michael Kelly, for example, argues that *Tilted Arc* was "merely a private sculpture in a public space, rather than a work of public art specific to a particular place." He finds Serra's conception of site specificity one-sided—more a formal-aesthetic critique of commodification than an effort to develop a public art.[58] Others believe that *Tilted Arc*, by failing to treat the public as people, merely exposed the hollowness of the arts community's radicalism, and stood as a "monument to the convergence of formalist art and 'formalist politics'—a politics . . . of theory without praxis."[59] In this regard, Deutsche finds that Serra's supporters, apart from pursuing the worthwhile tasks of challenging "the mobilization of democratic discourses to sanction . . . shifts to state authoritarianism" and countering the trivial reduction of "public spaces to harmonious leisure spots . . . (in which) to eat lunch," generally made "few efforts to articulate democracy, public art, or public space in more radical directions."[60] From this perspective, the whole controversy has perpetuated essentially modernist ideas about great artists and great works of art rather than solving or advancing the issue of publicly sited artworks.

At its trial, *Tilted Arc* faced all kinds of charges. It was accused of being profoundly ugly—a rusting pile of junk; of promoting totalitarianism and embodying the principles of the enemy, communism; of being responsible for public nuisances including graffiti, rats in buildings, and litter; of interrupting pedestrian traffic and public enjoyment of the plaza; of impeding police surveillance and thus of promoting crime; and (extraordinarily) of functioning as a potential blast wall capable of concentrating the effects of terrorist bombings. As Crimp reminds us, when such accusations are entered into a public record contributing to the removal of a public work of art, it is clear that the "federal sector" now considers everyone who uses public space "potential loiterers, graffiti scribblers, drug dealers, terrorists."[61]

Conclusion

Tilted Arc reflects the particular difficulties of creating site-specific artworks for the city's open spaces. Perhaps its curve was too subtle and its tilt too slight to create that convincing aesthetic space for the subject's phenomenological awakening, or to offset its pronounced horizontal extension. Serra's apparent response to the debacle was to work less with the single long curve and more with shorter, multiple plates configured so that the resulting curves and tilts more obviously and more decisively sculpted space. This is apparent in *Intersection II*, a work that carves out a multitude of spaces, including an obvious central grove, and whose power is amplified by compression in gallery space; and *Torqued Ellipses*, a production of massive twisted steel plates that provide an "enveloping experience . . . akin to architecture."[62]

Postmodern art is allegedly difficult and arrogant because it does not produce beautiful works that appeal to traditional consumers of art. Embodying Serra's interest in abstraction, monumental scale, and industrial materials, *Tilted Arc* contradicted popular conceptions, reinforced by culture generally, that art is essentially a retinal, visual experience requiring little of the viewer. Serra's steel sculpture, however, like the land projects to which it is related, advances the view that art is consumed as much by physical movement of the body as by vision. Such public art, however, lacking any discernible function and hence any excuse for its obdurate qualities, is likely to face greater criticism than the architecture, however hideous, surrounding it.

Yet it would be a mistake to ignore the many achievements of postmodern art. As *Tilted Arc* demonstrates, such art has a social and intellectual agenda, contributing to a dramatic broadening of the art object by applying and extending the intellectual achievements of minimalism. Site-specific public sculpture critiques commodification, investigates the aesthetic properties of new materials, and revolutionizes conceptions of the audience and the art consumption process. Thus it not only reworks the modernist art system but also makes us think more critically about the world around us.

Notes

The writing of this paper was supported by a Rider University Paid Research Leave and a Summer Research Fellowship. I would like to thank Lise Vogel for comments on an earlier draft and Karen Feinberg for excellent editing.

1. Hilde Hein, "What Is Public Art?" *Journal of Aesthetics and Art Criticism*, 54, No. 1 (1996): 5.

2. For a general discussion of the American avant-garde, see Irving Sandler, *American Art of the 1960s* (New York: Harper and Row, 1988). For open-space art, see John Beardsley, *Earthworks and Beyond* (New York: Abbeville, 1989); Henry M. Sayre, *The Object of Performance* (Chicago: University of Chicago Press, 1989); Rosalind Krauss, *Passages in Modern Sculpture* (Cambridge, Mass.: MIT Press, 1977).

3. An early appreciation of earthworks is John Beardsley, *Probing the Earth* (Washington, D.C.: Smithsonian Institution, 1977). A recent comprehensive overview is Gilles A. Tiberghien, *Land Art* (Princeton, N.J.: Princeton Architectural Press, 1995).

4. Sayre, *Object of Performance*, chap. 6, stresses the ephemeral aspect of open-space art. Also see Dominique Laporte, *Christo* (New York: Pantheon, 1986); and Alanna Heiss, *Dennis Oppenheim: Selected Works 1967–1990* (New York: Abrams, 1992).

5. The best source on dialectical landscape is Smithson himself. See Nancy Holt, ed., *The Writings of Robert Smithson* (New York: NYU Press, 1979). Also useful are Robert Hobbs, *The Sculpture of Robert Smithson* (Ithaca, N.Y.: Cornell University Press, 1981) and Gary Shapiro, *Earthwards: Robert Smithson and Art after Babel* (Berkeley: University of California Press, 1995). Ephemeral and dialectical landscape are discussed in greater detail in my essay "Journey into Space: Interpretations of Landscape in Contemporary Art," in *Landscape and Technology*, ed. David E. Nye (Boston: University of Massachusetts Press, forthcoming).

6. For urban public sculpture, see Harriet F. Senie, *Contemporary Public Sculpture* (New York: Oxford University Press, 1992); Arlene Raven, ed., *Art in the Public Interest* (Ann Arbor: UMI Research Press, 1989); Louis G. Redstone, *Public Art* (New York: McGraw-Hill, 1981).

7. Michael Heizer, "The Art of Michael Heizer," *Artforum* 8 (December 1969): 32–39; Sayre, *Object of Performance*, 211.

8. Brian O'Doherty, *Inside the White Cube* (Santa Monica: Lapis Press, 1986), 14.

9. Thomas McEvilley, "The Rightness of Wrongness: Modernism and Its Alter-Ego in the Work of Dennis Oppenheim," in Heiss, *Dennis Oppenheim*, 7.

10. Joseph Kosuth went so far as to argue for the reduction of art to philosophy. He rejected earthworks and much of the avant-garde because they retained visual and material references to traditional "morphological" art, which he

thought inhibited "the understanding of the linguistic nature of all art propositions." See Sandler, *American Art of the 1960s*, 69, 353. Also see Kosuth, "Art
after Philosophy," *Studio International*, (October 1969): 136, where he writes:
"Works of art are analytic propositions . . . they provide no information whatsoever about any matter of fact. . . . The validity of artistic propositions is not
dependent on any empirical, much less any aesthetic, presupposition about the
nature of things."

11. Robert Morris, "Notes on Sculpture, Part II," *Artforum* (October 1966):
30–23; and "Some Notes on the Phenomenology of Making," *Artforum* (April
1970): 62–66. Morris's essays from this period are now gathered in *Continuous
Project Altered Daily* (Cambridge, Mass.: MIT Press, 1993). A useful guide to
Merleau-Ponty is Monika M. Langer, *Merleau-Ponty's Phenomenology of Perception* (London: Macmillan, 1989). Michael Fried rejected artworks contingent on
"the duration of the experience" because he considered them "paradigmatically
theatrical," confronting and isolating the viewer with "the endlessness not just of
objecthood but of *time*." In contrast, in real art (i.e., modern art), the work is
"wholly manifest at every moment." See Fried's seminal critique of minimalism,
"Art and Objecthood," *Artforum* (June 1967): 12–23.

12. Lucy Lippard, *Six Years: The Dematerialization of the Art Object* (New
York: Praeger, 1973). Jack Burnham had already noted the reduction of modernist
sculpture to a "squiggle in the air" in *Beyond Modern Sculpture* (New York: Bra-
ziller, 1968), 364.

13. Sayre, *Object of Performance*, 216. Smithson's five "iconic" earthworks are
Spiral Jetty, *Amarillo Ramp*, *Partially Buried Woodshed*, *Asphalt Rundown*, and
Broken Circle/Spiral Hill. Most of these works now no longer exist or are severely
eroded.

14. Douglas Crimp, "Serra's Public Sculpture: Redefining Site Specifity," in
Richard Serra, ed. Ernst-Gerhard Guse (New York: Rizzoli, 1988), 32.

15. Armin Zweite, "A Steel Curve Is Not a Monument" in *Running Arcs Richard Serra* (Dusseldorf: Kunstsammlung Nordrhein-Westfalen, 1992), 22.

16. See, for example, Clare Cooper Marcus and Carolyn Francis, eds., *People
Places: Design Guidelines for Urban Open Spaces* (New York: Van Nostrand Reinhold, 1990), 10, 40–42, where *Tilted Arc* is criticized for fulfilling the criteria for
good public art only "insofar as it promoted communication among those who
resented its presence."

17. Crimp, "Serra's Public Sculpture," 37, 33.

18. Zweite, "A Steel Curve," 10.

19. Crimp, "Serra's Public Sculpture," 37.

20. Herbert Read, *The Art of Sculpture* (New York: Pantheon, 1956), 53, 55.

21. Read, *Art of Sculpture*, 56.

22. Burnham, *Beyond Modern Sculpture*, 372.

23. Read, *Art of Sculpture*, 58.

24. For accounts of minimalism, see Francis Colpitt, *Minimal Art* (Seattle: University of Washington Press, 1993) and Gregory Battcock, ed., *Minimal Art: A
Critical Anthology* (New York: Dutton, 1968).

25. Donald Judd, "Specific Objects," *Arts Yearbook* 8 (1965): 74–82.

26. David Bourdon, *Carl Andre: Sculpture 1959–1977* (New York: Japp-Reitman, 1978), 14.

27. Richard Serra, *Weight and Measure* (London: Tate Gallery, 1992), 21.

28. Crimp, "Serra's Public Sculpture," 28.

29. Crimp, "Serra's Public Sculpture," 26.

30. Clara Weyergraf-Serra and Martha Buskirk, eds., *The Destruction of Tilted Arc: Documents* (Cambridge, Mass.: MIT Press, 1991), 184.

31. Richard Serra, *Writings/Interviews* (Chicago: University of Chicago Press, 1994).

32. Zweite, "A Steel Curve," 16.

33. Weyergraf-Serra and Buskirk, *Destruction of Tilted Arc*, 184.

34. Weyergraf-Serra and Buskirk, *Destruction of Tilted Arc*, 12, 13, 11.

35. Krauss, *Passages in Modern Sculpture*, 254.

36. For materials relating directly to *Tilted Arc*, see Weyergraf-Serra and Buskirk, *Destruction of Tilted Arc*, and American Council for the Arts (ACA), *Public Art, Public Controversy: The Tilted Arc on Trial* (New York: ACA Books, 1987).

37. Zweite, "A Steel Curve," 70.

38. Weyergraf-Serra and Buskirk, *Destruction of Tilted Arc*, 3. For an account and photographs of the removal, see *Art in America* 77 (May 1989): 34–47.

39. Rosalyn Deutsche, *Evictions: Art and Spatial Politics* (Cambridge, Mass.: MIT Press, 1966), 228, points out that the documentary material assembled in Weyergraf-Serra and Buskirk, *Destruction of Tilted Arc*, is an important "act of historical preservation" providing "a solid foundation for future art-historical and legal scholarship."

40. Weyergraf-Serra and Buskirk, *Destruction of Tilted Arc*, 184; ACA Books, *Tilted Arc on Trial*, 65.

41. Weyergraf-Serra and Buskirk, *Destruction of Tilted Arc*, 184–85.

42. Weyergraf-Serra and Buskirk, *Destruction of Tilted Arc*, 185.

43. Weyergraf-Serra and Buskirk, *Destruction of Tilted Arc*, 185–86.

44. Weyergraf-Serra and Buskirk, *Destruction of Tilted Arc*, 186.

45. Weyergraf-Serra and Buskirk, *Destruction of Tilted Arc*, 186.

46. ACA, *Tilted Arc on Trial*, 148. Zweite ("A Steel Curve," 68, 70, 102) suggests that the shallow curvature and slight tilt of *Tilted Arc* made it seem "to be the segment of a cone and not a cylinder." As further complication, "(t)he conical shape created an additional moment of irritation in that the curve seemed to be unstable and, depending on the viewing position, gave the impression that it was leaning inwards or outwards." This appears to contradict Serra's own description of the arc as an embedded cylinder. Zweite complicates matters when he suggests that in the late 1980s "Serra developed a series of works, which in the final analysis, were all derived from *Tilted Arc* in that they operated with conical elements," but then adds parenthetically "For accuracy's sake . . . it must be pointed out that *Tilted Arc* was not in fact a conical element but rather a cylindrical curve which was let into the ground at both ends, resulting in the tilt and the greater height in the middle."

47. ACA, *Tilted Arc on Trial*, 148–49.

48. ACA, *Tilted Arc on Trial*, 133–34.

49. ACA, *Tilted Arc on Trial*, 24. For a discussion of public art in New York, see Deutsche, *Evictions*, 49–107.

50. Marcus and Francis, *People Places*, 20–24.

51. ACA, *Tilted Arc on Trial*, 5. The *Tilted Arc* debacle has had a chilling effect on public art commissions nationwide. For example, after the community panel advising on selection of an artwork for the Sacramento Federal Courthouse rejected Tom Otterness's original proposal, the artist asked the members what they wanted. "Eagles" was the reply, so Otterness created a series on Western culture: gold miners, covered wagons, building the railroad. Robert Cembalest, "Public Sculpture the Public Really Likes," *New York Times*, 21 September 1997.

52. ACA, *Tilted Arc on Trial*, 8.

53. ACA, *Tilted Arc on Trial*, 8, 7.

54. Weyergraf-Serra and Buskirk, *Destruction of Tilted Arc*, 5.

55. ACA, *Tilted Arc on Trial*, 25.

56. The GSA presented 3,791 signatures in favor of "relocation" and 3,763 against, out of a total workforce of approximately 10,000. Weyergraf-Serra and Buskirk, *Destruction of Tilted Arc*, 9.

57. ACA, *Tilted Arc on Trial*, 26.

58. Michael Kelly, "Public Art Controversy: The Serra and Lin Cases," *Journal of Aesthetics and Art Criticism*, 54, No. 1 (1996): 16–18.

59. Robert Storr, "*Tilted Arc*: Enemy of the People?" in Raven, *Art in the Public Interest*, 281–82.

60. Deutsche, *Evictions*, 267.

61. Crimp, "Serra's Public Sculpture," 37.

62. Michael Kimmelman, "Inventing Shapes to Tease the Mind and Eye," *New York Times*, 26 September 1997, 33, 36. Also see Roberta Smith, "Richard Serra's Temporal Monument," *New York Times*, 2 April 1993.

Sites of Symbolic Density:
A Relativistic Approach
to Experienced Space

Katya Mandoki

The way we experience space and signify it in our everyday activities is far more complex than Descartes' idea of *res extensa* might suggest. From physics' point of view, the elapsed notion of static Euclidean space filled with ether has been substituted by Hermann Minkowski's four dimensional space-time continuum. Albert Einstein further elaborated this idea into the general theory explaining gravitation as a result of the curvature produced by matter in this space-time continuum.[1] These concepts are not easy to understand, yet it seems that our experience of space in both private and public spheres intuitively follows similar assumptions. Certain objects and events seem to alter the configuration of space and become like spiraling points of higher spatial density. Space is increasingly being conceived closer to the idea of an organism developing in time than to Kant's a priori, timeless and empty background for perceptions.

Such view of space-time as unevenly bowed may be new for science but not, I contend, for common awareness. From very early times, social imaginaries have tacitly apprehended space as textured and bent both physically and symbolically rather than as an empty container. Particular places have been experienced as loaded with specific historical, noumenal and emotional value. The superposition of images in cave paintings suggests that certain places were conceived as having more magical power than others. Most religions have in common the enhancement of specific places as more symbolically dense than others. Peregrinations to sacred places such as Mecca, Jerusalem, Santiago de Compostela and many others indicate the belief that God may be omnipresent, but not all places are equal nor space even. Their hierarchy and significance is determined by their history and the quality of events that occurred exactly in a given place.

A prototypical case of space-time bending is Mount Moriah over which, according to the Bible, Abraham almost sacrificed Isaac. It was later the location where the Temple to house the Ark of the Covenant was built by King Solomon until the Babylonian Nebuchadnezzar II destroyed it in 586 B.C. Rebuilt on the same spot by King Herod (40–4 B.C.) and destroyed again by the Romans in A.D. 70, more than half a millennium later the exact same place marked for Moslem tradition the site of Mohammed's ascension to heaven on June 8, 632, and where, thirty years after, the gold-domed mosque was erected. This site is consequently a dangerous focus of friction between Moslems and Jews in the present.[2]

Another example of space–time symbolic implosion is the Kaaba in Mecca, Islam's most sacred sanctuary located in the courtyard of the Great Mosque. According to the Koran, the Kaaba was built by Adam and rebuilt by Abraham around a black rock that was given to Ismael by the Angel Gabriel. It was later a shrine for the pagan deities of the Arabs until Mohammed began to preach to the Meccans and rededicated it to Allah. Moslems, who have a duty of pilgrimage to Mecca at least once in their lifetime, face toward Mecca in their prayers (Jews face toward the Western Wall) as if space would bend toward these points.[3]

Jerusalem and Mecca are clearly not the only sites of symbolic density. The *Templo Mayor* in México-Tenochtitlán, physically built out of several layers of overlapping pyramids, is a perfect metaphor for the building of symbolic meaning of a place. As the Moslems with the Dome of the Rock, Cortés chose to keep the symbolic density of the main square of Tenochtitlán and used for himself the same parcel of the palace that belonged to the great Aztec emperor Moctezuma.

This paper is contributing to the elaboration of a symbolic cartography by focusing on a particular way of building and experiencing the character of a place. I will take the Aztec formulation of their settlement and meaning of their capital city, the great México–Tenochtitlán, and its symbolical layers developed through time as a case in point. Changing scales from private to public space, from the ontogenetic to phylogenetic meaning of place, we will explore how the entire region came to be symbolically coiled into a single spot and remains so to this day.

I. Toward Symbolic Topoanalysis:
Differential Signs and Charged Symbols

The locations of human settlements are determined not only by practical considerations, such as material resources (water, fertile land) and strategic position (panoptic and physical protection against attacks), but also by layers of meaning accumulated and enriched through time. A place, then, is not pure space nor the opposite of time: it is woven with time. Space is not only physically shaped by geographical and architectural elements but it is also symbolically configured by social imaginaries into quite complex symbolic organizations. Operating as strong gravitational fields, these symbolically dense places tend to draw towards them further layers of meaning by warping its surroundings.

In his effort to construct a phenomenological archeology of images and a topoanalysis, Bachelard has stated various categories of spatial qualification.[4] However, his attempt is limited to what he has named "images of happy space," which although expressed sincerely and movingly, mostly portray a sense of intimate space characteristic of a bourgeois sense of dwelling. For an archeology and a phenomenology of lived space, we need a broader, but no less specific, comparative approach of experiencing and signifying space. Paradigms from semiotics and the theory of relativity can provide tools to enable a more fruitful framework for this topoanalysis.

We signify places according to two distinct kinds of semiosic[5] orders. On the one hand, a strictly semiotic order is displayed by means of a system of oppositions and differentiations according to Saussure's concept of the sign.[6] Countries, mountains, rivers, cities, neighborhoods, streets, buildings and rooms are designated by different names and numbers to enable distinctions based upon conventional codes.

There is another sense in which places are defined, although we lack a cartography capable of depicting it. This is the symbolic order through which we experience places as being charged with specific personal or collective memories, stamped with emotional, historical, and material meanings. In other words, we experience space as a variegated and heterogeneous assortment of energetic, historical and material weight. Contrary to the semiotic system of conventional differentiations that is relatively flat and abstract, the symbolic is substantially charged with energy, time, and matter, motivated by specific events and highly culturally specific. This second conception of meaning as symbolic is the one referred to here.

II. Hubs in the Private Scene

More clearly than Bachelard, Jean Baudrillard[7] has elucidated how domestic space is organized and how it acquires meaning by a particular ordering of personal things within it. He defines it as a moral arrangement of objects that becomes a representation of family relations. Furniture are for the author like monuments that attest to and portray class status, stability, credibility, and lifestyle. Classical figures of rhetoric, such as alliteration, ellipsis, and hyperbole, are used to emphasize and express particular meanings of places and relations within a house. Flowers in the middle of a rounded vase on the center of a round tablecloth on the center of a circular table that stands in the middle of a round rug in the center of a room is a typical example of alliteration within this personal mapping of space. The rules of this apparently individual configuration of private space are mostly dictated by social status. Every home seems to have a center or an assortment of centers marking the most meaningful places for the family, like the classical living room center table, the dining room table, and the matrimonial bed. To enhance this particular place, decorative objects specially cherished by the owners are set there. In the case of the bed, expensive bed covers, handmade quilts, pillows, and dolls are placed over it to emphasize its importance as the center of the room. In these days, when cooking has lost its full time dedication as a consequence of women working away from home, the refrigerator has taken the central place that the hearth and stove used to have in the kitchen. We now see typical American homes with their huge refrigerators all decorated with children's drawings, notes, or a collection of decorative magnets. Baudrillard depicts how in past times, the hearth for cooking constituted the main centripetal point of a home in the countryside. Later, the fireplace was the main focal point, substituted in urban contexts by the clock and later by the radio around which sofas and chairs were arranged during the thirties and forties. During the 1950s, it was the television set that acquired the status of center, enhanced by a flower pot over an embroidered cloth placed on top (as can still be found in many middle and lower class homes in Mexico and other countries). The television set was later dispersed into the bedrooms and has been replaced recently by the personal computer as the centripetal spot in a home, around which family members linger and items accumulate. During December, an extra locus is added in Christian homes: The Christmas tree establishes not only a different order in space but also in time. All these items—the hearth, the fireplace, the clock, the radio, the television, and the computer—are experienced as symbols of time, hence framing around them the family's private main square.

Many low class families today in Mexico City still keep a centuries old tradition of arranging a niche for a holy creature within the house. The Virgin of Guadalupe, the "Niño Dios" (Child God), or the saint of the town are the occupants of such a niche as a focal point decorated with a special glass little chapel, candles and flowers.[8] Workplaces such as factories and car repair garages also have this special site in which the image of the Virgin of Guadalupe is carefully displayed surrounded by colorful lights, flowers, and other ornaments. Even taxi and bus drivers establish a focal point with some religious allusion more commonly over the central mirror.

Rudolf Arnheim defines the center as the point of convergence of forces and finds that elements in nature spontaneously agglutinate around a center (as in our planetary system, a tree, a crystal and the human body).[9] He states that we perceive asymmetry and anisotropy mainly by two bodily senses: sight and kinesthesia, the latter a sense that perceives physical tensions in the body and interprets gravitational force as weight. Gravitational attraction totally alters our perception of space, since what is up and down may not have particular meaning in neutral space, whereas according to gravity and body orientation, "up" requires an effort that "down" does not. In Einsteinian terms, "down" is literally moving toward the lower, bent part of curved space-time. Whether banal refrigerators or celestial figures, technological items or religious niches, this proclivity to enhance special places attests to a human tendency against an homogenous, neutral and flat space. There is a need to establish accents over space that makes it warp into denser, more meaningful sites in private as well as in public spheres.[10]

III. Personal Loops within Public Spaces

Private areas are not the only ones to be ontogenetically orchestrated: the city we live in is also symbolically configured for each of its inhabitants in a particular way. When we move through its streets and neighborhoods, we experience places according to both phylogenetic and ontogenetic meanings. For De Certeau, walking is a means of signifying places. I find it hard to agree with this idea that "the act of walking is to the urban system what speech act is to language or to the statements uttered."[11] We often walk so absentmindedly that these steps may be comparable only to talking in our sleep. Rather than simply walking, it is Dewey's "doing and undergoing"[12] that makes affective memory color places and perceive some as more densely meaningful than others. It is true that the streets we walked through in our childhood become especially meaningful to us, yet it is not by our walking through that we signify them nor what makes them meaningful, but it is rather due to the remains of the self they bring forth as an after image. More often than not, we are pulled in our transit by the area we want to reach, rather than explicitly stating each step of our route. On the other hand, places become personally significant by their fortuitous experiential result: we will always remember the spot where we were attacked or unpleasantly surprised, where we used to play or ride a bicycle, places where we met with significant people, where we sat with profound grief, where we discovered a different sense of ourselves. Each of us has gathered through life a collection of ontogenetically significant sites that seem to bend and make us slide through them into the past. For Hernán Cortés, the Spanish conquistador, the place that is today called "tree of the sad night" where he lamented defeat by the Aztecs on June 30, 1520, was an ontogenetically significant site that became philogenetically meaningful. This ontogenetic geography of meaning is complementary to the phylogenetic cartography of places for common celebrations, political protest, ritual gatherings, and recollection of social disasters.

Ontogenetically meaningful places emerge to the surface and are typically shared with others by means of literature. Mexico City's Colonia Roma is described by numerous authors such as José Agustín, William Burroughs, and José Emilio Pacheco among others. Some places become particularly vivid when associated with undergoing an experience, as in Elias Canetti's description of a certain place in Marrakesh, next to a fountain, where he saw up on a first floor a woman behind a grille. Margo Glantz recalls the bread ovens at Uruguay Street, and Luis G. Urbina ponders over the sense of fear and sadness he felt at the west side of Mixcalco Plaza, next to a wall that still kept bullet holes from public executions. Carlos Fuentes begins his story about "the most transparent region," alluding to Mexico City, at a single point: Plaza del Caballito, from which "an asphalt coffin" spreads. This is a coiling spot, marked by the origin of the city's main boulevard Paseo de la Reforma[13] to the west (later extended to the east all the way to the Villa de Guadalupe), by Bucareli to the south, as well as by Avenida Juárez flanking the great Alameda park down to the Palacio de las Bellas Artes. The name of the plaza comes from Manuel Tolsa's monumental equestrian sculpture of Carlos IV, which was moved west from the first square of the city to this spot to serve as a knot to tie up the centrifugal force of these avenues.[14]

As flower vases or lamps set in private homes, monuments are always placed for bending space and creating a centripetal movement. The nineteenth-century Plaza del Caballito mentioned above, the Monument of the Revolution, and the Angel of Independence are examples of this purpose. They manifest a need to balance the enormous weight of the Zócalo, or the main city square, and to create alternative dynamic centripetal points. This counterbalance, however, is not and probably will never be achieved. No matter how many additional squares, monuments, or esplanades will be scattered and sowed over Mexico City, the density of the Zócalo as the navel of the whole country is likely to endure. We will now examine how it emerged, or rather, in Einstein's terms, how it ebbed into the deep spatial crater it is today warping with it the entire Mexican territory.

IV. First Layer: The Mythological Site[15]

According to legend, the Aztecs emigrated from Aztlan following orders of their god Huitzilopochtli who commanded they should look for a place to settle (ca. 10 A.D.). This place was to be marked by an eagle standing on a special kind of cactus, the *nochtli*, scientifically named Opuntia. In the *Segunda Relación* of Cuauhtlehuanitzin[16] another element is mentioned: It is no longer the fortuitous encounter with the prophetic image that enabled the founding of the Aztec city, but it was rather the result of a calculated act. While living with the permission of the people of Malinalco, Toluca, and Texcaltepec, the Aztecs discovered a plan to attack them. The Aztec priest Cuauhtlequetzqui took the initiative and killed his equal, the Malinalcan priest Copil (nephew of the god Huitzilopochtli). He snatched Copil's heart and ordered his assistant Tenochtli to plant it as a seed among the canes and tulle plants. As time passed, he sent Tenochtli back to where the heart was buried and found out that a cactus germinated and grew from it, upon which an eagle was standing. This is where the city of Tenochtitlán was founded, on an islet right in the middle of the salty lake of Texcoco.[17]

There are other versions of this legend. In the 1528 manuscript, *Unos Anales de la Nación Mexicana*, the eagle was found in this place standing on a cactus whose leaves were covered with the bird's excrement.[18] Another version is in *Crónica de Mexicayotl*, written by Moctezuma's grandson, Fernando de Alvarado Tezozómoc.[19] According to this version, they saw the eagle standing on the Opuntia surrounded by feathers and the remains of birds it had eaten. In other versions, the eagle is devouring a serpent, always standing on the cactus. Finally, in the representation of the foundation of Tenochtitlan illustrated in the Mendoza Codex, we also have the eagle on a cactus of red prickly pears.

The eagle as an emblem of an empire is not exclusive to the Aztecs. Together with and previous to the bald eagle of the United States, its persistence in Western heraldry can be traced as early in history as Babylon, India, Persia, Greece, the Byzantine Empire, Prussia, Russia, Egypt, Rome, Austria, and so on.[20] What is unique in this case is not only its role as an index for the foundation of a capital city, but the presence of the Opuntia.

The eagle may have captured the people's imagination because of its fierceness, independence, predatory power, and courage. It also has a formidable visual sharpness of great value for a community dedicated to hunting and warfare. We could add other qualities such as speed in attacking, longevity, grace, its being carnivorous and, more importantly, the strength and robustness of its claws capable of destroying victims of a larger size than the eagle itself. In stratified societies, an avis that flies independently and to great heights is obviously eligible as a symbol and index of high status.[21] This solitary character, together with its fierceness, its habitat between earth and sky, between men and gods, may have motivated its being chosen as a symbol for the Aztecs and other cultures. Cuauhtlequetzqui, a name that relates to the eagle (*cuauh* means eagle in the Aztec language[22]) says to Tenochtli (from *nochtli, Opuntia* cactus): "the cactus or tenochtli will be you, you Tenochtli. And the eagle that you will see will be me".[23]

If aloofness and courage motivated the choice of the eagle, what were the qualities that justified selecting the Opuntia as symbol and index of a place? There were other major plants that had equal importance for the survival of the Aztecs. Among these, we have the mezquite or algarrobo (*Prosopis*), corn and the maguey (*Agave*).[24] However, Opuntia's symbolic importance for the Aztecs is not equaled by any other plant, as is testified by its numerous representations in almost all the codex available.[25] In addition, the symbolic importance of the Opuntia didn't decrease with the Spanish conquest. Sodi Pallares[26] mentions that in at least thirty Franciscan temples and convents founded after 1516, the image of the Opuntia appears in altars, carved chairs, fountains, sculptures, paintings, ceramics, crosses, *retablos*, open chapels, baptismal fonts, portals, carved chests and other furniture.

The symbolic preeminence of the Opuntia over other plants, such as *Agave* and corn, also basic for stable agriculture among ancient Mexicans, can be explained by the amazing number and variety of uses it had for these people: its fruits, leaves, and flowers were eaten raw or cooked, the plants were used to arrange fences, and the sap was useful as an emulsifier, a lubricant that enabled moving great rocks, a glue, and a material for construction, for covering and sealing. It was also used for coloring hair and for making vinegar, candies, and a beverage named *colonche*. The seeds of the prickly pear were crushed for making pinole, a high protein nutritive powder. The fibers could be woven or burnt, since they had the quality of producing a very long flame of slow combustion, and therefore used in the ceremonies of the New Fire.[27] Moreover, in this cactus lives the *nocheztli* or *grana*, an insect from which a very strong red colorant is produced for textiles, feathers, and body decoration. The leaves were used as shields in battle, the thorns for sacrifice and penitence. The Opuntia was also used as a medicine and to cure the effects of various hallucinogens.

This points to the fact that wherever the Opuntia could grow, life of the community could be secured. However, this cactus is so endurable that it is able to survive in quite extreme environments. Opuntia cacti can be found all over the country. That is why the index of the eagle was basic for distinguishing one place from another. The Opuntia represents the land altogether, matter, sustenance. The eagle was an indication from above to distinguish one territory from another, something like the will of the god. A cactus emerging from a whole lake and yet needing so little water is an image that echoes that of the eagle, able to fly enormous distances and heights and yet posing itself upon the thorny leaf of a cactus. This double image represents the Spartan quality of the Aztecs.

Apart from this impressive number of uses that the Opuntia had for the ancient Mexicans, an extra aesthetic and religious meaning springs from it. As I mentioned above, the *grana* insect, which yields a red dye associated with blood, is parasitic to it. Moreover, its fruit, the red prickly pear, was associated by its oval shape, color and size to the human heart. As is well known, the Aztecs believed they had to repay life with life, the life of the community with the life of the sacrificed, as fruits of the soil are sacrificed from immediate consumption for sowing, and the life of animals sacrificed for feeding humans. In the same sense, humans had to be sacrificed for feeding the gods. Huitzilopochtli, god of war and solar deity, had to be nourished with human hearts to gather enough strength for upholding its war against the moon every night and defeat darkness. The Opuntia cactus was literal food for men and metaphorical food for the god. In this sense, the whole city of Tenochtitlán (meaning in Aztec language *tetl* [stone], *nochtli* [Opuntia cactus], *tlan* [place]: "the place of the rock cactus"), was the cactus that fed the universe.

Whether the apparition actually occurred or not is hardly relevant for our analysis; what is important is the manner in which the meaning of a given place was constructed. We have here the basic survival conditions represented by the cactus, together with the signifying eagle to which an extra element was added: the cactus selected by the eagle was no ordinary cactus, but the one sprouting from a sacrificed priest's heart. There is a merging of two legends: a previous legend of Huitzilopochtli's command, and an after the fact legend of the victory of Cuauhtlequetzqui, the sacrifice of Copil and germination of his heart.[28]

We have a conjunction of two levels of meaning: the eagle represents metaphorically a heavenly and a political-military creature, while the Opuntia portrays a practical, earthly tribute to one of nature's species. Both the political and the practical meanings are synthesized in this mythical icon. These two elements, repeated and represented by the two characters of Tenochtli and Cuauhtlequetzqui by linguistic association, synthesize earth and sky, the natural and the divine, the feminine and the masculine, the human and the superhuman, matter and energy. The image not only endows the place of residence with meaning but gives coherence to the world view of the Aztecs, who saw themselves responsible for the subsistence of the world. More Humean than Hume himself, the Aztecs never took for granted that the sun would rise the next morning.

V. Second Layer: The Teocalli or Imperial Site

This highly significant space-time event for the Aztecs, the moment and place where the eagle stood upon the cactus, totally alters history and triggers the almost miraculous transformation during the brief period of about a century and a half[29] of a bare islet in the middle of a lake into what Hernán Cortés depicted as a marvelous city comparable in size to Seville and Cordoba.[30]

Apart from the mythological sense of the place, other strategical and economical considerations were involved. From a political point of view, the site for the foundation of Tenochtitlán was crucial: by being in the middle of three kingdoms (Atzcapotzalco, Texcoco, and Culhuacán), the Aztecs could always seek help from the other two whenever attacked by the third.

The Aztecs were not a seafaring people, nor was their diet heavily dependent upon fish. The image that appeared in the middle of Lake Texcoco forced the Aztecs to become fishermen and adapt to this aquatic environment ("this is when we are going to learn to fish with nets . . . There was the beginning of having to live by fishing with nets in the year 3 Rabbit, 1326").[31] However, since the Aztecs didn't use the wheel for transportation nor domesticated animals for hauling or riding, only vehicles on water enabled them to carry great weights and became their main means of transportation. This may be considered an important practical reason for establishing themselves on a lake.

The salty lake of Texcoco is also not good for agriculture. It is claimed, on the other hand, that there was a stream of sweet water in the middle of the islet, where the cactus emerged: "they found a beautiful eye of water. . . ."[32] "[T]hey went back to the fountain that they found the day before and they saw that formerly it was clear and pretty, and that day it was red, almost like blood."[33] This image of the clear water turned into blood almost literally represents the development of the theocratic hold over the Aztecs: The transparency of the original poetic mythical image later became a stream of blood.

Exactly there, on the site of this flow of sweet water, they marked a square and began to build a very modest temple to Huitzilopochtli, around which the rest of the city set forth. Two centuries later, this fountain was kept inside a chamber of the great palace built over it.

In the foundations of the National Palace in Mexico City, a monument called the Teocalli of the Sacred Stone was found. It shows an eagle standing on the Opuntia. Blood is leaking from the eagle's beak to whom prickly pears, turned into human hearts, are offered. This finding indicates that the site where the original eagle was supposed to have appeared was right there, where it later became the Palace of residence of Moctezuma and the great temple of Huitzilopochtli and Tlaloc. According to Alfonso Caso the Opuntia illustrated in the Teocalli is the tree of sacrifice to feed the sun with human hearts.[34] Since human hearts do not grow from cactus nor eagles feed on prickly pears, the metaphorical character of this image is obvious. The legend of the apparition is a rhetorical device, constructed as an indexical and iconic enthyneme, of the eagle as saying "this is where I will feed," which is culturally interpreted as "this is where the Aztec community will feed its god Huitzilopochtli and make the world abide."

That modest square, which the original Aztecs marked around the rock where the cactus grew and the eagle stood, was the radial point from which all the temples and palaces of the empire were built. Together with the two great palaces of Moctezuma and Axayácatl, as well as the *Templo Mayor*, other religious sites spiraled from this point: the temple of Tezcatlipoca, the temple of Quetzalcóatl, the *Tzompantli* or skull rack, and the ball court, surrounded by the *Coahtepantli* or wall of serpents. Everything in the Aztec world revolved around this square, site of religious celebrations and of the second greatest market in all Mesoamerica.[35]

VI. Third Layer: The Site of Colonial Assertion

On the afternoon of August 13, 1521, about two centuries after its foundation, Tenochtitlán was defeated by the Spanish conquistadors. Destroyed to the point of becoming uninhabitable, Cortés had to move to Coyoacán. It had to be decided where the capital city of New Spain was to be settled. Texcoco, Tacuba, and Coyoacán were considered, but against common sense and his peers' opinion, Cortés had a clear decision in mind: "that it had to be where they had won and where the old city of Mexico stood."[36] Cortés understood well the importance of symbolic accumulation of meaning in situ and of its indexical eloquence. He appointed Alonso García Bravo to design the new city plan. García Bravo followed the original arrangement, kept the main plaza where it originally stood,[37] and reproduced unknowingly that same little square around the rock of the cactus. The square continued to serve as the main market and site for religious and civil ceremonies. Moreover, on July 27, 1529, Cortés got for himself as place of residence the remains of Moctezuma's two main palaces due to a gift from His Catholic Majesty the Emperor Carlos V (of Germany and I of Spain): the Palace of Axayácatl or Old Houses of Moctezuma, and the New Houses of Moctezuma, respectively on the West and east sides of the main square.[38] The Palace of Axayácatl was where Cortés dwelled during eight months with his troops as a guest of Moctezuma, and also where this great Aztec emperor found death by Cortés' orders, his body thrown down that same roof.[39] The other palace, Moctezuma's New Houses, is where the emperor dwelled. The symbolic density of these places was essential for Cortés: by owning both of Moctezuma's palaces, Cortés symbolically and eloquently stated the substitution of his for Moctezuma's power.

Cortés was appointed Governor and General Captain of New Spain, but his power was soon eclipsed when two other governors were later commissioned and when the First and Second *Audiencias*[40] were sent by the Spanish crown. By the time the first *Audiencia* was established, Cortés was asked by the Spanish Emperor Carlos I to please lend his property for this aim. He referred to no less than the Palace of Axayácatl. Furthermore, by 1562, fifteen years after Cortés' death, the main colonial institutions, the *Audiencia* and the third *Virrey*, were moved to the other of Cortés' properties, the main palace of Moctezuma and his dwelling. Cortés' son and heir, Martín Cortés, who attempted to crown himself Emperor of the New Spain and failed, was consequently forced to sell the palace of the New Houses to the Crown of Spain in exchange for saving his neck following his attempted usurpation. This effaced any doubt about who was the real power in the New Spain: Rather than Cortés' descendants, it was the Spanish Crown substituting for Moctezuma. This fact was again spatially stated by the establishment of the Viceregal Palace on the precise site of Moctezuma's Palace.

In the *Ordenanzas de Audiencia* on April 23, 1528, it is stated that in order to keep the attendance to the meetings better and more orderly "a clock should be continuously placed in a convenient place so everyone can hear."[41] The first clock ever to be placed in Mexico was originally installed at the Palace of Axayácatl at the time when the first two *Audiencias* and the two first *Virreyes* were located there. Not surprisingly, it was moved later to the former palace of Moctezuma when these authorities moved. As the eagle and cactus had had a symbolic meaning for the Aztecs, so the clock did for the Spaniards. Both related to the sun and to the idea of time, the clock indicated a sense of order and integration of social activities. Valle-Arizpe mentions two other curious, but nonetheless symbolic, aspects of the site: that the first café of the city, symbol of the rising bourgeoisie's urban society, was placed on the site of the former Palace of Axayácatl, and that it was exactly there as well where the *Marseillaise*, quite symbolic of the future Republican order, was sung for the first time in the New World.

What is important to note here is that Tenochtitlán was almost totally destroyed. The remnant temples and palaces were further ravaged to use their stones for constructing the new houses for the Spanish conquerors. It is true there was enough material for construction, but it was still very inconvenient to build a city in the middle of a lake. The underlying economic structure and distribution of goods was taken into account, yet a similar structure also existed in the other three places considered, as well as in Tlaltelolco. One could think of no other reason for choosing the ruins of Tenochtitlán than the symbolic meaning of the place. Cortés was not alone in this awareness of the symbolic weight of a site, since the Spanish emperors, both Carlos I and Felipe II, insisted on placing their representatives in no place other than Moctezuma's previous properties.

VII. Fourth Layer: The Executive Site

After the administration of sixty-three viceroys,[42] the anticolonial war, two regencies and the First Empire of Agustín Iturbide, by 1827 the site of power still remained on the exact same spot. Hereinafter, the first president of the new republic, Guadalupe Victoria, moved to the National Palace followed by many others that succeeded him. The 1910 Revolution almost began in this palace where President Francisco I. Madero was imprisoned and later murdered at Lecumberri. The symbolic charge of the place has been kept beginning with Huitzilopochtli's appearance as an eagle over the cactus and continuing with the Aztec emperor Moctezuma's palace, the house of the Spanish victor Hernán Cortés, the Viceregal Palace, and up to the republic's presidents until the present *Palacio de Gobierno, Sede del Ejecutivo*. Each of these varying authorities has stood on the exact same site.

The place has been kept constant, yet a key item has varied in direct relation to the distinctive quality representing this particular location. The indicative role that the Teocalli had for the Aztecs and the clock for the colonial order was substituted by the bell during the independent republic. On September 14, 1896, at one o'clock in the afternoon, a bell was installed over the central balcony of the National Palace for the celebration of national independence. It was brought all the way from the town of Dolores, and it is claimed that it was the exact same bell that the Father of Independence, the priest Miguel Hidalgo y Costilla, tolled to call the people to fight against the Spanish Crown at dawn on September 16, 1810.[43] Since then (and even after an extra floor was added to the National Palace in the beginning of this century) this bell is made to ring only once a year, at eleven o'clock on the night of September 15, by the president in turn. After the revolution of 1910, another symbolic element was added: to prove the nationalistic advocacy of the *callista* government, Diego Rivera was hired to paint a mural in the main stairway of the Palacio representing the official version of the history of Mexico. The main subject was space-time: Mexico City from prehispanic times to the future.[44] Like the imperial Teocalli, the colonial clock and the bell of independence, Rivera's mural captured the idea of time precisely within this densely symbolic site.

The main city square of Tenochtitlán became the colonial Zócalo[45] during the sixteenth century and is still not only the city's main plaza but also the country's main center. It was there, of course, where the great Metropolitan Cathedral was built, with its combination of gothic, baroque, and neoclassical styles in fashion for the three centuries it took to build it, where the Inquisition's hangings took place, where a Montgolfier was elevated, where the main civic and religious ceremonies were performed, where goods and services were offered and acquired, and where revolts ignited. More recently, every six years, each new *regente* or city mayor has used the Zócalo as a site for symbolic expression of his power and individuality by changing its decoration. The final word was taken by the people who have used it as a site for protest under which no cute decorations could endure. The Zócalo is now a place of peregrination from all parts of the country to demonstrate against the president and express dissidence. Now a stripped extension of bare concrete, in the middle of which the Mexican flag is flown daily, protesters lodge temporarily in plastic tents, undertake hunger strikes, make political speeches, and march and demonstrate against the government. It is also the only place where Aztec traditions linger through dances performed on a daily basis and where the memory of the lost empire is still evoked five centuries after its defeat.

Mexico City is densely charged in many senses. First, as we have seen, in a metaphorical sense that we can trace at least as early as 1200 or earlier, since the time of the prophecy. It was the site of the most powerful empire in Mesoamerica before the conquest and of the worst massacres during the invasion. After the conquest it has been the center of viceregal political power that turned in our times into one of the most centralistic forms of government in the world. It is also the most populated city on the planet with close to 23 million inhabitants.

This year Mexico City was also the site of a major political change. The first elections ever for chief of government of the city, previously appointed every six years by the president, were, moreover, won by the candidate of an opposition party. This first elected chief of government of the city (remarkably named Cuauhtémoc, after the last emperor of the Aztecs and related by the eagle prefix to Cuauhtlequetzqui) is occupying his office south of the great Zócalo, a few meters from the place of apparition and of Moctezuma's palace.

Another significant event occurred on September 12, 1997. Eleven hundred eleven members of the Ejército Zapatista de Liberación Nacional came to Mexico City for the first time since their declaration of existence in 1994. The reason was to begin the process of becoming a civil front, rather than an army. They advanced from their gathering place in Xochimilco toward no place other than the Zócalo. We have the conjunction of practical, political, historical, and religious meanings all imploding continuously towards a single place. The character of political power has changed, the religion substituted, the language replaced, but the site remains immutable throughout time.

VIII. Center and Heart of Power

Originated in the Greek *agora*, the Roman traditional *forum* at the crossing point of the *cardo maximus* and the *decumanus maximus* has influenced many other cities' pattern to our day. The Plaza Mayor, however, followed a similar north-south *cardo* (Tepeyac-Ixtapalapa) and east-west *decumanus* (Texcoco-Tacuba)[46] independently from the Romans. Despite variations on the layout of many cities, the square seems to be universal in the same degree that the assortment of meanings each of them radiates is specific and unique: Tiananmen Square in Beijing, the Red Square in Moscow, St. Peter's Square in Rome, Djma el Fna in Marrakech, Trafalgar Square in London, Lafayette Square in Washington, and many others.

Lakoff and Johnson[47] insist that the metaphorical mappings we use in everyday language operate according to a clear systematicity and a law of coherence. The same can be said about the symbolic use of space, which establishes a systematic and coherent sense of place beyond a particular turn of events. In this sense, the perpetuation of power, despite changes in the type and character of government or ownership, is consistent with the idea of the perpetuation of a given site. Power is believed to be a magical and superhuman force emanating from a site, rather than the effect of human will or physical might. Whoever happens to control a given site automatically and legitimately is supposed to take possession not only of an abstract quantity of square meters but also of a location in the hierarchy of symbolic power. The individual person, regardless of the range of his or her heroic deeds, the quantity of popular vote, the evidence of birthright or the official legitimacy of his or her appointment, is not mighty enough per se to justify authority. The help of the accumulation of symbolic weight of place is necessary as the real and most eloquent crystallization of power. This weight is due to the gravitational field exerted by time-space or the history of a given site. Taking hold of a place is taking hold of power. Such a place, like a fetish, endows its occupants with an aura of worldly or divine power.

To mark this distinct quality of the place and to make power more explicit and categorical, other semiosic and aesthetic devices are required. Great investments of labor in luxurious buildings and decoration, rare expensive materials such as precious metals and stones, legends of immemorial times and unfathomable heroes, all add to the unequivocal character of hierarchy. Yet the place, as a sponge that has absorbed layers of time and history, is ultimate.

IX. Organic Space-Time

Like the Kaaba and the Golden Dome, Tenochtitlán is also related to a rock, the *tetl*, from which the cactus or *nochtli* grew. However, it is the *nochtli* rather than the *tetl* that expresses the primary meaning of the place. The Opuntia, as a living creature, was vulnerable and mortal. The sense that space was alive and could disappear, that not only great cities such as Monte Albán, Teotihuacán, Chichén Itzá, Mitla, and others so mysteriously abandoned, could vanish, but that the world itself, place of places, could be no more, was present in the minds of the Aztecs. They believed that they were living in the fifth of a series of worlds that had come to an end and that their fifth world could vanish at the end of each 52-year cycle. For the Aztecs, time beats in the heart of space. Space is a mortal organism whose destiny is determined by discrete "quanta" of time. This view marks a very great difference with Western monotheistic beliefs of one world, one God and one definitive end, which is echoed today in the contemporary cosmological view of a closed universe that will reach its limits and contract again into an infinitely dense point, disappearing in another big bang implosion.

Lakoff and Johnson also refer to what they call "orientational metaphors" that are spatially configured and relative to our body. In this sense, sites of symbolic compression are experienced as hearts of the national body in civic centers, or of the religious body in holy centers. Tenochtitlán, as organic space-time and cactus of hearts, was made to beat by the sound of the *huéhuetl* and the *teponachtli*[48] during sacrifice ceremonies. When this heart was snatched by the conquest, it was replaced by the clock of the palace pounding through the colonial body. After independence, it was substituted by Hidalgo's bell on an annual basis and by the drums of the military band accompanying every day the rise and descent of the banner (with the eagle and the cactus at the very center of the flag) in the center of the Zócalo.

X. Stars and Black Holes

Trying to explain the quality proper to sites of symbolic density in Newton's terms as a force of attraction of matter over matter clarifies the appeal that relics like the leg of Saint Theodore, the arm of Saint Magnus, the body relics of Gautama in Sanchi, or the remains of Saint James in the Cathedral of Santiago de Compostela have for the devout. As Newton's physics operate as a special case in the theory of relativity on a smaller scale, so the attraction of relics can explain the appeal of certain sites. They do not, however, help to elucidate matters on a larger scale to the degree that has impelled masses of people to peregrinate and to fight over certain places for centuries. Instead of looking at the effects of gravitation over matter as Newton did, Einstein tried to understand gravitation less as a force than as a distortion in the structure of space-time continuum due to the effects of matter. The Black Stone of Mecca, the bones of Saint James, the hidden Ark of the Covenant, and the mythical Opuntia alter the symbolic configuration of an otherwise neutral place, extending its influence beyond their material presence like the concentric ripples of a stone dropped in a pond.[49]

These particular sites seem to slow down time by making the past still active and alive, as if it would abide and overlap into the present. They may also be said to extend space: the single spot where a cactus grew was able to generate meaning in expanding waves through successive constructions that inherit and increase its original symbolic weight. This is what happened during the several layers from the original *tenochtli* to the present Palacio Nacional, configurations that do not stand adjacent to each other, but are contained, so to speak, within the concavity of a nipple that is elastic enough to bend further by the added symbolic weight of successive significant events. The eagle and cactus are no more, nor the material remains of the Ark of the Covenant, and yet the space in which they stood is irreversibly bowed.

Following the metaphorical mapping of relativistic cosmology, one could say that holy places radiate a great amount of energy to the pious, whereas black holes exert a tremendous gravitational field that absorbs all matter and energy. Pilgrims that go to Santiago and Mecca may feel instilled with warmth and a gentle radiance emanating from the symbolic glow of the place due to their faith. Yet not all stars are bright. Facing the events that occurred in Auschwitz and Treblinka [50] collapses our capacity of understanding and faith in the same sense as black holes deplete all energy, even that of light.

During the twentieth century, we have amassed an ominous list of space-time locations of appalling meaning: Amritsar, April 13, 1919 (a crowd of peaceful Indian civilians massacred by the British General Dyer); Badajoz, 1936 (civilians massacred after their surrender to Franco); Guernica, April 1937 (Spanish civilians bombed by Nazi aircraft); Katyn Forest, April-May 1940 (15,000 Polish officials massacred by Soviet secret forces); Babi Yar, September 1941 (33,771 Soviet Jewish civilians machine-gunned by the *Einsatzgruppen*); Auschwitz and Treblinka 1942; Sharpeville, March 1960 (South African police opened fire on a large crowd of black Africans); My Lai, March 1968 (300 unarmed Vietnamese civilians killed by American infantry); Sabre and Chatila, September 1982 (hundreds of Palestinians massacred by Phalangist militia); Tiananmen Square, June 1989 (about a thousand students killed by the People's Liberation

Army); Bosnia and Herzegovina 1992–1993 (ethnic "cleansing" of Moslems by Serbs); Rwanda and Burundi, 1972–1997 (violence between Hutu and Tutsi tribes); and Algeria, 1997–1998 (ongoing slaughter of Algerian civilians by Islamic fundamentalists).

We have been guided by stars for orientation in space and time. Our first star, the sun, has guided us to discern day from night, to understand space in our planetary system, and it is now leading us toward other suns, to the confines of the universe and to the beginning of time. Perhaps the idea of black holes may some day guide us to realize that the flexibility of our space-time might not be infinite and that its delicate fabric can be irreversibly punctured.

XI. Conclusion

I have proposed the application of a conceptual mapping adopted from a lay interpretation of the theory of relativity to elucidate the symbolic meaning of places. By focusing on the specific case of México-Tenochtitlán, I tried to show how this frame can be used. I hope it has provided tools to interpret how emotionally and historically charged events and objects have transformed the structure of their surroundings and how this organic unfolding through subsequent episodes tends to increase and sustain its lure beyond its original material presence. Other frames of reference might be equally useful, but in an effort to construct a frame for symbolic topoanalysis, we don't have that many theoretical alternatives. The examination of contemporary paradigms that deal with space such as topology and cosmology and the effort to construct an analogous version in regards to personal and social experience of place is worth attempting. After all, a physicist's intuition of space does not originate solely out of pure numbers.

Notes

I would like to thank my two anonymous reviewers for their careful reading and effective advice that enabled this manuscript to be presented in a much better form.

1. I may suggest the following readings on relativity for a broader audience: Albert Einstein, *Über die Spezielle und die Allgemeine Relativitäts theorie* [Relativity, the Special and the General Theory: A Popular Exposition]. Authorized translation by Robert W. Lawson (New York: Crown Publishers, 1961); Max Born, *Einstein's Theory of Relativity*, prepared with the collaboration of Gunther Leibfried and Walter Biem (New York: Dover Publications, 1965); James A. Coleman, *Relativity for the Layman; a Simplified Account of the History, Theory, and*

Proofs of Relativity (New York: William-Frederick Press, 1958); Robert Geroch, *General Relativity from A to B* (Chicago: University of Chicago Press, 1978).

2. A few meters from there, the Church of the Holy Sepulcher was begun in the 4th century A.D. and rebuilt by the Crusaders beginning in 1099.

3. Another significant place for its material and historical value is the Cathedral of Santiago de Compostela. The bones discovered in 813 (believed to be those of the apostle James) are kept in this cathedral erected by Alfonso II, one of the most important shrines for pilgrimage in the Christian world.

4. Gaston Bachelard, *Poética del espacio* (Mexico City: Fondo de Cultura Económica, 1986), 27.

5. I am using the term "semiosic" rather than "semiotic" as is usually employed, to mark the difference between two kinds of processes encompassed within semiosis in general, i.e. the semiotic as a specifically differential process and the symbolic as cumulative. From here on I will refer to the semiotic in this particular sense only and to the semiosic when related to both, the symbolic and semiotic. On this distinction between the symbolic and the semiotic orders, a brief summary can be consulted in Katya Mandoki, "Between Signs and Symbols: An Economic Distinction?" in *Semiotics Around the World; Synthesis in Diversity*, eds. Irmengard Rauch and Gerald Carr (New York: Mouton de Gruyter, 1997), 1015–1018. A broader version is developed in Katya Mandoki, *Prosaica: introducción a la estética de lo cotidiano* (México: Grijalbo, 1994), 99–120.

6. Saussure's great contribution to semiotics was eliminating the common idea that words carry their meaning as a receptacle or container. Instead, Saussure noted that meaning (or the signified) of a term (or signifier) depends upon its relations of differentiation and opposition within language as a system. Ferdinand de Saussure, *Course in General Linguistics* (London: Duckworth, 1983).

7. Jean Baudrillard, *Le Système des Objets* (Paris: Gallimard, 1968), chap. 1.

8. The saint is taken home from the church in special ocassions during nine days for prayer or "novenario." In the most traditional neighborhoods such as Xochimilco and Ixtapalapa, almost every family has a Niño Dios placed in a special cradle or chair during the whole year. It is undressed and placed with miniature figures depicting the sacred family on December 24, and remains there until February 2, the day of the Candelaria, when he is dressed again in new clothes and taken to church, blessed and symbolically baptized. It is returned home and stays in the niche all year until the next December 24.

9. Rudolf Arnheim, *El Poder del Centro* (Madrid: Alianza Editorial, 1984), 16–23. Original title *The Power of the Center: A Study of Composition in the Visual Arts* (Berkeley: The Regents of the University of California, 1982).

10. Designing excessively uniform spaces can produce a sense of anxiety that some feel, for instance, at airports, hospitals or prisons with long corridors and identical gates repeating themselves one after another.

· 11. Michel De Certeau, *The Practice of Everyday Life* (Berkeley: University of California Press, 1988), 99.

12. John Dewey, *Art as Experience* (New York: Perigee, 1980).

13. This avenue spreading west was originally conceived by Maximilian of Habsburg all the way down to Chapultepec park in similar fashion to the Champs

Elysees, with the intention that the Chapultepec palace, his place of residence, could be appreciated.

14. The sculpture was moved again to the street of Tacuba, in front of the Museo Nacional de Arte. In its place, there is a huge yellow geometrical abstract version of a horse by the artist Sebastián.

15. I have applied Peirce's model of three trichotomies for the analysis of this mythical image in "Guadalajara en un llano, México en una laguna, sobre el águiila y la tuna, un análisis peirceano"presented at the VIth International Congress of Semiotics; International Association of Semiotics Studies, Guadalajara 1997. That paper developed into the present version involving a different, more complete perspective.

16. Cuauhtlehuanitzin Chimalpahin, "Segunda Relación" in *De Teotihuacán a los Aztecas; antología de fuentes e interpretaciones históricas,* ed. Miguel León-Portilla (México: Instituto de Investigaciones Históricas, Universidad Nacional Autónoma de México, 1977), 159–160.

17. It is interesting to note several common elements with another foundational legend: chance/augury, murder, escape, gods of war. (1) Chance: the site at the foot of the Palatine was chosen for the foundation of Rome because it was right there where the trough, in which Romulus and Remus were placed, stranded. This element of chance is comparable to the posing of the eagle. Like the prophecy by Huitzilopochtli, the foot of the Palatine was also selected by augury. (2) Escape: the twin babies were hidden to protect them against their uncle Amulius (as the Aztecs had to escape persecution from the other tribes). (3) There is also a murder involved, as in the case of Copil: Romulus killed his twin brother Remus as a consequence of an argument about the foundation. (4) War: as the Aztecs followed Huitzilopochtli, god of war, Romulus and Remus were sons of Mars, Latin god of war.

18. Here it is Copil's head which was buried by Tenoch, while Cuauhtlequetz-qui buried his heart. *Unos Anales de la Nación Mexicana: Manuscripts 22-A and 22-B at the National Library in Paris* (Copenhagen: Facsimile edition of Mengin, 1945).

19. This text, written about 1600, is based on old texts of the Mexican Royal House. Fernando de Alvarado Tezozómoc, "El Águila y el Nopal" ca. 1600 in *La literatura de los aztecas,* ed. Angel Ma. Garibay (México: Editorial Joaquín Mortiz, 1970) 43–46.

20. It is commonly believed that the Mexican national emblem consists of an eagle devouring a serpent. Guillermo Boils has explored this image of the eagle and serpent as an emblem in several cultures and concludes that what is unique to the Mexican emblem is the Opuntia, rather than the eagle and the serpent, which is common to several other cultures. See Guillermo Boils, "Símbolos nacionales y simbolismo universal: águilas devorando serpientes en diversas culturas," *En Síntesis* 6, no. 20 (1995). It is interesting to note that this idea that the image of the eagle and the serpent is not unique to Mexico appeared sixty years earlier in an article of Alfonso Reyes, "Virgilio y América," *Monterrey* 10 (1933), where he states that this image of the eagle devouring the serpent can be traced as far as Virgil's *Aeneid* XI-751–58. Also in "Los romanos tenían también como símbolo

el águila y la serpiente de nuestro escudo nacional" in the Mexican newspaper *El Universal* (February 10, 1937), the same conclusion is presented. These two accounts are given in a note by Artemio de Valle-Arizpe, *Historia de la Ciudad de México según los relatos de sus cronistas* (México: Editorial Pedro Robredo, 1946), 34–36.

21. I am taking the term symbol exclusively in the sense I explain above in section 2 and according to references stated in note 1. The term index, however, does follow Peirce's definition. See Charles Sanders Peirce, "Logic as Semiotic: The Theory of Signs," in *Philosophical Writings of Peirce*, ed. Justus Buchler (New York: Dover, 1955), 98–119.

22. *Diccionario nauatl-español, español-nauatl* (Toluca, Edo. de México: Instituto Mexiquense de Cultura, Colegio de Lengua y Literatura Indígenas [no date]).

23. "El tunal o tenochtli serás tú, tú, Tenochtli. Y el águila que tú verás seré yo." Translation is mine. In Chimalpahin, "Segunda Relación," 160.

24. On the importance of these three plants since the origins of Aztec culture, see L. González Quintero, "Origen de la domesticación de los vegetales en México," *Historia de México* (México: Editorial Salvat), I: 81–86. According to Claudio Flores, the Opuntia was used since 25000 years ago, although evidence only traces it back to 7000 years from excavations in Tamaulipas and Tehuacán. See Claudio A. Flores V., "Historia del uso del nopal en México y en el mundo," *Agricultura y agronomía en México; 500 años*, eds. Juan de la Fuente, Rafael Ortega, and Miguel Sámano (Mexico City: Universidad Autónoma de Chapingo, 1993), 156.

25. Such as Mendoza, Aubin, Badian, Bodelian, Borbonic, Borgia, Boturini, Cospian, Cozcatzin, Durán, the Féjérváry-Mayer, the Florentin, Lord Kingsborough's, Magliabecchi, Quinatzin, the Texcocan of Tepechpan, the Xolotl and others.

26. Ernesto Sodi Pallares, "Las Cactáceas en las épocas pre-colombina y virreynal, y en el siglo XIX," *Cactáceas y suculentas mexicanas* 13, no. 1 (January-March 1968): 3–12.

27. On the uses of the Opuntia, see Helia Bravo-Hollis, *Las cactáceas en México* (México: Universidad Nacional Autónoma de México, 1978); Rafael Martin del Campo, "Las Cactaceas entre los Mexica" *Cactaceas y suculentas mexicanas*, 2, no. 2. (April-June 1957); Facundo Barrientos P., "El nopal y su utilización en México," *Revista de la Sociedad Mexicana de Historia Natural* 26 (December, 1965): 87–90; Secretaría de Desarrollo Agropecuario, *Algunos usos prehispánicos de las cactáceas entre los indígenas de Mexico* (México: Dirección de Recursos Naturales, 1982); and Flores "Historia del uso del nopal." Today it is used for the conservation of land, to reduce levels of pollution, as forage, for export of pectin, fructose, cellulose, viscose, nectars and colorants for the production of cosmetics and other uses. We also know now that it helps reduce cholesterol and sugar levels in the blood.

28. As I have stated above, since Copil was Huitzilopochtli's nephew, his order to kill him, his own blood, means a sacrifice by Huitzilopochtli himself.

29. It is interesting to note that the construction of the whole capital city of the Aztec empire took half the time that was necessary to build the Cathedral of

Mexico City, which lasted for about three centuries. Walter Krickeberg attempts, but does not really succeed, to answer his own question on how was it possible to build a city comparable to Venice in less that one third the time it took to build Venice (at least 500 years). Walter Krickeberg, *Las antiguas culturas mexicanas* (Mexico City: Fondo de Cultura Económica, 1961), 44.

30. Hernán Cortés, " Segunda Relación," in *De Teotihuacán a los Aztecas; antología de fuentes e interpretaciones históricas*, ed. Miguel León-Portilla (Mexico City: Instituto de Investigaciones Históricas, Universidad Nacional Autónoma de México, 1977), 172.

31. "Ahora es cuando vamos a aprender a pescar con redes. . . . Allí dió comienzo el tener que vivir pescando con redes en el año 3 Conejo, 1326," according to Moctezuma's grandson, Fernando Alvarado Tezozómoc, "Crónica Mexicáyotl" in *Seis siglos de la ciudad de México* , ed. Salvador Novo (Mexico City: Fondo de Cultura Económica, 1974), 15.

32. "Vinieron buscando y mirando si hallarían algún lugar que fuese acomodado para poder hacer asiento, y andando de esta manera por unas partes y por otras entre las espadañas y carrizales, hallaron un ojo de agua hermosísimo. . . " Fray Diego Durán, "De cómo los mexicanos, avisados de su dios, fueron a buscar el tunal y el águila, y cómo lo hallaron, y del acuerdo que para el edificio tuvieron," in *Historia de la Ciudad de México según los relatos de sus cronistas*, ed. Artemio de Valle-Arizpe (Mexico City: Editorial Pedro Robredo, 1946), 26–27.

33. "Tornaron a topar con la fuente que el día antes salía clara y linda, aquel día salí bermeja, casi como sangre" Durán, "De cómo los mexicanos," 29.

34. Alfonso Caso, "El águila y el nopal," *Memorias de la Academia Mexicana de la Historia* no. 2, (April-June 1964), 102–104.

35. The first was the older market of Tlaltelolco, also a highly symbolical site in Mexico City to the present date, as it was there where the 1968 killing of students occurred, and where high apartment buildings collapsed during the 1985 earthquake leaving not only hundreds of homeless but also many people dead.

36. "que había de ser donde habían vencido y donde se había sentado la antigua México." Luis González Obregón, *Las calles de México* (Mexico City: Editorial Porrúa, 1922), 125.

37. Francisco Cervantes de Salazar could be considered the first chronicler of the capital city of New Spain. He wrote a dialogue between the fictional characters, Alfaro Zuazo and Zamora, describing the main square. See Francisco Cervantes de Salazar, "La Plaza Mayor en 1554," in *Historia de la Ciudad de México según los relatos de sus cronistas*, ed. Artemio de Valle-Arizpe (Mexico City: Editorial Pedro Robredo, 1946), 241–251.

38. Artemio de Valle-Arizpe, *El Palacio Nacional: monografía histórica y anecdótica* (Mexico City: Compañía General de Ediciones, 1936), 32.

39. Artemio de Valle-Arizpe, "El Palacio de Axayácatl o Casas Viejas de Moctezuma," in Valle-Arizpe, *Historia de la Ciudad de México*, 215–27.

40. The *Audiencia* is a royal court first established in 1528 to consolidate Spanish colonial power in New Spain.

41. Valle-Arizpe, "El Palacio de Axayácatl," 216.

42. One of which, specifically Don Fray Garcia Guerra, both Viceroy and

Archbishop, went as far as to install a plaza for bull fights inside the National Palace. Quite a character, as Valle-Arizpe ironically depicts him in *El Palacio Nacional*, 41.

43. Valle Arizpe doubts that it was the same bell tolled by Hidalgo, but rather something like the lateral cowbells on that same church. However, as in the case of the eagle over the cactus, the true facts are not particularly relevant; what counts are the connotations and circulation of the object and its symbolic import. Valle-Arizpe, *El Palacio Nacional*, 151–152.

44. This mural (1929–1935) was later developed into the north and east halls of the first floor (1941–1951) of the prehispanic era until the conquest. For more information, see Ester Acevedo, Alicia Azuela et al., *Guía de Murales del Centro Histórico de la Ciudad de México* (Mexico City: Universidad Iberoamericana, CONAFE 1984).

45. Probably comes from *zoco*, "market" in Arabic.

46. On prehispanic urbanization, see Jorge González Aragón, *La urbanización indígena de la Ciudad de México; el caso del plano en papel maguey* (Mexico City: Universidad Autónoma Metropolitana, 1995), and María del Carmen León Cázares, *La Plaza Mayor de la Ciudad de México en la vida cotidiana de sus habitantes* (Mexico City: Instituto de Estudios y Documentos Históricos, 1982).

47. George Lakoff and Mark Johnson, *Metaphors We Live By* (Chicago: University of Chicago Press, 1980).

48. Both are prehispanic percussion instruments.

49. A very recent case that is also developing into a quasimythical affair is the precise point on the "Bridge of the Soul" in Paris where Princess Diana's car crashed on August 30, 1997. This spot will probably become a place of reverence and awe. The royal family of England will from now on be forever linked to this site in public emotional memory. The money offered for acquiring the crashed car is a good example of how an otherwise common object becomes charged with emotional energy and turns into a symbol.

50. And other numerous places such as Sachsenhausen, Ravensbruck, Flossenburg, Buchenwald, and Mauthausen.

Transformations in the
Myth of the Inner Valleys
as a Zionist Place

Izhak Schnell

The purpose of this article is to trace the rise and fall of the *Emek* myth in the history of Zionist settlement with regard to the perception of space and its relationship to human beings. It presents the elements of this myth as they took root over the years, and attempts, via a comprehensive conceptual framework, to understand the alterations that took place in the perception of the Emek as a mythical reality during the various periods of Zionist history. This essay is based on memoirs and poetic, literary, and political essay sources. Space not allowing an analysis based on diverse relevant sources, I have chosen to focus on a limited number of sources most familiar to the public at large, which I believe reflect the spirit of those perceptions. These sources illustrate the meanings that have been institutionalized in the community, and are broadly manifest in the society.

The first chapter introduces the chief concepts in terms of which the meanings of mythic spaces may be explained and assessed. In the next five chapters the various perceptions of the Emek as a mythic space—a Land of Milk and Honey expressive of the perception that preceded the pioneering settlement, a wasteland, a hostile nature susceptible to conquest, and a locale overshadowed by its myth—are presented as elements of the myth; and the Emek itself as a periphery exposed to discrediting of the myth. The last chapter presents these approaches as they fit into a comprehensive conceptual framework.

The Emek (the inner valley) or the *Amakim* (the inner valleys) became a mythic place in the annals of Zionist Settlement. It is there that the pioneering settlement venture reached its acme, and where the myth was born of the pioneer who conquers the wasteland, exhibiting heroic sacrifice for the sake of the venture's success. The concept of "the valleys" in its mythic sense usually refers to the region that was the cradle of the Zionist-Socialist workers' settlement movement. To be sure, the first roots of this settlement (the Sejera plantation and the Degania group) lie at the periphery of the region, but the majority of the pioneer settlements during the early years were established in the Jezreel and Harod Valleys, spreading from there to adjacent Beit She'an and Zevulun Valleys and other areas. In this locale the settlers were obliged to meet difficult challenges, chiefly the malarial swamps and the hostile Arab population. Moreover, this was the birthplace of the new forms of settlement (except the idea of small *kvutza*, which started at Degania) that gave rise to the principal political-social movements and from the first settlements in the Emek provided the leadership, at least ideologically, of the organized Jewish community in Palestine.

One may learn the essential content of this myth by touring the Yif'at Museum—the most prominent museum commemorating the Emek settlement enterprise. The museum tour, with the director's explanations of the settlement beginnings, exhibits a three-stage narrative:[1] The first stage depicts a wasteland prior to Zionist settlement. In those days the Emek was dominated by hostile natural forces, first and foremost the swamps and an Arab population strikingly wretched and negligent of its environs. The Arabs are presented as a foreign and hostile population that lacked the motivation and talent to cope with the challenges with which that environment confronted them. The second stage is the stage of conquest—of mastering nature in the broadest sense of the term. Conquest of the Emek means first and foremost draining the swamps, but also mastery of work and the Hebrew language. The goal was achieved by virtue of four commitments the pioneers undertook: hard work with a willingness for self-sacrifice, resourcefulness in solving problems, use of advanced technology, and stress on the importance of direct contact with the soil as a means of shaping a new human being. The third stage emphasizes the objective of constructing a new human being. The Emek pioneer makes do with few material rewards, lives a life of equality and cooperation, develops a new secular Jewish culture stemming from his connection with the Emek soil, and assiduously endeavors to sink roots in it.

Conceptual Background

The present study employs a hermeneutic methodology that makes it possible to examine texts such as memoirs and literary works in a broader frame of reference and to identify events as types that the selected frame of reference suggests. Reliance on literary works is justified by the appraisal that representational relations exist between art and reality. This means that art may capture some qualities of the way that the external world is socially constructed and may translate them into artistic language within a common interpretative scheme.[2]

Writers derive their world of images and meanings from the social-cultural and political milieus in which they operate, and play an important role in constructing the social reality of their milieus.[3] Hermeneutic investigation makes it possible to understand events in a broader theoretical frame of reference, which is proposed by the researcher during a reflexive process. The process of constructing a hermeneutic theory entails a dialogue between possible exegetic patterns and the text, in the course of which texts from the original authors' narratives are translated into the interpretative one. A hermeneutic theory is constructed from three simultaneous cycles of interpretation. First, the internal cycle, in which the researcher collects relevant quotes from the text itself and examines their overall meaning, seeking an internally coherent narrative. The second cycle, in which the internal meanings are examined in a broader sociocultural frame of reference.[4] A third cycle, which assumes that the hermeneutic patterns adopted by social groups are influenced by political, economic or even sectarian, interests.[5] The test of a hermeneutic theory is its simplicity, plausibility, coherence, and ability to enrich our understanding of the reality.[6] The geographical narrative I seek to unearth focuses on the perception of the Emek's space as it took shape in the Zionist myth. Beyond that, the Emek myth was considered in the frame of reference of the meaning of space, nature and environment in the immigrants' adaptation to a new environment.

This paper deals with construction and reconstruction of the relationship between human beings and the space of their day-to-day life as it crystallizes in extreme situations of immigration and adaptation to a strange and hostile new locale. I assert that dialectic relations develop between human beings and their day-to-day space, in whose context human beings shape the world around them at the same time that they are shaped by their environs. The Zionist settlement in the valleys is an example of an especially extreme case. Settlers were guided by an ideology that consciously sought to generate this dialectic process as a means of moulding a Utopian human being and society in a new environment cut off from the diaspora reality in which they were shaped.[7] The pioneers sought a secular process of redemption by living close to nature.[8] They made a deliberate attempt to transform their idealistic unearthly sense of motherland to a concrete territorial sense of place.[9] De-Shalit[10] notes the transition from a romantic sense of territoriality and nature to a classic one in Zionism. The romantic ethos was characterized by the pioneers' attempts to get closer to nature as a means to be reborn from the new land of milk and honey. The classic ethos was characterized by the pioneers' uncompromising determination to domesticate the bewildered nature. Unlike him, Gorni[11] and Shapira[12] emphasized the dominance of the romantic ethos of sense of heroism along the history of Zionism. The narrative of the Emek museum seems to confirm De-Shalit's conclusion concerning Zionist perceptions of environment and nature, highlighting the political relevancy of these two ethoses. However, there is still a need to investigate Zionist myth of the inner valleys' nature and environment in a broader interpretative context, as the core of the pioneering process. This study attempts to discover the structure of the valleys' mythic space as perceived in Zionism, and to trace the changes that occurred in the Emek myth.

The discipline of geography in general, and the humanistic approach in particular, has analysed the human-world dialectic from ethical, aesthetic, emotional, spiritual and power-relations aspects. The broad scope of research has obscured the conceptual clarity of these five aspects. I am adopting Porteous's[13] definition for conceptualizing the various aspects of this dialectic. The aspect that most stresses the relation between person and territory is the emotional: a sense of belonging or feeling "at home" as against a sense of strangeness and sometimes even alienation. Homelike territories provide a sense of order, meaning, security, warmth and autonomy that is requisite for renewal. Strange territories, in contrast, provide dangers and challenges along with opportunities for expanding one's experiential world.[14] From the aesthetic aspect, geographers analyze the sensory experiences stemming from discovery of the territory's physical "surface" elements (landscape). The environment and nature are concepts used by geographers to analyse the ethical aspects of space and human territoriality. The concept of nature refers to aspects of the world perceived as prehuman and not controlled by human beings. The concept of environment refers to those aspects that maintain synergetic relations with individuals and society.[15] The spiritual aspect bestows on space and territory a topophilic status, verging on sanctity in extreme situations. The present paper stresses the emotional and the ethical dimensions, which shaped the mythic meanings of the Emek as a distinct territory symbolizing the pioneering socialist ethos in the annals of Zionism.

A Land of Milk and Honey

One of the first Zionist groups—*Hibat Zion* (Lovers of Zion), those who lived in the diaspora or had settled in the land of Israel—perceived the Emek, like other parts of the country, as a land of milk and honey that was expected to comply willingly with the Zionist settlement endeavor. The economic crisis in the diaspora countries and the 1880–1881 riots spawned the Lovers of Zion movement and stimulated the adoption of a broader world outlook that preached denial of the diaspora, and a national solution to the Jewish problem. This outlook revived interest in the land of Israel. Descriptions in art, literature, and tourists' and immigrants' memoirs began to burgeon. Their descriptions of landscapes are influenced by the romantic European tradition, adapted to the special reality of the Zionist national revival at the turn of the century. They make mythic use of the materials of the country's reality to glorify it and make it every Jew's dream to go there. This tendency was so powerful that many authors played down the country's squalor for fear of being tainted with the blame of the biblical spies who "brought up an evil report of the land."[16] One of the more influential writers on the second wave of immigrants, Brenner accused authors and poets from the first generation of settlers of being overly zealous to create fine works imbued with the country's spirit. In his opinion those works failed because the traditional Jewish community in Palestine disengaged itself from nature and from the Zionist intellectuals, while the new settlement had not yet managed to crystallize.

The scenic descriptions are usually general and noncommittal, but alongside places in the new settlement they mention many more biblical sites than did the Enlightenment period poets. Nonetheless, they lack detail and evade dealing with the reality that meets the observer's eye. Frishman,[17] who only visited the country and did not have to struggle for his existence in it, adopts this narrative. In his book *In The Land of Israel* he describes the view of the Emek from the Carmel ridge. He marvels at the sight of the Kishon "flowing like a fine silk thread," but promptly embarks on imagining the prophetess Deborah's victory over Sisera and Elija's victory over the Canaanite Prophets—two heroic events that occurred there. Comparison with biblical scenes as manifested in Frishman's writing is another feature of the landscape descriptions. In the romantic outlook, the remote past is a source of inspiration for future life. For a romantic national movement, nostalgia for the biblical golden age is a crucial source of inspiration.

Another element of this narrative is a tendency to depict the "desirable as extant," as Govrin phrased it, and to contrast it with the negative present reality in the diaspora or with the desolated reality in Palestine under the control of gentiles. The descriptions of Bialik[18] (the national poet who succeeded in presenting diaspora as well as the pioneers' life) from the beginning of the twentieth century in one of his first Land of Israel poems, "In the Field," depict the chief elements of the desirable environment as a contrast to the diaspora reality. The dream-like Israeli reality is first and foremost that of fields of grain responding to the Jewish worker on the one hand and giving him his freedom and pride on the other. These metaphors as contraries of the diaspora are underlined in the following quote:

> As a pauper shall I face the glory of the bright glad grain field,
> and know but now how great my poverty is, ha, but now I'll see it,
> it was not my hands that moulded you, ears of grain, not my hands that
>   cultivated your stature,
> I did not scatter my power here, I will not gather it up.

The description does not refer to any specific area, but these motifs later became central features of the Emek's mythic landscape. Moreover, the colonizing institutions' decision to focus efforts on settling the vast fertile valley tracts seems to have been connected with an assessment of the region as suitable for founding an agricultural environment that fitted the pioneers' world of imagery. This imagery was influenced by the agricultural landscapes of the hardy peasants in Eastern Europe.[19] It is manifest in the memoirs of prominent members of the second wave of immigration like Berl Katznelson, who described his ideal expectations of the country before emigrating: "How did I imagine walking in the Land of Israel? The picture split into two: One of course was a peasant working the land and the second—there were very pretty gardens, flowers and plants in the vicinity."[20] Yishai Adler[21] gives his description: "We saw it in our imaginations as a heaven on earth, all immersed in greenery and flowers. We dreamed and longed to reach the hoped-for shore quickly." The disparity between the land of milk and honey narrative and the descriptions of the Emek as the settlers were exposed to it is strikingly expressed in Ever Hadani's accounts:

> I was a little surprised at the sight of the Khan (the lone Arab House) protruding desolately, especially after the wonderful descriptions we were given in the Diaspora about the grand splendour of the Emek city, its shopping centres, theatres and gardens, its tranquillity and now I see no road, no path, no trail, no tree the air was full of wonderful gossamer, of which dreams are spun, and of which they are woven the sun was already setting, and the sky had begun to wrap itself in the beautiful gown of night, but the crimson was hot and above it hovered light fumes as though it rose from the west's burning.[22]

In this passage the author contrasts the Emek of the future vision with the sorry reality of the present. The topophilic description is still emphatic, but the region's squalor and the harsh climatic conditions invert the crimson dream's meaning for the settlers.

Another prominent romantic motif in Bialik's descriptions is the human-nature dialectic and the poet's sorrow that he did not manage to enter into it. It was not he who expended his strength on working the land, not he who amassed vitality and power from the fruit of his labor. This dialectic is the essence of (the pioneers' most influential spiritual leader) A. D. Gordon's doctrine and is what, in his view, entitles us to the land of Israel.

> This bond of our creative participation with the country's soil and the country's nature—where we seem to be reviving the land and the land seems to be renewing our spirit—is a more lasting bond than any existing. It is also the most reliable and most forceful proof of the persistence of our historical right to the country, owned by us till this day and not by our neighbours, who did not form such a vital and firm bond with it, did not create anything in it, and have not been in the least renewed in it.[23]

But even the pioneers of the second and third immigration waves, whom A. D. Gordon's doctrine inspired to attempt to enter the dialectic process, discovered that the country was not responding to them as strongly as they had dreamt. This situation heightened the perception of the country as a wasteland.[24]

The Wasteland

The wasteland perception was born of the settlers' immediate day-to-day life experience of adapting to so harsh an environment. The sense of a wasteland emerged out of their poor living conditions and the backward technology coupled with their sense of strangeness and alienation in the hopeless reality of the uprooted, far more than any professional ecological evaluation of the lands' desolation. Achad Ha'am,[25] a significant leader who preached for a long educational transition among the Jewish people instead of a political revolution, visited the holy land in the beginning of the century. He made a clear distinction between the present condition of the country and its future potential, in his article "The Truth from the Land of Israel":

> It is enough to walk and travel through it for a few days, to see its mountains and valleys, its fields and vineyards, which yield their fruit despite all the Arabs' sloth, for one to know that it has not yet lost its vitality and is as capable now as it was in the past of giving life and felicity to its children . . .

The purchasers of tracts in the Emek also judged the land fertile and worth buying, the only obstacle to developing the region being the swamps that could be drained.[26]

Unlike the experts, the settlers were shocked by the Emek's desolation. Horowitz describes the wasteland to which they had immigrated:

> The soil was arid, meagre and sterile. The locale was wild and barren without tree or shade. At night the jackals howled and the danger of Bedouin robbers lurked. The entire area was strewn with rocks and boulders, and the fields were covered with jujube shrubs that had to be uprooted to make the ground fit for cultivation ... We were wrapped in solitude, which we felt many times more at nightfall, when we were alone in the great gloom, the howling of the jackals all around us heightening the sense of solitude.[27]

Dayan[28] describes the debate that took place on the eve of settling Nahalal. The group's doctor asserted that they must not venture onto the site because of the dire danger of malaria, but the members undertook to submit to that bitter prospect for the cause of conquering the wasteland and swamps: "We won't ask doctors. The Land of Israel with its wastelands and swamps is ours, and we must settle it, must heal it and heal ourselves."

The most important factor, then, in the wasteland myth's formation was the existential crisis into which the pioneers of the second and third immigration waves were plunged following their radical attempt to build and be built in the Emek, utterly cut off from their diaspora past. Their dilemma is described admirably by David Melz:

> We immigrated to the Land of Israel and communed with ourselves, leaving behind us the chronicles, the wars and the complications of the past ... All at once we were uprooted from the soil of our culture, on which thousands of years of history had nevertheless made their mark. We were uprooted, by force majeure cast here to this arid land, cast among white sun-seared fields, stood in front of nude boulders, exposed to brimming fire from above, stood before the universe, face to face with the primeval elements, body to body, without outer garments separating us, and in the midst of these we must master our lives.[29]

The disparities between the tourists' attitude and the settlers' are especially striking in Vilkanski's descriptions. On their journey to the Galilee, he and his companions cross the Jezreel Valley. Their first reaction as tourists is to marvel at the breathtaking scenery and at the mountain ranges that bound the valley. They "stand mutely amazed at the power of the landscape."[30] Vilkanski shifts swiftly to interpret the sights from a settler's viewpoint, and the enchanting landscape is transformed instantly into a barren scene, its scorching heat unbearable, its fields now perceived as terrible in their extent because they are either bare or cultivated by foreigners, i.e., Arabs. The wasteland is manifested in the alienation between the author and the expanses of valley enclosed by mountain ridges whose Arab denizens imperil Jewish identity.

> And on both sides of the road are fields, fields terrible in their extent, bare fields and tilled fields. And among the fields are roads, highways: and camels bearing loads traverse the roads. Where are they coming from and where are they going, and what is in this world? And what is the relation between them and us? And there are beautiful houses on the mountain ridges and the mountain tops. What is there? Certainly not Jewish colonies.

Brenner expresses, in his pessimistic way, the Merhavia (one of the first settlements in the inner valleys) pioneers' alienation from their surroundings in the story "Redemption and Change" from 1935.[31] It depicts the settlers' hope for a better future after the British conquest of the country, as though redemption depends on an outside conquering army. Brenner is actually asserting that the pioneers' distress stems from a sense of existential disruption, confusion and non-belonging. "Everything was consumed by dryness, dust and thirst . . . everything was eerie, without meaning, without sense." The valley is presented here as a venue insensible to the misgivings of the settlers who are anxious about their fate, feeling deeply foreign to the place they live in, to their way of life, and to one another. The wasteland experienced by the pioneers is, then, an existential desolation stemming from their failure to enter the dialectic process they sang about, "We came to the Land to build and be built in it." The difficulty stems from the intolerable climate and devastating swampy environment.

Facts that patently belie the wasteland perception—like the Arabs' having lived in the valley for centuries, and the Zionist leaders' assessment that the valley's soil is fertile and that swamp land possesses a high botanical potential—do not shake the pioneers' estimate of the valley as wasteland. We learn from A. D. Gordon's writings (1925–1929), that the Arab adapts to the environment in a life devoid of any awareness of the dialectic potential of human being and land, accepting the meagre life to which he is doomed by circumstances. Non-realization of this dialectic potential makes the valley Arabs part of nature, denying them any national right to the country. But assessment of the land as fertile turns out to be an insufficient condition for entering the dialectic process. In the Jezreel Valley, for instance, some 40 percent of the settlers had malaria in 1923.[32] In the Harod Valley, Horowitz[33] reports that the swamp drainers were caught in a vicious circle: Disease impaired the group members' output, as a result of which their income decreased, their standard of nutrition declined and their vulnerability to malaria increased. At the end of the draining period, 90 percent of those engaged in the reclamation work were ill with malaria. Hence the swamps were in fact a true obstacle that took a heavy toll of those who sought to make the valley their home.

To the pioneers during the first settlement years, the valley is a wild expanse governed by the hostile forces of a nature indifferent to their fate and to their attempt to enter the dialectic of upbuilding new individuals within a new society and environment. This expanse becomes the venue of a battle to create a domestic space. It is not, however, an open space that extends beyond the horizon, but a limited space bounded by mountains that are populated by firmly established, hostile alien Arab settlements. Existential bewilderment and hardships of adaptation intensified the perception that the valley environment is a wasteland despite its fertility.

A Hostile Nature

The heroic tale of conquest of the wasteland is the crux of the Emek myth's narrative. It is a tale about a perversely recalcitrant milieu that could only be tamed by violent action such as conquest, harrowing etc. Great determination and sacrifice were required of the pioneers in order to curb nature and subordinate it to human utility. The purpose of this mastery was to enter the dialectic process of creating a new human being and society alongside transformation of nature into a new environment. Therefore this is not merely a tale of heroism, but a description of heroic performance of a sacred task, analogous to worship, which is the only way the evil forces of nature may be mended. Only renewed intervention in God's work will afford the pioneers the right to national ownership of the Promised Land, and to a place enjoying a sacred status parallel to that of Jerusalem.

The first component of the tale of conquest is an attempt to magnify the wasteland in order to glorify the heroism of its conquest. In this context the swamp is portrayed as a perverse act of immense natural forces. In the jubilee issue of the Jewish National Fund's magazine, Granot describes the swamp as a wild and hostile landscape produced by disruption. "The scene of the desolate valley, of a lovely landscape ravenously devoured by marshland, is the result of ferocious castration of the primeval order by a huge ancient geological rift." Though the reference was to the Hula swamps, it expresses a general attitude towards the swamps in all the valleys.

The second component of the story is magnification of the settlement venture and the sacrifices it entailed. Zalman Schneour, in his collected *Poems of the Land of Israel*, gives a dramatic touch to the struggle against nature. In "The People's Plow,"[34] the poet makes use of the biblical belief that the wasteland is God's decree so long as the land is governed by Gentiles, but infinite sacrifice is required of those returning to Zion to redeem the land from its desolation:

Then we ourselves will pull the yoke, like horses in harness bound hungry
    and unshod, smitten sore;
complain not, pioneers, make no sound
be strong and more!
through malarial swamps, boulders and sand
joyously penniless we'll pull the people's plow
searing Asian sun by day, bleak cold by night
. . . and if the laggard stumble and fall in the gruelling toil—
we shall pass over and leave his weary bones by the wayside,
a song on our lips and our soul saddened:—
in judgement there is no mercy and in redemption no compassion,
Let us make ourselves strong! Let the sweat stream and the blood drip,
to soften and crumble
the wasteland's clods,
to make the adonis flower red and the grain golden.

The new environment constructed and controlled by the settlers was glorified in the Emek myth, fed by the hardships of draining the swamps and the need to give meaning to the fallen victims sacrificed on the altar of the wasteland's conquest. The three songs that attained the status of hymns—"Fields in the Emek," "Rest Comes to the Weary," and "And the Watchman shall Sing"—stress this motif.[35] The fields of grain and fodder, the flocks of sheep, the odor of manure and the fragrance of hay in the Hebrew settlements are components of the new environment and no longer of a wasteland nature. These landscapes evoke an outburst of positive emotions, of peace and tranquillity whose source is the broad expanses shaped and controlled by Hebrew workers to whom Levi Ben-Amitai, who wrote "Fields in the Emek," chose to express his happiness in a song of thanksgiving.

The conquest of the terrible wasteland demands supreme sacrifice, and action whose importance is analogous to a secular modern incarnation of holy works. Three authors played a leading role in exalting the Emek myth to the degree of sanctity: Avraham Shlonsky, Sh. Shalom, and Uri Zvi Greenberg before he identified himself with the Revisionist movement.[36] These three engage very little in describing the natural landscape. Their descriptions are mainly domestic scenes that are the pioneers' handiwork. Most salient are the pastoral motifs that have become permanent assets of Israeli authenticity. Central scenic motifs are the fields of grain, the flocks of sheep, etc. Here the cycle was completed, the scenery of the *Hibat Zion* poets' future vision had become that of the dream come true.

The work invested in converting nature into a home environment is a holy labor analogous to ritual worship in the Temple in Jerusalem. Greenberg expressed the sanctity of labor in his essay "Towards Ninety Nine": "The Godhead finds its liturgy precisely here: in our secular life and in back-breaking labour in the Holy Land" performed by "the Jezreelites without earlocks or beard." The comparison between the sanctity of Jerusalem and that of the Emek is expressed explicitly in his poem "Glowification": "Ein Harod, Tel Yosef and Beit Alfa, two fervid Deganias / Jerusalem—head phylacteries, and the Emek—arm phylacteries."

Shlonsky's poems itemize pioneering as sacred labors and the components of the Emek landscape as a sacred place. The fields become "the holy milk of your breasts, oh God," the sheep and cow dung are "droppings of gold and sanctity," the sun rises like a cow emerging from God's barn, and its setting is likened to "the loading of a sheaf of wheat on a wagon by a great God who stands with trident in hand."[37] Sh. Shalom's writing stresses the motif of the new Israeli's sacrifice and rebirth: "If a man die in the Jezreel Valley / let the ears of grain be still. / The Jezreel Valley is the Holy of Holies / and one does not weep in the Holy of Holies." Shalom's hero, On Ben-Peleh,[38] flees the holy but corrupt Jerusalem seeking to heal his heart somewhat in the pure and fresh Emek. Sacrifices are required there which sanctify the place. "Happy are those who fall" to sanctify labor, because "the Holy of human Holies" is the striking of roots in its soil. The sacrifice is not made in vain. From the heroic man-world dialectic in the Emek is born the new Israeli who embodies redemption: "He is born, the new man, I have seen him / in the morning radiant in the fields, in Jezreel."

The conquest of the wasteland underlines even more the perception of a closed and bounded space, fed by the contrast between the sense of home in the valley and the foreignness and wasteland of the mountain expanses at its periphery. This was finely expressed by Fichman in his work *Seed Beds:*

In the searing end-of-summer heat, on a day of intensely dry desert wind, I travelled the road through Wadi Ara. I saw the heart of the mountains, the Shomron Mountains that have always drawn me like a mystery. And I again realised that wonders do not always appear where we expect them. Here, too, the earth was white with scorching dry rocks, the stones breathed flame, and dusty thistles grew dolefully grey all about. God only knows what sustenance the sheep found in the brown stalks they bent down to nibble with long suffering serenity, as the rays of the sun beat mercilessly on their backs. "The true wonders came to light in the olive grove of Tel Yosef, . . .

The hour was wondrously still. A primordial Biblical glow spread over the white-hot grass, over the trees that stood rooted on the slope with no leaf stirring. I had never before seen the valley breathe as heavily as on that day, but even the hot desert wind had its charm here. And I had not yet got over my joy at having finally reached the Emek fields despite my exhaustion, with the Shomron and Gilboa Mountains separating me from the city . . . However unenthusiastic I may be about the frequent holidays in this land, the greatest for me is the day on which a settlement is established. It is a holiday that bears a sort of mark of redemption—a sort of miniature exodus from Egypt . . .

The haze of the hot desert wind hanging over the fields of the valley below blurred the Gilboa Mountains opposite and the wood above the spring, which the eye strove to see, but their overhanging presence was palpable, like every primeval corner in which the remembrance of wonders is retained forever.[39]

Even after the wasteland's conquest, Fichman distinguishes three bounded spaces characterized by distinctly different identities. The neighboring mountainous area of Shomron, still depicted in terms customary in describing wasteland zones, partitions the urban coastal plain from the wondrous valley in which the feat of redemption has materialized. The same hot desert wind that lashes the Shomron wasteland envelopes the valley in biblical radiance. The sharp demarcation between the spaces is no longer hostile, but the Gilboa mountains still overhang the wondrous valley and separate the sacrosanct from the profane, the valley as symbol of pioneering from the urban space or wasteland. Fichman concludes his description of the Jezreel Valley with an outpouring of nostalgia typical of all the intellectuals who have been quoted in this context. "This place now looked like a primeval scene, and from the roof of the Sturman House (a cultural centre in memory of one of the leading Emek pioneers) my gaze dwelt on it with yearning for the early days." The days of conquering the wasteland were highly meaningful in their lives. It had been a time of changes in the primal order—by virtue of which the wasteland was conquered, a pioneering space generated by the settlers' Zionist-Socialist vision was constructed in the valley, and the settlers struck root in their homeland's soil.

In the Shadow of the Myth

In the shadow of the myth that flourished chiefly outside the valley, its inhabitants and their children lived their daily routine. For them, the Emek was the home in which they led their day-to-day lives, and not a sacrosanct space that was the subject of a mythic cult. It was the venue of the events of their childhood memories and the routine of their life, a routine conducted in the shadow of the myth but not in the mythic space itself. The poet Yehoshua Rabinov, who passed his adult life in Kibbutz

Gvat in the Emek, asserts that alongside the myth is a concrete reality of the earthy vintage.[40] Indeed, descriptions of the landscape become more specific and concrete, as though the disparity between mundane reality and mythic vision is for the first time not tolerated. Fania Bergstein, who lives in Kibbutz Gvat, expresses the immediate contact between nature and the person rooted in his locale:

> These tilled fields of Jezreel will blacken and grow verdant before your eyes, will shake your heart with fear when drought threatens, and with them your lungs will expand with the odours of merry showers . . . This landscape has become part of you. It is imprinted in your eyes, accompanies you like an unforgotten vision wherever you go.[41]

O. Hillel, in an interview on the occasion of receiving the Fichman Prize, described his attitude toward nature:

> I was born in Kibbutz Mishmar Haemek, where the land is not just a place but a part of existence. Every normal farmer all over the world is attached almost biologically, almost erotically to land, as is the case with me. I feel that I am part of the land. That is also the way I feel about the landscape, the stone, the forest, the grass—everything that the land puts forth. The land's experience is a fundamental experience for me.[42]

The breakdown of the conflict and hostility between human beings and nature which the above testimonies indicate are manifest in the works of art as well. Hillel considers himself at one with nature to the extent of blurring the boundaries between them. In his poem "At the Kfar Saba Junction," he expresses his feelings: "And on the fifth of the month the world flowered upon me tempestuously . . . and I heard all the blossoms of light and tinkles of water calling my name: Here! Here!"[43] In his poem "On Scorpion Climb" Hillel expresses total identification with nature: "God Almighty, why did you create me a man, when my heart yearns to be a desert or a mountain or a wind!" Natan Yonatan describes a similar harmony of people rooted in their environment: "All the fields breath as their bread is sliced, / and their joy is imbued in toil / and their sadness is vital and innocent."[44]

These descriptions demonstrate the success of the pioneers' attempt to enter a dialectic process with nature, in whose context both environment and man are transformed. The old-timers' generation and especially the members of the second generation no longer live a struggle against a terrible nature but are at one with it. S. Izhar[45] presents an attitude different from Hillel's. He does not unite with nature, but neither does he sense the dialectic tension between nature and human being. A domesticated nature becomes for him a neutral context for human commentary. In his plains stories he asserts,

> These azure baked skies are distant, dazzling, and care for nothing. The mountains—if you like they ponder sublime thoughts; if you like they are just clumped in mocking abandon. And these fields are merely soil, soil and nothing more.

In the story "Ephraim Goes Back to the Alfalfa" Izhar refrains from severing the human-nature dialectic:

> Ephraim goes down to the alfalfa field in the valley, stamping his footprints where the sand has absorbed those of yesterday and the day before, keeps on walking, and the same familiar delight always creeps in, without waiting for the storm whose onset is imminent, that delight of liberty, of easy relaxed breathing, of idle whistling entwined with hopeful contemplation and covert gaiety, and the heart again responds willingly, clinging to longings on the bright terrain, hinting at thickets whose dusk puts out of mind their solitude in the surrounding dark, and the stubble in the fields is yellow.[46]

But loss of dialectic tension has its price, too. Routine begins to eat away the settlers' sense of the locale and their vitality. Nature, here described as concrete and neutral, again symbolizes the mental state of Izhar's hero, and the human-nature dialectic is again salient, manifested in the hero's desire to couple an inner change with an outer change:

> Behind the valley of fields, they are encompassed by known and familiar mountains, like a huge ring within which are familiar roads, known hills and a dusty silence of light, too familiar and devastatingly known . . . A change must come, an inner change involving an outer change, which is why I want to switch to the citrus grove.

The switch to the citrus grove might seem trivial, but in the mythic environment it is profoundly meaningful. The valley is identified with the fields of grain and field crops that extend from horizon to horizon in the "Emek sanctuary", while the citrus grove is identified with the private agriculture that exploits Arab workers in the profane space of the Sharon and the coastal plain. Hence switching to the citrus grove may be perceived as a betrayal of the Holy of Holies—the conquest-of-the-wasteland ethos—and thereby the constitution of a new human being and society. But the harshest motif that recurs in many works is the need to compromise with man's inability to purify himself entirely of his faults, even in the intensive melting pot of nature in the valley. The story hints at the fact that many of the pioneers' commitment to social justice and moral high standards were not completely internalized.

In his autobiographical novel *A Genesis*, Shlomo Reichstein, one of the first members of the Emek kibbutzim Tel Yosef and Ein Harod, describes the need to come to terms with "the anguish of dark and conflicting instincts." In moments of despair the hero wants to destroy everything, but on ordinary days it is hard for him to distinguish between "the light of a dying day" and "the radiance of a new day." Only on special dates and in isolated moments of grace is it possible to restore the sense of exaltation that attended the experience of conquering the valley wasteland. Reichstein was caught between his sense of failure to reach the high moral standard he tried to struggle for and the fall into meaningless habituality.

Relegation of the Valley to the Periphery

Challenges of the myth's validity began to be voiced in the 1960s but gathered impetus in the 1970s and 1980s, chiefly on the part of the generation of grandchildren of the founders. Several elements recur at this stage. The founders are represented as naive and extreme idealists, certain of their rectitude to the point of oblivion to the changing environment: the predilections of the members of the next generation, the new immigrants, and the new socioeconomic reality. The closed-mindedness of the generation of titans evokes an ironic or mocking attitude in the new generation's writers. These usually tend to appreciate the pioneers' tenacity to the up-building of the country but stress their failure to create a new person liberated from ugliness in interpersonal relations. Ben-Ner[47] in his novel *Protocol* underlined his admiration of the Zionist enterprise his parents shared in, which led to the founding of Kfar Yehoshua, creating "a place that is home" out of the impossible. But in his collected stories *Village Sunset*, the author stresses, besides his admiration for the founding generation's enterprise, their inability to create a system of united and altruistic social relationships. The society is portrayed as a cramped, strife ridden human milieu in which the pioneers do not overcome jealous and vengeful emotions. And, too, the pioneering ethos of rapprochement with nature through working the land also began to be undermined together with a weakening of faith in the human-world dialectic. Agricultural work is depicted as an increasingly heavy burden, and the beautiful valley landscape with its domestic scenes (squared fields, round settlements, etc.) no longer encourages the settlers.

Meir Shalev in *Russian Novel*[48] presents a more complex attitude which like Ben-Ner's combines great admiration for the founders' generation alongside penetrating criticism of the pioneers' naivete and shortcomings as human beings, to the point of presenting the myth as ludicrous. The founders' salient trait was their tenacity to nature and its conquest. The agricultural workers belittled the nonagricultural workers in the village, except for Pines, the teacher who identified his pedagogical work with tilling the soil. He makes much use of phrases like "virgin soil," "errant vines," "irrigation troughs," "saplings," and "seed beds" in describing his pupils and his work as educator. In the description of how the dairy sheds were built, there is a mixture of appreciation of the self-sacrifice entailed, alongside mockery at the overritualization that attended the pioneering activity. "When the founding fathers went up on the land they invested the first construction budget in concrete barns for the milch cows, because the cows were less hardy than they themselves were against the ravages of the climate, generations of domestication and breeding having removed from their hearts any aspiration to return to nature." The pioneers also adhered with demonstrative extremism to the values of frugality. "Yosef sent money from America to buy a frigidaire. Grandpa threw the letter into the cow barn's manure gutter and told Grandma he would never use a capitalist traitor's money." Only in the social sphere does Shalev accuse the pioneers of failure. They didn't succeed in overcoming jealousy, malice, and other human frailties. A cynical expression of this is given in the description of the pioneers' attitude toward a widow in one of the valley villages. "The Rabbi asked the village people to make him a match with her, and they were glad to get rid of her because she had been putting the principles of mutual aid to a difficult test."

The pioneer world was relegated to the sidelines of Israeli life and even of the valley's life, as the pioneering generation grew old. "Like an old machine whose parts have reconciled themselves to one another's movement, the village persisted in its nightly routine." Not many of the sons followed in their footsteps. "The spiders built their dense funnels in the modern milking stalls . . . pimples of mould and rot formed on the concrete walls, putting an end to the last traces of crop and prudence . . . desolation reigned everywhere." The pioneers entrenched themselves in defensive positions. The valley's space is again perceived as a closed space in which the hyena threatens the farmer's serenity, symbolizing the threat to him and his environment posed by the Arabs and city life, as well. After the hyena killed the boy Baruch, as the Arabs had killed his parents, we read: "The hyena is dead, Yaakov, Grandpa told him. Who knows as well as you do that it is dead? You can relax. Every generation grows new enemies, said Pines and went out." Nature keeps threatening to return the wasteland to the valley at any moment. Especially, "The legend bellowed from them all: the swamp that the founding fathers imprisoned awaits a sign of doubt." The fewer the pioneers and their successors became, the more need they felt to buttress and glorify their enterprise. But the greatest threat came from the city. When Levin leaves for Jaffa, which he defines as "a city without stones, a soft city", he himself is defined as a "defector" by the founding fathers. The city is not merely a soft space that contains no hostility or challenge, but a source of temptations. "When he looked west he saw the orange glow of the big city's lights beyond the mountain, a sunrise of the seductions of exploitation and corruption, easy profits, flirting flesh and winking eyes."

The young generation's reaction to the pioneer pathos was one of estrangement, and the pioneers' failure to bring about individual and social change accelerated the pioneering enterprise's fall from grace. On the one hand, the second and third generations are the valley's children, shaped by its rugged natural milieu. On the other hand, they exhibit no willingness to embrace the founders' pioneer ethos. The most striking expression of this is the founders' cemetery that the narrator builds on his grandfather's land, which yields him cynical riches from the pioneer myth. His grandfather, wishing to avenge himself on his comrades, first proposed the idea, and Buskila from the *ma'abara* (temporary housing camp from the mass immigration of the fifties), which represents another group of people that the founding fathers spurned, assists him. The narrator's desire for cynical enrichment from the outdated myth notwithstanding, the author leaves hope for the valley. The narrator's cousin chooses to go back to cultivating the fields among the gravestones.

Eli Amir's work, *Sacrificial Cock*,[49] stresses the estrangement in an Emek kibbutz between an immigrant youth group and the old-timers and kibbutz-born youths. The author's confrontation with Dolek illustrates the cultic self-orientation into which the pioneers had sunk and their inability to accept the new reality. Eli Amir, too, treats with awe the pioneers' sincere attempt to build and be built through proximity to nature and to agriculture in the valley soil. At the same time, it is hard for him to forgive the closed-mindedness and sense of superiority that have been instilled in the hearts of the kibbutz's younger generation.

The last of the bewailers of the valley myth's relegation to the sidelines of Israeli life is Amos Kenan, who has difficulty retaining optimism in his novel *The Road to Ein Harod*.[50] When a dictatorship seizes power in Israel, Ein Harod, one of the leading kibbutzim in the Emek, remains free. The author sets out on a highly perilous journey to reach it. When he arrives he experiences what Vilkanski experienced at the beginning of Zionism, or rather an ancient primeval experience: "Here and there a Tabor oak copse, here and there a green gulch, the entire valley a verdant meadow. Blossoming almond trees, patches of anemones, first spring flowers, . . . but there's nothing, I don't see anything." Once again the wasteland is more a loss of control over reality and an existential crisis than an ecological assessment of natural conditions. In Kenan's opinion, the failure lies in the pioneers' having stopped to rest on their laurels and forgetting "that there will always be one more swamp left." If there remains any measure of optimism in what Ein Harod represents, it is the fact that that is where everything started. It is where the spirit of freedom burgeoned and if it will revive, Ein Harod is the place from which it will all start again. This time it will not be possible to expect that rapprochement with nature will enable us to surmount the diaspora Jewish past or the reality surrounding us, lest we remain estranged from our environment.

Conclusions

The most salient feature that emerges from the testimonies cited above is the dialectic relationship prevailing between human beings—especially modern ones—and the world around them. The human-world dialectic is clearly manifest in the experiences of the Emek pioneers, as well as in the doctrine of A. D. Gordon (the father of the Zionist-Socialist movement), and in the immediate experience of the Bittania Ilit Group's members. This relationship assumes various forms, depending on the experiences of those describing the Emek reality. The dialectic is described in five different ways: as a land of milk and honey that is going to respond willingly to the Jewish settlers; as an empty and alienating wasteland; as a hostile nature requiring heroic conquest; as a place in which human beings and environs are defined by one another; and as a space that has been relegated to the periphery of Israeli life, its fate determined by spaces external to it.

Various perceptions may typify different individuals or groups owing to the specific context of their experience. But there is no doubt that a different perception was dominant in each period, and that the historical order of these perceptions of nature and environment was not random.

The land-of-milk-and-honey myth characterizes the first Zionist generation on the eve of settling the Emek. Most salient in this group are Jews who dreamed about or visited the country but did not have immediate experience of the settlement enterprise, or pioneers who described their experience prior to immigrating. The harsh reality of the two first decades of the century with which the members of the second immigration wave were obliged to cope, contributed to deposition of the land-of-milk-and-honey myth and adoption of the wasteland myth. It is against this background, too, that we must understand the rise of the hostile-nature-requiring-conquest myth, from the early 1920s until the 1930s. This myth was fed chiefly by the utterances of leaders and authors who were in the valley for only a brief time, while most of their fame stemmed from their activity outside it.[51] According to the testimonies of some of them, their sojourn in the valley was perceived as decisive in shaping them when they came to the country, and so the period evoked great nostalgia in their hearts. One might assume that apotheosis of the myth also served political interests of the workers' elite in the country, which entrenched its national status on the strength of its pioneering activities. It is well known that national leaders were asked to come to the Emek kibbutzim for years to meet the labor parties' ideological leaders. The generation of those born in the valley and the veteran settlers who stayed on the land, chiefly in the 1930s and 1940s, celebrated the birth of the new rooted Jew ("Sabre") who was born out of this erotic relations with the land of the inner valleys. But after the establishment of the state in 1948 the inner valleys' settlers faced the need to bridge over the disparity between their drab day-to-day life as marginalized sociospatial group and the glamorous myth. The 1970s and onward are characterized by a breakdown of the Emek myth and a more sober examination of the reality created in the valley in the course of a century of settlement. It may be concluded from the interpretation that each transformation in Zionist perception of nature and environment in the inner valleys must be understood to a large extent as a response to a former stage, leading to human-world successions of fusion and separation.

Notes

I would like to thank Mr. Yigal Shenkman for his excellent English translation of the literature and the poetic quotations.

1. Avner Galili, "The Museum in Yif'at," in *The Jezreel Valley*, ed. Mordechai Naor (Jerusalem: Yad Ben-Zvi Publ., 1993), 253–262.

2. Nelson Goodman, *Languages of Art*, (Indianapolis: Hackett Publishing Inc., 1976). Rut Lorand, *On the Nature of Art* (Tel-Aviv: Ma Da, 1991).

3. bell hooks, *Yearning, Race, Gender and Cultural Politics* (London: Turnaround, 1991).

4. Paul Ricoeur, "The Model of the Text: Meaningful Action Considered as a Text," *Sociological Research* 38, 3 (1972): 529–562.

5. Dennis Cosgrove, *The Ideology of Landscape* (Cambridge: Cambridge University Press, 1988). Raymond Guess, *The Idea of a Critical Theory* (London: Cambridge University Press, 1981).

6. Ze'ev Levi, *Hermeneutics* (Tel Aviv: Sifriat Hapoalim, 1986).

7. Izhak Schnell, "Nature and Environment in the Socialist-Zionist Pioneers' Perceptions: Sense of Desolation," *Ecumene* 4, 1 (1997): 69–85.

8. Shmuel Almog, "Redemption in Zionist Rethorics," in *Redemption of the Land of the Eretz-Israel*, ed. Ruth Kark (Jerusalem: Yad Yizhak Ben-Zvi, 1990), 7–19.

9. Zali Gurevitz and Gideon Aran, "On the Place," *Alpaim* 4 (1991): 9–44.

10. Avner de-Shalit, "From the Political to the Objective: The Dialectics of Zionism and the Environment," *Environmental Policies* 4, 1 (1995): 70–87.

11. Yosef Gorni, "The Romantic Foundation in the Second Wave of Immigrants' Ideology," *Asufot* (1966): 47–56.

12. Anita Shapira, *The Dove's Sword* (Tel Aviv: Saul Avigdor Society for Research, 1994).

13. J. Douglas Porteous, *Environmental Aesthetics* (London: Routledge, 1996).

14. Anne Buttimer, "Grasping the Dynamism of the Lifeworld," *Annals of the Association of the American Geographers* 66 (1976): 277–292. Edward Relph, *Place and Placelessness* (London: Pion, 1977). Izhak Schnell, *Israeli Arab Perceptions: Territoriality and Identity* (Aldershot: Avebury, 1994).

15. Terry Ingold, *Culture and the Perception of the Environment* (London: University of London, 1990, unpublished manuscript). Schnell, "Nature and Environment," 70–74.

16. Nurit Govrin, *Honey from Rock* (Tel Aviv: Defence Ministry Publication, 1989).

17. David Frishman, *In the Land* (Tel Aviv: Achiasaf, 1913).

18. Haim N. Bialik, *Complete Writings of Haim Nachman Bialik* (Tel Aviv: Dvir, 1938).

19. Schnell, "Nature and Environment," 70–74.

20. Berl Cazanelson, "My Way to Israel," in *The Book of the Second Aliya, Vol. A*, eds. Avraham Shochat and Bracha Habas (Jerusalem: Am Oved, 1936): 68.

21. Yishay Adler, "How I Made Aliya," in *The Book of the Second Aliya, Vol. A*, eds. Avraham Shochat and Bracha Habas (Jerusalem: Am Oved 1936): 37.

22. Ever Hadani, *The Town of Yizrael, Afulas' 25's Anniversary* (Afula, 1951).

23. Avraham David Gordon, *Writings of A. D. Gordon* (Tel Aviv: Central Committee of Hapoel Hatzair Party, 1925).

24. Schnell, "Nature and Environment," 70–74.

25. Achad Ha'am, *Complete Writings of Achad Ha'am* (Tel Aviv: Dvir, 1947).

26. Zvi Shiloni, "Zionist Land Acquisitions and Settlement," in *The Jezreel Valley*, ed. M. Naor (Jerusalem: Yad Ben-Zvi Publ. 1993).

27. David Horovitz, *My Yesterday* (Jerusalem: Shoken, 1970).

28. Shmuel Dayan, *The Village of Nahalal* (Tel Aviv: Kupat Hasepher with JNF, 1926).

29. David Meltz, *The Locked Gate* (Tel Aviv: Am Oved, 1959).

30. Meir Vilkanski, "To the Galilee," *Haomer* (1909): 243–245.

31. Yosef H. Brenner, *Complete Writings of Y. H. Brenner*, (Tel Aviv : Steibel, 1937).

32. Ilan Zaharoni, "Swamps in the Valley," in *The Jezreel Valley*, ed. Mordechai Naor (Jerusalem: Yad Ben-Zvi Publ., 1993), 253–262.

33. Horovitz, *My Yesterday*.

34. Zalman Schneor, "The People Plow," in *From Poems of the Land of Israel* (Tel Aviv: Dvir, 1958).

35. Zippi Fleischer, "The Valley is a Dream" in *The Jezreel Valley*, ed. Mordechai Naor (Jerusalem: Yad Ben-Zvi Publ., 1993), 228–242.

36. Avner Holzman, "A Land Heavy with Vision and Wine," in *The Jezreel Valley*, ed. Mordechai Naor (Jerusalem: Yad Ben-Zvi Publ., 1993), 204–228.

37. Holzman, "A Land Heavy with Vision and Wine," 204–228.

38. Shin Shalom, *We Were As Dreamers* (Tel Aviv: Yavne, 1954).

39. Ya'akov Fichman, *Seedbeds* (Jerusalem: Mossad Bialik, 1954).

40. Holzman, "A Land Heavy with Vision and Wine," 204–228.

41. Fania Bergshtein, *In the Field of Jezreel* (Tel Aviv: Reshimot, 1952), 263.

42. Aharon Levitt, O. Hill Receives Fichman Prize, *Maariv*, May 1986.

43. Oien Hillel, *Nonetime Country* (Tel Aviv: Siphriat Hapoalim, 1950).

44. Natan Yonatan, *That We Loved* (Tel Aviv: Siphriat Hapoalim, 1957).

45. Izhar Smilanski, *Plains Stories* (Merhavia: Hkibbutz Hameuchad, 1963).

46. Izhar Smilanski, *Ephraim Goes Back to the Alfalfa* (Merhavia: Hkibbutz Hameuchad, 1964).

47. Itzhak Ben Ner, *Village Sunset* (Tel Aviv: Am Oved, 1976).

48. Meir Shalev, *Russian Romance* (Tel Aviv: Am Oved, 1988).

49. Eli Amir, *Expiatory Rooster* (Tel Aviv: Am Oved, 1984).

50. Amos Kenan, *The Road to Ein Harod* (Tel Aviv: Am Oved, 1984).

51. Holzman, "A Land Heavy with Vision and Wine," 204–228.

Democracy and Sense of Place Values in Environmental Policy

Bryan Norton and Bruce Hannon

An important problem of modern society is to understand how constraints on resource use can be democratically imposed. Recent authors have expressed deep concern about the possibility that resource shortages will lead to totalitarian governments. They hypothesize that such governments would be the only effective means to enforce constraints on resource use and protect the environment from the inevitable consequences of human population growth, overconsumption of natural resources and social chaos (Hannon 1985, Heilbroner 1974, Kennedy 1993, Ophuls 1977, 1992). Ludwig et al. (1993) have recently provided an elegant argument—based in fisheries management but apparently susceptible to startling generalization—which calls into question the ability of democratic governments with free market economies to protect renewable resources once there has been heavy capitalization and development of exploitative industries. Must societies of the next millennium be undemocratic if they are to protect their natural resources?

In this paper we address one important aspect of the search for a democratically supportable policy that will sustain resources for future generations—the comparative role of national/centralized, regional/state, and local communities in the development of environmental policy. We distinguish two approaches to the evaluation, development, and implementation of policies to protect resources and environments. The two approaches (we will call them "top-down" versus "bottom-up") differ most essentially in that the top-down approach emphasizes centralized control and decision making, while the bottom-up approach attempts to protect, to the extent possible, local prerogatives in setting environmental policy. We will then show that the different approaches would require very different methodologies for gathering and aggregating data regarding envi-

119

ronmental values, and that application of the two methodologies results in differing conceptions of the overall good of a society. We conclude with some general applications of our theory to the future of environmentally sensitive planning.

More and more authors and commentators on the environmental crisis endorse sense-of-place values as important components of our enjoyment and valuation of the environment (Ehrenfeld 1993; Norton and Hannon 1997; Sagoff 1993; Sale 1985; Seamon and Mugerauer 1985; Tuan 1977). The idea of sense of place is addressed in the literature of several disciplines—we will mention here key works in geography, anthropology, sociology, environmental ethics and social criticism, and especially ecological history, as well as in architectural and planning theory. We find the concept intriguing, in that the idea/concept is highly praised as important in several subdisciplines (such as phenomenological geography, historic preservation, and environmental ethics), but the concept itself has remained somewhat peripheral to the main subject matters of each of these disciplines. Perhaps the transdisciplinary nature of the concept, which has prevented its development within a single disciplinary paradigm, explains why the concept has not been given precise operational meaning or application. This lack of a shared operational meaning might at first recommend abandoning the term as too imprecise to serve as the basis for a scientific approach to policy formation and evaluation. We prefer, in contrast to this defeatist approach, to define the term within a transdisciplinary discourse rich enough to express aspects of the idea emphasized in several disciplines.

The concept of place has been most developed by *geographers*, especially by geographers in the phenomenological tradition (outstanding in this tradition is the work of Gould and White 1974, 1986; Relph 1976, Seamon 1979, Tuan 1971, 1974, 1977; also see the essays in Seamon and Mugerauer, 1985). While this work has created interesting conceptual ties with the tradition of philosophical phenomenology—especially the work of the German philosopher, Martin Heidegger (1958, 1962; and Vycinas 1961), it has not attracted much attention from more quantitative geographers. Consequently, while this literature has greatly expanded our qualitative understanding of the place-relatedness of humans, their institutions, and their cultures, it unfortunately has not been fully integrated into the broader theoretical and quantitative work of geographers. One promising direction in this area is geographical work that incorporates ecological theory—specifically hierarchy theory (an application of general systems theory to ecological systems) into large-scale, landscape-level geographical analysis. This work employs the ideas of hierarchy theory to develop more integrated conceptions of scale and interconnectedness in landscapes (Allen and Hoekstra 1992; Allen and Starr 1982; Collins and Glenn

1990; Holling 1992; Johnson 1993; Lavorel et al. 1993; McMahon et al. 1978; O'Neill et al., 1986). What remains puzzling, here, is how exactly the objectivist, hierarchical models, which seek scientific and culture-free "objective" truths of physical geography, relate to the subjectivist and culturally determined models of phenomenologists (Norton and Hannon, 1997).

Anthropology, sociology, and related social sciences have contributed to literature on the relationship of local and regional cultures to their environment and resource base; especially important have been several excellent accounts of successful systems of resource access and protection among indigenous cultures (see, for example, Gadgil and Berkes 1991; Gadgil and Guha 1992; Rappaport 1968). The relationship between societies and their resource base has been effectively studied in a new way by a group of environmental historians—the *ecological* historians—who have used a combination of ecological and social historical data to reconstruct the role of human institutions in the "development" of the new world by colonial and post-colonial societies. The breakthrough book in this area was William Cronon's *Changes in the Land* (1983), which surveyed the changes in the New England countryside as a result of the arrival of European colonists. Crosby (1986) offers a broadly similar account, but Crosby emphasizes introduced species as the agents of "ecological imperialism," while Cronon details the intricate interrelations of ecological processes with the dynamic of human institutions (Cronon 1983, 1991); we find Cronon's institutional/ecological account more illuminating in the context of issues emphasized in this paper. Cronon, Crosby, and also Worster (1979, 1985) have all added to our knowledge of the interrelations of social and natural history. This theoretical work has been followed by numerous studies which have applied similar methods to the social and ecophysical transformation that occurred in the landscapes of every region of the United States and a few foreign countries (see, for example, Gadgil and Guha 1992; Gutierrez 1991; Silver 1990). Many examples of this literature do not consider place relatedness explicitly, but it provides many local and regional examples of how changing social and economic institutions alter, contribute to, and in many cases destroy the distinctiveness and identity of a place.

The idea of place has also been discussed, although not extensively, in *environmental ethics and social criticism.* Murray Bookchin (1965, 1982) articulated the idea that ecology and social criticism both point toward smaller, decentralized communities with strong commitments to place, in opposition to centrally controlled societies and resource management regimes. Other popular authors and essayists, including Wendell Berry (see, especially, 1977) and a whole literary movement sometimes called Southern Agrarians, have been highly critical of top-down management of resources and have advocated a strong commitment to the distinctiveness of local places. Alan Gussow (no date, 1993) has explored sense of place in art and aesthetics. Sale (1985) provides a useful overview of the role of place in understanding human cultures, advocating a "bioregionalist" approach, while Sagoff (1992) explores the cultural and aesthetic aspects of sense of place values. Sagoff, incidentally, argues that Americans generally have a weak sense of place, and attributes this to both the mobility and commercialism of American society. Deep ecologists have advocated more attention to the concept of place, but in our view they have not successfully resolved the apparent conflict between the localism implied by emphasis on place, and the centralist, universalist, and Eurocentrist implications of their theory that all life has equal intrinsic value. In general, interest in these universal, extra-cultural values among environmental ethicists has reduced the importance of the concept of place in that discipline (Norton 1995a and b).

Among architects, planners, and designers there was considerable interest in place-relatedness in the late 1960s and 1970s, and there has been a revival of interest in the concept in the 1990s. Important early work ranges from concern for the cultural and physical distinctiveness of local communities (Briggs 1968; Lynch 1960, 1972; Moore et al. 1974) to phenomenological/aesthetic studies in architecture and planning theory (Norberg-Schulz 1979). Norberg-Schulz sharply separates objective from subjective aspects of place awareness, and then argues for a geographical determinism according to which cultural attitudes are determined by the physical structures of the environment (see, especially, chapter III.1). These issues have become intertwined with the question of the nature of the "spirit of place" or "genius loci," as it is sometimes called, as definitions of these ideas can vary according to the mix of physical and cultural factors assumed to determine the spirit of a place. More recent work ranges across the spectrum from approaches mainly descriptive of distinctive features of physical places (e.g., Hough 1990) to work with greater emphasis on cultural and perceptual aspects of place relatedness (e.g., Jackson 1994; Steele 1981). Daniel Kemmis (1990) provides both a provocative discussion of regionalism versus federalism in American politics and a useful application of the idea of place in local politics; also see J. K. Bullard (1991) for an account of professional specialization in a specific local place. Interestingly, Kemmis and Bullard have both been elected mayors of their cities (Missoula, Montana, and New Bedford, Massachusetts, respectively).

There has also been serious study of placelessness and loss of place. Important theoretical work by Relph (1976) was preceded by empirical studies, funded by the National Institute of Mental Health in the 1960s and 1970s, which examined the lives of residents of Boston's West End before and after it was levelled for urban renewal. This work emphasized the psychological importance of attachment to place, and of a sense of grief at loss of one's place, even in an area considered by outsiders to be a "slum" (Brett 1980; Duhl 1963, including especially Fried 1963; Gans, 1962).

One area where consensus has not been reached is in the area of boundary-setting, and the related question of how rigid boundaries between places are assumed to be. This difference spans geography and planning, with physical geographers usually employing physically measured boundaries, while planners and phenomenological geographers follow anthropologists in emphasizing perception and cultural factors in the determination of boundaries between places.

Even if most individuals orient from a place, it is not clear whether this perceptual position translates into "neighborhoods" or whether neighborhoods have more shifting boundaries, depending on human issues and cultural similarities. See Galster (1986) for an incisive, empirical approach to these complex questions.

One important agreement among psychologists, geographers and planners is on the importance of distinguishing *place* from *location*. Despite their local mobility, migratory peoples can have a strong sense of place. This distinction was made sharply by the aesthetician Langer (1953), who argued that a gypsy camp is a *place* which is reestablished in many separate *locations* during migrations. In this case, the placement of wagons, etc. can create a sense of constant "place-orientation" at multiple locations. The ideas behind this distinction—that a sense of place emerges from an interaction of cultural and natural setting and that commitment to place is somewhat independent of location—may prove important to planners and environmental managers, because it raises the possibility of consciously building upon and strengthening a community's sense of place identity, even in the face of extraordinary mobility of populations. Of special interest here is the work of Proshansky (1978; Proshansky et al. 1983), who suggested the possibility that place-bonding may be to *types* of settlements as much as to particular locations, and thus may function transpatially. Feldman (1990), working in this tradition, reviews literature on "spatial identity" and presents data establishing loyalty to types of places, such as city, suburb, or small town. Hull (1992) explores Proshansky's hypothesis empirically, developing an operational notion of "place congruity."

If it is possible for individuals and communities to actively promote a positive sense of place, and if sense of place values in a community encourages protection of their local environments, it becomes an important question whether it is possible to adopt a policy of promoting a sense of local responsibility through strengthening the sense of place in a community. Unlike Sagoff, who, as we noted above, explains lack of sense of place by invoking population mobility, this approach treats the relationship between mobility and sense of place commitment as an empirical matter, and as an important area for active participation by local planners, who may function to develop a stronger sense of place commitment in highly mobile communities. We return to this point in the conclusion.

A survey of these varied literatures suggests that the concept of sense of place is much better understood, theoretically and empirically, than it once was, and that the concept may present opportunities for important applications in planning and in environmental management. Despite the increasing interest of environmentalists and planners in the idea of place, however, little has been done so far to operationalize this intriguing but elusive concept, and it has been given little emphasis in actual analyses of environmental values. As a result, important applications have not occurred because of the inability of practitioners of multiple disciplines to settle upon a concept that is operational and sufficiently transdisciplinary to unify insights from the disciplines, all of which address the subject of place from different perspectives and with differing emphases.

This lack of agreement regarding operationalization and application is well illustrated in a recent exchange published in *Resources*, the newsletter of the economic research institute, Resources for the Future. In response to a proposal by Mark Sagoff (1993), that protection of sense of place values be articulated as a criterion of good environmental management, the economist Raymond Kopp (1993) expresses disdain, rejecting the concept as "problematic as a basis for policy. If Congress and the regulatory agencies can figure out how to define environmental policy on [the basis of the concept of place], more power to them."

Kopp's summary dismissal of Sagoff's proposal as unworkable rests upon a key, implied premise. Kopp implies that sense of place values must prove themselves useful in guiding *national* environmental policy (through guidance to Congress and the regulatory agencies). Notice that this apparently unquestioned assumption functions in effect as a methodological stipulation, requiring that any measure of environmental values must be easily aggregable across space. Further, the remark might be taken to imply a preference for centralized control of resource use, a top-down system of environmental management that assumes federal sovereignty over state and local governments in conflicts regarding resource use. We hope we are not imputing too much to Kopp's remark; we worry, however, that a strong methodological preference for cross-scale aggregation of all values up to the national level may well bias environmental economists against sense of place values. Kopp, if we have understood him correctly, argues that sense of place values cannot be aggregated to guide a national environmental policy and, therefore, so much the worse for sense of place values as policy guides. This commitment to aggregating environmental values at the national level quite naturally discriminates against sense of place values, the accounts for which—almost by definition—must be kept local. Setting aside centralist and aggregationist biases, however, Kopp's argument can be reversed. If there is strong evidence for place-relativity of important environmental values, and local values and sovereignty are favored, it might be concluded: So much the worse for measures of value that aggregate at the national level but which cannot account for these locally placed values. Our purpose in this paper is to present a twofold argument. First, that there are local, place-relative values which are systematically missed if all environmental accounts must be kept in nationally aggregated accounts (such as market prices recorded as dollar values). And, second, that these values have an important role in charting a course toward a democratically acceptable approach to environmental policy and planning.

An Example

We introduce our argument for sense of place values by discussing a particular example—a farm family who has owned the same farm for several generations—and inquire how this family values its property, hypothesizing that some of these values cannot be captured within a market analysis of social values. We recognize that the example is a favorable one for our case, but we use it simply to establish the existence of nonmarketable sense of place values in one case. We discuss how widespread and how significant these values are below. For simplicity, we formulate the case as applying to land values, although we believe it applies to environmentally sensitive values more broadly, and perhaps to every "public good" in environmental valuation.

Consider the plight of a fourth-generation farm family who learns that an adjacent property is to be purchased under eminent domain provisions and provided as the site for a toxic waste treatment facility under a contract with the local municipality. Our family is offered a choice. If they wish to stay, they will be compensated for the decrease in their residential property value resulting from the siting or, if they prefer to move, they will be bought out at the estimated market value of their property before the siting. The amount offered in compensation, in case they stay, should in theory represent their property value lost by the change in the adjacent site. Determination of just compensation in the law is usually based on market values (Freeman 1993). It seems fair to ask whether in this case a "fair market value" approach does indeed represent complete compensation. Does fair market value capture all the values that are lost if the family decides that, while they do not want to move, they cannot accept the new risk and disruption, and decide to leave?

Apparently not. If the family accepts fair market compensation and then uses the money to purchase a farm elsewhere, they will be compensated for their economic loss, but they will not be compensated for the loss of their "home." Place-relative information such as how to avoid poison ivy on the way to the pond, what time of day to catch the largest fish, and a plethora of other practical and aesthetic details will not be transmitted with the deed to the property cannot be carried to a new site.

These nontransferrable values are the countless pieces of information and experiences that are entwined with daily life, impossible to separate into fact and value. They represent generations of wisdom accumulated from specific experiences and encoded in the cultural information and attitudes passed from generation to generation. We believe that these place-relative values appear in all cultures, though we expect that their specific form and content will be highly variable across cultures. To see the environmental connection, consider the extent to which loss of vernacular tradition in Florida architecture in favor of generic building techniques has both reduced the cultural distinctiveness of that semi-tropical state and also greatly increased demand for electrical energy.

At least some less technologically advanced cultures, especially those that have survived for many generations, have developed myths and cultural practices—often religious in nature—that have the effect of protecting the resource base (see, for example, Gadgil and Berkes 1991; Gadgil and Guha 1992; Rappoport 1968). These local myths and practices, which are part of the "cultural capital" of a region, are often eroded by "development," leaving local populations with neither traditional practices or trained scientists who might gauge the impacts of resource use. Because place-relative cultural values must be developed with intimate knowledge of local conditions, migration, especially toward modern cities, diminishes this cultural capital.

Return to the case of our family. If the loss of these values—the loss of a special relationship between people and a place—leaves the family diminished despite having received "fair compensation," what does society risk when these values are ignored in analyzing and shaping our environmental policies? There are specific experiences—a particular granddaughter learning to *like* to fish at her grandfather's side, or an apprentice learning the tricks of the trade for building a more comfortable Florida house, for example— which transmit values and information through experience, practice, and enjoyment that are too personal and place-specific to be exchanged with the sale of property. The sum of these values, practices and strategies constitute locally based cultural capital.

Now suppose our family sells and another, nonlocal, family, willing to accept the risks and disutilities of the site, subsequently purchases our family's property at a lower price (determined by its postsiting market value). Most of the place-relative values associated with the first family's long association with the land will not be transferred in the sale. The original family will leave the farm diminished, and the new family will acquire these positive place-oriented values only slowly, if at all. These effects represent a part of what economists have called "adjustment costs" (Hanemann 1993). This concept, which has been developed as a category of easily missed costs in computing the impacts of global warming, may be particularly applicable to locally originating values. Because long-term estimations of changes due to global warming compare two temporally distinct equilibria, Hanemann argues that it is important to consider the disequilibrium costs incurred in adjusting to accelerating environmental change. Values lost during a forced transition may represent a systematically undercounted category of costs, and locally disruptive changes such as sitings of noxious land uses can involve significant costs of this type. If we suppose, alternatively, that the siting goes forward and the land is no longer considered suitable for residential use at all, the land may be rezoned, making it a site for further difficult-to-site industries and facilities. These changes may make it an "attractive" site for further disputed industrial uses. The market value of the farm may then even increase as important place-related values are completely eradicated.

If this argument proves sound, it apparently entails that there exist significant, systematically overlooked externalities associated with large-scale development activities, and with economies and regulations that encourage movement of industries, etc. These losses are losses in the cultural capital of a community, the bits of particular information and experiences that unite a people in a relationship with their resource base or, in ecological terms, their "habitat." At this level, a culture's integration with the larger biotic community—the plants, other animals, and physical forces that make up its habitat—represents both cultural capital and also an important part of the local identity of that culture. Having offered one (admittedly favorable) example to illustrate this local cultural capital, we proceed to examine some of the characteristics of this capital to determine how widespread this phenomenon is, and to inquire whether this cultural capital and the values it embodies could and should have a role in environmental policy analysis.

Characteristics of Sense of Place Values

It is worth noting several unusual characteristics of these sense of place values. We will describe five features of place-relative values: (1) conditionally transferrable, (2) local, (3) culturally constitutive, (4) pervasive, and (5) partially measurable.

Conditional Transferrability

First we must note that nontransferrable sense of place values are not the only type of place-relative values. Indeed, many types of place-relative values are easily recognized and readily incorporated into a market-based analysis. A wonderful view across a valley or the sea, for example, is highly relative to a given site, but is readily included in a market analysis in societies in which such value is common; since the view is obvious to any buyer, the added value is reflected in the market price. Similarly, location near an already existing noxious industrial use lowers purchase prices. Our special concern here is with values that are similarly place relative but which cannot be observed by prospective buyers and which cannot therefore be reflected in the purchase price. Prices in free markets reflect values that are discoverable and exchangeable. The experience of a grandfather teaching his granddaughter to fish in the lake cannot be discovered by potential buyers, nor can it be exchanged. It can have value only to those who experience it and, therefore, if it has value, it is an extra-market value. Both transferrable and nontransferrable place-relative values affect the character of a place; our interest, here, is in the nontransferrable ones, however, because those will be most likely to be missed in a market analysis.

Locality

All sense of place values are place-relative in the sense that they emerge in a specific, local context. Philosophically, this means that actions constitutive of a culture gain their meaning in a specific place, and they are expressive of locally distinctive and highly variable culture, biogeographies, and physical features. Development by a person of a local sense of place is an important part of developing a sense of personal identity (Fried 1963; Relph 1976).

Place-orientation is complex and many-layered (Norberg-Schulz 1979). To paraphrase the geographer Yi-fu Tuan, "we need a sense of place and a sense of the space around our place" (Norton and Hannon 1997; Tuan 1971). Anthropologically, this means that one should expect as many senses of place as there are unique combinations of culture with varied types of natural communities that form the contexts of those cultures. Practically, it means that no environmental policy that ignores local variation and local experience can be expected to protect biological or cultural diversity. If the only values that get counted in our analyses of policy options are ones that can be aggregated without reference to perspective and scale, then the nontransferrable, place-relative values identified here will be "washed out" in the process of aggregation to higher levels.

Cultural Constitutivity

The contextual knowledge that results from multigenerational interactions between a culture and its distinctive plants and animals ensures that sense of place will be highly variable across cultures and across natural physical systems. This variability expresses the creativity involved in a culture's adapting to varied challenges and opportunities as offered by their biogeographic context. These values can be thought of as representative of "options"—choices to enjoy particular experiences—as viewed from a local perspective. But they are also a series of possible connections to the land, connections that are mediated through patterns of choices. It will be the choices that our generation makes regarding these places, whether to lose or to continue them, that will determine the options of future generations. The fabric woven across generations by this process of interaction with local resources sets the broad outlines of the identity of a culture within its surroundings. It determines the physical context to which subsequent generations will adapt.

In this sense, the choices made by one generation create the context for the next generation's choices; but it is the combination of physical/ecological constraints and the reactions of a culture to them that constitute meaningful activity. Sense of place values, in this sense, capture the "options" open within a community (the patterns of learned behaviors and possibilities for innovation) *and*, at the same time, those behaviors give expression to locally based cultural meanings—they are individualized responses to a particular environment (see Norberg-Schulz 1979; Relph 1976).

Pervasiveness

While we have developed a quite specific example of private property values associated with experiences that are place-specific, the type of values identified here are by no means limited to this narrow case. We could re-tell the above story of the family, simply moving the experience of a grandparent teaching a grandchild to fish at the public access to the best local fishing lake. The difference in the cases is that, if an undesirable land use is sited near the public fishing site, the experience will be diminished, and the stock of sense-of-place values enjoyed by the family will decrease, but the family will almost certainly not be offered compensation of any kind. Indeed, it appears that there are similar losses in nonmarket values associated with many changes in the context of common access resources such as occur when the Forest Service clear-cuts land near a recreation area, because this action can negatively impact the quality of the experience of visitors to the area.

The type of values introduced in the favorable example can now be broadened. It is as if the fabric of future possibilities for a local culture is woven from choices in the present. Defense of place-relative values reflect the collective will of a people—the common embracing of a cultural identity—a collective decision to maintain an authentic relationship to its past, to its future, and to its natural context. The search for a cultural identity must respect and build upon the natural history of a place, which includes the practices that emerged historically, and it must also project values into the future.

Sense of place values emerge at the local level and are highly dependent on the context at that level; they represent the positive sense of community that, in best cases, arises between a people and the place in which their culture has been defined. These values are therefore "scaled"—they are associated with a particular level of a multiscalar system (see Norberg-Schulz, 1979; also, for some ecological theorizing relevant to this point, see Allen and Hoekstra 1992; Allen and Starr 1982; Collins and Glenn 1990; Holling 1992; Johnson 1993; Lavorel et al. 1993; McMahon et al. 1978; O'Neill et al. 1986). If one attempts to connect local values to a common scale (such as a monetary scale), and then to aggregate the community-level values of many communities to arrive at a "sum" for the nation, all of the richness and context-dependence of these locally originating values will be lost. These sense of place values cannot therefore be meaningfully monetized.

These values are also "scaled" in time—they emerge intergenerationally as the community accommodates itself to its habitat; new practices are adopted and passed from generation to generation in an ongoing process of culture-building. It may be useful to think of these values as "aspirations" or "community preferences" in contrast to economists' "individual preferences" as a second, and essential, aspect of human valuation (Norton 1994). Whereas preferences exist in the present and are taken as givens, aspirations exist on an intergenerational scale and they represent choices on the part of a society regarding the type of society it will be. The values that emerge on this level require intergenerational continuity, a continuity that should reflect itself across generations on the landscape. Choices each generation makes concerning the landscape govern the range of freedom of the future in the precise sense that the landscape will determine what options are open and what experiences are possible in the future (Norton 1995a). A commitment to sustainable use is a commitment to hold open certain options and the possibility of certain experiences. Because of this dynamic, intergenerational quality, sense of place values cannot be captured in a "snapshot" approach to ascertaining the aggregated preferences of a population at a moment in time.

Partial Measurability

Sense of place values can be expressed as measurable differences in human behavior. We have argued that many sense of place values will not be captured in market transactions because they are so intimately intertwined with bits of knowledge and experience that are too place-specific to transmit at a real estate settlement. Again, our example is instructive. If the family had no positive attachment to the farm—if they were absentee owners or if they had just bought it and had not moved in yet, for example—they would probably be fully compensated for their loss if the price offered is indeed the fair market price. We can hypothesize that, if a family has a large stock of sense of place values, they will be more likely to refuse to accept a fair market price for their property, and their efforts (including, for example, legal fees and volunteer work) expended to protect the place itself provide a rough—or, lower-bound—measure of the strength of their commitment to their particular home place. Our emphasis on locally developed values as indicative of commitment to place leads us to take these costs very seriously in evaluating environmental impacts of large development projects and of national management of resources such as national parks and national forests. As an example of the power of local feeling, consider the State of Illinois' eighty million dollar attempt to site a radioactive waste storage facility in Martinsville, Illinois. A local citizen group of the small rural community with relatively high unemployment obtained contributions of nearly one-half million dollars in intervenor funding to organize expertise to defeat the project on several gounds. This remarkable effort was undertaken despite a state offer of over one million dollars per year in compensation to the community.

Willingness to accept the market value indicates an *economically* defensive stance—its motive is to protect the economic investment of the private landowner, but not the place itself, which is treated as having acceptable substitutes in alternative properties. Willingness to fight on against a siting *after fair market compensation has been offered* is indicative that something other than economic interests are being defended. In these cases, the economic model, which assumes there exists a rate of compensation that will make the person indifferent to loss of their home, seems inapplicable to an analysis of a positive commitment to *this* place, rather than to this and comparable places that could be purchased elsewhere.

The values of home are in this sense separable from economic values embodied in the property; indeed, they are in an important sense nonfungible with economic values because they become obvious only when economic interests have been fully protected. When owners reject fair market value for their home, it is always possible to interpret their refusal to sell as economically motivated gaming. The difficulty of controlling for this confounding variable represents one of the major deterrents to the development of a more precise and measurable conception of sense of place values. But sense of place values, however difficult to measure directly because of the gaming effect, are necessary to explain behavior that is likely to be counter-productive economically. Citizen actions to protect parks and preserves are often motivated by noneconomic goals. Another approach to quantifying values associated with particular places might be to pay attention to private landholders gifts and below-value land sales by private landowners to environmental groups for preservation (Robert Mitchell, personal communication). Sense-of-place values therefore manifest themselves in connection with private goods (as in the case of our farm family) or they can be motivated by a public spirit. The point to be emphasized here is that these are significant and pervasive values and they are often systematically ignored in market valuations.

We feel justified in calling these place-relative values that cannot be measured in market transfers *positive sense of place values.* These are the values, the positive commitments—the aspirations that are tied up with a particular place—which are not compensable in dollar terms. These values express commitment to a non-interchangeable connection to a particular place. A strong stock of positive sense of place values would represent intimate experience and relationships with the plants, animals, and ecosystems that are distinctive to their region. The idea of aspirations captures the sense of a cultural future, which must of course grow organically from a storied past, and it is these features that give distinctive value to a particular place (Rolston 1988). These aspirations, which correspond to intergenerationally created and protected cultural capital, cannot be understood independently of the resources—the opportunities and options expressed in the local biotic community. Nor can they be separated from the constraints that have been conquered by local technologies and local wisdom. These constraints give meaning to actions of individuals and communities who are integrated into a place (Norton 1995a). They emerge not so much in connection with particular acts and purchases, but rather as expressions of cultural identity and character (Page 1992). A good example of this type of value, from the political realm, would be the type of underlying political ideals (such as rule of law) that express themselves as a community writes a new constitution (Page 1977; Toman 1994). Whereas preferences expressed in markets may represent individual values as felt in the present, aspirations are group values that express themselves on a longer, intergenerational scale.

Notice also that aspirations can be more complex than preferences in the sense that, if one has an aspiration that one's children and grandchildren share and enjoy an experience (such as learning to fish in the family fishing hole) in the future, two conditions are implied: one hopes, first, that the fishing hole be unspoiled and accessible and, second, that the youngsters will enjoy that experience. So, in addition to the implied value of accessibility to means to fulfill a preference, aspirations represent also second-order preferences regarding what preferences future individuals will have and express. This feature of aspirations (Norton 1987; Sagoff 1986) introduces a level of complexity—they represent preferences over preferences—into the analysis that is impossible to capture in a uniscalar analysis such as that exemplified by microeconomics.

A Classification of Place-Relative Values

Drawing on our analysis of the example, we offer the following taxonomy of place-relative values:

1. Preferences associated with place
   a. publicly observable benefits, risks, and disutilities associated with a place and adjacent land uses
   b. recognizable and transferrable amenities (a nice view, fishing opportunities)
2. Place-oriented aspirations
   a. enjoyments that depend for their value on the history and future of a place. These intimate values are expressed in a culture's relationship with their physical and ecological context—the geography, plants, and animals that constitute their environment/habitat—and they only emerge through participation in, and acquisition of knowledge about, the natural and cultural history of a place. They are values that are transmitted and experienced only by intimate contact among people who interact in a culture with a sense of natural as well as social history.
   b. the value of the cultural and community continuity conserved when experiences of type (2a) are protected over generations.

While the values in category (1) are presumably captured in market transactions, values in category (2) cannot be so captured, as argued above. They are, however, the very essence of any positive connection between a human culture and its place.

Measuring and Aggregating Sense-of-Place Values

Nontransferrable, place-relative values have measurable behavioral consequences. For example, we predict that communities with a large stock of
these values are more likely to continue to contest land use decisions,
incurring measurable costs, even after they have been offered compensation. Many of these costs are easily measurable—legal fees, for example—
others are difficult to measure, but offer no problems in principle—such
as donated time and efforts, etc.—while others, such as emotional pain
experienced during a long legal battle, will never be measured accurately
(Varlamoff 1993). The quantifiable expenses of opponents of a development plan (after having been offered market compensation) would nevertheless appear to provide a lower bound measure of place-relative values
that are not transferred in fair-market sales.

The problem with these values is not so much that they are unmeasur-
able or unquantifiable in particular situations—any method of quantifying social values will include some easily measured and other difficult-to-
measure values. But these values are so highly context-dependent that
their character is lost when an attempt is made to aggregate them across
many communities. We must therefore revisit Kopp's assumption in favor
of nationally aggregatable data. Even if we were to develop quite precise
measures of positive sense of place values for a given community, Kopp
may well be correct in believing it is impossible to aggregate these "values" together to guide federal policy decisions because these values contain a nonfungible commitment to characteristics that are place-specific.
These values are not additive with other values to achieve a grand, national
total of welfare, because these values exist in so many different, and in
some sense, incommensurable contexts. In particular, they embody values
that emerge on multiple levels. These values do not aggregate because they
are scale-specific (Norton 1995a).

The dispute here is not one about whether to *quantify* values; it is
rather about whether to vertically aggregate values across hierarchical levels, once a quantification has been achieved. And it is also about whether
it is worthwhile to seek and use information that cannot be monetized
and aggregated at the national level. Whereas a decision maker following
the top-down approach would aggregate information to the highest decision level, treating decision making as a matter of computation of single-
scaled values, a decision maker acting from the bottom-up would first
sort decisions into various categories according to a scalar criterion. In
the version we have developed, these categorizing decisions are based on
an assessment of the scale of the problem and the social scale at which a
response is appropriate (Norton 1995a; Norton and Ulanowicz 1992).
Then, the decision maker asks, given the scale and level of dynamics at

which we must address this particular environmental problem, what decision rule should apply in this context? Once a decision rule is chosen and goals have been formulated at the relevant governmental level, it should be possible to quantify data about the physical world and to quantify data regarding citizens' values affecting the decision. But on a multiscalar approach one would not expect that all of the data should be analyzable in terms of a single utility function of individuals and thereby aggregable upward in the decision hierarchy.

To illustrate the importance of the difference, consider two ways of making a decision regarding the placement of a long-term, low-level radioactive waste storage site. Suppose, first, it is noted that the risks and costs to society (considered as the set of all citizens in the nation) attendant upon having many decentralized storage sites are computed to be very large because, for example, security arrangements at many sites are either expensive or risky; or because there will be widespread stress on individuals because far more people will live near multiple sites than would live near a centralized site. A nationally aggregated decision made in the computational style, in other words, would apparently favor the choice of a single storage site in a remote area. But suppose that every local community refuses to accept the site. If we consider the siting to be a matter of the "right" of each local community to self-determination, respecting this right amounts to offering each local community a veto power. With such a multiscalar view of our governing system, in other words, it makes a lot of difference which questions are addressed first. And in this sense the decision systems we offer are not computational, but emphasize careful categorization of risks and the values associated with them, seeking to characterize environmental problems in terms of their appropriate scale, and matching decisions to the appropriate governmental scale.

With a multiscalar view, every decision maker would accept the right to self-determination on the local level and would treat this universal veto as a given. The search for a national policy on radioactive waste storage would now be formulated with a whole different set of policy options. All options considered would be ones that respect the decisions of local governments not to accept the site. Admittedly, this approach may be idealistic in that we already possess—because of past decisions and activities—large stockpiles of waste requiring storage somewhere, which makes the apparent implication of the bottom-up approach inoperative as a complete solution. But this practical complication does not obscure the clear implication for future decisons of a commitment to local self-determination and enforceable local veto powers. Placing a high priority on local self-determination in effect constrains the options for a national policy, perhaps imposing the outcome that there must be a vast reduction in activities that create such waste. The point of such examples is to show that the choice of an aggregative approach to measuring environmental values tends to devalue local considerations that seem persuasive to members of local communities. If all communities reject a particular land use or even if a great number of them do, the message to the higher level would be to stop the imposition and seek another alternative. For example if no place can be found (due to local vetoes) for storage of low-level radioactive waste, then stop generating it and find substitutes. We could then dispense with cynical reports such as "Building Citizen Support for Responsible Low-Level Radioactive Waste Disposal Solutions: A Handbook for Grass Roots Organizers" (1995), published by the Nuclear Energy Institute, a trade organization consisting mainly of nuclear power utilities and manufacturers.

The special characteristic of hierarchically organized decision processes is that they recognize and meaningfully represent the apparently unavoidable asymmetries in space-time relationships. If actions of individuals are viewed as scale-specific within a multiscalar system, then the larger-scaled systems that provide the context for individual decisions appear as both constraints and opportunities available, locally, to individuals. The amount of forested land in an area offers an opportunity for a timber industry; but a limited quantity of high-quality forest also places a constraint on the development of such an industry. Opportunities provide an explanation of the behaviors of individual actors such as timber companies and their employees, but the constraints embodied in the limited extent of forest cover will determine, on a longer scale of time, the evolving character of the community in relationship to its natural context. Sustainable forestry, thus understood as including the sustenance of local culture and local ecological integrity, would in this sense be a *local* commitment and include local responsibility for forest protection (Norton and Hannon, 1997).

The problem is that in a nationally or internationally organized economy it is possible to "export" opportunities in the form of timber, but the associated constraints—the results of near-total deforestation such as erosion and siltation of streams—necessarily "stay at home". Thus it is "rational" for decisions made by multinational corporations in the context of international markets to change the character of a local community by deforesting it and then moving to a new forested area. Their profits will be exchangeable in the currency of larger-scale systems such as world markets (Clark 1974); the costs of their aggressive exploitation, the degradation of the natural resource, will be felt at the local level and will be lost from computations as the profits are summed at higher levels of geographic, social, and economic organization. Aggregated measures of rationality and single-scaled approaches to decision making therefore tend to over-estimate benefits and under-estimate costs because, in the arena of national economics, wealth will be created by the systematic transferrence of externalities to local communities as a byproduct of the exportation of their opportunities. Especially when international corporations can command federal subsidies through lobbying at the federal level, local communities will be hard put to resist such exploitation.

We have questioned Kopp's assumption that measures of environmental value must be expressed in terms that are aggregatable across space and time, exploring hierarchical systems of analysis which, unlike the single utility measures of mainstream economics, analyze values in a contextual and scale-sensitive manner. Multiscalar systems retain information of local importance in the process of developing a national policy, at the cost of giving up aggregability across scales. Sense of place values exist on many local levels and, within a hierarchical approach, these sense of place values would be satisfied locally before going on to address larger-scale questions of valuation. This creates a burden of proof on the powers of centralization to show why expressions of local goals should not trump centralized interests. If one favors local control and reestablishment of local responsibility, a multiscalar system of analysis which favors a bottom-up approach is more likely to achieve a democratic outcome than a policy process that emphasizes those values that can be aggregated to a national level. We should clarify that our preference for local control is not based on the assertion that all problems are local problems. Indeed, we expect that there will be many cases in which local governments must address large-scale environmental problems, including their contributions to global changes. Our point is that even to address international problems while ensuring democracy at the local level, decison structures must be organized in a bottom-up fashion.

Applications to Policy and Planning

We have sketched two approaches to environmental policy formation and valuation, and have noted that aggregation of values across all levels of environmental policy formation will promote policy goals—and the values that support them—favorable to a centralized decision process. Alternatively, a multiscalar organization of the process can be designed to be scale-sensitive and to encourage processes of valuation that emphasize locally developed environmental values. This approach eschews cross-level aggregation of values and instead recognizes the asymmetry of time-space relations, protecting local values at a local level. While we recognize that local cultures do sometimes destroy their resource base, local control has the advantage that information feedback loops are shorter and local populations may have to live with the consequences of reduced opportunities and economic options more directly than do national and international corporations or national governments.

The evaluative, informational, and decision models we have proposed have been built from the bottom up, in that we have avoided the methodological requirement of cross-scale aggregability of value measures we propose. Our methodological choices have in this sense been guided by a persistent attempt to favor localism and values that are articulated locally, because we believe that centralized goal-setting for economic growth will inevitably favor large economic interests. These large interests will systematically export opportunities, leaving results of ignoring constraints behind as they move to fresher exploitable areas.

In closing we can return to the very large question with which we began this paper: is there any general approach to environmental policy formation that both protects resources *and* can be established democratically? If we think of democracies, broadly speaking, as governments that are responsive to the will of the people, it is possible to ask "which people?" and "How will their wills be aggregated?" In systems which are multiscalar (such as federal systems), it is possible to identify communities that exist at more than one level. It is comforting to think that, when such a system is working properly, "democracy" occurs at all levels, with the government at each level pursuing policies that are favored by the relevant community. A democratic national government would therefore pursue policies that are acceptable to people at all lower levels.

In the process of analysis, we have uncovered an important ambiguity in this conceptualization of the democratic process. We have shown that aggregating values from smaller to larger communities can bias policy analysis against local communities. We saw that Kopp and other neoclassical microeconomists set, as a methodological constraint/expectation, that all values expressed on all levels must be aggregable in common, fungible terms. On the view of democracy that emerges in this case, a democratic national government would pursue those policies that are indicated by the sum total of the aggregable preferences of all individuals, *qua* individuals, at all lower levels of the society. It allows no statement by a local community of nonfungible, place-relative values. We have seen that, on the system assumed by Kopp, it will often be "rational" to impose a land use on a community despite opposition from that community because the strong local values of the opposition are swamped by the "common good" of millions of people from other communities who will reap the rewards of the government's imposition of a siting on this small community. The harshness of this approach can of course be mitigated by insisting, for example, that the few in the local community should be compensated from the gains of the many, perhaps with direct payments or with new schools, etc. These mitigative "bribes" take the form of subsidies flowing from the federal to the local level; they have the same impact as other federal subsidies for local resource extraction: they confuse the signals so that local governments will not perceive the consequences of nonsustainable use of their resources. This mitigation does not change the fact that the aggregative approach presupposes a "top-down" flow of control in the system. Policy is set on a national level and local communities are left with no choice but to negotiate the best "compensation package" they can get. The "good" of the society is determined at the national level through an aggregation of individual preferences; any local "goods" such as positive, nontransferrable sense of place values will have been lost because they are invisible among the market values that, on the view of mainstream economists, should guide national policies.

If, on the other hand, we relax the aggregability requirement on environmental values and think of environmental policy as hierarchically organized from the bottom up, locally developed values that are highly context-dependent may be instrumental in building many strong local communities in which individuals act upon a strong sense of local place. These local communities might, on this view, reject "fair compensation" for a siting simply because it is not consistent with their conception of their community. Values will be counted, voting will take place, etc., but the political outcomes at local community levels will stand on their own. They cannot be swamped and overridden by values that are aggregated at a larger scale. This difference in conception of the public good is the operational significance of the difference between a multiscalar and bottom-up approach to conception of environmental values and methods, and an aggregative and computational approach to policy with a national focus only.

Our theory suggests no less than an about-face in current trends toward centralized control in environmental policy formation. To some extent, we are calling for an end to federal and state sovereignty, and an end to "top-down" thinking in environmental policy. Our approach would, for example, shift the initiative for environmental policy development away from the federal to the local level. But it is important to realize that the approach can only work if devolution of federal control is accompanied by an end to federal subsidies and bail-outs. The point is to reestablish local *responsibility* for resource use and planning decisions, which requires both local control *and* a system in which local populations must accept the consequences of their actions.

One advantage of a compartmentalized, multiscalar, bottom-up system of many local controls is that it will reduce the impact of national economic lobbies. In the current system in which environmental policy goals are set on a national level, it is much easier for national industries to centralize their lobbying efforts. We hypothesize that it will be more difficult for national economic interests to control environmental decision making if it is decentralized.

Our argument also implies that we should provide local activists with resources by which to resist encroachment upon local prerogatives. In particular, new laws are needed to empower local activists to challenge proposed impositions of decisions that are motivated by the concerns of centralized, governmental power, often in collusion with large international businesses (Varlamoff 1993). More generally, our argument has several implications for planning and for the planning process.

First, once one draws the distinction between location and place, recognizing that it is possible to create a sense of place even among populations that change locations regularly, it is possible to advocate a strong role for planners as facilitators of a process of building and strengthening local sense of place. This process of community value articulation should be designed to build a stronger sense of place and a stronger inclination to defend the distinctiveness of local cultures. Planners, on this approach, could become key players in ecosystem management projects, encouraging local communities to articulate and develop their sense of place and local identity as a general guide to setting goals of environmental policy. This approach might also encourage closer cooperation of environmental and cultural/historical preservationists.

A second, related implication is that the process of devolution of responsibilities for environmental quality and regulation from the U.S. federal government to the states—a process that is certain to be accelerated by strong budget cuts at the U.S. Environmental Protection Agency—should be met with a process of social learning (Dewey 1984; Lee 1993). Local communities may, with the help of planner/facilitators, be able to seize as an opportunity the current trends away from federalism, using these events to strengthen local responsibility and control, and to build a healthy sense of the distinctiveness of particular places as broad guides to resource use and environmental protection (see Kemmis 1990). The processes of social learning described here must be iterative; they must encourage ongoing discussion of environmental goals and how those goals interact with socially and culturally expressed statements of the distinctiveness of particular places. This iterative process, well described by Lee (1993) and Gunderson, Holling, and Light (1995), emphasizes the interaction of professional scientists, environmental planners and managers, and the public in an experimental approach to proposing and testing environmental policy goals and policies.

These general implications all follow, directly or indirectly, from the main argument of this paper, that social values can only be protected if local communities can exert self-determination and a veto power in favor of locally originating and locally supportable norms to guide resource use. In general, then, a strengthened and more scientific conception of sense of place values, based on improved understanding of the role of place in developing a sense of community and a willingness to accept responsibility for local resources, may encourage a stronger role for planners in facilitating the articulation, public discussion, and revision of the goals of environmental management.

We recognize that return to local responsibility will be difficult and will require time to develop stronger, local senses of place and a commitment to protect the integrity of local places. But this may be the only route toward a democratically supportable approach to sustainable use of resources. We believe that it would also represent an important step toward introducing true democracy, which on the hierarchical bottom-up view of policy involves actions of government that are responsive to the needs of people and communities who live most intimately with their resources and within their habitat.

Notes

Allen, T. F. H., and Hoekstra, T. W. (1992). *Toward A Unified Ecology*. New York: Columbia University Press.

Allen, T. F. H., and Starr, T. B. (1982). *Hierarchy*. Chicago: University of Chicago Press.

Berry, W. (1977). *The Unsettling of America*. New York: Avon Books.

Bookchin, M. (1965). *Crisis in Our Cities*. Englewood Cliffs, NJ: Prentice-Hall.

———. (1982). *The Ecology of Freedom*. Palo Alto, Calif.: Cheshire Books.

Brett, J. M. (1980). "The Effect of Job Transfer on Employees and Their Families." In *Current Concerns in Occupational Stress*, ed. C. L. Cooper and R. Payne. New York: John Wiley and Sons.

Briggs, A. (1968). "The Sense of Place." In *The Fitness of Man's Environment*, Smithsonian Annual, II. Washington, D.C.: Smithsonian Institution Press.

Bullard, J. K. (1991). "The Specialty of Place." *Places* 7, no. 3: 72–79.

Clark, C. (1974). "The Economics of Over-Exploitation." *Science* 181: 630–634.

Collins, S. L., and Glenn, S. M. (1990). "A Hierarchical Analysis of Species Abundance Patterns in Grassland Vegetation." *American Naturalist* 135: 633–648.

Cronon, W. (1983). *Changes in the Land: Indians, Colonists, and the Ecology of New England*. New York: Hill and Wang.

Cronon, W. (1991). *Nature's Metropolis: Chicago and the Great West*. New York: W.W. Norton.

Crosby, A. W. (1986). *Ecological Imperialism: The Biological Expansion of Europe, 900–1900*. Cambridge: Cambridge University Press.

Dewey, J. (1984). "The Public and Its Problems." In *The Later Works, 1925–1953, Volume 2*. Carbondale, Ill.: Southern Illinois University Press.

Duhl, L. J., ed. (1963). *The Urban Condition: People and Policy in the Metropolis.* New York: Basic Books.

Ehrenfeld, D. (1993). *Beginning Again: People and Nature in the New Millennium.* New York: Oxford University Press.

Feldman, R. (1990). "Settlement-Identity: Psychological Bonds with Home Places in a Mobile Society," *Environment and Behavior* 22: 183–229.

Freeman, A. M., III. (1993). *The Measurement of Environmental and Resource Values: Theory and Methods.* Washington, D.C.: Resources for the Future.

Fried, M. (1963). "Grieving for a Lost Home." In *The Urban Condition,* ed. L. J. Duhl, Basic Books: New York.

Gadgil, M., and Berkes, F. (1991). "Traditional Resource Management Systems." *Resource Management and Optimization* 18: 127–141.

Gadgil, M. and Guha, R. (1992). *This Fissured Land: An Ecological History of India.* New Delhi and Berkeley: Oxford University Press and University of California Press.

Galster, G. C. (1986). "What is a Neighborhood? An Externality-Space Approach." *International Journal of Urban and Regional Research* 10: 243–263.

Gans, H. J. (1962). *The Urban Villagers: Group and Class in the Life of Italian Americans.* New York: The Free Press of Glencoe.

Gould, P., and White, R. (1974). *Mental Maps.* New York: Penguin Books.

———. (1986). *Mental Maps.* Second Edition. Boston: Allen & Unwin.

Gunderson, L., Holling, C. S., and Light, S. S. (1995). *Barriers and Bridges to the Renewal of Ecosystems and Institutions.* New York: Columbia University Press.

Gussow, A. (no date). *A Sense of Place: The Artist and the American Land.* San Francisco: Friends of the Earth/Seabury Press.

———. (1993). *The Artist as Native: Reinventing Regionalism.* San Francisco: Pomegranate Artbooks.

Gutierrez, R. (1991). *When Jesus Came, The Corn Mothers Went Away.* Stanford, Calif.: Stanford University Press.

Hanemann, M. (1993). "Assessing Climate Change Risks: Valuation of Effects." In *Assessing Surprises and Nonlinearities in Greenhouse Warming,* ed. J. Darmstadter and M. Toman. Washington, D.C.: Resources for the Future.

Hannon, B. (1985). "World Shogun." *Journal of Social and Biological Structures* 8: 329–341.

———. (1994). "Sense of Place: Geographic Discounting by People, Animals and Plants." *Ecological Economics* 10(2): 157–174.

Heidegger, M. (1958). "An Ontological Consideration of Place." In *The Question of Being.* New York: Twayne Publishers.

———. (1962). *Being and Time.* New York: Harper and Row.

Heilbroner, R. (1974). *An Inquiry into the Human Prospect.* New York: W.W. Norton.

Holling, C. S. (1992). "Cross-Scale Morphology, Geometry, and Dynamics of Ecosystems." *Ecological Monographs* 62(4): 447–502.

Hough, M. (1990). *Out of Place: Restoring Identity to the Regional Landscape.* New Haven: Yale University Press.

Hull, R. B. (1992). "Image Congruity: Place Attachment and Community Design." *Journal of Architecture and Planning Research* 9: 181–191.

Jackson, J. B. (1994). *A Sense of Place, a Sense of Time*. New Haven: Yale University Press.

Johnson, A. R. (1993). "Spatiotemporal Hierarchies in Ecological Theory and Modeling." From *2nd International Conference on Integrating Geographic Information Systems and Environmental Modeling*, Sept. 26–30, 1993, Breckenridge, Col.

Kemmis, D. (1990). *Community and the Politics of Place*. Norman, Okla.: University of Oklahoma Press.

Kennedy, P. (1993). *Preparing for the Twenty-First Century*. New York: Random House.

Kopp, R. J. (1993). "Environmental Economics: Not Dead but Thriving." *Resources for the Future*, Spring 1993, (111), 7–12.

Labao, L. (1994). "The Place of 'Place' in Current Sociological Research." *Environment and Planning A*, 26: 665–668.

Langer, S. (1953). *Feeling and Form*. New York: Charles Scribner's Sons.

Lavorel, S., Gardner, R. H., and O'Neill, R. V. (1993). "Analysis of Patterns in Hierarchically Structured Landscapes." *Oikos* 67: 521–528.

Lee, K. N. (1993). *Compass and Gyroscope: Integrating Science and Politics for the Environment*. Covelo, Calif.: Island Press.

Ludwig, D., Hilburn, R., and Walters, C. (1993). "Uncertainty, Resource Exploitation and Conservation: Lessons from History." *Science* 260 (April 2, 1993): 17–19.

Lynch, K. (1972). *What Time is This Place?* Cambridge, Mass.: The MIT Press.

———. (1960). *The Image of the City*. Cambridge, Mass.: The MIT Press.

McMahon, J. A., Phillips, D. A., Robinson, J. F., and Schimpf, D. J. (1978). "Levels of Organization: An Organism-Centered Approach." *Bioscience* 28: 700–704.

Moore, C., Allen, G., and Lyndon, D. (1974). *The Place of Houses*. New York: Holt, Rinehart and Winston.

Norberg-Schulz, C. (1979, U.S. Edition, 1980). *Genius Loci: Towards a Phenomenology of Architecture*. New York: Rizzoli.

Norton, B. G. (1987). *Why Preserve Natural Variety?* Princeton, N.J.: Princeton University Press.

Norton, B. G. (1994). "Economists Preferences and the Preferences of Economists." *Environmental Values* 3: 311–332.

Norton, B. G. (1995a). "Ecological Integrity and Social Values: At What Scale?" *Ecosystem Health*: 228–241.

Norton, B.G. (1995b). "Applied Philosophy vs. Practical Philosophy: Toward an Environmental Policy Integrated According to Scale." In *Environmental Philosophy and Environmental Activism*, ed. D. Marietta and L. Embree. Lanham, Md., Rowman and Littlefield.

Norton, B. G., and Hannon, B. (1997). "Environmental Values: A Place-Based Theory." *Environmental Ethics* 19: 227–245.

Norton, B. G., and Ulanowicz, R. E. (1992). "Scale and Biodiversity Policy: A Hierarchical Approach." *Ambio* 21(3): 244–249.

Nuclear Energy Institute (1995). "Building Citizen Support for Responsible Low-Level Radioactive Waste Disposal Solutions: A Handbook for Grass Roots Organizers." Nuclear Energy Institute.

O'Neill, R. V., DeAngelis, D. L., Waide, J. B., and Allen, T. F. H. (1986). *A Hierarchical Concept of Ecosystems.* Princeton, N.J.: Princeton University Press.

Ophuls, W. (1977). *The Politics of Scarcity: A Prologue to a Political Theory of the Steady State.* San Francisco: Freeman.

———. (1992). *The Politics of Scarcity Revisited: The Unraveling of the American Dream.* New York: Freeman.

Page, T. (1977). *Conservation and Economic Efficiency.* Baltimore: Johns Hopkins University Press.

———. (1992). "Environmental Existentialism." In *Ecosystem Health: New Goals for Environmental Management,* ed. R. Costanza, B. Norton, & B. Haskell. Covelo, Calif.: Island Press.

Proshansky, H. M. (1978). "The City and Self-Identity." *Environment and Behavior* 10: 147–170.

Proshansky, H. M., Favian, A. K., and Kaminoff, R. (1983). "Place Identity: Physical World Socialization of the Self." *Journal of Environmental Psychology,* 3: 57–83.

Rappaport, R. A. (1968). *Pigs for the Ancestors: Ritual in the Ecology of a New Guinea People.* New Haven: Yale University Press.

Relph, E. (1976). *Place and Placelessness.* London: Pion Limited.

Rolston, H. (1988). *Environmental Ethics: Duties to and Values in the Natural World.* Philadelphia: Temple University Press.

Sagoff, M. (1986). "Values and Preferences." *Ethics* 96(2): 301–316.

———. (1992). "Settling America: The Concept of Place in Environmental Ethics." *Journal of Energy, Natural Resorces and Environmental Law* 12: 351–418.

———. (1993). "Environmental Economics: An Epitaph." *Resources (Newsletter of Resources for the Future)* Spring 1993 (111): 2–7.

Sale, K. (1985). *Dwellers in the Land.* San Francisco: Sierra Club Books.

Seamon, D. (1979). *A Geography of the Lifeworld.* London: Croom Helm.

Seamon, D., and Mugerauer, R., eds. (1985). *Dwelling, Place, and Environment.* New York: Columbia University Press.

Silver, T. (1990). *A New Face on the Countryside: Indians, Colonists, and Slaves in South Atlantic Forests, 1500–1900.* New York: Cambridge University Press

Steele, F. (1981). *The Sense of Place.* Boston: CBI Publishing Company.

Toman, M. (1994). "Economics and 'Sustainability': Balancing Tradeoffs and Imperatives." *Land Economics* 70:399–413.

Tuan, Y.-F. (1971). *Man and Nature.* Resource Paper no. 10. Commission on College Geography, Washington, D.C.: Association of American Geographers.

———. (1977). *Space and Place: The Perspective of Experience.* Minneapolis: University of Minnesota Press.

———. (1974).*Topophilia: A Study of Environmentral Perception, Attitudes, and Values.* Englewood Cliffs, N.J.: Prentice-Hall.

Varlamoff, S. (1993). *The Polluters: A Community Fights Back.* Edna, Minn.: St. John's Publishing.

Vycinas, V. (1961). *Earth and Gods.* The Hague: Martinus Nijhoff.

Walters, C. (1986). *Adaptive Management of Renewable Resources.* New York: MacMillan.

Worster, D. (1979). *Dust Bowl: The Southern Plains in the 1930s.* New York: Oxford University Press.

——. (1985). *Rivers of Empire: Water, Aridity, and the Growth of the American West.* New York: Pantheon Books.

From the Inside Out: The Farm as Place

Ian Howard

Let us state, without argumentation, that there is something environmentally amiss with modern industrial agriculture. Let us also state, with minimal argumentation, that at the farm level current thought looks to the relatively new science of ecology to fix the problems. The main thrust of this thought is that universal ecological principles should drive farming practices. Yet, ecological complexities and the influences of social and cultural arrangements on agriculture make it difficult to pin down exactly which principles are relevant, and in what spatial and temporal framework relevant principles will be important. While the ecological approach is complex and problematic it does have something basic to say. It points out that modern industrial agriculture has attended too little to geographical information in its development, and that localized geographical information is paramount to good farming. Similarly, over the last fifty or so years, considerable research and development have gone into attaining high productivity, sustaining productive capacity, and environmental improvement. While not divorced from farming, we might describe most of the research and development as coming from institutions that are outside of farming, and in practice unable to attend to specific geographical information. In what follows, I suggest that the notion 'sense of place' can address the inattention to geographic information. And, as a way to clarify its role in determining good farming practices, place highlights an outsider's versus an insider's view of farming. After a brief introduction to the environmental problem as a problem of design, the paper looks at sense of place, the influence of place on personal identity, and how that identity can shape farms and farming. From there, it suggests that the insider's view of farming—the farmer's view—is the best bet for land improvement, farm aesthetics, and human fulfillment.

The Environmental Problem as a Problem of Design

C. A. Hooker, in his analysis of agriculture, suggests that, "the whole world is shifting from reacting to what has happened, to designing what will happen." The transformation that Hooker sees rapidly occurring is the creation of an artifactual future and this leads to one immediate conclusion—it suggests an immediacy and urgency for the primacy of design. As Hooker sees it, the urgency means that we must "understand the designs of the complex systems which we are and in which we live, so that our actions may be appropriately related to the dynamics of those systems." If Hooker is right, the design of complex systems will require, among many economical, ecological, social and cultural considerations, a deep understanding of the places in which we live.[1]

To date and especially from the view of farming as a business, the design process has been driven by relatively simple systems centered on production and profit, and maintained by the application of external inputs. The defense of the dominant, conventional, resource-intensive western farming techniques is that millions would be malnourished or starve without them. Generally, while satisfying economic self-interest, the justification is one of preventing a great harm. The most acerbic criticism of this economic perspective is that the profit motivation has seldom, until quite recently, let noneconomic environmental values enter into the accounting.

The tendency to understand agriculture by concentrating on economics has led to a concentration in the power politics of food, changed rural demographics, and produced neglect in agriculture. Alternatives to the economic magnet downplay the economic interest of producers, or argue that long-range productive capacity and the needs of future generations trump methods that lead to short-term profit. Yet, if short-term profit is defined as, and geared to, economic viability from season to season then short-term profit is important. It measures the producer's success at making a livelihood—growing crops, raising livestock. At the same time, good farming need not be profitable, indeed, on a farm "that does not entirely support its family . . . , the values of the family-owned and family-worked small farm are still available."[2]

The design process from an environmental perspective centers on the application of ecological principles, and in some ways it seems to be the most promising vision for the future. Its defense is driven by the desire to prolong agroecosystem stability through the maintenance of resiliency and high internal recycling, and perhaps its appeal comes from the study of ecosystems that seem successful (e.g., climax forests). A major infrastructure reorganization is envisioned when natural ecosystems are mapped onto agroecosystems. Indeed, the history of agriculture has been the opposite with agroecosystems being mapped onto natural ecosystems.

Clearly, difficulties lie ahead, and ecological rules may not be at all appropriate to the tinkering with nature that farming requires.

Without discounting the utmost importance of site specific ecological facts, ecological principles might not take us far. First, a vision of agriculture based on nature goes too far with its metaphor of nature as a farmer. Second, it gives too little direction for what will count as acceptable tinkering. Simply, misdeeds in wild ecosystems are those acts that drive a system away from the mean of the functioning ecosystem. On the other hand, misdeeds in agroecosystems are those acts that drive the system away from directed productive stability and high resilience, or move it to the equilibrium of the wild ecosystem.

Without the ability to make livelihoods individual farmers cannot continue. Without practices that maintain the stability and resilience within particular agroecosystems farming cannot continue. So, the design for agriculture, so that producers are motivated to conduct it in sustainable ways, must connect economics and ecology. Finally, farming needs the support of social and cultural arrangements that permit farmers to satisfy long-range economic requirements and environmental farsightedness. In effect, I am claiming that economics and ecology are not enough: some real value beyond commodities and means of production needs to be attributed to farming. Therefore, in what follows, I will make some tentative claims about the human *psyche*, and contend that farming in sustainable ways can be fostered, even if not completely driven or explained by, the important *connectedness* people have to place. This connectedness offers the benefit of placing the 'politics of food' in the hands of those most likely to care the most about the land, that is, producers. It posits that farming (or anything else for that matter) can be environmentally sound only through the attention of those who work and live in close connection with nature. Agricultural sustainability will be as much a product of an intimacy with the land as it will be of economics, ecology and agricultural policy.

A Characterization of Sense of Place

Intimacy with the land can be stated in two ways: (1) "people identify themselves and their local community by natural landmarks;" and (2) "the setting . . . represents a quality of interaction." These statements give the starting point to the notion of sense of place.[3] The idea that personal identity is often sought in terms of place can be used as an organizing theme for resolving environmental issues. It can connect the entire environmental issue of ways we, as individuals, have come to see and shape our world. In the farming context, the notion of sense of place can elaborate an awareness of a social position within an ongoing life process that defines *one's place* in the ecological and agricultural situation, and

a perception, as in a sense perception, of what is entailed in the experience of the physical location in which the ecological and agricultural situation is played.

It is easy to demonstrate how we see and shape our world. We are all aware of the extent to which places are becoming increasingly homogeneous. At the rural level, we see the dissolution of local markets with their local produce, and the rise of products that exemplify a truly global reach. Stereotypical components of modern landscapes—shopping malls, high rises, urban sprawl, monocultures, feedlots, battery barns, etc.,—are all at the expense of seeing and shaping the world according to the local and unique. I, like many others, think that when we see and shape our world according to global perspectives we find ourselves uprooted without any clear sense of where we belong. To be uprooted is not merely the manifestation of an emotional attachment to something that we think we have lost. It is the effect of changing rural demographics, commodification of food, and alienation from the means of food production.

The history of human conflict speaks volumes about how personal identify is bound up with place and territoriality. In this human beings are not unique. Many animals exhibit behavior that is territorial, and patterns of mating, reproduction, and survival explain such behavior. For humans, survival extends beyond the physical to include the need for meaning in life. As such, the perception of belonging to a community and a commitment to places once signified meaning, and was expressed in the social and cultural traditions of the local and unique. Perhaps we ought to again think in terms of roots, commitment to the ecological facts of the local and unique, and the social support of, and commitment to, community.

To redesign agriculture to not only reclaim land, and increase such things as fertility and biological diversity (i.e., improve working land), but also establish commitment and community, a person must belong to the place, and know that the work done there is of generations. To belong to a place can mean that one is permanently settled there. Indeed, to stay at home is necessary if one wishes to farm well. There is no other way to grow a garden, tend to animals, fields and orchards, to mend and maintain buildings, and study the accretions of time. "For those who stay at home, there is no figure of speech here, no metaphor." There is a list of real chores, hauling water, chopping wood, hoeing rows, planting trees, raising children, tending animals, "by which the notion of home, both of house and of landscape, is made and defined."[4]

In a trivial sense all of us are in some measure a product of a place. We are all born and live someplace, and some people live in places more because of their choosing than chance and legality. More profoundly, we can be homesick for places, reminded of places, and the sights and smells of places can provide a measure of our past and present. In a farm context, the sights and smells of a place can tell what was done in the past, is being done in the present, and if that work is completed how the place will be in the future. The understanding and awareness of the past and present will inform us about the vision for the future, and gives us some ground by which to evaluate what is being done.

There are qualities of certain places which certain persons respond to with love. In part then sense of place can be considered as a capacity akin to love. As one may talk about caring for a loved one, one may talk of a sense of place as the feeling entailed in caring for one's land. Similarly, sense of place is about landscapes of which people are proud: they are landscapes influenced by human work and craftsmanship, and the perception that this work is done well for good reasons. It is also about landscapes in which people live comfortably: they are landscapes that are understood and known as hearth and home and where people feel they belong. For farming, sense of place is a dimension beyond the geographic space in which the farming drama is played.

One essential feature of the farming drama for those who belong to a place is that it supplies meaningful and worthwhile work. Work that is ennobling or conducive to human fulfillment. One can account for many cases in which farmers appear to argue for farming as 'a way of life' on the basis of its success in fostering that way of life; that is, they like doing it. That someone cares for the land and the farming way of life is a good enough reason for that person to explain why they would care for the land and live a certain kind of life. Such a position would explain *one's place* as a life process and location. Yet, clearly, we have no moral obligation to save everything to which we are attached. Many unique ways of life have faded into obscurity, and there is no particular reason why we have a moral obligation to preserve them. To base the whole conception of good farming on an appeal to emotion may carry any particular farmer in its wake, but it will not support the general conclusion that society and the individual are the better for farming.

However, if we reflect on the notion that a human being living well is bound up with a multiplicity of complicated cultural and social values then we have a justification for the acceptance of farming as a way of life. The complexity of human life is compounded by the fact that we are all connected to agriculture in one way or another, and agriculture is irrevocably connected with the environment. To sever the connection, for so many, between farming and meals is to sever the best opportunity that

people have to connect the social, cultural, and environmental with livelihoods.

Farming is the source for a lifework. The person who is motivated to
have a responsible relationship with the land, where certain basic and necessary patterns of life are repeated endlessly, will set as her goal healthy,
continuous farming. The temporal aspect of this choice is significant. A
long-term commitment to a particular place requires an understanding of
that place: a particular knowledge of the life of that place over time.

Knowledge, work, and living are all situated aspects of human life.
Knowledge of how and when to work toward, or for, something entails
knowing whether one ought to so work. One must be disciplined to work
and to choose whether that work is worthwhile. Such choices involve not
only moral abstraction, but the lived place.

> Under the discipline of unity, knowledge and morality come together. To
> know anything at all becomes a moral predicament. Aware that there is no
> such thing as a specialized—or even an entirely limitable and controllable—
> effect, one becomes responsible for judgments as well as facts.[5]

Whether they are rich or impoverished, the situated aspect of human
life and farm work occurs in communities. The scale and design of any
farm must be tailored to the capabilities, innovation, and aspirations of
the particular farmer, and the scale by which farming will be successful
(i.e., production and stability) is related to the knowledge that both consumer and producer have of a particular place. This knowledge is not
taught in agricultural colleges, but is personal, intimate, and learnt by
doing. Knowledge, in this sense, is an unspoken grasp and understanding
of the lived situation.

While much of farming is of a solitary nature, and for some people
farming may be simply lonely, to till, plant, harvest and process crops
requires the cooperation of many. To sell what the farmer produces requires the further collaboration of those who purchase the farmers' produce.

> Organizing a landscape into an agricultural purpose, even a small one of six
> or seven acres, is no solitary labor. Of necessity it is a pre-eminently cooper-
> ative and social one, even in the heart of a nation awash in the media myths
> of self-sufficiency and rugged individualism.[6]

In places and in time the common ground is found not by some resolution brought about by conflict, exercise of power or even ethical theory,
but by virtue, etiquette and being indispensable to one another. In a sense,
this is self-interest, but it is the self-interest of being neighborly. One can
only be a good neighbor by bringing virtue and etiquette to the practical

issue of living in a community. The real tasks of living that need to be done by everyone require cooperation not because it is to the particular advantage of one individual over another. It is not the kind of advantage one gets when someone else is less favorably placed, but the advantage to living for all. The tasks at hand cannot be done without the help of others. To think otherwise is arrogance and hubris. To think otherwise about nature and others is fatal.

We can also think of belonging to a place in terms of describing farming from the perspective of an 'insider's view' and 'outsider's view' of place. While both views require more work than this paper can devote to them, the distinction can be set up briefly as the distinction between those features of agricultural situations that are mapped onto the lived-space of a particular individual or group, and those features, such as social organization, economics, ecology, and ethics, that may be universal to any inhabitant of the planet.

From an outsider's view the description of place concerns artifacts such as farmsteads, land use patterns, energy flows, agroecosystem boundaries, global economics, conservation, hydrology, etc. The outsider's view is amicable to centralizing or decentralizing themes in agriculture. Benefits and harms are derived from various ways of structuring agriculture. So, from the outsider's view the moral dimension can be couched as the moral goods or evils that flow from a centralized or decentralized agriculture. For the outside observer, there are analyzable patterns of ecological, agricultural, and social activity. Historically, most of the discussion of agriculture has been from an outsider's view.

From an insider's view, the description of place concerns an ongoing process of living within the reach of a particular horizon that is personal and part of lived experience. For the resident, the personal and lived experience involves patterns of life that are not usually reflected upon. So, from the insider's view the moral dimension can be couched as the moral goods or evils that flow from belonging. Invariably, most of the discussion of sense of place will be from the insider's view. Given this brief description of place and the insider's view of farming let us tie both of them into farming's objectives.

Farming's Objectives

I hope to show that there is a set of non-controversial objectives for farming that the notion of sense of place meets better than either the economic or ecology perspectives. For the most part, the objectives of farming are fairly obvious. Overall, the objective is to sustain a way of living well in which abundant, good quality and healthful crops can be raised in a way that is non-destructive to culture and the environment. I am sure many people consider that agriculture should be directed essentially to inexpensive and abundant food production. And, the argument that farmers are to be responsible for producing abundant food and fiber is familiar and obvious. But, recent changes in the understanding of agriculture have led to a widening of this responsibility to include the impact of farming practices on the environment. Let us put this widening of the farmers' responsibilities in the following way. A person's obligation may not be to make 'a better world,' but there is certainly the requirement to make it no worse. That, at least, was the moral obligation; now, farmers are under the obligation to leave their farms more valuable than they found them, particularly in today's social climate of environmentalism.

To leave the land 'more valuable' can mean improving its capital value, or its productivity. From what we know about farming and natural history, it seems to be a fairly small step to saying that a purpose for working landscapes is the improvement of productivity. To leave the land more valuable can also mean improving its environmental value. Given the stresses on land caused by industrial agriculture, it seems to me that one goal of farming is not the preservation of some agricultural status quo or even the maintenance of original optimal productivity, but the actual environmental improvement of already worked land.

These two features, productivity and environmental improvement, do not capture the full extent of farming's objectives. On a deeper view of farming's objectives, productivity, at least, will be attained almost as a by-product. So, beyond productivity and environmental improvement we add the following other tasks:

>to make farms more beautiful, and by extension nurture the wilder habitats;
>to promote or inculcate good moral character;
>to keep human beings in touch with biological entities and living processes and the places in which they flourish.

In many ways, these objectives are justified on consequential grounds. The production of safe and nutritious food and environmental responsibility lead to the socially desired benefits of food and the maintenance of productive capacity. The justifications on a wider view of farming are in some ways just as obvious. They also lead to desired outcomes. For example, a reversal of the migration from the farm to the city that is entailed in smaller production units, dispersed populations, and land reform, could supply work for what appears to be increasing unemployed populations. An emphasis on increased food self-sufficiency could help supply basic necessities and relieve pressures on increasingly costly social assistance programs. On an even deeper view of farming, the justifications are not as obvious, and, in what follows I will outline the deeper justifications as they pertain to place.

The Improvement of the Productive Capacity of Farm Units and the Improvement or Repair of Damaged Land

To say that humans can and ought to improve working landscapes is a relatively easy claim to defend. Widespread environmental concerns, changing agricultural practices (e.g., integrated pest management, conservation tillage, etc.), and increased biological knowledge are good indicators that we can improve the land, and when 'can' is grounded in widespread social benefit then we 'ought' to so improve land. For example, the reclamation of an eroded hillside or the increase in soil tilth and fertility are relatively easy to quantify as improvements on damaged lands. When we are able to reclaim eroded hillsides then, by the above argument, we ought to do so.

To say what an improvement on any particular farm would ultimately amount to is difficult. While we can come up with a number of indices that will measure the improvement of damaged lands, it is difficult to state what a further improvement would achieve. Is an increase in soil nutrients, soil fauna, etc., beyond those needed to maintain production, an improvement? If so, are we obliged to constantly improve the land? For example, is a producer who buys a television culpable because she could have invested the cost of the television in land improvement? Does a happier farmer count as an improvement? If so, are we obliged to support the farmer who wants more time to reflect and enjoy the pleasures of farming at the cost of harvesting a crop? Part of the difficulty in deciding what an improvement for any farm would be is that it will be dependent on the particular features of that farm, and the personal aspirations of the farmer. What is done on each farm beyond maintenance and production will be the result of each farmer's vision, that vision will rely on a matrix of economical, ecological, ethical and social values.

At some point we will have to rely on the intimate knowledge and deep feeling individual producers have for their farms. This intimate knowledge and deep feeling will be an essential feature of the insider's view and a view the outsider will most likely lack. In other words, we may have to rely on the producer saying that this is good enough, or that she has gotten it right. For example, there will be a point when all the outbuildings are in the right place, when all the permanent fences are built, when the feeding and housing regimen produces healthy and comfortable livestock, when all the stones are picked, when the orchard is planted, etc.

While speculative, the general argument about the improvement of farm land turns on the idea that a sense of place can generate a certain synergy between farmer and place. This synergy best positions the farmer to meet the stated objectives. The individual attending to the dictates of place is in a more advantaged position with respect to meeting the goals of improvement than is the individual attending merely to the dictates of either economics or ecology. In other words, the place-based farmer is in the best position to make the call as to what counts as an improvement.

To Make Farms More Beautiful, and by Extension Nurture the Wilder Habitats

To a large extent the argument for making farms more beautiful follows the argument for improving them. However, unlike arguments for improvement that can fall back on empirical judgements, arguments about making farms more beautiful must come face to face with the subjective nature of aesthetic experiences. To argue for what, in particular, would count as more beautiful over what would count as less beautiful would drive us far off topic. So, here is not the place to attempt more than a cursory comment on the aesthetic and the subjective. Roughly, I take subjective to mean a psychological assertion to the effect that 'this is beautiful' that some particular individual has, or would have in the appropriate circumstances. By aesthetic experience, I mean the kind of mental attitude that some particular individual has, or would have in the appropriate circumstances, that is expressed in the subjective statement 'this is beautiful.' In spite of this rough description of the aesthetic and subjective, we can make at least one objective statement about the beautiful, and I will rely on G. E. Moore's thought experiment about extremely beautiful and extremely ugly worlds to do so. Roughly, Moore asks us to choose, based on preferences, between a beautiful and ugly world. He considered that human beings have a preference for the beautiful over the ugly and when we are faced with a choice between the beautiful and the ugly in the actual world we would choose the beautiful. It is a short step to saying that in situations where we can make an aesthetic difference then we have a case for making things more beautiful insofar as we can.

If the above thought experiment is acceptable, in that we have an obligation to make things beautiful insofar as we can, then we have a case for making farms more beautiful. However, because the beautiful is expressive of a subjective mental attitude held by an individual or class of individuals, we cannot expect any public policy in a pluralistic society, regarding the nature of a beautiful farm, to be anything more than arbitrary. In other words, regulatory or legislative control of the beautiful will be inadequate. Public sentiment as to what is beautiful is fickle: it changes as social conditions change. Furthermore, it will change with particular farms in particular regions, and socially driven decisions regarding the description of beautiful farms by populations that are predominately urban may be completely inappropriate. So again, to make farms more beautiful must rest with those most likely to be in a position to have a vision of beauty concerning particular farms, the farmer. Hence, to make farms more beautiful requires not only the possibilities of agricultural production but also a vision of how a farm is to be designed. It will require an aesthetic sense particular to the particular place, the farm. Perhaps the beautiful farm is one in which the types of improvements mentioned earlier have been applied. Nonetheless, to beautify and improve farms will require strength of character to carry out the projects.

To Promote or Inculcate Good Moral Character

I must admit that I have no definitive idea about how we could go about instilling or reinforcing good moral character. I suspect that it can be fostered by socially relevant and worthwhile practices *vis à vis* Alasdair MacIntyre. Nonetheless, in this section I offer a theoretical case of the synergy between farmer and place in action. In many ways, it is the old circularity of agrarianism: good farming inculcates the virtues and the virtues are needed to farm well. Here the position takes the form place-virtue-place: place creates virtues while serving as the point of application for the virtues.

In spite of my earlier criticisms, there exist some ecological and social standards by which treatment of the land can be measured. For example, we have the duty to prevent immediate and foreseeable harm by producing food and doing it in sustainable ways. Socially, we can take abundant, safe, and nutritious food as the standard that this is being done. Ecologically, we can take the maintenance of the productive capacity of farm units as the standard. However, what is it that will prompt the producer to meet these standards if we accept the claim that conventional thinking has been counter-productive to at least the second standard? An examination of the way things are in the world will show that from the existence of a moral obligation or responsibility it does not follow that individuals fulfill them. To achieve the very real obligations or responsibilities entailed in farming, or anything else for that matter, we must rely on the moral character of the participants.

Just as it is difficult to state what will amount to an improvement on a particular farm, it is difficult to state the moral character required to farm well. Certainly, the good farmer will require physical strength, managerial skills, etc., but good farming, as does any worthwhile task performed well, also involves personal constraints. In part, these constraints supply their own standard for judging the appropriate moral character needed to fulfill the farmer's obligations.

Constraints will be bound up with a multiplicity of complicated moral and social values, but we might suggest that the particular knowledge associated with good farming is essentially knowledge relating to what is good or bad for a human being—qualities such as prudence, justice, temperance, honesty, that is, the virtues.

A virtue can be variously described as "being a disposition of character to choose or reject actions because they are of a certain ethically relevant kind"[7]; as *correctives*, each relating to "some temptation to be resisted or deficiency of motivation to be made good"[8]; or as "commitments to forms of behavior that we, as a community, reasonably require of one another."[9] It is in these broad descriptions that we find the particular range of ethical considerations in which virtues are recognized. We might consider the range of ethical considerations as bounded by being fulfilled as a human being, i.e., being rooted, placed socially and geographically in relationships where what we do affects others and our place in the world. We might consider the constraint, discipline and amelioration of culture and nature mean the living of lives of modest desires, hard work and geographic permanence.

As Peter Geach understands them, the virtues are normative for any worthy enterprise. I would think they are particularly so concerning farming. Farmers need courage to persevere in face of the setbacks, difficulties, and dangers working with nature entail. They need temperance to avoid the distractions of short-term satisfactions so that fertile land, sturdy buildings and durable fences can be built. They need humility to overcome hubris in our choices relating to nature. They need justice to ensure cooperation and mutual trust in any large-scale social enterprise, but especially so because far too few humans are involved in farming or even know how to farm. Last, farmers need the wisdom to understand those practices that foster use and improvement.[10]

The objective basis for the virtues required for 'good farming' relies on it being a practical art, and it depends as much on character as on agricultural knowledge. It is by way of the constraints on human character that good farming can be defended. Since good farming destroys neither farmland nor farmers, it requires intimate knowledge, attention and care. Moreover, good farming is a process of the improvement of the land, not the extraction of its life. That one ought to lovingly use land and not extract the life from it is, in some respects, based on instrumental values. For example, both conventional and alternative forms of agriculture are practiced to produce benefits for humans. These benefits are not forthcoming without appropriate knowledge, care, and attention. With human character, one is to be centered and not enticed away from the center. To lose the center—a sense of place—is socially and culturally dangerous and in the agricultural situation irreparably damaging. Indeed, to have an attachment to the land is ipso facto to have good reason for practices that care for the land even at the expense of other goals. The knowledge and skill required to farm well will come from the past. Such an argument has its antecedents in agrarianism. It is a practical argument based on agricultural experiences. Practically, it is based on a principle that, to be successful, human designs for farms should be made only on the most modest assumptions about changes to nature, and the safest assumption is to rely on what worked in the past; that is, practices that have maintained, or improved, production and the land's productivity. It is through these practices that we find a possibility of human fulfillment. The matrix of human capacities and disciplines once made farms sustainable and that is the only way they will be sustainable in the future. The matrix of human life comes, in part, from the commitment to, or faith in, the values of one's community, and while this is irrevocably relativistic, it is not absurd for social creatures to think in terms of their social and cultural situation. Similarly, it is not absurd for farmers to think in terms of their environmental situation.

To Keep Human Beings in Touch with Biological Entities and Living Processes and the Places in which They Flourish

One thing that is quite striking about the shift in agricultural production over the last fifty years is the shift from methods that were relatively favorable to some wildlife to methods that are an anathema to some wildlife. Mixed rotational farming systems involving both tillage of crops and the rearing of livestock offered a certain amount of variety in wildlife habitats. There was a robustness in multiple-enterprise farming that was favorable to supporting diversity through the availability of varied breeding habitats and food supplies.

In contrast, the impression that modern farming is biologically simple or contains less biological information is substantiated by farmers who produce only one or two crops. It is further substantiated by the decrease in animal species occupying and breeding in farm environments. The impression that there is less diversity relates to the fewer varieties and types of crops that tend to be grown on modern farms. The decrease in diversity is the result of changes in cropping practices that can be understood partially by the seasonal pattern of farm work.

How individual farmers deal with wildlife can indicate how personal identification with a particular landscape might be manifest in farming. The seasonal nature of farming is something to which every animal inhabiting farmland must adjust, but by way of explanation I will refer to wild birds. An important effect of mechanization has been to compress the period in the farming year in which food is available to birds. The effect of this compression has been adverse on the populations of several species. This is especially prevalent where spring cultivation has given way to autumn-sown fields that are unsuitable as feeding areas. Similarly, modern harvesting methods have seriously reduced food availability. Prior to mechanization, harvesting involved several stages—cutting, stooking, carting, stacking and threshing—that were spread over the fall and winter months and resulted in much grain spillage. However, spillage was exploited by birds and other animals that, from their perspective (if we can talk of birds having perspectives), was not waste but largesse. In contrast, modern combining starts later but is completed earlier and in a single operation with less spillage, and under one form of accounting less grain is wasted. There is less food available for birds, and over a shorter time. Subsequently, there has been a decrease in nesting pairs on farms that have mechanized.[11]

We might say that we need wild places and wildlife in farm environments. Perhaps such places act as a standard of civilization and as models for an accurate sense of farming's impact upon its natural sources. Perhaps—for reasons practical and humane—we need to *see* the differences farming makes to wildness to keep these differences as small as possible. To know, by way of statistical analysis, government reports, and academic papers, the environmental impact of agriculture is to dissociate that impact from personal lives. To see the difference farming makes to soil, fertility, and bird populations reconciles the possibility of a conservation impulse with sensitive and intimate knowledge of particular places. The possibility of conservation, in other words, is about its effect on personal lives. Conservation, as it affects personal lives, will be in part about the economies that the people who live those lives practice. For example, the economies that led to changes in cropping practices over the last fifty years affected the lives of birds. The effect on the lives of birds is reflected in the sensitivity brought to wild places and wildlife as shown in the following example about pesticide use from O'Connor and Shrubb's interpretation of the British Common Bird Census.[12]

In the late 1970s a survey of farmers' attitudes to various risks associated with pesticide use revealed that most farmers favored pesticide use on financial grounds but were averse to its use on health and environmental grounds. Yet the financial argument tended to be the one that had influence on the actual use of pesticides. This was particularly the case in insurance use, where pesticides were applied to reduce risk of loss even though no evidence of pests was found. For our present purposes, this part of the bird survey indicates that the perception of risk to wildlife relates to attitudes toward wildlife and place as well as an indication of the concentration on economics. The result from four English shires is most telling:

In Lincolnshire, where hedges, scrub, and related habitat have long been scarce, most farmers were aware of wildlife but only as 'vermin'. In Norfolk and Suffolk, where the distribution of hedges is patchy, many farmers were unaware of wildlife. In Bedfordshire, where wildlife habitat has long been abundant, most farmers were both aware of and in favor of wildlife.[13]

Perhaps we can extrapolate from the above that the existence of wildlife habitats (e.g., hedges, scrub and rough pasture) heightens awareness of wildlife. By extension, the preservation of wildlife habitats requires the perception that farms are homes for more than high yields and can heighten the awareness of the biological world around us. Again we must rely on the producer's grasp, or sense of place, for the possibility of such awareness. The results from the four shires indicate that if wildlife habitats exist, then farmers are more aware of wildlife. The more aware that they are of wildlife the more it seems that they are prepared to maintain wildlife habitats. In design terms this translates into farms with permanent borders and some nonproductive land. Physically such farms would have hedges rather than wire fences; copses, riparian habitats, wetlands, and ponds rather than drainage and fields plowed from fence row to fence row. Often, the vision for the economy of such farms is mixed rotational farming, or diversified specialty farms that grow plants and rear livestock. The economies of high yields are kept at a distance; that is, the farmer's objectives are centered somewhere between the apices of economy and ecology.

Lastly, mixed farming systems support not only a preservation impulse but an ideal of a free market where the preservation impulse reaches beyond the farm's borders into a local and regional community. Obviously, rural wildlife habitats increase the availability of wildlife for everyone. Similarly, traditional mixed farming and marketing systems increase access to local produce for everyone. The farming economy is tied to sense of place and the social and cultural order because farmers, as members of the community to which they sell, have direct access to the needs and desires of their customers. Both farmers and consumers can determine the design of a place.

The Justification for the Notion of Sense of Place as It Relates to Farming

Generally, ethical dimensions related to farming must assure us that the correct attitude is universal and disinterested: the account and justifications are decided on the outsider's view of farming. By disinterested is meant objective, generalized, and applied without consideration of differences between individual farmers and individual farms. Much can be made of the differences between individual farmers and individual farms on an insider's view compared to the outsider's view that is limited to understanding all farmers and farms alike. A central feature of the outsider's view is that it is essentially cognitive as distinct from emotive and acts of volition. To understand farming, or to approach the tasks of farming from a purely generalized, cognitive perspective, drives a wedge between the producer and the working landscape.

We can think of the globalization of agriculture as part of the trend that breaks down the boundaries between different cultures. The global food system has a truly global reach, and as one multinational company used to suggest, "I ought to buy the world a soft drink." In contrast, there is desire for intimacy where ecological and agricultural differences among farms are most visible to those who work them. It is not surprising that in an era of ecological crisis many of the cultural differences are being worked out on the land itself. While we look to the promise of global cooperation, to resolve the problems of agriculture requires an intimacy with the productive, ecological, and communal situation.

The wedge being driven between the producer and the working landscape is analogous to the growing gap between the global citizen and place-based environmental duties. It is the gap between the "breaking down of boundaries among people" and the intimacy of the local and unique. For example, we can think of the intimacy found among family members who live in close approximation and those who live far apart. In close approximation, differences in behaviors and attitudes are often manifest in arguments over minute, often trivial, detail. Probably, we can all recall the childhood squabbles we had with our siblings and parents over differences that, at a distance, break down. At a distance, differences are often manifest in tolerance for behaviors and attitudes that are at great variance to one another. It is as if differences matter more in the lived situation than in any other.

Yet, as the sociologist J. Meyrowitz notes, the "differences among people are most visible when they are at least present."[14] The intimacy of family members can lead to conflict, and distance can appear to foster tolerance. However, the actual resolution of family conflict requires a close connection among family members rather than the tolerance of distance. While intimacy may lead to conflict, and of course love and cooperation, the immediacy of conflict allows for the possibility of resolution. This is also the case for farming. The possibility of sustainability requires a similar intimacy and immediacy, because "land is too various in its kinds, climates, conditions, . . . to conform to any generalised understanding or to prosper under generalised treatment."[15] And, "if you do not pay close and constant attention to your fields—always at the expense of what the rest of the world is up to—you risk losing all you have poured into them."[16] The intimacy and immediacy of place presents an insider's view of sustainability. In the ideal, it diminishes the wedge between the producer and the working landscape.

We can use the idea of a wedge between farmer and landscape to further the idea of an insider's view of farming. The idea is to center the producer more firmly within the context of sense of place. The experience of a place and the personal identification people have with the local and unique is about feelings of welcome, of safety, of wonder, of humility, and of certainty in the cycles of nature. To feel the comfort of hearth and home after a lengthy absence exemplifies the feelings of safety and comfort. There is no choice but to live at the expense of other life, but here sense of place encompasses wonder and humility in the realization that it is in nature and by nature that we live. Here one's sense of place acknowledges that environmentalism begins with how one lives in, and by the nature of, a particular place. One nice feature about the sense of place thesis is that it does not rely on vague generalizations about the supposed goals of nature. Nature repeats its patterns endlessly: we make our way in those patterns as best we can.

The experience of place is visual and spatial in that a thing is "what it is in part by being *where* it is."[17] Land that can feed us has a distinctly human purpose and importance. The purpose in the design of working landscapes tells us much about what the designer thinks other entities and the land are worth to herself and others, and much about the social purpose of farm land. Confinement-fed veal calves are, loosely understood, meat machines. Comparable bull calves in India are, as locally understood, sacred. An eroded hillside probably tells us about the economic and nutritional pressures that the farmer was under. Similarly, the homogenous strip of fast food restaurants and car dealerships that are the introduction to most North American cities tells us something about how people think about food and the land as do well-tended household gardens.

Though we can assume that designing a farm will be a lifetime's work, to belong to a place is also historical and cultural. Historically, families can be permanently settled. From this we speculate that designing a farm will be the work of generations. Granted, the bucolic farm and the large feedlot are both experienced as places, and there is no formula for experiencing places, but there is a sense in which the experience of place can be present in, and a part of, an historical and endless continuity of human life and endeavor. Places can be experienced as exemplars of human life where 'good' farms are the fulfillment of human work done well over generations.

Culturally, agriculture's reach extends beyond the farm gate to markets and social interactions, and the converse is also true. Social, cultural and ethical constraints affect the design of agriculture. This interchange between the rural and social affects personal identity and how an individual sees and shapes the place in which she lives. In this the local and unique environmental and ecological situations of agriculture might serve as an awareness of the primary importance in living in, and wanting to live in, a particular farmstead and community. This awareness might serve as a concrete influence on a particular environmental, ecological and cultural situation. If farms are perceived as food factories, as some critics of agriculture would have it, then farming will follow all that the metaphor connotes. If farms are perceived as homes, where individuals are rooted in their community, then the conducting of farming might be perceived as the sustaining of the territory, the place. Sense of place plays a role in self-identity, roots and what one is, because, in part, these things are determined by where you live. We all know that you can tell a lot about people by observing their homes.

The experiences of place, as vague as they are, form 'connectedness' in the sense of kinship with places, a sense of being rooted and belonging somewhere. Therefore, sense of place can be likened to kinship with the life of a place. Though some of the relations may not be all that beneficial to agricultural operations (e.g., weeds or insect pests), the idea that they can flourish and be controlled within the life of a place requires experience of them flourishing and being controlled. Part of knowing one's fields is knowing where weeds and insects dominate, and knowing how many weeds and insects can be tolerated. To summarize, we can say that the values associated with working a particular place involve an intimate awareness of, or closeness to, the distinguishing features of a place. Both the attributes of, and the attitudes toward, particular places motivate how they are treated.

Obviously, to be connected with a place is a difficult concept to spell out, because it is in part experiential, in part non-cognitive, emotional or affective, and in part aesthetic. In the practical, it might involve the design of working landscapes that are (1) uplifting and give rise to the very countryside panoramas that are expected of the countryside, (2) ecologically sound, and (3) economically responsible. This design can be found in fertile farms whose economies are domestic. It can be found in the kinds of farms envisioned and experienced as a partnership with working landscapes where balance is struck between managing productive farmland, the millions of entities that thrive in and on soil, and the development of infrastructures and economies (e.g., suburbs, highways, airports, products and markets, etc.) that support such a partnership.

The Critique of Sense of Place

Even if sense of place has little to do with the purposes and practices of modern agriculture (is, indeed, too self centered for that), it may still have much to do with the proper validation of good farming. The most forceful criticisms will center on the claim that personal identity associated with, or derived from, commitment to community and place smacks of relativism and subjectivity. Moreover, even in a homogeneous world people do have a sense of belonging to a community, for example, a global community, and this belonging does not have to be associated with an agricultural situation. Indeed, in some cases it is a belonging that fosters tolerance.

Clearly, the notion of sense of place is relativistic insofar as it concerns the immediate and the intimate. Its reach or horizon is the local and unique. It is from the understanding and knowledge of the local and unique that the possibility of solutions to agricultural problems arise. It is from the assessment of the local and unique that a sustainable agriculture will be designed. It is from intimacy with particular social, cultural, and environmental situations that we will learn what to do with farms, and it is from immediacy that we learn whether to do it. However, we do not have in mind the vicious kind of relativism as one finds in cultural relativism where moral rules are limited to social norms. The environmental influences on agricultural situations merely forge an alliance among local social values, cultural arrangements, and behavior that is appropriate to the community. The horizon is the intimate and immediate and this horizon includes ethnological and sociological considerations. It is immediate to what is at hand, and intimate in its practicalities.

The notion of sense of place is subjective, because it is about personal identity and meaning in life. It is not subjective to the extent that it is thoroughly egoistic. Values of good moral character extend beyond the egoism of self-preference. In a sense, the relativism of sense of place conveys part of the metaphysical message underlying writing about agriculture. If we want to get our societies right then we must get our agriculture right, and in the process we will supply worthwhile and meaningful work in which to find the possibility of human fulfillment. Given we all eat and live in a world not of our choosing but partially malleable to our choices, the perception of our particular situation is manifest in our agriculture.

It is true enough that few people are involved in an agricultural situation (except as consumers), and that people still enjoy or participate in some form of community. However, the claim that has been made here is that this participation is distanced from the local and unique and the perception of belonging to physical place is becoming increasingly weaker. I do contend that the price for belonging to a global community and the tolerance that it entails is at the expense of what is valuable in the intimacy of the local and unique. Under the rubric of environmental and social concern, belonging to a global community threatens human and environmental health. For example, people whose diets rely on products shipped thousands of miles run the risk of losing control over safety and nutritional quality. Furthermore, products that are shipped long distances add to environmental costs through the infrastructures required to move them. Under the rubric of the local and unique, people can enhance their lives and communities.

Summary

Many readers will feel that ethical justifications in agriculture must refer to production and/or sustainability. So we have one class of concerns that refers to aspects of production. We have become increasingly aware of the dangers involved in agricultural production. Currently, much public awareness is centered on substances that are added to food either by producers or processors. Similarly, much concern is centered on genetic changes to common crops. The second class of concerns refers to the reasons for farming in sustainable ways. The ecological approach holds up nature as the ideal farmer and attempts to have it supply the method for sustainability. The sense of place perspective refers to the deep commitment people have to particular places, their communities, and the role place plays in personal identity. While I acknowledge economic, ecological, and communal considerations, it is the immediate and intimate practicalities of farming that are especially relevant to sustaining the social, ecological, and cultural dimensions of human life.

Insofar as we can make any general claims about the practices involved in farming, they are going to resemble the vision for an ecological approach to farming. Where they differ is that the organizing theme of sense of place supplies a different set of rules for farming. In fact, it does not rely on ecology to find the rules even though many practices will be similar (e.g., polycultures, or mixed rotational farming). Central to the notion of sense of place is the contention that agriculture is sustained (i.e., maintained and prolonged) by a settled human population striving to live well. Just as we lack guarantees that the satisfaction of obligations concerning future generations will satisfy future generations, we lack guarantees that such a conception will make agriculture sustainable. We have no idea how future generations will turn out, or how to tell what future technology will be. However, we do know that sustainable agriculture is possible if farms and farming are assessed on an insider's view.

Notes

1. C. A. Hooker, "Value and System: Notes toward the Definition of Agri-Culture," *Journal of Agricultural and Environmental Ethics* 7 (1994): 35.

2. Wendell Berry, "A Defense of the Family Farm," in *Is There a Moral Obli-*

gation to Save the Family Farm?, ed. G. Comstock (Ames: Iowa State University Press, 1987), 348.

3. Many readers will find the notion rationally inadequate because it is difficult to extract universalizable, moral abstractions from what is essentially associated with the private and personal spheres of life. But, the ability to extend personal sentiments to a more generalized concern is an old theme in philosophy. From my sentiments about my kith and kin I can, both cognitively and emotively, extend those sentiments to other humans, to some other animals (e.g., the great apes), to all animals, and so on. It is to be hoped that these sentiments map onto the moral intuitions that respect life, tolerance, some basic freedoms regarding personal choice, and avoid harm, as well as produce good.

4. Stanley Crawford, *A Garlic Testament* (New York: Edward Burlingame Books, 1992), 193.

5. Wendell Berry, *The Unsettling of America: Culture and Agriculture* (San Francisco: Sierra Club Books, 1977), 47–8.

6. Crawford, *A Garlic Testament*, 105–06.

7. Bernard Williams, *Ethics and the Limits of Philosophy* (Cambridge: Harvard University Press, 1985), 9.

8. Philippa Foot, *Virtues and Vices* (Berkeley: University of California Press, 1978), 8.

9. James Wallace, *Virtues and Vices* (Ithaca, N.Y.: Cornell University Press, 1978), 127.

10. For these insights that I have adapted to farming I acknowledge Peter Geach, *The Virtues* (Cambridge: Cambridge University Press, 1977), 16.

11. Raymond J. O'Connor and Michael Shrubb, *Farming and Birds* (Cambridge: Cambridge University Press, 1987), 79–102.

12. O'Connor and Shrubb, *Farming and Birds*, 212–13.

13. O'Connor and Shrubb, *Farming and Birds*, 213.

14. Joshua Meyrowitz, *No Sense of Place* (New York: Oxford University Press, 1985), 317.

15. Berry, *The Unsettling of America: Culture and Agriculture*, 31.

16. Crawford, *A Garlic Testament*, 190.

17. Andrew Brennan, *Thinking About Nature* (Athens: The University of Georgia Press, 1988), 173.

Commonplaces

David Glidden

Haec ergo argumenta, quae transferri in multas causas possunt, locos communes nominamus.

—Cicero, *De Inventione* II 25.48.

Philosophy has proven too fond of generality. Disdain of particulars in face of theory often led to studied cruelty toward persons, whose complex lives simply would not fit the elegant simplicities of rationalized reality. Even before the days of Aristotle the philosophy of man rode roughshod over women, children, barbarians, lesser creatures in the chain of being, all typically disregarded as inferior, defective. The pretense of universality too often preened itself in spite of history, place, and context, forgetting that everything humanity conceives of changes. Ignorance of differences among peoples, places, times, and cultures gave misplaced confidence to the timelessness of eternal truths about humanity, until the day inevitably came when such truths came to be replaced by newer, improved eternal truths. So, the game of confidence renewed itself upon its victims.

The history of philosophy is a litany of failures. Yet history proved to be of little cautionary value. In this century, Heidegger's hands-on ontology, so self-consciously stylized by ancient Greek philology, proved to be no respecter of persons either (especially Jews). Foucault's culturally sensitive archaeology of knowledge was itself too delimited within its own historical and geographical boundaries to serve as a universal foundation for a philosophically inspired study of cultures, of the kind Vico and Schleiermacher earlier had yearned for and also failed to deliver. Nor did Foucault's final thoughts on power stand up enough to scrutiny to forestall disputations and dissertations, despite the compelling texture of his imaginatively reconstructed stories about other times and places.

In the search for wisdom another way is needed than the choice first outlined by Parmenides: the way of being or the way of seeming. A third alternative less trodden-on might prove more suitable, one that might abandon paved-over generalities entirely. A priori laws of reason prove too straight and narrow, the formal legacy of deduction too directed. Quasi-empiricist constructions building up inductions into systems leave too much territory unexplored. Parmenides' highway to wisdom has long ago been moved and rolled, leveled, set, and surfaced in concrete, time and time again, in thralldom to the sciences' empiricist or formalist demands. Philosophy might do better traveling cross-country.

Aristotle once hinted at the existence of a rough-and-ready knowledge. Occasionally he called it *epagoge*. Aristotle explained, we first collect a variety of experiences together, and long before we begin to rationalize them and re-order them, we take up whatever cues of nature we can seize upon and simply make an effort to consider how nature presents itself to us. We do this in the form of rudimentary notions and tentative assumptions, which Aristotle called *hypolepseis*. All such collected experiences and preliminary observations, Aristotle suggested, would take place long before the traditions of philosophy came into play, to bracket in or bracket out what does or does not matter to the systematic process of abstraction.

The Epicureans emphasized, in turn, a somewhat similar commonplace wisdom to contend against philosophical abstraction. Sometimes the Stoics followed suit, acknowledging the force of Epicurus' 'traversing common ground', or *metabasis tou homoiou*, where salient similarities trigger associations connecting particulars together, without requiring the forceful linkage of a more rigorous abstraction which would strip away the separately defining identities of individual cases and localities. This assimilation of common similarities would not itself erase differences of time and place or varieties of experience. It would instead respect them when contained within an anecdotal epistemology, such as that made memorable in the writings of Lucretius.

Hellenistic Pyrrhonists embraced a parallel version of *metabasis* themselves in conceding the authority of ordinary preconceptions (*prolepseis*) and common notions (*koinai ennoiai*) which inform the way we guide ourselves through life, without becoming dogmatic about why things appear to be the way they are to such rudimentary common sense. These ancient skeptics allowed for a way of looking and of living that employed concepts, notions, forms of recognition which all the while remained sufficiently inchoate to license living without dogma.

Those ancient Greek and Roman physicians who were vigorously anti-dogmatic took up a similar methodology themselves. They remained content to consider the symptomology of the human condition, to witness and record the regimen that led to health as well as the sequence of symptoms that led to particular illnesses, diseases, death. So too, the medicines and diets they suggested were themselves a consequence only of what seemed to work, without becoming dogmatic about how. Often the therapies of antidogmatic physicians proved more helpful or at least less harmful than the practices of scientists.

Perhaps it would occasionally be better, when it comes to the contemporary study of humanity, to stick with something like ancient *epagoge*, to be content with the *hypolepseis, metabaseis, prolepseis,* and *koinai ennoiai* of ordinary experience. Perhaps it would prove useful to learn from the antidogmatic physicians and leave ordered, more formal inquiry to the brave or foolhardy, at least when it comes to pursuing certain questions about humanity. By restraining itself, contemporary philosophy might possibly rediscover and savor those details of human experience which inspired philosophy's existence in the first place, the particulars of the human condition and habitation, those personal, shifting, local values which a professional, more technical philosophy all too often passed over in the rush to dogmatize.

Instead of trying to conceive how nature, or some final science, sees the world, it might be good enough first to reconsider how the human world looks to human beings, but not in the way, say, Kant might formalize experience into a theory-laden epistemology. Rather, one might instead stop short of imposing an order of one's own invention, by not immediately converting how things locally present themselves into universal philosophical speculations, at least when it comes to the consideration of human lives and values situated locally.

To be sure, common sense assumptions often have a way of suggesting covert dogma, even theories. Yet, what saves such apparently artless notions from becoming terms of art is the commonplace consensus of a human community that shares a local form of life by traversing common ground, sharing similar experiences, intuitions, values and assumptions, describing them in rough-and-ready ways sufficiently agreed upon to establish genuine local consensus, prior to developing more elaborate, less shared interpretations, disagreements, conflicts. Such a Pyrrhonist or Wittgensteinean respect for common considerations and the ordinary notions of a consensus locally derived might prove too lowly for those, like Plato, with developed dogma of their own (or those with an ax to grind against their neighbors). But it might be exactly what is needed to return to philosophy a genuine respect for the rich varieties of human experience and cultures, within the ever changing continuum of human values variously at play in an ever changing world. On the other hand, for many contemporary philosophers and possibly even some geographers such a turn toward local communities and their situated values could be seen as positively threatening to what nostalgic neo-Cartesians take to be the absolute value of autonomous abstraction.

In what follows let us at least try out this bit of methodology borrowed from the ancient world. We shall be wandering cross-country, responding to particular experiences, without attempting to direct local observations toward laws and social systems. What results will not be skepticism toward the high art of theoretical abstraction so much as an exercise in approximation, more story-driven and localized than anticipating wide-ranging, ambitious conclusions. In particular, I shall try to regain the middle ground between universal systems, on the one hand, and, on the other, the singular preoccupation with the particular alone. Montaigne defined this middling ambition well, in his essay "On Experience" in a passage borrowed from Augustine's *City:* "If our faces were not alike we could not tell man from beast; if they were not unalike we could not tell man from man." Montaigne then glossed his text: "All things are connected by some similarity; yet every example limps and any correspondence which we draw from experience is always feeble and imperfect; we can nevertheless find some corner or other by which to link our comparisons."

One particular topic well-suited to this middling method of inquiry concerns situating community itself. The way residents and visitors regard and hold a common ground cannot be abstracted from actual experience, places, persons. Purely hypothetical examples, counterfactual thought experiments, armchair speculations cannot supplant field reports of places fleshed out in sufficient detail to make such localities come imaginatively, instructively alive. At the same time it is important to know when to refrain either from further generality or dwelling too much on details. What draws people together in those places where community appears appealing? Why does place matter so to those who prefer to live lives belonging to some greater, healing whole? Such general questions can be addressed by systematic arguments, by abstract propositions, but I believe they also can be answered by the kind of local portraiture Montaigne, for instance, practiced.

An apology is due those scholars who write more technically of the haecceity of place and community identity. This is not my originating position. As a classically trained philosopher and essayist, I am addressing community from a different point of view, more akin to Seneca, Plutarch, and Montaigne. More to the point, my contemporary sources of inspiration on this topic are other essayists on place who have commented artfully in an artless way, in particular Wallace Stegner, Wendell Berry, and Kathleen Norris. The anecdotal epistemology I shall employ here is a result of fifteen years or so of purposeful wandering about California, extensive interviewing, reading local papers and bulletin boards in grocery stores, and also writing occasionally about assorted California places as a freelance journalist and *flâneur*. I shall focus on specific stories and attempt to keep these stories primary, without rendering them as fodder for abstraction. I shall be traversing common ground. With this in mind, let us take a look at the North Beach district of San Francisco.

I

In 1994 Matteo Casserino was 81 years old. For the preceding quarter of a century he played mandolin on Saturdays at the Trieste Coffee House in North Beach. When he first began performing operatic melodies and Italian songs, he was accompanied by piano and guitar. After the guitarist, who was blind, had died, another mandolin came on and then another pianist.

The trio typically began in a rather desultory fashion shortly before noon. By early afternoon a full-fledged concert would be underway with singers joining in. Pavarotti once sang at the Trieste in September of 1975. Gino DiMichele sang tenor there for years. Like Matteo, he also worked in the café, cleaning dishes, taking orders. Men who play mandolins and sing arias from opera are still working and performing Saturdays at the Trieste *sub specie aeternitatis.* Yet, eternity never remains the same; things change. The year 1994 was emblematic of such changes underway in San Francisco.

Chinatown stands adjacent to North Beach. In recent years Chinese homes and businesses gradually moved into what was once San Francisco's staunchly Italian neighborhood. Chinatown expanded; Little Italy became increasingly Chinese. And so, on February 26, Matteo Casserino's Saturday afternoon of Italian opera was followed by the Chinese New Year's Parade, celebrating the year 4692, the Year of the Dog.

Ethnicity and geography have historically been bound together. In the United States whole sections of cities were traditionally blocked off into ethnic neighborhoods: Polish, Jewish, black sides of the tracks, Chinatowns, for instance. In time ethnic homelands proved unstable, leading to uncomfortable and sometimes violent transitions, as one population yielded space to another.

Territorial expansion displaces what went before. Depending on who is winning, sometimes the struggle over neighborhood is seen as a victory over segregation and oppression—so Spike Lee made the case for black Brooklyn, in *Do the Right Thing.* From the point of view of the replaced those very same transitions can be seen as killing history and tradition, whether Algonquin natives driven from New York or Italians from Brooklyn. *Do the Right Thing* ended with a racial riot. Where there are winners, there are losers.

Under the pressures of transition many urban neighborhoods and villages suffer the loss of identity entirely. Pride of place often yields to opened space at the cost of any abiding ethnic character whatsoever, the price paid for democracy perhaps. Pride of place produces conflict. So, ethnic communities sometimes peacefully dissolve into collections of individuals who just happen to be neighbors, even though they may not socialize together or identify with each other or even know each other's names.

Then again, the pressures of affluence sometimes gentrify ethnicity entirely away, creating affluence zones in cities, welcoming whoever has the money. Southern California's Palos Verdes and San Marino are today more propertied than partisan. And Old Town in Pasadena was recently transmogrified into an equal opportunity haven for the educated middle class, with bakeries, bookstores, restaurants, coffee houses, upscale varieties of shops. Once boarded-up brick buildings became businesses again. Old downtown was resuscitated, albeit more mechanically transitioned than resulting from a spiritual rebuilding from within.

Where ethnic districts and neighborhoods give way to fusion, for every economic gain there seems to be a private loss. Personal histories attach themselves to places. Once gentrification sets in, it can rob residents of any sense of place that is theirs, once stores are standardized in malls or homes are built in tracts and phases, gated off. After the places and their names have changed and changed again, where will the sources of familiarity be found to locate memories into niches where they fit? Can there be a sense of home without a corresponding tribal sense of homeland?

The ethnic changes underway in San Francisco's North Beach suggest redeeming answers to these questions, with the mere hint of a suggestion that amalgamation can occur without a corresponding loss of feeling, that ethnicity and local pride can survive within a culturally identified and diversified neighborhood, by re-imagining ethnicity and personal, familial history without requisitioning a separate space, without requiring an exclusive sense of place. Yet, some sufficient sense of locality is needed to acquire a feeling for one's own cultural and ethnic identity, to fend off anonymity. There is this tension to the concept of microbrewed communities, strained between the merely personal proclivities of gathered residents and larger cultural identities, often sparking friction with each other's other histories.

II

Since 1971 I had been coming to the Trieste for breakfast, once a month or so, flying up at first on business, to participate in a Saturday reading group at Berkeley on ancient Greek philosophy, scheduled later in the day. After twenty years I left the seminar, but continued to find excuses to wind up occasionally in North Beach on Saturdays, four hundred miles from my home.

Mamma Trieste, as I called her, knew me by my order and invariably greeted me with the words "cappuccino grande," once her eyes apprised me, though I often had a dolci, too. Waiting in line early on the morning of the Chinese New Year's Parade of 4692 (or 1994), I collected my order at the counter and then settled down on an old bentwood café chair at my usual table, facing a wall of opera photos which served as backdrop for performers. I took out a book to read but soon found myself in conversation before I even turned a page.

Previously, by reading ancient Greek, I had kept my distance from other customers, which allowed me to watch them relatively undisturbed in between snatching lines of Aristotle. People peering over shoulders who saw me reading Greek quickly turned away again, as if I were too foreign or too serious. But once I changed authors and gave up any pretense of preparing for the seminar, I engaged in conversation more than I had done before. Meanwhile, the clientele gradually had changed from the bohemians and beats of the early 1970s. Regulars now included tourists and lawyers, families with children.

Across from me that morning sat a Washington bureaucrat on business from D.C. He was frustrated over his espresso. Civil servants are not allowed by law to take initiatives of a certain order, he dutifully explained, and the agency he worked for was still waiting on political appointments from the Clinton administration. He lived in Chevy Chase, but his life appeared to be his work. To my right were two recombinant DNA physicians from Harvard Medical School, in town for a convention. Soon we were talking up the biochemical revolution, where the genetic codes are cracking. Then the mandolins began to play.

Conversation slowed, some took up reading once again, others let the tunes play in their head. Looking across the crowded tables, seating maybe fifty, there was nothing that we seemed to have in common, except our choice to be there, for whatever reason. Poets, philosophers, physicians, gays, businessmen and bums, persons of assorted color, professionals and travelers working on their memories in several different languages—we were what collected there, taking in the cosmos of Trieste. Italian was in the air, though most of us were not Italian. Yet most of us were there precisely because the Trieste Coffee House seemed quintessentially Italian, even though, of course, Trieste really never has been an authentic part of Italy.

The Trieste remained too seedy to be gentrified, at least in 1994. Changing its decor would have ruined the ambiance advantage which the Trieste café enjoyed over all the newer, cleaner coffee houses springing up in North Beach. The Trieste had history in its corner. Strangers who strolled in joined regulars who composed that history, customers for decades. By entering the scene strangers became part of that same narrative. Indeed, the Trieste thrived upon the presence of strangers in its mix whose presence shored up its identity.

Strangers play a crucial role in creating a community. If one could understand that riddle, one might gain insight into what makes some ethnic neighborhoods survive and sometimes prosper, even when tightly wound around each other, while other ethnic neighborhoods adjacent to each other become war zones of hostility.

Here especially anecdotal witness proves more valuable than abstraction. The sensitivity one acquires from looking at places which successfully sustain communities remains too locally bound to time and circumstance to yield grander generality. But it does not follow insights cannot be gleaned from witnessing what works locally, in places like North Beach. Ad hoc insights take the form more of portraiture than hypotheses which might be scientifically tested and systematically confirmed. Such insight is best informed by local knowledge, local lore. There are few laws of human nature, if any, worth systematizing, but there is a wealth of humanity to observe and ponder in detail.

Many contemporary philosophers who otherwise would welcome abstract thinking readily acknowledge the superior force of stories in comprehending and advancing moral values. So, too, the moral health of communities is well attested and measured by the stories of those who live there. What wisdom that can be found in the goodness of a good community is typically pictorial in character, the way insightful moral or social philosophy must be scenic, or so it seems to me. What is needed for understanding the art and essence of a thriving community is a complex, mind's eye vision of its particular goodness.

III

During a break in the performance at the Trieste that afternoon, I decided to take a walk about the neighborhood, as part of my North Beach ritual, wandering about with assorted Italian tunes lingering in my head. Today it was "Rondine al nido," by Vincenzo de Crescenzo, a Neapolitan immigrant who first came to the States in 1903. The song describes the swallow who returns on the same day every year, crossing mountains and the sea, but the singer's loved one does not come back. And so the singer ends his song with the lament, "You ran away, never to return."

I walked over to Washington Square at the heart of North Beach, thinking of the lyrics and the melody, savoring the sadness of being disconnected. The fog had cleared, the day was turning warm. The park facing

the Church of Saints Peter and Paul had already filled with children playing, old men sitting on benches, thinking of lost loves perhaps, or at least
pondering the lives they lived.

I remembered how, some years past, I was sitting on one such bench
myself an early summer morning, when an elderly Italian struck up a
halting conversation. He seemed sad enough to be Vincenzo de Crescenzo
himself, old enough as well. He pointed to the walk-up apartment where
he lived, overlooking Washington Square above a corner restaurant, and
he told me how he had been corresponding with his family's village in
Sicily to find relatives to take him in. He had, that very week, found
friends of relatives who promised to make a place for him. So, he was
leaving in a month, returning alone to the country from which he came
when he was young. He wanted to share his joy over going home again,
even if he had to share it with a stranger.

Mario, or so I shall call him, had never married and had lived in that
apartment several decades. From what he told me, he had lived alone, with
few friends or acquaintances. Primarily they were those he worked with
at the restaurants which employed him. He had lived his life that way and
spent it. Though he did not strike me as a particularly unhappy person,
he was certainly melancholic.

Mario expressed anguish over what I took to be the continuing sense
of isolation he had experienced in the States, even when living in the Italian section of San Francisco. He had always missed his village, he confessed. An immigrant Italian neighborhood was not community enough
for him, it seemed. He missed familiar places, familial voices, so he said.
An ethnically invented district could not compensate for that. He came
because he needed work. Now that he did not, he could return.

After we had talked, I presumptuously considered Mario's life, in the
way readers contemplate characters in novels: had Mario's life been a failure? The ethnic familiarity of North Beach had kept him living in San
Francisco and sustained him enough to work, survive, and one day return
to Sicily, where he would be well received. On the one hand, he had by
choice remained a stranger in a neighborhood where so many persons
knew each other well. On the other hand, North Beach took this stranger
in and gave him enough of a homeland to live for. He may have remained
a stranger, but he was not estranged.

There were other lives that Mario might have led, far worse for him in
fact had ethnic placement in his neighborhood not saved him. Here at
least there were people he could talk with natively and work for. Here he
was able to remain spiritually in sufficient continuity with his beloved
Sicily, in the same way so many Irish emigrants from the Potato Famine
stayed Irish and alive at a time when their homeland would have starved
them. Since time immemorial, from North Beach back to Greek colonies

surviving on the remote edges of the Mediterranean and even before Europa was conceived, first generations of migrants kept their hopes alive by living within recreated versions of an approximating homeland. So it must have been for those brave souls crossing over from Asia to the New World ten thousand years ago or so. A tenuous sense of home remained with them wherever they would wander, and so it had been for Mario.

Perhaps the ethnic solidarity of immigrant neighborhoods too strenuously contrives to relocate a place across the mountains and the sea because of the futility of doing so. The new world cannot age quickly enough to become familiarly old. Memory cannot attach itself so quickly to new spaces; it runs away, *sei fuggita e non torni più.* To the immigrant whose heart remained at home, an Italian neighborhood afforded only someplace to survive, not thrive. Nostalgia possibly became a curse and not a blessing to such a person locked within a past he would not overcome. To Mario, North Beach was not an especially good community; it was simply someplace safe for him to live, a place to reminisce. Most other places he might have moved to would not have been safe havens.

What made North Beach work better for the children playing joyously in the park and the old men sitting contentedly on their benches, chatting with each other, required some surrender to the place as theirs, some surrender of their past identity. This in turn required a commitment Mario had missed, some subtle, shifting sense of one's identity from someplace else to here and now. To see North Beach as home seemed far more characteristic of the local clientele in the Trieste, those wandering into and out of assorted local bakeries, flower stalls, the post office, talking animatedly, than it did for Mario talking haltingly with a stranger on a bench.

Yet, it seems every successful ethnic haven contains a space for Marios, since not every resident of a local neighborhood will fully participate in its democracy. Many are too passive for that, too melancholic, too limited in their ambitions, what they came for, why they fled. For those who live their lives with rigid borders, they too need a sense of place as theirs. An ethnic neighborhood can provide that comfort, if only because the language of their homeland still is spoken there and the style ordering their daily lives is more or less preserved. For this reason language and cuisine provide rudimentary habits for the heart, especially for immigrants who came to work but not to change their lives. Most economic migrants find themselves in this predicament at first, and ethnic homes away from home prove necessary for their survival and for those who would employ them. Some can move beyond that space and place; others won't and cannot. Even though Mario remained a stranger to his neighbors, he was no stranger to the neighborhood. This was his home, where he belonged, even though his heart and dreams were in the Old World.

IV

North Beach had been Italian since San Francisco first settled down to city life, after absorbing all the forty-niners. The Fior d' Italie Ristoranti was established in 1886, preceding the Dante Building and the Church of Saints Peter and Paul, erected at Washington Square in 1922. Figoni's Hardware, down the street from the Trieste, opened up for business the year after the 1906 earthquake. It still sold bocce balls in 1994, though in recent years old-fashioned brass hardware competed for space with pottery, kitchen gadgets, Cusinarts. Figoni's became something of a museum piece, precisely because it remained more old than new, with people often dropping in to reminisce instead of purchasing goods, so a salesman complained to me. Yet, Moliari's Deli on Columbus was still the place to buy excellent Amarone and genuine prosciutto. Bordi's Art Imports, across the street from Moliari's, had been selling hand-painted Tuscan pottery long before it went from kitsch to in. Even so, the neighborhood was no longer what it was.

Once upon a time Sex, Italy, and China met discretely at the intersection of Columbus and Broadway, demarcating three separate zones. But the Condor, with the famous neon bust of its celebrity stripper, was now a bistro selling espresso. Many of the porno performance places closed. And Mario's Bohemian Cigar Store Café now stood kitty corner at Washington Square across from the re-named Pagoda Theater, playing kung fu films. The Caffé Roma, the Caffé Molvina, Stella's Pastry, Rossi's Market, or La Pantera now were juxtaposed with Hoo Wah Florist, Yick San Barber, Chinese cleaners and apothecaries, not to mention assorted imitation ristorantis, the Caffé Puccini or Calzone's Pizzeria adjacent to Chinese take-out. The Ace Hardware Store down the street from Figoni's and kitty-corner from Trieste had gone Chinese.

Of course, the City Lights Beat Poets' Bookstore still existed, and I suppose Allen Ginsburg's howl could be heard at night, but the classically Italian North Beach Restaurant was somewhat out of fashion by 1994, just as there were now no-smoking tables at the Trieste. The neighborhood had been modernized and mixed. Although gentrification was gradually eroding ethnic identities entirely away, introducing a Gap and Tower Records into the equation, the North Beach neighborhood in 1994 continued to be more Italian and Chinese than anonymously middle-class, as it might become someday.

Mario never made North Beach his home, no matter how Italian it appeared. The ethnic familiarity of his new neighborhood never could compete with memories from his village life in Sicily. So, it really didn't matter much to him, I suppose, that his neighborhood slowly was becoming more Chinese and less Italian, as long as it remained sufficiently Italian to get on. Mario's vision remained focused on a particular village, not a nationality. Generic identities often prove too flimsy to build a life upon.

To those who made North Beach a real home, their vision of the community was albeit different. Yet such neighborhood changes did not seem to them to be that threatening either, judging from Chinese drinking cappuccino or Italians using chopsticks. The children playing ball in Washington Square were speaking Chinese, English, and Italian, and they mixed with one another. Witnessing their parents also interact, fetching balls that went astray, I came to appreciate the ethnic miracle of North Beach. It had become a real village to those who lived more active lives there. Sufficiently familiar spaces continued to exist to make the neighborhood still seem to be Italian, to those who wished to see it so. But now there were also places which were sufficiently Chinese to extend the welcome mat of Chinatown for those who wish to live Chinese. Combining these together gave North Beach a specifying identity that could overcome mere nostalgia and still remain familiarly Chinese or Italian when it needed to be so.

What remains so interesting and promising about North Beach circa 1994 is that very different, ethnically identified locales can be found adjacent to each other on any block within the district. It is an interethnic zone, not a case of ethnic fusion or of effacing specific ethnic identity away. Instead of ethnic rivalry, there is instead a relatively peaceful ethnic coexistence. And this mixture gives the district its own particular identity, in much the same way any village in Guangdong or Sicily would offer a localized place for residents to live. But here the local village is ethnically diversified while still remaining unified as a single neighborhood. Real places retain complex, local identities. The migrations into North Beach have made the district over into an authentic Chinese-Italian community, something that might be unthinkable in theory and fairly rare in world history.

Many older Chinese and Italian residents living, working, shopping side by side still possess so little English they cannot talk with one another. While their children may eventually become bilingual or trilingual, they start out speaking different native tongues at home. So, while walking up Filbert Street one morning, climbing sidewalk stairs up Telegraph Hill on my way to Coit Tower, two Chinese children stopped me, as they tumbled out of the apartment building where their family lived. One had his quilted jacket all buttoned wrong and he pointed at me to fix it for him, asking me to do so in Chinese. Neither could speak English. After I rebuttoned the jacket, they scampered on their way, seeing I was too foreign even to be thanked, but not too foreign to be asked for help. They felt secure enough within their neighborhood to ask a stranger for assistance, even if I couldn't speak with them. They readily accepted strangers in their midst.

When they are old enough, these same children will be learning English in the schools, even though they might continue to speak their mother tongues with relatives and some Chinese residents. They are already learning something of the customs of their neighborhood and its many visitors, just as they are picking up Italian. They are growing up within a district where the world is literally their neighborhood: Asian, European, old and modern, the English language spoken in juxtaposition with an assortment of native tongues and dialects sometimes occupying the very same apartment building. Children growing up in such a place can come to see their lives as shared with differing ethnicities. In this way personal associations multiply cross-culturally and memories are made more cosmopolitan, all the while remaining local. Perhaps a new kind of neighborhood history is being written in North Beach. Such interethnic toleration would have been unacceptable in other, older Eastern cities in the States or even in San Francisco during the days of violence and bigotry against Chinese, when Chinese migrant workers were thrown into the bay to drown.

As long as the respect remains to share a single space with other customs, other kinds of place-names, diversity can co-exist peacefully within a single neighborhood. Economic interests help fuel that respect by doing booming business among diverse local residents, along with a steady flux of tourists who have also learned to become eclectic in their tastes. Yet, there remains sufficient space and business to continue on as Italian or Chinese in North Beach, if one would prefer to. Native habits and languages are not excluded, they are included. In this way, such habits could in time be changed again and expanded even further by other generations who come to live in North Beach, as additional languages are incorporated with the arrival of new migrants and the introduction of their children into such continuing waves of changes. What appears to remain constant in this mix is a mutual respect sufficiently shared in large enough numbers for none to feel genuinely threatened by other residents whose ways of life are foreign.

V

On February 26, the Year of the Dog, 350,000 San Franciscans turned out to watch the annual Chinese New Year's Parade, broadcast live across the nation and on Hong Kong television. Fire-breathing dragons, dancers, lions, and spectacular floats passed before the reviewing stand at the corner of Kearney and Columbus. The city celebrated its Chinese heritage, as it does its Italian heritage during the Columbus Day Parade.

The San Francisco Police Department contributed a lion dance group passing in review. There were also floats from Disneyland (Pluto, naturally), China Airlines (a colossal shar pei made of flowers), and children from the Sutro School singing "It's a Dog's World After All." There were martial arts performers, stilt-walkers, giants tossing firebombs. There was even a dragon made of lavender balloons, animated by the city's Asian lesbians and gays. This was their first entry in the New Year's Day parade, made possible by a kind of local cultural diffusion, broadening the horizons of traditional Asians, just as Chinatown transformed North Beach. To old-fashioned Chinese, or Italians for that matter, it once would have been unthinkable to publicly come out as gay or lesbian. In time the influence of the Castro community made its presence felt in other districts of the city and expanded the cultural horizons and values of the Chinese community, as part of Castro Street's contribution to San Francisco's life and times. Those who once were considered strange now were welcome in the mix across very different ethnic lines. The presence of such diversity also extended San Francisco's welcome to tourists and other strangers passing through, as a place where they might visit comfortably.

In this way, by following the model of North Beach, we see how stereotypical ethnic neighborhoods can transform themselves into more welcoming local identities. Heritage and culture can be adapted to survive by acquiring added individuating histories, with a myriad of changing and expanding local loyalties. And so a patchwork quilt becomes stitched together from the most diverse of interests and backgrounds. A Chinese and Italian neighborhood comes into co-existence. And the benefits are realized across the wider community.

Ethnic harmony in North Beach is worth noticing and prizing. It could be seen as a role model for other localities too, at a time when so many places on our planet are waging civil wars, mired in the politics of place and hostile ethnic exclusivity, even engaging in ethnic cleansing (i.e., genocide). Yet, the way North Beach might serve as a role model cannot be as a source of universal generalities about the essential nature of local ethnic communities. Each locality has its own particular circumstances which resist systematic generalizations used to cover them. The particularity of circumstances cannot be abstracted away. One size more or less fits one, not all.

Consequently, one must approach the case of North Beach from a different angle, less systematically and scientifically. One can, instead, envision model communities more anecdotally, as if one were walking into a picture. By drawing out a portrait of North Beach's ethnic mix and admiring its beauty as a successful community, one is then in a position to sketch other landscapes, too, of other localities where ethnic harmony and kindness toward strangers might be welcome there as well. So, storytellers such as Garrison Keillor or novelists such as Wendell Berry create fictional places of their own invention to model landscapes of human decency as moral aides to listeners and readers. And observers of places that work well can report their observations as inspirations to us all.

The inspiration value of North Beach, like that of Lake Wobegon, Minnesota, or Port William, Kentucky, is derived from what observers can sense about these places, what they see in them, and why they so admire them. Readers of Wendell Berry or observers of North Beach form pictures in their own minds of what makes such places so appealing. Such imaginative reconstructions do not lend themselves easily to theories, since systematic abstractions have, instead, a way of covering over paintings, washing out detail. But taken by themselves these portraits of healthy communities convey a wisdom in detail that can be shared by a diversity of persons with very different points of view.

One reason why such portraits prove to be effective, appealing, and inspiring, is that those who savor them must by reason of their own lives have had sufficient experiences to recognize the beauty of communities that succeed, as well as possessing familiarity with those that fail. What makes, for example, Jan Karon's fictional Mitford so popular in her series of best sellers is that her readers eagerly want to picture Mitford's village and make themselves at home there, the way visitors actually do at North Beach's Trieste. John Berendt's nonfictional *Midnight in the Garden of Good and Evil* has similarly made Savannah, Georgia, into an appealing, quirky, familiar place—raising the number of tourists visiting Savannah by several hundred thousand. No doubt, all such persons, residents, readers, visitors, might thoughtfully disagree among themselves regarding general politics or any particular theory of community, but the popularity of such places, imaginative or real, suggests a prior, common wisdom of shared notions and assumptions concerning what makes a community good.

Prior to the possible formulation of some particular theory of community of one's own invention, most of us as human beings have a wealth of experiences with local places we have found appealing as well as with those places where we have never felt at home. Added to this wealth of experience is a set of rough-and-ready notions and assumptions about neighborliness, public parks and family-friendly places, openness, decency, kindness, and respect—notions and assumptions that we bring to bear on our own pictures of what we imagine to be an ideal community to live in. We share these visions of community with one another just as we share these same experiences. They constitute a common ground, a common grounding.

Sometimes we do this passively, as tourists or as interpreters of portraits which paint compelling pictures of communities we come to cherish, from the *Saturday Evening Post* covers of long ago to contemporary stories. These compelling landscapes can empower their own beneficial, even political effect on the lives of actual communities depicted, the way Kathleen Norris's *Dakota* did or *Prairy Erth* by William Least Heat-Moon. Those who already live in such pictured communities will feel enriched by recognition and will want to try to keep their local places alive to a continuing vision shared both by themselves and visitors. Often local historical societies then go to work to preserve, protect, and defend their place histories from erosion. As long as the resulting efforts retain the originally shared vision of the goodness present in such communities, the result is also to the good, building up such communities even further.

Sometimes we come to share a common vision of community more pro-actively, as neighborhood alliances organize around local issues or as townsfolk get together to make decisions, master plans. The consensus building and public participation in local government that results from such activities often is too messy for theoretical philosophy. Yet as distinguished a theoretician as Habermas proudly points to his own town hall meetings as a far more valuable contribution to society than his theoretical writings. Public participation is increasingly the hallmark of a working community, a grassroots democracy. As long as the effort is sustained to reach genuine consensus with a shared vision in which all voices/visions of the community are continuously hearkened to, the community can grow stronger, better, reaching toward its future by building on a sense of common ground.

In this way, North Beach in San Francisco, with its activist community groups, can prove to be a model for the kind of ethnic community which retains and respects its diverse ethnic history, while at the same time welcoming strangers in to visit and to live. And if we leave ourselves open to contemplating such landscapes of humanity, savoring their beauty without a rush to theorize, the opportunity is there to learn from local lore while remaining alive and sensitive to the ever differing diversity of persons and locales. In this way we can extend the beauty of this human landscape to our own neighborhoods and neighbors.

It is important to keep such a vision of the good community ever present before our minds. So often those who rush to systematize and abstract away from examples do not then live the lives they originally envisioned, once the landscape of a good community is replaced by systematically organized propositions, rules, regulations. Hence, in recent years in the United States communitarianism —as theorized by political scientists or legislated by community associations— turned out to be a sorry shadow of its splendid initial vision.

VI

In *Democracy in America*, Tocqueville claimed America was the most Cartesian of nations, since in the 1830s it seemed to Tocqueville to be the stalwart custom of America's citizens to form their own opinions of their own free will, to rest all judgment upon their solitary souls, thinking on their own, as Descartes himself apparently had advocated in the *sum res cogitans* of his *Meditations*. Tocqueville wryly observed that although most Americans did not know the name of the most famous French philosopher, they were Cartesian in their souls: "Every one shuts himself up in his own breast, and affects from that point to judge the world." Tocqueville's thesis proved misleading.

For one thing Descartes had played us false with his philosophy. Human beings acquire their identity more socially than hermetically, more by the experiences we share in common than the reflections which we form apart. Unlike other animals, we human beings do, of course, fashion our own identity from within, through self-reflection, thoughtful images we form within our hearts and heads depicting who we are and who we want to be, the lives we want to live. Yet these self-reflections are never born entirely out of our own consciousness, as Tocqueville apparently thought and Descartes seemed to have said. We borrow bits and pieces from those who live around us, from what we see and hear and read, from the society we live within.

These borrowed bits are typically local, in the form of socially evolving concepts and categories geographically situated. The status of such local ways of thinking can, of course, prove controversial, especially when social conventions go morally astray—hence the appeal of solipsistic Cartesianism. Should a particular society prove false or merely prejudicial, its common concepts and categories can prove all too artificial, and those who would subscribe to them can readily and inadvertently become cartoon versions of themselves, instead of becoming more richly human, varied in their interests, diverse in tastes and talents. The more homogenized and stereotypical local lives become, the more vulnerable we are to becoming hollow humans, instead of what we might have been.

Nevertheless, the concepts and categories which we live by locally, or if you will the common ground experience traverses, cannot be invented in our heads or abstracted ex nihilo. These shared recognitions and common notions are themselves dependent on specific places for their articulation and evolution. Common memories and assumptions about humanity, whatever they may be, all are probed daily by local communities, as well as privately by our own differing experiences of living where we live. Although, at any point in time, such categories and assumptions can be deeply flawed, other local concepts normally rise up to contend against

them, and so over time common sense extends itself, provided that the
society is open enough to let sufficient voices be heard and various visions
be noticed. In this way enlightenment expands and communities improve
themselves.

Eras of slavery, racism, or misogyny often had more to do with philosophical theories about humanity than the collective experiences of hu-
mankind. Had Africans been themselves consulted, they would not have
been enslaved. Had women's voices been acknowledged, women would,
from the beginning, have had the right to own property and vote. Historically, common sense notions of fairness and human decency eventually
rise up to counter-attack the latest theory supporting some particular bigotry. The well of social reform typically draws from the bottom up, not
from the top down, starting with one community at a time, beginning
with Rosa Parks getting on a bus, for instance.

Of course, oppressive concepts often are themselves embraced by those
whom they oppress. But other notions and shared assumptions floating
through local communities work against oppression, provided that such
concepts and categories are not forcibly imposed by some upon the many.
Perhaps shared common sense provides a guide good enough for a society
to get on locally and even grow, if it is a participatory society sufficiently
governed by consensus in matters which matter deeply.

It would not be especially productive to attempt some general thesis
regarding the local power of the common good and the situated virtues
of public participation. It is more revealing to appeal to actual instances
—case studies of public participation and consensus building, examples
which model and even shape common notions and assumptions regarding
a good community. So, let me conclude this essay with another portrait
of a place in California: in this case, Mammoth Lakes.

VII

In the state of California, as with many other states, cities govern themselves for long-term planning with the use of general plans. These plans
serve as blueprints for the city's future and are used, for instance, to prior-
itize construction projects and zoning regulations into the next decade
and beyond. Re-visiting and revising the general plan is regularly required. Such exercises can be highly controversial, especially since general
plans carry considerable legal authority. The greater the consensus
around a general plan, the better it is for the particular community, since
constructing the general plan affords an opportunity for a common voice
about the evolution of the town, allowing both its citizens and outside

developers, for example, to have a clear sense of how the community sees itself.

Mammoth Lakes in Mono County, California, is a small town on the eastside of the Sierra Nevada, adjacent to the Ansel Adams Wilderness and Devil's Postpile National Monument. It is also quite well known in southern California, where more than twenty million people live, for superb skiing and splendid opportunities for mountain recreation. Recently, Mammoth Lakes was in the process of revising its general plan. And it appeared the process would prove painful, since village life in Mammoth Lakes was torn between developers and environmentalists, ski enthusiasts and hikers, local residents and migrant workers, the actively employed and the retired, among so many factions. In particular there were disputes about building another ski resort, providing affordable housing for service employees, whether to expand the local airport, in addition to hard-fought issues involving water, sewage, fire protection, and the development of a community college.

Instead of listening only to a privileged few, Mammoth made a strenuous effort to forge a genuine consensus around its general plan, by contacting all interested parties the city's officers could think of, as well as advertising general meetings in which anyone could speak to voice concerns. There also was a continuous feedback from meeting to meeting, designed with a view toward finally presenting the revision of its general plan to the Mammoth Lakes city council as the product of consensus. The entire process was far reaching and quite complex, more than I can delve into here. Rather, I wish to focus only on one particular, initial meeting when competing interests first came together.

The room was filled with representatives of different interest groups, including some who regarded one another as enemies. The gathering was truly representative of the factions facing Mammoth Lakes. As the meeting started, after everyone introduced themselves and the general process was discussed along with the day's agenda, an assignment was handed out by the facilitator. Each person in the room was asked to draw a picture of what an ideal Mammoth Lakes would look like in ten years. They were pointedly requested to draw a picture or a sketch without employing words. Once the drawings all were finished, the pictures were then displayed upon a wall for all to see. Each participant was then invited to explain his or her own vision of Mammoth's future in the sketch that he or she had drawn.

This is hardly an exercise one might expect from traditional philosophers, who would typically prefer a statement of initial principles and proceed from there to deduce an appropriate city plan, or else proceed with such principles implicitly in mind, in the way Plato wrote out his *Republic* or his *Laws*. The specific exclusion of employing language in producing sketches of community visions side-stepped traditions of philosophy and ideology, blocking the use of slogans, the language of allegiance to a cause, the words of argument, competition, confrontation. But it did not leave the participants entirely speechless, since each would present an interpretation later.

Nevertheless, once the pictures of "Mammoth Lakes ten years from now" were initially displayed, they exhibited surprising similarities with one another. The disparity depicted among them was so much narrower than the differences those who went to the meeting would have expected to see. Indeed, there appeared to be a proximately similar vision of Mammoth's future. Furthermore, the use of pictures was humbling to everyone present, who were as a group generally more facile with words and arguments. The gathered audience consequently came to see each other more as fellow human beings than as representatives of interest groups alone.

When each individual came to explain the drawing he or she had made, the explanations too seemed astonishingly in line with one another. Although many differences were visibly expressed and explained, the range of differences seemed manageable. The prospect of developing a general plan seemed possible. As the day progressed, the atmosphere changed. Once all the pictures had been displayed, explained, and discussed by those with questions, the time was ripe to proceed with the next stage of the process of consensus building, which would continue on for several months.

As a witness to the process, I came to notice how those local residents from the greater Mammoth region clearly had more in common than they realized about themselves. Mammoth Lakes was precious to every one of them, and they began to appreciate this fact about each other. As each described their vision of Mammoth's future, they spoke in general notions which they soon found they shared, common assumptions about public places, safety, fairness, decency, respect for persons and the environment. Whatever specific differences they had with one another—and there were many—what was more compelling was the ground they found in common.

Residents of Mammoth Lakes had gathered, expecting to be embroiled in interest group antagonisms. Instead they were directed to visualize what they had in common, to witness the ingredients of a common vision which they shared about the town. Once the picture of their future city became central to them, rather than the competitive ideologies of words in conflict, the way was opened to resolution of differences and the creation of a general plan. The process as it continued was by no means simple or free from antagonism. But the point is rather this: the day to day notions and assumptions of local people characteristically yield commonplaces about what it takes to be a good community, a decent, healthy, just, and friendly place for people to work and live in, where strangers will be welcome. Once these notions become sufficiently focused, as if one were walking into a portrait of a cherished homeland, such commonplaces can lead to a common sense of place and a true community.

VIII

By limiting our philosophical ambitions, we are able to appreciate how members of a neighborhood, a village, a community might come to see and prize this homeland, even though the community itself might appear unstable to theorists of race, ethnicity, or urban conflict. We come to appreciate how a sense of place can be largely visual, a pictured landscape where residents can recognize their home within the scene and learn to be tolerant of each other's differences, just as visitors to that village or neighborhood can derive a sense of moral comfort there. The common notions and assumptions which enclose this landscape and its locally shared sense of a common place prove stable and morally reliable, once a commonplace consensus can be formed around such shared assumptions, in the service of community.

The Cicero quotation that prefaces this paper is translated "we call these arguments which can be transferred to many cases commonplaces." This statement reflects the ancient origins of logic and its attempt to rationalize rhetoric, in particular as it applies to the legal adjudication of different cases. The sentiment expressed suggests that there are standard arguments, common situations, a host of common experiences which carry over from case to case so as to be persuasive to a thinker, listener, or juror. This metaphor of commonplaces was also carried over from ancient rhetoric to literature, to label the *loci communes* of experience with which we ground familiarity from topic to topic. Relying on such 'places', authors write and readers read.

Perhaps the force of the originating metaphor suggests those familiar local places and public spaces which serve to locate persons' lives within a wider, shared, social existence. It is part of the argument of this essay that in traversing common ground in one particular community we can become equipped with common notions and common values with which to ground a moveable conception of community, in much the same way Cicero invoked the use of commonplaces as a transferable device of common sense.

What makes this ancient rhetorical claim and geographical metaphor so controversial is a prevailing cynicism that just as common sense is culture bound, so too the notion of a good community can be highly prejudicial locally. It was, of course, also an ancient sardonic observation of Pyrrhonism that common sense is the one quality no one thinks he lacks. The irony was not lost upon Montaigne, who recited this ancient adage in his essay "On Presumption." It was, in turn, famously plagiarized and memorialized by Descartes in his *Discourse on Method*. People are forever presuming their particular point of view is widely shared, just as they presume local customs are universal. So, modern cynics ask, what wisdom can be found in local commonplace consensus?

Here I have tried to suggest that notwithstanding local presumptions and prejudice, common sense is sufficiently aligned with shared experience to be at least locally reliable. Even a skeptic such as Sextus could insist persuasively that there are sufficiently shared notions and ordinary presumptions to enable even skeptics to get on with living, without being taken in by dogma. Indeed, it seems as if traversing common ground is requisite for mutual understanding, even if such commonplaces are locally derived. A community of commonplaces is fundamental for communication. So like Cicero before him, Montaigne can say in his final essay "On Experience" that "the most ordinary things, the most commonplace and best-known" can convey an almost miraculous wisdom.

Can a Sense of Place
Be Preserved?

David Wasserman, Mick Womersley, and Sara Gottlieb

This paper explores some of the tensions in attempting to preserve a sense of place in the contemporary United States. It considers the case of Calvert County, Maryland, a largely rural region on the edge of the Chesapeake Bay and of Washington, D.C.'s expanding suburban frontier. It examines the extent to which the natural features of the bay, celebrated by generations of writers, shape the personal and social identities of those who live along it and the extent to which a sense of place depends upon the interaction of the residents with those natural features.

There is now an extensive literature on the significance of place as a dimension of human experience. Much of this literature explores the loss of traditional communities and the attenuation of ties to the particular and the local. Such changes have been attributed to various aspects of contemporary life, from increased mobility to architectural standardization;[1] there is a lively debate about how pervasive the changes have been, and why, or whether, they should be regretted.[2] There is also a growing literature on the importance of place in environmental ethics and policy, as a basis for grounding preservation in the lives of local communities and overcoming the dichotomy between nature and human activity.[3] We hope to make a modest contribution at the intersection of these two literatures by examining the changing relationship of nature and place on the suburban frontier.

In traditional societies, the physical features of a landscape largely determined the livelihoods of its inhabitants. The role of geography in the lives of farmers, millers, miners, and watermen was pervasive (and sometimes oppressive). Of course, economic activity often despoiled natural settings, but it also strengthened people's attachments to them. This irony is nicely illustrated by the recent history of the Chesapeake Bay. While commercial fishing and coastal farming caused severe ecological damage to the bay, they also kept people in close contact with the sea and land.

With the gradual but relentless decline of these activities, the bay has lost much of its importance as an ecosystem in, along, or through which people wrest their living from nature. Although recreational uses of the bay, like sport boating, flourish, they provide a livelihood for a much smaller segment of the population than fishing and farming once did, and involve less intimate contact with the bay's natural features. A sense of place may be harder to acquire for the rapidly growing proportion of Chesapeake residents who are commuters, spending most of their waking hours in places that have nothing to do with the bay.

In the past generation, there has been a concerted effort to save the bay both as a significant economic resource and as a place of great natural beauty. But measures designed to preserve the bay for economic, aesthetic, or spiritual reasons will not always enhance—and may sometimes threaten—the sense of place of those who live around it. Zoning and environmental protection measures, for example, may restrict the independence of watermen and farmers, even as they attempt to preserve the material conditions of their livelihoods. At the same time, self-conscious efforts to preserve culture as well as nature may often be self-defeating, turning once vibrant and eclectic communities into outdoor museums. The very attempt to save rural communities may contribute to their cultural annexation to the suburbs and their disappearance as independent places.

At Home in Calvert County

We selected Calvert County for a study of these issues because of its strong historical orientation towards the bay, and because it has already made a concerted effort to control and channel development. Most of the county is a peninsula, bordered by the main stem of the Chesapeake and the mouth of the Patuxent River, but reachable from downtown D.C., Baltimore, or Annapolis in less than an hour.

Not surprisingly, Calvert County has shown rapid growth in population over the past two decades, most of it consisting of homeowners who work elsewhere.[4] To examine how the growth of the county is affecting the place attachments of its residents, we conducted four focus groups with different segments of the population: recent arrivals, old-time white residents, African-American residents, and watermen.

We chose the focus group as our method of inquiry because it allows a single topic to be explored in depth by a small group of people with similar interests and backgrounds. It relies on the dynamics of group deliberation to yield a great deal of information in a brief time. Unlike a survey, it allows the researcher to see how people frame and talk about an issue, yielding insight into the structure of their beliefs and values.

Group 1: Newcomers

Our first group consisted of new residents in the middle-to-upper income range, the fastest-growing group in Calvert County and the vanguard of suburbanization. Members of the group displayed an enthusiasm for the natural and rural character of the county. Most of them had clearly been drawn to the region by its rural character, and by its coastline. But their appreciation of its natural and social attributes was not very specific:

> #14: You move down here because the people are nice. . . . Everyone seems to have a different attitude down here. You know, like you're on vacation all the time.

> #15: The first time I came to Calvert County . . . I was stunned, you can hardly see anything from Route 4. I mean you have these nice berms on the side of the road, you have trees. It's like driving through the Great Smoky Mountains National Park on the horizontal sections.

> #1: It just seemed more rural. It just seemed more country. . . . I think what I really love is the animals. All the different wildlife that is here in Calvert County, you know, I feel in touch with the animals here . . . they're just abundant. It's like living in a wildlife preserve but being so close to Washington. . . . You are really totally in touch with nature if you choose to be.

Other research has suggested that a strong attachment to or identification with a place does not require extended residence. In a survey of recent migrants to Cape Cod, authors Cuba and Hummon found that "fully 95% . . . reported that they felt 'at home' on the Cape, suggesting that some minimal level of place identification is achieved by these migrants."[5] But unlike the newcomers to Cape Cod, where much of the commuting may be internal, more than half of the participants in this Calvert County focus group commuted to jobs elsewhere, mainly in Washington, D.C.

For all their appreciation of the county's rural character, many participants in the first focus group also confessed to a sense of isolation. A combination of limited time and physical separation in subdivisions with multiple-acre zoning appears to contribute to this isolation and to limit the newcomers' active involvement in both the natural and social environments.[6]

For example, one focus group member responded impatiently to a question about the decline of the Chesapeake oyster beds: "What's an oyster got to do with where you live?" The group's one lifetime resident (the spouse of a newcomer) suggested that this comment reflected a broad ignorance on the part of the newcomers about a whole way of life:

> #4: I think #10's comment is probably more common, at least in my discussion with new people that have moved into the county. They weren't raised with the culture of oysters and mussels and crabs. When I was a kid we walked out and picked up oysters and mussels . . . and these people aren't used to doing that. They don't even think about it.

The same lack of connection to the life of the bay is reflected in the comments of other newcomers: the one who regards life in Calvert County as "a permanent vacation"; the one who describes his backyard as "a wildlife preserve"—a place where visitors are supposed to observe the fauna without interacting with them.

Can "the culture of oysters and mussels and crabs" be imparted to, and preserved by, the newcomers before their influx overwhelms it? Their migration, and the development accompanying it, have already made parts of the county seem less like home to its older residents. As the old-time resident described her own experience:

> #4: It's changed over the years. I used to be home just about the time I hit Forrestville. And then I was home by the time I hit Marlboro, and then I was definitely home when I hit Lyons Creek, which is where 260 branches off Route 4. Now I guess I'm home when I hit 260. I do not feel at home on Route 4, especially in rush-hour traffic. . . . So now I'm not home till I'm close to Owings, and I guess one of these days I won't be home till I get to Camp Roosevelt.

Group 2: Old-Time White Residents

The old-time white residents in our second focus group, each with more than 40 years in the county, had a deep sense of rootedness, shared memories of a tight-knit community, and very direct and personal connections to the land and water around them. Several members of the group had long family histories in the county, some dating back to the original white settlers. But even those who had moved into the county had a considerable investment in its past and future. One relative newcomer recalled that her father had built the county's first paved roads. Most—whether they were teachers, farmers, or administrators—worked in the county or had done so before they retired. They all considered Calvert County "home."

A striking moment occurred before the taping of this group session began, when the participants first arrived. Every person in the room knew every other one, and many of them also knew one another's family histories. (Recruitment of the group members was as random as possible, given that natives at present make up only about 4 percent of the county's population.) In contrast, the members of the first group were all strangers, except for two women who were in an organization together. Throughout this focus group session, participants completed each other's sentences and nodded vigorously in agreement when they listened to a story about what the county used to be like. Members of the group rarely disagreed about the issues under discussion.

In the histories of the old-time residents of the county, family names were obviously important. The women in the group were referred to by their maiden names on several occasions. Many of the participants remembered a time when they knew where someone in the county lived just by hearing his or her name. All white children in the county went to the same high school a generation ago, and, as one man pointed out, the teachers used to know the families of every child in their classes. The schools clearly were the heart of the community; three of the female participants had been teachers, several other participants had family members involved in the school system, and all of the younger participants ascribed great importance to the social interactions they had had while in high school.

The sense of place of these old-time residents has not always extended to the county as a whole. Members of the focus group recalled having once had far more localized attachments. One participant noted that "if you lived on the water, you were okay, but if you didn't live on the water, you were in the forest." It was also important at one time whether one's family lived on the bay side or the river side. People living in some parts of the county did not get along with people from other parts. Those from the southern end (from Prince Frederick to Solomons) regarded their part of the county as far more isolated than the northern end and found that people who lived north of Prince Frederick rarely ventured south of the county seat.

The geography of Calvert County pervaded the early lives of the members of this group. Several of the participants had been raised on farms and looked back fondly on what they admitted was a harsh way of life. Several had learned to swim in the bay or the river, and many had been involved in the culture of the water. The bay had been vital for transportation before the major roads were built: Children once traveled to school by means of a "school boat," and administrators visited the various schools by boat. Also, several members of the group had first arrived in the county by steamer.

The old-time residents regarded themselves as having lived in "the golden age" of Calvert County, but saw that age as coming to an end. The rapid influx of people to the county affected everyone; group members complained that they no longer knew most of the people they saw in church or in the store. One woman went so far as to say that she would never give strangers directions to the county, for fear they might decide to move in.

Participants recalled a process of acculturation that is breaking down in the face of rapidly increasing migration. Newcomers were always welcomed—about half the group had been newcomers once—but they usually came as the spouses or relatives of county natives, and they quickly adapted to the rhythms and pace of rural life. The recent arrivals live in insular enclaves and demand wholesale changes, making little attempt to understand or appreciate the communities they have entered. The session ended on a positive note, however, as some of the older participants recalled that their parents had faced what seemed to them to be insurmountable challenges, and that children of every generation come to terms with the world around them in their own way.

Group 3: African-American Residents

The African-American focus group had a perspective on Calvert County quite distinct from those of the preceding two groups. Its members brought almost every question about the physical setting back to the struggles of race. For example, when the moderator asked about "hardships associated with living that close to the water," a county native "remember[ed] hurricanes," but a 39-year resident quickly shifted the subject to "another thing that sort of pains me about the water as it relates to black progress, or lack of progress," and went on to describe the tribulations of a black developer stymied by racially motivated overregulation. The one account of growing up in a special place came from a woman whose family had managed an historic house, giving them elevated status and responsibility in a poor community. But her reminiscences about their role as "overseers" culminated in uneasy thoughts about playing the role of intermediary between the anxious white and restive black communities.

While all the older residents had personal experiences of segregation in the county, and almost all members of the group voiced some skepticism about racial progress there, none expressed resentment or anger toward the county or a desire to live elsewhere because of its racial history. In part, the moderator observed, this was because "they doubted whether any other part of the country would be more hospitable." There was also a general appreciation of the fact that Calvert County did not (yet) have the problems of crime and drugs that burdened African-Americans in the nearby inner cities and suburbs.

The oldest member of the focus group, who fought to borrow books from a segregated library and buy bus tickets at the same place as whites, expressed the deepest attachment to the county. At the same time, no one in the group waxed nostalgic about the old days; no one talked, as had several members of the second group, of "the golden age" of Calvert County. Finally, the members of this group had less experience with, and less apparent attachment to, the water surrounding Calvert County than did the old-time white residents in the second group.

The moderator suggested that the group's relative lack of interest in the concept of place reflected the oppressive priority of racial issues in their lives: "They talked about limited financial resources because of past salary inequities, limited scholarship opportunities because of prejudice and stereotyping that endures in the county's school system, and even limited recreational opportunities that haunted their past as children wanting to play on the beach. In earlier years, whites feared that black children would 'contaminate' the water. Perhaps as a result, today members of this group mentioned few pastimes linked directly to the water."

There was more prodevelopment sentiment in the third group than in either of the others, but also, underlying and related to the preoccupation with race, a great deal of ambivalence about development and preservation. On the one hand, a 39-year resident wanted a "nice indoor shopping mall like they have in Annapolis . . . and in Waldorf" and suggested that there was money to be made buying up land along the highways as the county population continues to grow. A 14-year resident who welcomed the arrival of shopping centers wished for "more industry here and the opportunity for a career." Yet that same resident recognized that the commercial development he welcomed had made the main highway more congested, and he declared that "the main thing I like about Calvert County is that it's still relatively rural." An older resident described herself as "one of the people that want to keep Calvert country"; another thought things had gotten worse because of overcrowding. These sentiments would have been right at home in the second group, of white old-time residents.

In conclusion, the experience of segregation, which had deeply touched the lives of all the older African-American residents, did not appear either to have estranged them from the county nor to have deepened their attachment through their struggle with adversity. Rather, the preoccupation with race shared by old and new residents appeared to make a sense of place less important or central to their lives. Most of them liked the rural character of the county, but, except for two of the older residents, they liked it in almost as generic a way as the new arrivals did in the first group. Their lives had more to do with race than place, and this limited their attachment to, and identification with, the county. Some appeared willing to sacrifice the rural character they appreciated for economic opportunity, which was a greater concern for them than for the members of the other two groups.

Group 4: Watermen

This group, composed of watermen born or living in Calvert or St. Mary's County, was the smallest of the four: Only ten watermen signed up, and only four actually appeared. But it was a very passionate and thoughtful group. All the participants had once been full-time commercial fishermen; two no longer were. All of them saw their way of life as dying—"[W]e're going the way of the whaling fleets of North America." Each had made adaptations to changing conditions, about which they expressed strong but complex attitudes.

On the one hand, they were resigned to change, and seemed tolerant, if not approving, of the influx of people to the coast. Acknowledging that tourism would be the "coming thing here, more so all the time," one waterman explained, "Lookit . . . we can't deny people access to the Chesapeake Bay. People love it just like I am." At the same time, perhaps because there was so little they thought they could—or should—do about it, the watermen expressed sharp resentment toward the agents of change, particularly wealthy professionals who bought up their land and transformed their communities:

> They buy the property, they go the price and buy the property, and the next thing you know—and don't take my word, walk down to Solomons and you'll see about two blocks of nothing but solid junk shops. When he don't make a livin' he gets out and sells and goes. See, that is the difference in the people we're gettin' in Solomons. . . . And eventually, it won't be no, what we'd call a real watertown. Because, we don't go down the road, er, we don't meet no watermen, we don't meet no crabbers, the only thing you see is a charter boat loading up, he's goin' in the bay for fishin'. Well . . . , you don't have too much to do with that.

But they did have an increasing amount "to do with that"—all of them derived some income from tourists. One built a skipjack—the traditional Chesapeake sailing vessel used to dredge oysters—for education and tourism. He took schoolchildren out on the bay to show them a vanishing way of life, and ran a charter boat operation as well. Another worked part-time at a maritime museum he had helped establish. Even the remaining two occasionally crewed on charter boats for fishing and tours.

These accommodations did not make the watermen any fonder of tourists and migrants. The skipjack operator heaped aspersions on the young professionals who complained when the shoreline became cluttered with netting and crabpots, and when their sleep was disturbed by the outboard motors of commercial fishermen heading out in the predawn hours. Another man referred to the masts of the fiberglass sailboats filling the harbors as "yuppie poles."

Despite this disdain for newcomers, these men still seemed committed to a live-and-let-live philosophy that opposed restrictions on where people could travel, move, work, and build. That philosophy may have been well adapted to an open-access fishery of historically immense productivity. But it has left the watermen largely defenseless against the forces of development: if they "can't deny people access" to the bay, they also may not be able to deny them the "right" to do as they wish with their property and thus to control development.

One man (the quietest member of the group) was the first to give us a hint of this constraint. When pushed by the moderator to state "one wish for the Chesapeake Bay," his prescription to restore the fishery, he thought he knew what had to be done, but could not quite bring himself to say it—to advocate restrictions on *people*:

#1: Ah, er, I don't know what to tell you . . . I'm the kind of feller, kinda like t'be fair t'everybody . . . and what I think about sayin' wouldn't be fair . . . [long pause]

Moderator: Ah. OK. . . . How about if we take people out of it and look just at the water? What would you do to make it a difference in the water?

#1: Well, there's people related in there too . . .

There is an admirable underlying consistency in the watermen's fierce independence and their reluctance to call for government intervention against others. In describing what he valued most about his work, one waterman declared, "You have nobody there with a hatchet over your head, telling you when you've got to do this, when you've got to do that. . . ." Now, he complained, "It's getting to where there's going to be a hatchet over our head." As another elaborated, "Things are getting tighter all the time, ah, rules and regulations." These watermen were reluctant to wield against others the "hatchet" of government regulation they see hanging over their own heads. Freedom for oneself implies a reciprocal freedom for others.

This vernacular libertarianism is reinforced by a strong fatalism that sees both the decline of the fisheries and the spread of development as inexorable. One waterman remarked that development is "just a big steamroller and it's just like a big shark. . . . [I]t's got a big mouth on it and it just keeps eatin' up anybody in its way. And there's a lot of stuff you can't do nothin' about." Interfering with the influx of tourists and migrants would not only be unfair, then, but futile as well.

Yet the watermen *were* vociferous about pollution, which they saw as the main threat to the fishery. It was the one threat against which they seemed willing to permit regulation:

> It's not that the ravenous gluttonous watermen has over-fished this. . . . The people, as they've done everywhere's else in this world, they've polluted our rivers and our streams and our oceans as to where they won't, they won't produce.

The watermen in our group clearly recognized the connection between development and pollution: "we've got too many people living around the Chesapeake. . . . they're the main problem." Interestingly, however, they did not seize on that connection to justify restrictions on development, even when the moderator invited them to do so.

For these men, the pollution of the bay was making an already difficult livelihood unsustainable. None of them saw their children earning a living as they had. The skipjack-owner emphasized the irreversible depletion of the fishery and the increasing difficulty of earning a living from it: "We haven't any good facets for our kids to try to get them to go into." Another member of the group emphasized the hardships of their way of life, and his desire to spare his children its rigors:

> They may stay here, but they won't do what we do. It's too hard of work. We're not raising them to work like we are. We're trying to get them to go to college, so they don't have to break their backs and their arms and wear their bodies out. When they get old enough to retire they can enjoy it. When we're old enough to retire, most of us are going to be history.

Yet this was said with as much regret as relief.

Emerging Themes

Two broad themes about place have emerged from our focus groups. The first concerns the plasticity of place attachment: its shifting focus and geographical scope; its expansion and amplification in response to social change and external pressure. The second concerns the future of place attachment: the diminishing role of interaction with nature in the contemporary sense of place; the difficulty—or contradiction—in preserving a sense of place rooted in nature by strategies used to preserve the natural environment.

1. The Changing Character of Place Attachment

The writers who introduced the notions of "place" and a "sense of place" into common academic parlance regarded the transformation of space into place as a product of sustained human interaction with the physical features of an environment, an interaction that endowed those features with a singularity and emotional significance that Cartesian geography could not capture.[7] Because place attachment reflects a history of human interaction, it is shaped by the changing understanding people have of that interaction, and it is subject to retrospective revision in ways that are not always obvious to those who experience it.[8] It is also political, in that it inevitably highlights or "privileges" the remembered histories of some people and groups, although not always those of the social and economic elites.[9] These aspects of place attachment are illustrated by several findings from our focus groups.

Sense of Place as Retrospective

The discussions of the old-time white residents suggest that place identification was far more localized when they were children: There was Solomons, Broomes, and Chesapeake Beach, or at most north/up-county and south/down-county. Back when Calvert County encompassed most of their social universe, it was not nearly as much of a locus for explicit identification and attachment. Now, as their own cosmopolitanism has increased and the outside world encroaches on Calvert County, it has become more of a distinct place.

Ironically, though, as development has shrunk the area they call home, it may also have broadened the area with which the residents identify. Calvert County as a place is appreciated largely in retrospect, as the specter of suburbanization highlights the commonalities among what once seemed like very distinct parts of the county. It seems that place attachment often becomes self-conscious and expansive at times when the character of the place is in jeopardy. This suggests the role of external challenges in shaping a sense of place.

Place Attachment as Oppositional

Among both the old-time white residents and watermen, the attachment to place appeared to become sharper in response to the influx of

newcomers. That influx had overwhelmed the locals' capacity for incul-
cating local culture, making them strangers in their own land. This threat
led them to emphasize, and exaggerate, the extent of the social cohesion
that existed when they were growing up.

The oppositional quality of place attachment is reflected in the carica-
ture of newcomers that prevailed in both groups. The recent migrants
were seen by local gentry and watermen alike as lacking any appreciation
of the values and sensibilities that group members attributed to themselves, and as corrupting the simplicity of small-town life and the beauty
of the landscape with their insatiable demands for suburban amenities.
From listening to these groups, one would never have suspected the enthusiasm, however indiscriminate, that the newcomers had for the rural
character of the county, nor the consistency with which they voiced support for measures to limit growth and preserve that rural character.

This tendency to define oneself and one's place in opposition to outsiders is nicely described by Charles Jedrej and Mark Nuttall in *White Set-*
tlers, a study of the impact of recent migration on rural Scotland:

> The ambiguous figure of the stranger is not only perceived as a generalized
> threat according to indigenous utterances and texts, but also makes possible
> precisely the articulation of what is threatened, tradition and community.
> The relationship between the ideas of local and outsider enters into the very
> heart of people's feelings about themselves and their historical identities.[10]

It would be hard to find a better illustration of this than the before/after
picture of Solomons painted by the senior member of the watermen's
group, in which the heart of a thrifty, hardworking, "real" watertown is
reduced to "two blocks of nothing but solid junk shops."

Whose Sense of Place?

The old-time white residents of Calvert County regarded themselves as
having grown up in a "golden age." Yet the age in which they were growing up—the 1930s through the 1960s—was a time of racial segregation,
agricultural decline, and an economy propped up by a twenty-year regime
of legalized casino gambling. The old-timers do qualify their expressions
of nostalgia with the acknowledgment that agricultural life was hard and
isolated, but they display a striking naivete about race—oh yes, we had
segregated schools back then, but we corrected that problem in neighborly Calvert County style and even left a large surplus in the school
integration fund. There was no expression of embarrassment at their nostalgia for a segregated past, and no sense that race continued to divide the
county.

The contrast with the African-American group is stark. No one in that group regarded herself as having lived in the "golden age" of Calvert County, even if several thought that things had gotten worse since their childhood. The integration of the schools was not a footnote, but a watershed event in the lives of the older African-American residents.

The sense of place which appears to dominate preservation efforts in Calvert County is that of the dominant social groups. (In much the same way, upper-class places, events, and memories often hold sway in urban restoration—a predominance that has only recently been challenged, most notably by Dolores Hayden.[11]) Given the nature of place identity in rural communities, where the continued ownership of a homestead integrates family and geography, this class bias is hardly surprising. As Barbara Allen observes of south central Kentucky:

> [A] sense of place is inseparable from a sense of the network of relations, past and present, that bind people in a neighborhood together. They read the landscape as a historical record in which people are related both to each other and to the land itself through their homeplaces. . . . [But] because only *owners'* names are given to places, the people who do not own the land they live on are automatically excluded from the genealogical landscape.[12]

It is in this context that the female members of the second group were referred to by their maiden names—those names linked them to specific landholdings in the county, and to a network of social relations among the landowning population.

Yet the local gentry do not have a monopoly on the past. The historical vision of the watermen, equally romanticized in its own way, has had a powerful impact on public thinking about the past and future of the Chesapeake Bay. Although watermen have always been a small numerical minority in Calvert County and other Chesapeake communities, their work maintains the link between those communities and the surrounding waters that is integral to the sense of place of most older residents, whatever their own livelihoods.

A Sense of Place in the Built Environment

Schools played an important role in the recollections of all groups but the watermen's, and education was a unifying theme. Several of the local gentry and at least two of the African-Americans had been schoolteachers. The attachment to particular schools was also very strong. The process of integration had a bittersweet quality for blacks as well as whites, because it often involved the loss of valued places. By the same token, perhaps the most triumphant moment in the struggle of African-American residents to integrate the Calvert County schools came when the county school board chose what had been the black high school as the high school for the entire integrated school system.

It is very likely that the children of the newcomers will form the kind of strong attachments to their schools felt by long-term residents. And if a sense of place can attach to such generic structures as public schools, it can also attach to libraries, stores, subdivisions, and even shopping malls. As residents shop and fraternize, they give these very generic places a patina of personal and social history. As Jedrej and Nuttall note, "even separated from place-based communities, there persists a human need to impose meaning on new places, to nurture a sense of identity and feeling of belonging as an antidote to the possibility of individual estrangement and despair."[13]

The next generation of county residents may well encounter a built environment more conducive to place attachment than the suburban sprawl of nearby areas. County planners are strongly committed to the creation and expansion of *public* town centers to accommodate the new migrants—areas of concentrated population and diverse uses, with the human scale, pedestrian orientation, and, it is hoped, the intimacy of small towns.[14] But the place attachments the new residents form may still be very different—less rich, intense, and fulfilling—than those of the county's older residents. This is the prospect to which we now turn.

2. The Future of Place

There are interesting parallels in the vicissitudes of "place" and those of "community." Since the publication of *Gesellschaft und Gemeinschaft* in 1887,[15] scholars have been announcing the death of community and consigning the citizens of modern society to isolated, fragmented, socially impoverished lives. In the past generation, though, there has been a recognition that news of the death of community was premature, and that communal life continues to flourish, albeit in different forms. In particular, scholars have noted the detachment of community from place, and the replacement of locality by shared interests and experiences as organizing principles.

A similar shift may be occurring in the scholarship of place. Since 1976, when Edward Relph announced the "death of place" and raised the grim specter of "placelessness," there has been a small but growing literature on the adaptability of place attachment in the face of residential mobility and cultural homogenization. But just as the forms of community that flourish a century after *Gesellschaft und Gemeinschaft* are quite different from those of past eras, the character and quality of place attachment may also be changing.

Our research has suggested one significant change: the diminishing importance of the particular, idiosyncratic natural features of a region for its residents' attachments. As we noted earlier, the sense of place experienced by residents of scenic and relatively undeveloped areas like Calvert County is attenuated by the loss of any connection between their livelihoods and the area's natural features.[16] This attenuation is apparent in the contrast between the very generic and passive appreciation of the landscape expressed by the newcomers, and the vivid, detailed narratives of encounters with nature provided by the watermen. These men have all had a rich, personal involvement with the bay and the shoreside environment from a very early age. They are proud of that relationship, and it is the source of their fondest memories:

[T]o be able to go out of the Catholic Church, Potomac Side, catch these little tailor blues, right after, it was kind of a ritual, after we would start school in September. When we get home, we'd have this old canoe with about seven and a half Palmer engine in it, we'd go out catch, catch those snapper blues. Little ones, about like that, you know. S'a big deal. And the water'd be so clear you could see all the way across St. George's Creek in the fall of the year.[17]

Even if the new migrants to Calvert County and their children develop strong attachments to their communities, they are unlikely to forge such intimate bonds with the natural landscape. They will surely acquire a stronger, more particularized sense of place than they now evince. But it is unlikely to be centered on the nooks and crannies of the bay, or on the sight, smell, and feel of freshly caught fish. A focus group of the newcomers' children in twenty years would probably reveal a strong attachment to the county's schools and town centers, some enthusiasm for its recreational facilities and open space, a bookish appreciation of its maritime history and lore, but little trace of the "culture of oysters and mussels and crabs" described by the old-timer in the first group.

This is not to say that nature will not matter to the next generation of Calvert County residents. They may pay an increasing premium for access to the water, and they may eagerly support measures to preserve the natural features of the county. But their love of nature is likely to be Platonic, in both senses of the word: They will value nature as an abstraction, not in its idiosyncratic detail, and they will value it largely as observers, not as partners (or adversaries). For most of them, nature will be green space and wetland, not the little snapper blues in the clear fall water of St. Georges Creek.

Those fortunate enough to live in close proximity to water or woods may acquire a more particularized attachment to the land- or seascape around them. A couple who designed their weekend cabin on a tributary of the Patuxent River to wrap around a 100-year-old live oak declared that "we have a relationship with every tree here."[18] But people with the opportunity to form such attachments are likely to be a small minority of new residents, and those attachments will often fade as their lives take them out of regular contact with their natural surroundings.

The absence of regular contact with nature may leave most new residents with a sense of place that is less rich, visceral, and enduring than that of the older residents. But it may also foster an attitude towards nature that is poorly suited to the maintenance of a rural landscape shaped by centuries of human habitation. The newcomers who see nature as a "wildlife preserve" display the kind of respectful, hands-off attitude for which the preservationist movement is often criticized. At best, this attitude will lend support to the preservation of lands that would otherwise have been paved over, but not in a form that will encourage or permit their regular use for hunting, fishing, or trysting. At worst, it will degenerate into an appreciation of nature as a valuable amenity, with wetlands regulation serving to "preserve" property values in much the same way that three-acre zoning does. Such a proprietary attitude toward the landscape has been observed by one critic of gentrification in rural Vermont: "They treat the land like any other possession, object, they own, set it aside, watch it, passively . . . thinking it abhorrent to engage in a living relationship with it."[19]

Thus, although much of the impetus for preservation comes from the recent migrants to waterside communities, who recognize that further development threatens the rural, small-town character that attracted them, what many of them seek to preserve is a tidy, sanitized simulacrum of rural life: pastoral landscapes, gentle wildlife, and the civility and intimacy of small-town life as they imagine it. They have little tolerance for the noisy, unsightly aspects of commercial fishing; for the very activities that create "a living relationship" with nature.

Yet the watermen, with a far more robust sense of place and relationship with nature, have not developed a more appropriate preservationist ethic. The difficulty goes deeper than their resistance to regulation. Their very relationship with nature may be incompatible with a preservationist orientation. Men who have grown up regarding the bay as a formidable presence—harsh, recalcitrant, and unpredictable—may be hard-pressed to see it as a fragile ecosystem, whose survival requires constant restraint.

These ironies of preservation pose a challenge for policymakers seeking to maintain a close relationship between people and nature. Two general approaches have been proposed to sustain or re-establish a naturalized sense of place in contemporary society. One, associated with Gary Snyder and David McCloskey, attempts to inculcate a naturalized sense of place by promoting grass-roots involvement in ecosystem maintenance and restoration. The aim of this approach is to create "bioregional communities," in which social boundaries will conform to watershed or other natural boundaries. Rural residents will acquire or deepen a sense of bioregional community through farming (organic, of course) or traditional crafts, urban residents by maintaining or restoring streams, greenways, and public space.

This approach has enthusiastic proponents and success stories, but both come mainly from the Northwest, where the contours of the land and the flow of the water are salient and often dominant features in the daily lives of its residents. It would be far more difficult to introduce a sense of bioregional community to the compartmentalized, work-oriented lives of much of suburban America. The difficulties are acute in an area like Calvert County, where geography has a receding role in the lives of its residents and where too many other communities, based on work, interests, or ideology, compete for their identification and commitment. Beyond its small core of farmers and homesteaders, the movement to create bioregional consciousness seems far more likely to mobilize people for occasional restoration efforts than to make their bioregions or watersheds integral to their sense of place or identity.

The second approach is to maintain, at environmentally friendly levels, those resource-based vocations which, by their very nature, create strong attachments to nature. This approach is embodied in the "smart growth" and "rural legacy" policies recently adopted in several jurisdictions, including our watermen's home state of Maryland.[20] These policies come too late for Calvert County, where the decline of the fishery, development pressures, and cultural conflict have already driven out most of the watermen. But they might help to keep watermen in place on Maryland's Eastern Shore, where small-scale commercial fishing is still viable and watertowns are, relatively speaking, intact.

The new legislation is based on a recognition that government initiatives in the past fifty years have helped to create suburban sprawl through an array of shortsighted policies, ranging from the construction of interstate highways to the appraisal of rural farmland at residential market rates. The new policies seek to reverse this trend by concentrating growth in already-developed areas and maintaining what is left of the rural landscape and economy.

These policies also reflect a significant change in the philosophy underlying state environmental initiatives. In the past, state policies have tended to reflect a utilitarian approach associated with the conservationist tradition of Gifford Pinchot, which sought to maintain the productivity of the commons (e.g., by restricting entry to a fishery, raising disease-free stock in hatcheries, and limiting harvest size). The newer initiatives belong to the preservationist tradition of John Muir, emphasizing moral, aesthetic, and cultural values over economic ones. But in contrast to classic preservationist policies, these new initiatives protect environments that are largely the product of human activity—pastoral landscapes rather than primeval forests—as well as the human activity that is integral to those environments. The question is whether a preservationist approach can be adapted to vulnerable ways of life as well as to vanishing landscapes.

There are several challenges in extending the new preservation programs to traditional commercial fishing. These policies have been largely directed towards farmers' holdings and the rural landscapes farmers help maintain.[21] Watermen are a more elusive target, and their relationship with valued environments more ambiguous and complex. What comprises a waterman's holding? The stretch of the bay or the tributary estuary he uses most? His yard with "six rigs rusting out"? Or his share of watertown life and community? All three seem to be necessary to maintain watermen on the bay. The challenge will be to find analogues to farmland easements—the centerpiece of rural legacy programs—in the case of watermen. While a focus on the tools of their trade—boats, rigging, traps, and docks—may be too narrow, a focus on their communities as a whole may be too broad. This challenge is heightened by the fact that the physical structures which sustain watermen and form an integral part of their sense of place, from the piles of rigging they accumulate to the packing sheds, gas stations, and "greasy spoons" where they congregate and exchange information, often offend preservationist sensibilities.

A second difficulty is that government preservation initiatives may conflict with the vernacular libertarianism of the watermen, which opposes restrictions not only on catch size and fishing seasons, but also on new construction and commercial activity. We have seen that the watermen are reluctant even to discuss, let alone demand, limits on the kind of development they see as threatening their way of life. It is difficult for them to regard curbs on growth as anything but state interference with the freedom of people to live and build as they choose.

The watermen tend to see suburbanization as an inexorable "natural" phenomenon, however regrettable, not as the direct or indirect effect of government policy. Because they do not recognize the state's hand in the proliferation of new homes on the land and "yuppie poles" on the bay, they tend to view curbs on growth as a simple denial of access to the bay, which they oppose, rather than as an effort to correct or balance past government intervention on behalf of development, which they might find easier to accept. Of course, the watermen's cooperation is not necessary to impose limits on development. But a culture that values personal freedom so highly might be compromised if it were heavily dependent on coercive state action for its survival.

If restrictions threaten the integrity of the watermen's culture, so do subsidies. Many watermen understand the worth of their work as inhering in their confrontation with the hardships and caprice of nature; its beauty and dignity lie in their struggle to sustain themselves and their families from the life forms around them. Subsidies designed to preserve their livelihood for its moral and aesthetic value would attenuate the connection between nature and subsistence.

Admittedly, that connection has never been quite as close as some watermen and observers would like to believe. Unlike Jeffersonian farmers, watermen have never aspired to narrow self-sufficiency: they and their families could hardly hope to consume even a sizeable fraction of the catch they bring home. Their confrontation with nature has always been mediated by an equally capricious market for seafood. Moreover, watermen, like most other resource-based workers, have not been economically self-sufficient in any strict sense for generations. They have long received indirect public subsidies, in the form of oyster seeding, disease eradication, and even the despised "sustained yield" conservation programs. The total spent by federal and state agencies to study and maintain the Chesapeake Bay fishery runs to hundreds of millions of dollars annually.[22]

Given this history, one might think the watermen could be persuaded to support new policies that recognized the intrinsic worth of their way of life and sought to preserve its beauty and dignity. However, in a society long dominated by utilitarian thinking, there is a strong temptation to interpret claims of "intrinsic worth" merely as demands for certain kinds of intangible consumer goods, and to see preservation merely as serving the interests of a certain kind of consumer—the tourist.[23] Watermen would be no more cynical than most resource economists if they concluded that their livelihoods were being preserved merely for the delectation of observers.

Preservation might thus threaten to transform the livelihoods it seeks to maintain, in what Erving Goffman calls the "keying" of an activity from one frame to another: from natural to social, from hunting-gathering to entertainment. If watermen are kept in business to preserve rural appearances, by people with a taste for their lifestyle rather than their catch, they may be seen (and, more critically, see themselves) as reenactors—even if it is their own past lives they are reenacting.

The fact that they still produce and sell food will hardly guarantee the authenticity of their enterprise. The "farmers" and "millers" at restored colonial villages often sell their products to tourists, but they are selling souvenirs as much as food. With their intense concern for authenticity, many watermen would find it demeaning to be kept at work in order to ornament the bay with their skipjacks, entertaining the tourists driving over the Bay Bridge or staying at Eastern Shore bed-and-breakfasts.

It is not inevitable that cultural preservation should have this corrupting effect. The experience of several Western European countries, particularly Britain and Norway, reveals a gradual evolution from the subsidy of agricultural output for prudential and political reasons to the subsidy of rural livelihoods and communities for their moral and aesthetic value. A broad consensus has emerged in those countries that the maintenance of dignified and humane ways of life is a matter of fundamental national interest.[24]

But there is no such consensus in our own society, least of all among the watermen themselves. Our policy discourse has long been dominated by a confident and dogmatic utilitarianism that, again, can only reject or distort claims of intrinsic value, and by an assumption that valuable activities will be economically self-sustaining. Ironically, the problem is not that the watermen's culture diverges from the mainstream, but that it is, in this regard, too much a part of it. Watermen are hardly thoroughgoing utilitarians, but they share the prevailing conviction that direct public subsidy is inherently demeaning, and that an enterprise that is no longer economically self-sustaining can only be preserved as pork barrel, charity, or public entertainment.

The explicit transformation of watermen into performers has already begun without direct state intervention. Our final focus group revealed an interesting divergence between the watermen's inflexible theory and their more accommodating practice. While they talked of themselves as a dying breed, who would rather move on or retire than change their way of living, they had already begun to adapt. As noted earlier, one has turned his skipjack into a floating classroom; another helped to start a local maritime museum; the others crew on charter boats.

In one respect, this transformation is encouraging. It will keep some of the more enterprising watermen on the water, whatever the state of the fishery or the local economy. Moreover, the transformation of watermen into educators and reenactors may give future generations a deeper appreciation of their natural and social history than they would otherwise have had. But museum talks and educational boat trips offer no opportunity for the kind of grueling, exhilarating, place-making encounters with nature that enriched the lives and animate the memories of contemporary watermen. It is doubtful that this transformation can either preserve or impart a sense of place rooted in the natural environment of the Chesapeake Bay.

Perhaps, however, there are other ways of preserving the livelihoods of watermen that maintain the connection to food gathering and harvesting on which the integrity of their work depends. Price supports for local fish, harvested by traditional methods, might well offend the watermen's sense of independence. But by placing added value directly on their catch, price supports might preserve the character of their work as resource extraction, and evince a social recognition of its dignity and worth. And perhaps the state can support the watermen less directly, by cultivating the kind of consumer demand for traditionally produced local products that has created a cottage industry in organic and boutique farming. Perhaps local fishermen could sell their catch at urban and suburban "white-markets." While the demand for the local is susceptible to abuse, and may express a patronizing taste for the yield of an idealized rural economy, it might sustain some watermen in their traditional vocations without the heavy hand of direct government subsidy.

To the extent that pollution is responsible for the bay's declining harvests, effective environmental policies might enable the diminished ranks of watermen to earn a comfortable living without any government intervention beyond that required for improving water quality. Of course, prosperity would have its own risks, as watermen used their increased income to reduce their labor and seafood harvesting became a less chancy and picturesque enterprise. But the bonds formed by adversity will endure a few good seasons, and renewed competition for the bay's replenished resources should keep the watermen from becoming too complacent about their livelihoods.

The revitalization of "real watertowns" would go a long way toward reviving the "culture of oysters and mussels and crabs" among those who live along the bay. It would be very gratifying if a solution to the most persistent threat to the bay's physical environment also helped to preserve or restore the sense of place of those who live around it.

Notes

The research described in this article was funded by Maryland Sea Grant and the National Science Foundation, Grant No. SBR 9422322; Mick Womersley and Sara Gottlieb conducted the research as Maryland Sea Grant Trainees. The authors are grateful to Mark Sagoff for his sponsorship and encouragement, to Jack Greer, Merrill Leffler, and Michael Fincham of Maryland Sea Grant for their support and guidance, and to Larissa Grunnig for conducting the focus groups with great skill and sensitivity.

1. See Allan Pred, "Stucturation and Place: On the Becoming of Sense and Place and the Structure of Feeling," *Journal for the Theory of Social Behavior* 13 (1983): 45.

2. See, e.g., E. C. Relph, *Place and Placelessness* (London: Pion, 1976); Yi-fu Tuan, *Space and Place: The Perspective of Experience* (Minneapolis: University of Minnesota Press, 1977); W.V. Walter, "The Places of Experience," *The Philosophical Forum* 12, no. 2 (Winter 1980–81): 159; J. Nicholas Entrikin, *Betweenness of*

Place: Towards a Geography of Modernity (Baltimore: Johns Hopkins University Press, 1991).

3. See, e.g., Wendell Berry, *The Unsettling of America: Culture and Agriculture* (San Francisco: Sierra Club Books, 1977); Alan McQuillan, "Cabbages and Kings: The Ethics and Aesthetics of New Forestry," *Environmental Values* 2, no. 3 (Autumn 1993); Mark Sagoff, "Settling America or The Concept of Place in Environmental Politics," *Journal of Energy, Natural Resources & Environmental Law* 12, no. 2 (1992).

4. See Maryland Department of State Planning, Office of Planning Data, *County Profile Series* (Annapolis, Md.: Department of State Planning, 1988).

5. Lee Cuba and David M. Hummon, "Constructing a Sense of Home: Place Affiliation and Migration across the Life Cycle," *Sociological Forum* 8, no. 4 (1993): 547–573, 555.

6. Robert Putnam, "The Strange Disappearance of Civic America," *The American Prospect* no. 3 (Winter 1996): 34–48, 37.

7. See note 2.

8. Tad Tuleja, ed., *Usable Pasts: Tradition and Group Expressions in North America* (Logan, Ut.: Utah State University Press, 1997); Eric Hobsbawn and Terence Ranger, *The Invention of Tradition* (Cambridge: Cambridge University Press, 1983).

9. Dolores Hayden, *The Power of Place: Urban Landscapes as Public History* (Cambridge, Mass.: MIT Press, 1995).

10. Charles Jedrej and Mark Nuttall, *White Settlers: The Impact of Rural Repopulation in Scotland* (Luxembourg: Harwood Academic Publishers, 1996).

11. Hayden, *The Power of Place*.

12. Barbara Allen and Thomas J. Schlereth, eds., *Sense of Place: American Regional Cultures* (Lexington: University Press of Kentucky, 1990), 161–162.

13. Jedrej and Nuttall, *White Settlers*, 142.

14. Calvert County Department of Planning & Zoning, *Vision Statement*.

15. Ferdinand Tonnies, *Gemeinschaft und Gesellschaft, Grundbegriffe der Reinen Soziologie* (Darmstadt: Wissenschaftliche Buchgesellschaft, 1963 [1887]).

16. It has also been attenuated by changes in the pattern of land uses and ownership. As Allen observes of the residents of the rural community she studied (*Sense of Place*, 163):

Their ties to the land have dwindled to the raising of small vegetable gardens for family consumption and perhaps a "patch" of tobacco. . . . "Places" are bought and sold and subdivided with increasing frequency; old houses slowly collapse in corn-fields, or serve as hay barns, or stand as ironic back-drops to new ranch-style brick houses or double-wide trailers. Yet association with a homeplace and its concomitant integration into a kinship network remain the unalterable grounds for the social recognition of an individual as a full-fledged member of the community. The genealogical landscape . . . is an anachronism, keeping the past alive in the present.

17. This kind of intensely personal attachment to the landscape is found in the Scottish Highlands, where, as Jedrej and Nuttall report (*White Settlers*, 123):

[A] footpath through a peat bog might be named after the person who first cut it . . . or specific places may have particular associations with individuals, such as . . . the place where Niall almost drowned when he was out poaching. . . . By naming places after people or by commemorating an event with a name, people are located in the landscape, giving a sense of social continuity. This linking of persons with local topography is a characteristic feature of agricultural and maritime societies throughout the North Atlantic region.

18. "On the Waterfront," *Washington Post Magazine*, 21 May, 1995, 24, 28.

19. David Budbill, quoted by Lucy Lippard, *The Lure of the Local: Senses of Place in a Multicentered Society* (New York: New Press, 1997), 153–154.

20. See, e.g., Parris Glendening, "The 1997 State of the State Address," in "The State of our State is Sound. It is Good," *Washington Post*, 16 January, 1997, D5.

21. See Tom Daniels and Deborah Bowers, *Holding our Ground: Protecting America's Farms and Farmland* (Washington, D.C.: Island Press, 1997), 1–13, 241–242.

22. See, e.g., Nancy E. Bockstael and Kenneth E. McConnell, *Benefits from Improvements in Chesapeake Bay Water Quality* (Washington, D.C.: U.S. Environmental Protection Agency, 1987), 3, 7, 139–148.

23. On tourism and the commodification of place, see John Urry, *The Tourist Gaze: Leisure and Travel in Contemporary Society* (London: Routledge, 1990); *Consuming Places* (London: Sage, 1995).

24. More likely, there were always moral or aesthetic impulses buried under prudential reasoning. For original farmland schemes, see John Bryden and George Houston, *Agrarian Change in the Scottish Highlands* (London: M. Robertson, 1976); Kirk H. Stone, *Norway's Internal Migration to New Farms since 1920* (The Hague: Martinus Nijhoff, 1971). The U.K. gave per unit subsidies and protected farmland from development (1940s through 1960s); then added subsidies for amenity, habitat, and tourist facilities (1970s and 1980s); all now incorporated into "sustainable development" (late 1980s and 1990s). The recent convergence of historical, biodiversity, and farmland protection into regional "Heritage" agencies underlines our point. Those areas designated as national parks came under explicit moral and aesthetic scrutiny from the late 1940s; U.K. preserves are grazed and populated by native farmers. See U.K. Town and Country Planning Act of 1947 and the National Parks and Access to the Countryside Act of 1949 (London: Her Majesty's Stationery Office); also John Moir, "The Designation of Valued Landscapes in Scotland," and Kevin Bishop, "The Challenge of Convergence: Countryside Conservation and Enjoyment in Scotland and Wales," both in Roderick Macdonald and Huw Thomas, eds., *Nationality and Planning in Scotland and Wales* (Cardiff: University of Wales Press, 1997).

New Meanings of Place:
The Place of the Poor and the Loss of
Place as a Center of Mediation

Lea Caragata

This paper explores certain aspects of the meaning or experience of *place*. I suggest that our experience of and thinking about place is undergoing significant change. As technology and globalization create new possibilities for transcending the locality of place for some, others are excluded from this experience. More fundamentally, the importance of place as a space of mediation, of places and spaces with common cultural and social meanings, is diminished.

Place as described here has two functions: It provides the *spaces* essential to association and mediation *and* it *represents* a city to its inhabitants. Thus, this latter symbolic meaning helps shape what "citizens" expect to occur in the spaces of their community and their understanding of what kind of place it is. A common understanding of place acts as a social "unifier" and helps to forge a "public" identification and ownership of the spaces of the city.

The concepts of space and place require elaboration. Space is without the narrowing limits of place. Space is unbounded, and encompasses both physical and social space. And, although unbounded, space is never empty but is inscribed with particular cultural and social meanings. The referencing of place is both specific and spatial although we also use place to describe metaphorical and psychological space. We know our place, or the place of women, or the place from which women speak; these indicate the multiplicity of uses of place. So, although for my purposes, place *is* spatial, these other uses, the richness of place, adds to its spatial or territorial significance and to its conceptual possibility. And, while "place" represents both geographical and spatial features, it also *conveys* social meanings. The mention of *a* place brings to mind, both its physical and spatial features as well as social meanings. The physical space and its ambience or atmosphere are interpreted along with information which we "read" about who uses the space, the uses for which it was intended and about the social relations of the users.

Both space and place, whether local or global, are partially constituted by social processes, based on shifting definitions.[1]

This paper argues that cities are important as places of mediation among the different social and economic groups which together inhabit urban spaces. (The cities referred to here are North American, perhaps also those of Western Europe.) The extent to which such mediation occurs is, I suggest, one of the characteristics that defines a "healthy" city for it evidences the engagement of the citizenry in a public or civil discourse.

The existence of a public discourse implies a mediation of needs and their expression in the spaces of the city. In this context, mediation refers to the negotiation and contestation over and in the spaces of the city by the interest groups and subcultures which comprise that particular place. When the spaces and places of the city enable and are shaped by such a mediated process, two important things occur. First, the city reflects those who live there, not just those who govern, or those who vote, but more broadly reflects in its spaces, the needs, interests and issues of its residents. Second, through this process of mediating, the citizenry *becomes* a public, takes on a form and stature beyond individual interest. It is in such a public realm, through negotiating shared and conflicting interests, that a *common* interest is constructed, acknowledged and reflected (reproduced). The mediation between city dwellers comes about because it is sustained and reproduced by certain kinds of social relations and city spaces and because it *has been* a condition necessary to groups with different needs and interests coexisting in a common urban framework.

The use of "framework" is intended to convey that in sharing urban space, much more is involved than just a sharing of physical place. Cities are developed as particular places, as a result of social/political agreements about how space is to be developed and places constructed, how the city will be governed, and by whom, and how city spaces will be used. When the structures of governance, development and services are to be *used* by all of the residents of the city, residents have a common interest in the forging of an agreement about the nature of this framework. (I stop short of claiming that cities develop on the basis of a social consensus, as any observer of the modern city will be aware that some needs and interests are served more fully than others.)

As globalization increases the disparity between rich and poor, it also acts to minimize the extent to which we must share urban space as for some people, shared or communal place is more easily transcended through the purchase of increasingly privatized lifeworlds. The major thesis of this paper is that broad and critical social consequences derive from this emerging divergence in our experience of space and place. The loss of a common meaning and experience of place which I postulate to be occurring as a result of globalization, has at least three significant impacts which warrant consideration. First, we face cities in which both space and place are increasingly segregated along social, economic and ethnic (racial) lines. This increased social segregation is enabled as globalization has helped to fuel increasing income disparity. As a result, it has become possible for some of the citizenry to "buy-out" of the process of mediating an urban framework.[2] Instead of mediating their needs, which, with respect to things like streetspaces, education, recreation and even to some extent housing and shopping, they had previously had to do, they appear now to be able to literally buy exclusive, privatized, individualized urban space which extends beyond the house in an exclusive neighbourhood of previous times, to an entirely privatized community. Second, as this change occurs, the extent to which people from the same city have common needs or a mutual interest is diminished. And this mutual interest was the driving force in all of the parties of the city acting as a public, the experience of which is necessary to valuing a public realm. Finally, these losses further affect the reproduction of space and act to sustain the ongoing marginalization of those who are poor.

The line of argument pursued first establishes the nature of the relationship between place, social structure and human behavior. This understanding is necessary to explore the significance of the city, as it relates to the structures of global capitalism and democracy and the interests and aspirations of human "actors." I suggest that the city both reflects and reproduces the dominant social relations, tempered and influenced by human "agency," which, in turn, creates alternate spaces in the city which support, sustain and nurture other human needs. The human interactions and social relations which arise in certain spaces, and are then supported by them, are an important part of what translates urban space into local place. In this context I discuss the city as "center", and the center of cities as places of mediation. The city has historically been a place in which the public is made visible. Place and a common understanding and experience of it are critical to the maintenance of a public realm which as Nancy Fraser suggests, must be broadly accessible to have continued meaning.[3] Globalization threatens our common understanding of the city and the center, diminishes our shared understanding of and access to the public, and further traps those on the social and economic margins of our society.

Interrelationship between Agency, Place, and Structure

The relational nature of the environment, "built form" or place, and human behavior has typically been acknowledged only insofar as the environment impacts *on* individuals. While we readily conceive of the impacts of crowding, inadequate shelter or the lack of particular physical amenities, we lack clarity about *how* they affect people. All too often, we perceive these environmental impacts to be uni-directional and determinative of human behavior and the more subtle analysis of how people act both socially and spatially to shape place has only begun more recently.[4] At play is an interchange; human behavior is both impacting on the environment and being affected by it. Until recently, these environment/behavior or place/agency debates did not directly encompass reflections on how these elements or forces impact on our social structure.

The relationship between agency (human behavior) and structure has also long been a focus of debate[5] which also did not, until recently, explicitly consider how human behavior and our social structure are reflected in, and reflect, the built environment or place. That the social structure does not "determine" human behavior has been a long standing critique of a Marxist analysis of capitalism. In spite of the power of capitalist economic relations, of the significance of the "base" in shaping the "superstructure," there continues to be an unresolved struggle about how to account for social change, for what at times have been obvious and significant manifestations of human agency.[6] Thus the argument is that human behavior, social structure and place must be considered together as three interrelated elements which impact with and on each other. While the relative importance of each of these elements remains the subject of continued debate and analysis which Gottdiener adeptly discusses, this question is not the primary focus here. This paper focuses on the interplay which results from a change in the social structure (economic globalization) and the pressure which results from this change, on human actors and the built environment. I am not, however, claiming victory for structure, agency or place, rather, I wish to draw attention to the dynamic, and to the importance of cities as places which produce and reproduce our social structure. Further, I will discuss some of the impacts which I see deriving from this interplay if current globalizing trends remain uncontested and unchecked. In summary, this paper sheds light on how the spaces of the city and particular cities (places) reflect these global processes *and* manifest local difference.[7]

City as Reflector, Reproducer of Social Relations, as *Local* Place

Several theorists support the notion that in the modern city we see represented the confluence of all of the agents or forces by which our society is produced and reproduced. It is this question, the significance of the *city* against the backdrop of the processes of production and reproduction, that is at the heart of *The Urban Question*, in which Castells argues that the city is a theoretically significant context. Soja adds further definition, arguing the presence of "a socio-spatial dialectic—not implying a resurrection of geographical determinism—and that the socially produced spatiality of society also conditions and shapes society." Jencks comments more specifically that architecture, the built form, is a crystallization of the dominant social values and conveys social meanings.[8]

Given then a relationship between the spaces of the city and the reproduction of the social structure, it follows that in the city we might "see" expressed the "spheres" by which the activities and functions of our society are categorized and organized—which can be formulated as the marketplace, state, family and civil society. This description includes as a sphere of life practice, a "social" sphere or "third sector"[9]: civil society, which I believe to be critical in understanding the interrelationship between human behavior (agency), social structure and place.

The relations between the state and the marketplace, and the life practices supported by them, are expressed and represented in the physical and social spaces of our society. Through these relations and their representations in space, our society reproduces itself. These relations are particularly visible in urban, city space, where the life practices of people (their "lifeworlds"[10]) can be seen juxtaposed against these representative realms. Indeed, the city is an exemplar of all of the elements that combine to shape our society:

> Capitalism has survived into the twentieth century through the production of space and [it] has been an increasingly urbanized space that has been produced. A study of the urban process tells us much therefore, about the mechanisms of capitalism's successful self-reproduction. Secondly, increasing urbanization makes this the primary level at which individuals experience, live out, and react to the changes going on around them. To dissect the urban process in all of its fullness is to lay bare the roots of consciousness formation in the material realities of daily life.[11]

Although as Wolch and Dear describe it, geography both facilitates and constrains the practice of everyday life, as yet there is no *universal* everyday life. These activities are grounded in gender, income, class, culture and ethnicity. So too, are they grounded in both time and space, including both national, political and environmental space, economic and social space, rural/urban space and finally, the more detailed physical structures of the buildings, streetscapes, and patterns of land use that prevail in the capitalist, industrialized cities of the West, which is the context in which this work takes place.

Translation of Urban "Space" into Local "Place"

Although I characterize "cities of the West" in fact, the very ways in which I suggest that the practices of everyday life are grounded argues against any such construction, because cities are particular places. (Although some are more alike than others, which is the basis of my construction.) And while globalization promotes uniformity it has not, at least yet, overcome the particularities of places which are constructed by their unique histories. These unique histories are reflected in the reproduction of these places as are the varied life practices which occur there. Space and place continue as well to be particularized, made local and specific, by the nature of the particular urban framework mediated in *that* place. Oncu and Weyland summarize:

> It is only by taking into account the cultural frames and life strategies of social actors who are positioned within the power constellations of a different social order, with its own logic, that it becomes possible to make practical and political sense of metropolitan experience in the globalizing world.[12]

We need to understand the nature and cause of local difference as we note that even as global pressures create similarities, all cities are not the same. Oncu and Weyland further suggest that metropolitan culture is the locus of hybrid forms, they are particular and unique but are based on exchanges, elements added and deleted, over time and space.

There is no one global urban space; cities remain particular places wherein one can see the intersection of global economics with the specific local, political, and social institutions and relations that have been forged there. City space is local place, reflective of the life practices and life/place struggles and aspirations of *that* citizenry. It is in this sense that every city remains local, providing spaces and places unique to the way in which struggles for life space have played out among the interest groups and subcultures of the city. This outcome, the particularity of the places of the city, representing local needs, presupposes an arena in which the diverse groups of the city struggle *together* to contest their needs and interests and define their life spaces. Such an arena takes multiple forms, broadly represented by what I will describe as the public realm, a variant of the Aristotelian polity, and central to our democratic traditions. As I will discuss in more detail, a central aspect of the polity important to this argument was that it was a realm of discourse for the citizenry (although still selective with respect to *who* might be a citizen). Beyond their casting of a ballot (a representational public), people in cities are more likely to debate, in various forums, the nature of their social and political relations and the structures by which such governance shall be represented. In a city, these social and political relations issues are "close to home" and debates about new city halls or downtown redevelopment, discussions about daycare and schooling, park usage and lighting and whether to allow "squeegee kids"[13] their street space are likely to spark interest and engagement by the citizens. Partly by engaging in such a discourse, a citizenry becomes a public and comes to develop a common experience and understanding of public. This understanding in turn supports the further reproduction of the public. Deutsche suggests that acts which support our experience of the public promote the survival and extension of democratic culture.

Before proceeding, I will further clarify my use of public given a long history of multiple, diverging and at times conflicting use. While a debate swirls over whether civil society is to be included or not, or whether feminist theory conflates governance, bureaucracy and a public discourse and in doing so masks important issues and questions, the concern which I raise in a sense encompasses these issues of what we mean by "public". My claim is that what is threatened by globalization is a public discourse, or even the opportunity, the *spatial possibility* for a public discourse. Because we come to value, or experience the need for a public discourse through interaction, through an experience of "commonness" or mutuality of interests, we require space which supports this common experience. Sennett suggests that we come to a realization that we require a public, because we experience our own inadequacy, the acknowledging and experience of which is at odds with liberal self-sufficiency. The self-sufficiency which Sennett describes is an important part of what fuels the desire of some of our population to transcend place, to remove themselves from "society," the structures established in common with *all* others.[14] Those who can buy their way out of mediating space and place with others they have marked out as different from themselves are sustained by social values which tell them that they are better for their independence and autonomy. They have both a right and an obligation to first (and perhaps only) take care of themselves, to be self-sufficient.

It is in opposition to such self-sufficiency, rather, a common interest or purpose, or what we might describe as civil interconnectedness, for which in times past we chose to develop a formal system of governance and a bureaucracy. These structures are manifestations of a public, not the public itself. So, my quest for a public and its continued presence and importance is not about the structures of governance but about the civil discourse and experience that underlie it. The public is a realm in which *all* of the sectors of a society have an opportunity or, even better, a compelling purpose to engage in a discourse about the forms, structures and nature of their city, in whatever ways these issues arise for them. In this sense, I share Fraser's critique of Habermas' public and similarly argue the need for multiple arenas and a multiplicity of discourses.[15] The precise way in which this concern expresses itself here is the extent to which places in the city previously provided forum(s) for such expression and whether these city centers are being lost as "public" space.

Contact as Precursor to Connection

Jan Gehl describes San Vittorio Romana, a town in which the houses were constructed so that they all faced on to a central square where until quite recently, there was a communal well. The practice in the town was to leave your pail at the well, in this way when someone turned up and you wanted to talk, there was always the excuse of "going to get the pail". Gehl suggests that human beings need an excuse to engage in such discourse and painstakingly identifies the kinds of spaces and social circumstances in which people—not friends or coworkers—talk to one another. This talking, "going to get the pail" is of course the social intercourse which underlies establishing a common interest or a public. Necessary to this social intercourse is place, the spaces like the well in the village square, which attract a broad cross section of the community and convey a sense of belonging, of common citizenship. It is this common citizenship which has disappeared in so many American cities, as places and services have increasingly been segregated by income and social class. Robert Kuttner notes that "with in-kind, universal services, people of all classes actually meet and interact with each other and with those doing the servicing. They wait together, flirt, swap sob stories and advice, save each other's place in line, keep an eye on each other's kids. The middle class is . . . reminded that poor people are human" and a common bond is built. Although the bond may not be deep—it is and has been sufficient that through such social contact we see others as people with similarities, rather than marking them out as the "other."[16]

The places which have historically provided these spaces for building social solidarity have been city centers, public spaces and places, institutions and unstructured space and place, which like the well in San Vittorio, encouraged discourse. As Oldenburg illustrates, private places such as taverns and coffee shops also fulfil, under the right conditions, some of these same functions. Although the place might then be either public or private, its importance is the role it plays in creating a "public," enabling people to have a forum, to engage with others beyond their family or select group of friends. A more casual civil engagement is what is being described, like the civil possibilities provided by the well in San Vittorio. The centers of cities historically provided spaces which attracted all of the disparate groups in the city. In cities where the *use* of these spaces has been retained, there generally continues to be interaction between diverse constituencies which, in turn, is important to the vitality, safety and growth of urban place. The absence of such interaction leads, as Castells' has suggested, to the creation of "urban reservations" for the poor and office tower sanctuaries for the middle class, who flee from city centers by evening. There is an increasing middle class assumption, revealed in the literature, that once a place has been "taken over" by the poor and/ or marginalized that it can only be "taken back". This view reflects exclusivity—it's either mine or theirs and is precisely what I suggest to be problematic. This issue is nicely explicated by two illustrations. Kaus describes a Los Angeles park which locks the basketball hoops, preventing "undesirables" from playing a little late night basketball. The same issue is revealed as Deutsche describes the *New York Times* reporting of the battle over Jackson Park in Greenwich Village. This tiny green space located on a traffic island is "taken back" from the homeless by the erection of gates which are locked until the public, in the form of middle class neighbors, unlocks them during the day. These views of how spaces are reclaimed or made public again are fundamentally at odds with a notion of public that is inclusive. While the issue of one public, the middle class, needing to feel that the space is *also* theirs is reasonable, the notion that they are the final or only arbiters of what is appropriate public use is not. Contrasting with the locking of basketball hoops or park gates, is Jane Jacobs' view of how a process of "unslumming" occurs. Jacobs described a process of spaces being made safe and *public* by the presence of multiple and different users which ensures the "safety" of the place for all, rather than, as is described in the illustrations from Kaus and Deutsche, a place becoming safe for one group by excluding the other. For this latter process to work, more, and more effective, gates and locks will be endlessly required. In this latter process, there is no negotiation or contestation, replacing it is "the arbitrary claim of one group that it *is* or *represents* the 'public.' The mediation necessary to the construction of a 'public,' which is based on all of the parties to a process being represented, and is the basis of democracy, does not occur."[17]

Traditionally, "place" has been essential as meeting, negotiating and contesting space for all of the constituencies represented in our society. Two phenomena appear to be changing our experience and expectation of place. First, because of increasing income disparity and globalization, we share less space and, as the above illustrations indicate, we appear to have diminished expectations about the very possibility and the desirability of sharing space. These factors are self-reinforcing and both act to minimize the opportunity for negotiation and contestation, further limiting the meaningful contact between different social groups.

Having a memory, relating to others, participating in a larger story, calls for involvement, requires presence. This presence, naturally, is lived out in particular physical settings, like piazzas or streets, mountains or seashores. And these locations are in turn imbued with experience past and present. They become places of density and depth. . . . And it is there that people share a particular vantage point and that language, habits and outlook combine to constitute a particular style of being in the world.[18]

The style of being in the world described in the above citation is a being in the public. Cities have been critical for providing the spaces and places which have translated democratic theory into functional democracy, enabling diverse publics to negotiate, contest and mediate how they will live together in space. In this way the city has been "center" and the centers of cities through varied public, quasipublic and private spaces have served as important sites of mediation. And, the act of mediating is important in constituting a "public."

Globalization

Globalization is, as Giddens describes it, "the intensification of worldwide social relations which link distant localities in such a way that local happenings are shaped by events occurring many miles away and vice versa."[19] Made possible by advancing technology, globalization is changing the economic infrastructure of our societies which in turn effects pressure on our political and social institutions. These shifts have been accompanied by a well constructed and widely disseminated doctrine that they are to be welcomed, represent advancement and possibility, and that to express skepticism or opposition is to mark one out at least as regressive.

Globalization and the social and economic relations which are described by the term are relations of power and reflective of unequal distributions of power. As Oncu and Weyland describe these power relations, "some social groups initiate flows and movement, others do not; some are more on the receiving end of it than others; some are effectively imprisoned by it."[20] Sassen describes with precision the nature of the globalizing economic process, including the way in which globalized economics have fragmented and polarized the workforce. She notes new forms of inequality arising at several levels. There are increasingly unequal relations between firms competing for work in the global market, a factor relating to the increasing inequality between cities, and then, also related, is a growing inequality for those in the low-wage workforce who must compete for housing, space and consumption services, making their living in the city more difficult, which further reduces the competitiveness of the industrial core . . . And these disparities are no longer ameliorated by the nation state, also weakened by this process. These effects play out in space, play out in the real lives of people and their relations with each other that are revealed in the spaces of the city.[21]

Globalization changes our understanding of place; the image is of a borderless world, less limiting and defining. The image created is, at least in part, false. Boundaries which were to be transcended are reinforced as they become the site of struggles by groups seeking to reclaim or redefine their borders in the spaces of the city (the need for which intensifies as a function of increasingly unequal relations among the inhabitants of the city). For some, spatial limits are transcended by means of rapid and frequent travel, and by developments such as fibre optics and satellites which permit communication instantly across vast expanses of space. Sorkin suggests:

Main street is now the space between airports, the fibre-optic cables linking the fax machines of multinational corporations' far flung offices, an invisible worldwide skein of economic relations. Liberated from its centers and its edges by a new world order bent on a single citizenship of consumption, the new city threatens an unimagined sameness even as it multiplies the illusory choices of the TV system. . . . The new city replaces the anomaly and delight of such places [traditional cities] with a universal particular, a generic urbanism inflected only by applique. Here locality is efficiently acknowledged by the inclusion of the croque-monsieur at the McDonald's on the Boul' Miche or the Cajun Martini at the airport lounge in New Orleans . . . The idea of the city as the site of community and human connection [has been sacrificed].[22]

Sorkin's comment is illuminating because it captures an essential element of globalization, the promise or possibility of something new. What is promised, however, derives singularly from economic relations and therefore can only be what the marketplace can produce. In other respects, the comment misleads as it universalises; cities remain local. While the *functions* of city centers as spaces of mediation, as centers, are being lost, the borders between the centers and edges of the city are being fortified rather than erased, as only some particpate in the "citzenship of consumption". "It is not the city as a whole that becomes part of the global society but certain strongholds and citadels, clearly demarcated social, economic and spatial parts of it."[23]

To return to that element of globalization which focuses on the singularity of the economic relations which it reproduces, much of what we have traditionally valued in "modern" urban life derives not singularly from the marketplace, but from the interplay between what we might describe as the spheres of life practice which have been categorized as the public and the "private", or more meaningfully and completely as the marketplace, the state, the family and civil society. Sorkin argues that globalization has contributed to the weakening of these other spheres. It is reducing the significance of the state as it retreats from its protectionist and welfare functions and Sassen and others describe the diminishing significance of the family as a social institution and the more general polarization of the social from the economic. And, of course within the economic realm itself, polarization occurs between those who have the so-called "good" jobs and those with part-time and/or poorly waged jobs. The life practices of these two groups have moved apart and the spaces and places in which their lives are lived are also increasingly separate. A third group which is even further economically, socially and spatially marginalized is of course that group with no jobs. City space *both reflects these emerging social and economic relations and acts to further shape them.* "The immediate juxtaposition of global and local, rich and poor, of skyscrapers and squatter shacks is characteristic of every metropolis and at least partly caused by globalization itself . . . Imagined differences between cultures and classes become social and spatial boundaries that divide the city into different localities."[24] This echoes Castells' view of globalized cities as fragmented, with sharp boundaries.

The representation of our social structure and social relations in the spaces of the city has historically ensured the presence of spaces—and their use—which enabled divergent people and their views to be mediated. How we see ourselves and the relations we forge with others occur relative to the spaces in which they take place, and our view of ourselves and others is reproduced in part by our spatial experience. A consequence of globalization has been the increasing segregation and for some, privatization of families and family space. Those who can, "buy-out" of civic life by buying space away from the city with others they determine to be of their own social and economic class. In such spaces, private schools and recreational spaces and a lack of "public" create a different experience of place, one in which economic, social and spatial relations are separated by class, income, type of work and so on. As private or family life becomes less intimately connected with *all* of the spaces of the city, two changes occur. First, there is less contact between divergent social groups. As families work longer hours and live less of their lives in and near to public space there is correspondingly less time for community and neighbourhood activities which builds families' identification and comfort with their neighbourhood. The absence of this means that neighbourhood children no longer fill their spare time playing together in the parks and street spaces of their neighbourhoods, through these informal ways of socializing also engaging with a more diverse group than their parents might choose. Instead, children too face increasingly commodified social and recreational options, which reduces their public presence further as previously discussed to the image of there being no public life. This in turn impacts on how "public place" is perceived, used and structured. As well, the sense that "public" space is not *for them* further contributes to an increasing social/spatial distance. Secondly and relatedly, our urban spaces will reflect this change—place will be less developed and utilized as a space of mediation. As the absence of such mediation shapes the lives of children, the likelihood of spaces of mediation being reproduced becomes further diminished as a generation is raised with no experience of contesting social goals and values. For those for whom buying-out is not possible, the public that remains is an abandoned public which no longer serves the larger social function of sustaining some level of social equality and probably no longer even serves well its more specific purpose of providing educational or recreational space. As it ceases to be fully "public", the resources to sustain such space will be provided with increasing reluctance. Public institutions and spaces are reinvented as charity to those who cannot sustain themselves.

As we move to other less spatially "fixed" social representations, transcendent communications make "place" less necessary for interaction. Relatedly, as the structures and spaces of our cities are transformed, marked differences in the types of social relations that are supported and available via "place" will further impact on the human relations occurring there and ultimately on the kinds of social structures that might be sustained: they become more likely to be congruent with globalization. These changes will, I suggest, support social, political and economic interactions which are more selective, exclusive, and purposeful. This is likely to result in diminished mediation between disparate social groups, a diminished "public" realm and understanding of its importance.

Globalization and the Poor

Work increasingly identifies *who* we are, economically and socially. It shapes where we live—urban/rural, inner city/suburb, private community/public housing—and it appears to be dividing more exclusively into three camps—good jobs, Mcjobs, and no jobs. A "good" job implies a number of important things about choice and place: place is transcendent. Air travel, instant communication by phone or Internet, global social networks, control over one's hours of work, home as private community, private recreation, the pleasures of tourism as consumption are all readily available. To those in both other groups, "place" remains fixed in time and space. For those without work, life becomes increasingly limited, without "life chances." And, globalization is creating disrupture and disparity in the world of work. While significant benefits have accrued to some, for another group of workers—those in an increasingly part-time, without benefits work force—work commands most of the waking hours of the day in the quest for sufficient income to sustain a family. And, although their lives are difficult, these people at least have work. For those without work, lacking the definition of work not only means that they are economically poor but they are also without the status and life-defining role that work provides—the dominant and most important "life practice." The absence of work increasingly correlates with the form of the family (led by a single mother) and with its urban, geographic expression in public housing. In the U.S., these forms of family and of housing are likely in the inner city and are further correlated with race and ethnicity (black and Hispanic). In the case of the poor, the family role in the reproduction of children outside of the most narrow biological function is even further reduced by the intensive bureaucratic interventions of child welfare authorities, school truancy officers and police. As economic relations become more dominant and eclipse other kinds of social relations, to be poor, without economic relations, is to be more completely marginalized. The absence of work, the homogeneity of life spaces and the lack of an integrating centre or public further reduces the life chances of those who are poor.[25]

As Kaus notes, in previous times, the poor were socially and geographically less isolated from those who were middle class. The benefits which accrued from the welfare state also helped to mask some of the difference. This circumstance has changed and adding to it is a neoconservative view, widely disseminated, that the poor are authors of their own misfortune, too dependent on social programs, taking advantage of "us" and so on. This campaign, as I believe it can fairly be described, has created mistrust and suspicion, in effect served to widen the social gap between the "haves" and "have-nots." These changing public perceptions of the poor are both reflected and reinforced by their spatial reality.

Before proceeding, it is perhaps necessary to make a point about what I suggest we might be leaving behind. Our cities are stratified places and have always been so. However, with the development of a welfare state and the massive economic expansion of the postwar years in the West, more of the citizenry became engaged in mainstream social and economic life than ever before. This is what built the level of social equality which Kaus refers to and what helped to create spaces and places in our cities which were fully public and reflected a public interest. I am not claiming that these phenomena have completely disappeared and nor am I claiming that we previously had some sort of social utopia. Rather, I am suggesting that there are features of globalization that are causing this fragile level of social equality which did exist to become diminished.

For those on the extreme end of the work/not-work continuum, home is the street or a shelter and even the latter likely dictates a life on the street during the day, and difficulty, no matter how determined the person, in maintaining a standard of personal hygiene even remotely acceptable to the middle class. Thus, differentness is made more apparent and all of these circumstances combine to discourage mediation. In fact, as the illustration described by Deutsche reveals, the middle class increasingly appear to feel no need to mediate, *they* are the public, these are "others" whose use of city space is to be controlled by the *true* public. Attempts to remove "squeegee kids" from the streets and the "cleaning up" of the community by removing "street people" before major national and international events are further illustrations of this view.

The same spatial distancing has accompanied the increasing social distance between the middle class and the other poor, those who at least have homes. The social and spatial distance is expressed and reinforced as we no longer share neighborhoods, we no longer even share dwelling types. The homes of the "poor-without-work" are grouped together, a forced homogeneity, often in poorly constructed "projects," located in inner city neighbourhoods where *everyone* is fearful for their personal safety. These homes do however compare favorably to jails, shelters, and other "options" which those without work may rely on as "home."[26]

In San Francisco, a well-intentioned architect has designed 4x8 foot plywood dog houses at $500 a piece to house the local homeless. . . . In the United States, it is also possible to find a $15,000 miniature Victorian mansion for a [dog]. . . . in these instances [housing] symbolizes foremost the prevailing national commitment to a view of housing as a commodity.[27]

The Notion of Choice

Place, especially the place where we *choose* to live, is a powerful symbol in western society of who we are. Such representation implies (or hides) a number of factors of importance to this discussion. One of these is clearly the notion of choice, that we have and choose among various options. The notion of a free market and the ability to act freely in the marketplace of homes disguises that for most people in North America the choice of home and where it should be located is severely circumscribed. Home may need to be very close to work because of the difficulty of otherwise getting to work, or it may have to be remote from work and other interests because being closer costs too much. The cost of home is the most significant factor affecting our choice; for many such, choice is illusory.

Other factors affect choice, including the increasing size of some cities and, correspondingly, the decreasing jobs available in cities which are losing the global competition battle. In the first case, the number of renters, and hence competition for place, increases. In the second, the need for a home in such a city, declines. Another element of the choice game is that some are dependent on where someone has chosen to build rental housing. The location, almost always, is less desirable and desirability and access to community services and spaces usually declines in direct relation to the rents charged. Choice is also further constrained by our place in the life cycle, affecting needs such as unit size, physical accessibility, neighborhood, schools etc. Beyond choice of location are further cost constraints that impact on whether we buy or rent, share bedrooms, share apartments, have living space. In spite of these obvious and limiting constraints we continue to embrace the notion that the marketplace enables us to "choose" where and how we live. "Place" is indeed a powerful representation of who we are but for many it is imposed rather than chosen and, as Sassen suggests, the shifting nature of the economic marketplace and places of work for those competing for less skilled jobs further exacerbates the problems of "choice" of where to live.[28]

Implications for *All* of the People Living in Urban "Place"

The impacts of these changes to place are individual and personal but also have broader social meanings. It may not yet matter to those for whom place remains replete with possibility if there are others who are excluded. It is however my contention that over the long term it will matter to us all. First and most obvious has to be a consideration of what happens when a significant proportion of the population of our cities becomes so marginalized as to become a permanent underclass. I suggest that such a consideration is motivated by both morality and self-interest. A society that can effectively discard so many of its members will, even from the perspective of market economics, not fare as well as those which are inclusive and developmental, supporting the education and training of their citizens to the highest possible level. That of course is the self-interest argument; the moral one is an argument for equality.

At the root of this discussion, thus far largely implied, is a claim for *some kind of equality*, likely the social equality which Kaus claims to be increasingly less supported (and evident) in American life. While American, Canadian, most western European societies are stratified and we are unlikely to support an argument for money equality, Kaus argues that we used to have a much higher level of social equality. Fraser similarly notes that our social system generates inequality, what she describes as "groups in relations of dominance and subordination." Given this, Fraser argues, we are unlikely to see equal participation by all groups in public discourse and so argues for a plurality of publics that creates the widest possible avenues for public participation. A public or multiple publics, however the discourse is structured, must provide access to and engage the citizenry. A public(s) and spaces that support engagement, contestation, and mediation are critical to democratic society and without these, the society will begin to break down—even for those who *can* transcend place. The basis for this claim is the connection between equality and democracy. Democracy is based on a notion that citizens are a public, can participate in decisions which affect them, and that democratically organized political life is a central part of all people's lives. Some measure of equality is necessary to the realization of this and it is equality—perhaps equality of possibility—which is being eroded by globalization and the impacts of this are made manifest in the places of the city. Beck suggests that "in a society without consensus, devoid of legitimating core, it is evident that even a single gust of wind, caused by the cry for freedom, can bring down the whole house of cards of power". He further describes ghettos as "side-effects" in the centers of modern cities, an imagery which is perfect for its vitality and inhumanity. For they are just that—they are unintended, unfortunate and result inadvertently from what some regard as another quite satisfactory pursuit.[29]

Consequences of the Loss of Spaces of Mediation

For some, those who are marginalized and poor, not only is place fixed in time and space but so is opportunity and possibility. Jencks and Edin provide a compelling account of the social costs of this exclusion from the economic mainstream. The poor are casualties—their skills are no longer required in a global marketplace and support for them is no longer sanctioned by a "public" which is in decline, which often fails to make decisions according to the "public" interest. Indeed, the very idea that there *is* a public interest, distinct from aggregate individual preferences, is increasingly brushed aside as irrelevant.[30]

A question which arises from these considerations is in whose interest is a "public"? It has, I believe, been assumed by the tax paying public that the benefits of the public realm accrued unreasonably to the poor. Others could meet their own needs and do so more effectively in the marketplace. For members of all three groups, I suggest that the "public" realm and its representation in our local urban spaces is critical to the city as "place."

Contrasting with the claims made for the ability of technology to transcend space, Zukin reminds us of a theme that is recurrent in many contemporary conflicts occurring across the globe.[31] These are about localism and personal identity whether defined by ethnicity, religion or attachment to place. In spite of the transcendent promise offered by technology, people maintain attachments that are important beyond what may be rationally deduced. Zukin's claim is not surprising given that community is structured by social bonds formed in place and these contribute to feelings of local attachment. These bonds to place are supported by community activities and the experience of *shared* community life. The implication for the current discussion is that as place becomes particularized, homogenous and segregated—not shared—the social bonds of the community diminish. Further, many have suggested that our political bonds only continue to work because "civil society" or "interest groups" support the representation of non-market needs and demands in the political arena. Civil society requires structures and spaces which support it, especially given that mediation is now likely to involve mediating needs and interests between groups locked at one extreme, in their "urban reservations" and at the other extreme, in their private communities. Mediation becomes more difficult, because there is nothing that compels it, perhaps even little that suggests it to be necessary. Thus, the ready acknowledgement, by all of the populace, of the assumption on which such mediation is predicated—that there are or might be *common* needs and interests—has already fallen significantly from view.

The public realm has found its primary expression in the centers of cities. The expression and reflection of the public has however been more diverse, located across cities and oriented to the needs of all (most?) of its citizens. Public schools, parks, street space and sports arenas as well as cultural facilities, libraries and the more direct structures of government are manifestations of this public in most communities. These spaces tie us together as citizens of a place. Their use, even mediating disagreements over their use, involves us in a kind of local democracy. As a national public becomes harder to find and even harder to defend in a global marketplace, it is these local attachments which are likely to remind us of our areas of sustained public interest. Local attachments are supported and sustained by place and it is therefore at this level that we might most successfully argue that there remains a "public" interest, the mediation of which requires a public sphere. To these ends, the city must provide spaces which enable the experience of the public interest, the discourse and its further reproduction into space and place.

Conclusion

The genius of capital is . . . a relentlessly parasitic capacity to appropriate and saturate social life . . . But this capacity is not ineluctable; it is not a structurally foregone conclusion. Rather it is the dialogical tension between capital's rapacity and cultural resistance that is often central to the construction of urban forms.[32]

This paper has illustrated some of the impacts of globalization on place. An encroaching marketplace is transforming the traditional spheres of society and the structures and institutions by which they are represented, all of which results in profound changes to place. The city, as both mirror and map of change, plays a critical role as the site or place of "society"— wherein groupings of diverse people have been able to engage in a discourse about shared and conflicting social goals and interests. Thus, the city, and especially the centers of cities have provided places of social, political and economic mediation. These places or "centers" of mediation have been essential to resolving and/or managing the competing needs and interests of diverse social groups and developing sufficient shared values to enable the social engagement of *most* of society's members. Place has been a construct central to this political, economic and social discourse.

Among many changes being wrought by globalization, there appears to be less need for *economic* mediation between disparate social groups as the marketplace requires more specialization, fewer participants and fewer marginal workers. Workplaces are as likely as neigborhoods to be segregated on class and income lines. Head office workers remain downtown, in the center, while increasing land prices drives firms to relocate other parts of their operation which can indeed be linked through technology rather than by place. Mediation is also less necessary in the work place because so many people are simply no longer there. At the same time, work has become more central as the defining life practice. These phenomena have led to an assumption, largely by those who have secured their private lives, that social mediation in a public sphere is no longer essential or even desirable. This view, similar to the doctrine of globalization and free trade, suggests that the poor must simply "get competitive" and ignores the social and economic reality of those who have been economically marginalized. The perspective that the poor can effectively be dismissed because of their own failure, their lack of self-sufficiency, legitimizes the social and spatial disengagement of those who are middle class and "better." Both the structures and places that previously facilitated the mediation of social groups and the development of social bonds have suffered a loss of use and, correspondingly, a loss of meaning.

Consequences of these changes include an increasingly differentiated and homogeneous "place" in which sectors of society differing by race, ethnicity, level of prosperity and education, stage in the life cycle and participation/non-participation in economic life live in segregated seclusion. There are fewer naturally occurring opportunities—such as used to occur in city centers—for diverse representation and engagement in a public discourse. Zukin comments that "without a traditional centre cities . . . can only be seen in fragments." And the consequences of this will be many, including only "fragmented" representation in the "public" sphere and a fragmented and limited understanding of what such "public" issues might be. All of which reduce the ability of cities—*as places of people*—to offer resistance to what Ursula Franklin, a noted theorist on the social impacts of technology, describes as the global, economic "mining" of our cities.[33]

And, if the picture wasn't already sufficiently pessimistic, as these transformations occur in the places of the city, "place" is differently reproduced, with a different history and experience and meaning. Therefore, the spaces and places which result are less likely to be sites of alternative or resistant life practices that might help to shape changes in the prevailing social structure. As we lose sight of the city through the retreat into our respective realms, the likelihood that it will be viewed as a jungle—an environment hostile to that "public" which Deutche describes as having the keys to the park—increases, hastening the retreat—for those with economic choice—to private space, which in turn limits the possibility of seeing that heterogeneity was what kept "place" from being a jungle.

Notes

This paper has benefited from helpful comments from several friends and colleagues and from two anonymous reviewers from *Philosophy and Geography III* to whom I express my appreciation.

1. On the distinctions between space and place see Ayse Oncu and Petra Weyland, "Introduction: Struggles over Lebensraum and Social Identity in Globalizing Cities," in *Space, Culture and Power*, ed. Ayse Oncu and Petra Weyland (London: Zed Books, 1997), 1–20, 14; David Harvey, "From Space to Place and Back Again: Reflections on the Condition of Postmodernity," in *Mapping the Futures*, ed. Jon Bird, Barry Curtis, Tim Putnam, George Robertson and Lisa Tucker (London: Routledge, 1993) 3–29; and Edward Casey, *The Fate of Place* (Berkeley: University of California Press, 1996).

2. See Michel Chossudovsky, *The Globalization of Poverty* (London: Zed Books, 1997), and Saskia Sassen, *The Global City: New York, London, Tokyo* (Princeton, N.J.: Princeton University Press, 1991). For a discussion and analysis of the impacts of globalization, including increasing income disparity see Mickey Kaus, *The End of Equality* (New York: Basic Books, 1992). Kaus makes specific reference to this notion that some people expect to "buy" their way out of social mediation.

3. See A. Touraine, *Return of the Actor* (Minneapolis: University of Minnesota Press, 1988) for a discussion of people as "actors," and M. Dear and J. Wolch, "How Territory Shapes Social Life," in *The Power of Geography*, eds. J. Wolch, and M. Dear (Boston: Unwin Hyman Inc., 1989), 3–18, and L. S. Bourne, ed., *Internal Structure of the City* (London: Oxford University Press, 1982) for a discussion of how social and structural relations are played out in the spaces of the city. For further discussion on the "public," see Nancy Fraser "Rethinking the Public Sphere" *Social Text* 25/26 (1990): 56–80.

4. See W. Michelson, "Congruence: The Evolution of a Contextual Concept" in *Housing and Neighbourhood*, ed. Willem van Vliet et al. (New York: Greenwood Press 1987), 19–28, and David Popenoe, *Private Pleasure, Public Plight* (New Brunswick, N.J.: Transaction Books, 1985). Both argue the need to understand these relations more fully.

5. S. Pile and M. Keith, *Place of Politics of Identity* (New York: Routledge, 1993).

6. See E. Laclau and C. Mouffe, "Post-Marxism Without Apologies," *New Left Review* 166 (November/December 1987), 79–106, for a full discussion of this issue and the possibilities of human agency.

7. M. Gottdiener, *The Social Production of Urban Space*, 2nd ed. (Austin: University of Texas Press, 1994); also see S. Pile and M. Keith, *Place of Politics*, and Laclau and Mouffe, "Post Marxism Without Apologies."

8. M. Castells, *The Urban Question* (London: Edward Arnold, 1977); Soja as cited in Lagopoulos, A. P., "Postmodernism, Geography and the Social Semiotics of Space," *Environment and Planning: Society and Space* 11 (1993): 255–278, 262; C. Jencks, *Modern Movements in Architecture* (Harmondsworth: Penguin, 1985).

9. J. Cohen and A. Arato, *Civil Society and Political Theory* (Cambridge: MIT Press, 1992), use "civil society" to describe a sphere which encompasses life practices outside of the state, marketplace and family, which has the same intentions and is intended to rectify the same conceptual problems as the use of the term "social" sphere as it was used by H. Arendt, *The Human Condition* (Chicago: University of Chicago Press, 1958) and built on by K. Hansen, "Feminist Conceptions of Public and Private: A Critical Analysis," *Berkeley Journal of Sociology* 32 (1987): 105. The construct was used to correct for a significant array of life practices which are not encompassed in the traditional "public," "private" construction and was hence the third sector, contrasting also with the state and marketplace.

10. This is a term which I borrow from J. Habermas, *The Structural Transformation of the Public Sphere*, trans. T. Burger (Cambridge: MIT Press, 1989). I use it here because it so completely explicates the point that represented in the city is the whole world of life, life practices and the mediations between the life practices of the whole society.

11. D. Harvey, *The Urban Experience* (Baltimore: Johns Hopkins University Press, 1989), 230.

12. Oncu and Weyland, "Introduction," 11.

13. "Squeegee kids," who approach vehicles at traffic lights unsolicited and wash windshields hoping for payment are now a presence in many cities in Can-

ada and the United States and have sparked a considerable debate which is reflective of issues of inclusion and to whom the "public" belongs, as the middle class often argues that these kids have no right to be on public streets. The issue might be seen as one group effectively "forcing" a discourse and mediation with other socially and economically diverse groups.

14. See Fraser, "Rethinking the Public Sphere," whose notion of "public" this work most closely subscribes to, and Christopher Bryant, "Of Matters Public and Civil" in *Debating the Future of the Public Sphere*, ed. Stephen Edgell, Sandra Walklate and Gareth Williams (Aldershot, U.K.: Avebury, 1995), 257–268, for a discussion of these issues; Richard Sennett, "Bodily Experience in Public Space," in *Debating the Future of the Public Sphere*, eds. Stephen Edgell, Sandra Walklate and Gareth Williams (Aldershot, U.K.: Avebury, 1995) 165–176.

15. Fraser, "Rethinking the Public Sphere."

16. Jan Gehl, *Life Between Buildings* (New York: Van Nostrand Reinhold, 1987 [English trans., orig. publ., 1980]); Robert Kuttner, *The Economic Illusion* (Boston: Houghton Mifflin, 1984), 231.

17. Ray Oldenburg, *The Great Good Place* (New York: Paragon House, 1989); "use" is intended to convey wide usage by more than one constituency, across a wide span of time. How space is perceived to be used is also important—a particular group may not in fact use a space but consider that they could see it as being available for their use and in this sense it registers as "theirs"; M. Castells, *Urban Question*; Kaus, *End of Equality*, 55; Deutsche, *Evictions*, 276; J. Jacobs, *The Death and Life of Great American Cities* (New York: Random House, 1961).

18. W. Sachs, "One World," in *The Development Dictionary. A Guide to Knowledge as Power*, ed. W. Sachs (London: Zed Press, 1992), 111.

19. Anthony Giddens, *The Consequences of Modernity* (Stanford: Stanford University Press, 1990), 64.

20. Oncu and Weyland, "Introduction," 3.

21. Sassen, *The Global City*, 1991.

22. M. Sorkin, "Introduction," in *Variations On A Theme Park*, ed. M. Sorkin (New York: Hill and Wang, 1992), xi–xiv.

23. Erhard Berner, "The Metropolitan Dilemma: Global Society, Localities and the Struggle for Urban Land in Manila," in *Space, Culture and Power*, ed. A. Oncu and Petra Weyland (London: Zed Books, 1997), 98.

24. Berner, "The Metropolitan Dilemma," 100; also see Oncu and Weyland, *Space, Culture and Power*; Chossudovsky, *The Globalization of Poverty*; Sassen, *The Global City*; and Castells, *The Informational City: Information Technology, Economic Restructuring, and the Urban-Regional Process* (Oxford: Basil Blackwell, 1991) for an extensive discussion and analysis of the impacts of globalization.

25. Sassen, *The Global City*, and Saskia Sassen, *Cities in a World Economy*, (Thousand Oaks, Calif.: Pine Forge Press, 1994), describes in detail the process by which globalization widens the gap between not only rich and poor but between cities and between regions. Chossudovsky, *The Globalization of Poverty*, describes both the structures and impacts of global economics and details their particular nature in several regions of the world, Christopher Jencks and Kathryn Edin, "Do Poor Women Have a Right to Bear Children?" *American Prospect* 20

(Winter 1995): 43–52, more directly describe the economic life chances available to those who are marginalized; the point being made is not that the spaces of the center have disappeared, but that they become less important to those with the "opportunity" to transcend them.

26. We sometimes assume that the only people who are fearful of our inner cities without centers are the middle class. This "story" is of course inaccurate, as inner city crime is perpetrated by a comparatively small number of people and the most common victims are other poor people. See James Midgley, "The Radical Right, Politics and Society," *The Radical Right and the Welfare State*, ed. Howard Glennerster and James Midgley (Hempstead, U.K.: Harvester Wheatsheaf, 1991) 3–23; Margaret M. Severson, "Adapting Social Work Values to the Corrections Environment," *Social Work* 39, 4 (1994): 451–456; Gary Teeple, *Globalization and the Decline of Social Reform* (Toronto: Garamond Press, 1995). These works discuss the increasing reliance, especially in the U.S., on the criminal justice and penal systems to "serve" those previously attended in a social service setting.

27. Willem van Vliet, *Housing and Neighbourhoods* (New York: Greenwood Press, 1993), 559.

28. Sassen, *The Global City*.

29. Kaus, *The End of Equality*, argues for a return to "social equality," and to key structures and institutions which have been lost and contribute to our loss of social equality. Among these he acknowledges the importance of "place." See also Fraser, "Rethinking the Public Sphere," 66; Ulrich Beck, *The Reinvention of Politics*, trans. Mark Ritter (Cambridge: Polity Press, 1997), 100.

30. See, for example, R. Sennett, *The Conscience of the Eye* (New York: Alfred Knopf, 1990); Jencks and Edin, "Do Poor Women Have a Right to Bear Children?".

31. Sharon Zukin, *Landscapes of Power* (Berkeley: University of California Press, 1991), 217.

32. J. Caulfield, *City Form and Everyday Life* (Toronto: University of Toronto Press, 1994), 229.

33. Zukin, *Landscapes of Power*, 217; Ursula Franklin, "Local Democracy," Public Lecture, Innis College, University of Toronto, October 28, 1997.

Space-Shaping Technologies
and the Geographical Disembedding
of Place

Philip Brey

Places are not what they used to be. Rapid transportation systems have shrunk the distance between places, transforming them from isolated spots to junctions in the global village. Electric media like telephony allow places to blend into each other, making it possible to be closer to someone thousands of miles away than to a person in the next room. Computer networks have generated new places in cyberspace, that are frequented and inhabited like physical places. All this has dramatically altered the nature of places, as well as our sense of place. Or so I will argue.

Specifically, I will defend the thesis that over the past two centuries, the role of geographical features in the constitution of the identity of places has decreased; this devaluation has resulted from the employment of various space-shaping technologies, used by human beings to transcend the limitations of their local environments. I call this thesis the *geographical disembedding thesis*: places have become geographically disembedded, that is, they are less and less determined and defined by physical-geographical features. This thesis will be explained and defended in this essay, and it will be discussed how this process of geographical disembedding has impacted the identity of places, and even our very concept of place.

The structure of the remainder of the paper is as follows. In the next section, I will further expound the geographical disembedding thesis, focusing on key concepts like place, geographical disembedding and space shaping. In sections three to six, four geographical disembedding processes will be discussed along with the space-shaping technologies that sustain them. They are time-space compression, time-space distanciation, space blending, and space generation. Each section will describe one such process, the technologies that sustain it, and its role in the geographical disembedding of place. It will also be analyzed how these four processes cohere. In a concluding section, I will discuss how the geographical disembedding of place that results from these processes is transforming place identities, and even our very conception of place.

Conceptual Preliminaries: Place, Geographical Disembedding, Space Shaping

This essay is concerned with the changing identity of places. But what do I mean by "place"? To begin, I of course mean "geographical place," that is, a part of a geographical region. But then there are many conceptions of geographical place. Place is sometimes defined objectively, as a mere location in physical space. Many, however, have emphasized the importance of human activity and human conception in the definition of place. David Seamon has argued that places should be understood as human constructs that arise out of routine physical interactions with the environment.[1] Yi-fu Tuan has described place as "an organized world of meaning" that emerges out of human interpretation and valuation of space: "What begins as undifferentiated space becomes place as we get to know it better and endow it with value."[2] David Canter has proposed that places are the product of physical attributes, activities, and conceptions and that any definition of place should refer to these three ingredients.[3]

Taking the suggestions of these authors into account, I will define place as *an area or space that is a habitual site of human activity and/or is conceived of in this way by communities or individuals.* This definition includes many spaces identified intuitively as human places, such as cities and villages, farms and beaches, market places and graveyards, favorite nature spots and cross-roads, homes and drilling platforms, as well as smaller places like living rooms and reading corners. In this essay, the places I have in mind will usually be larger places that are sites of social life, such as cities and office buildings, or what have been called "locales," the places of operation of collectives.

Turning now to the notion of geographical disembedding, this notion is intended to denote *the decreasing importance of geographical features of places, both their internal geographical features and their geographical location in physical space, as important aspects of their identity.* The identity of a place, its *place identity*, can be understood as those features that constitute a place as a meaningful site of human activity, and that situate it relative to other places and locations. Traditionally, geographical features of places have played a strong role in their identity, and they still do. For example, the identity of a city like San Francisco is determined in large part by its physical layout, its characteristic buildings, its site in a hilly terrain near a large bay, and its location on the West Coast of the United States. However, I will argue that in many places, understood as sites of human activity, such geographical markers are increasingly superseded by other identity markers. This is because place identity is to a large extent determined by the significance of a place for human activity, and geographical markers are becoming less influential as determining factors of the significance for human activity of a place.

By the significance of a place for human activity, I mean two things: (1) the kinds of activities that it enables as determined in large part by the kinds of objects and structures available in it and (2) its nearness to other places and spaces that contain different opportunities for human activity. The kinds of activities that a place enables are determined in large part by the *goods*, or amenities, that a place offers. I intend to use the term 'good' in its broadest possible sense, to include any structure, object, person, or event that affords certain human activities or experiences. Example of goods are buildings, foods, services, information, vistas, festivals, social communities, weather, and local customs. The significance of a place for human activity, as defined by the goods it contains and its nearness to other places, largely defines its identity. By illustration, a village with no drinking water for which the next well is twenty miles away will acquire a different place identity than a village that has a well nearby or within its confines. Similarly, the place identity of a town square would be significantly altered by the addition of an information booth or a number of benches, as it would support different kinds of activity and afford different experiences.

The geographical disembedding thesis can now be reformulated to say that both the nature of the goods found in a particular place and its nearness to other places with different goods are less and less determined by its geographical features alone. This transcendence of geographical constraints is the result of a continual historical effort by human beings to overcome the limitations imposed by their physical environments. Historically, there have been two means by which human beings have pursued such transcendence. A first route has been *local development*, the modification and enhancement of local geographical elements: plowing the land, building homes, constructing a well, and installing air conditioning. Such development makes human activity less dependent on geographical contingencies of places. For example, air conditioning makes it possible to regulate temperature, and therefore to break free from the temperature contingencies of a particular geographical place.

A second route has been *connectivity development*, being the construction of more and better linkages between places, so that (1) goods from other places can become more quickly and easily available in a place and (2) people can themselves move more quickly and easily to other places to gain access to goods in them. Extensive transportation, information and communication systems have been developed to this purpose, including structures like roads, automobiles, airplanes, airports, canals, oil pipes, satellites, and television sets. In recent years, connectivity development has even included the development of and connection to novel places that have no identifiable location in physical space, i.e., places in cyberspace.

In this essay, I will refrain from discussion of the role of local development in geographical disembedding, and will instead focus on the role of connectivity development. I take connectivity development to be an attempt by human beings to overcome the limitations of geographically situated places through efforts to "shrink" or even abolish their distance to other geographical places, or to even create novel, "virtual" places that link to them. I will call these attempts to "shrink" and "create" space and place *space shaping*. Space shaping is performed through the deployment of *space-shaping technologies*, that are technologies that are able to "shrink" or "create" space.[4] These include the aforementioned transportation, information and communication technologies.

Connectivity development geographically disembeds places by making their nearness to other places less a function of geographical, physical distance, and more a function of various kinds of *relative distance*. The notion of relative distance has been used in geography to denote conceptions of distance between places that are defined in pragmatic terms, such as the time and cost it requires to move from one place to another.[5] I will construe this notion similarly but more philosophically to denote the ease by which (aspects of) goods in one place can be made *available* to individuals located in another place. Space-shaping technologies enhance the availability of goods in other places. Goods may be made more available by enhancing their use availability, perceptual availability, or informational availability. *Use availability* is the ease by which goods can be made available to use, modify, or otherwise affect them. *Perceptual availability* is the ease by which goods can be made available to be perceived (in particular, to be seen and heard). *Informational availability* is the ease by which (perceptual or linguistic) information about goods in other places can be gained. To illustrate, television has served to enhance the perceptual availability but not the use availability of places, whereas airline connections have also enhanced their use availability.

Space-shaping technologies have made the geographical distance between places increasingly inadequate as a measure of the relative distance between them. A place like Johannesburg may in many ways be closer to a geographically distant place like New York, with which it maintains high connectivity, than to a small town eighty miles away in the South-African countryside. Indeed, the intensification of space-shaping processes in the twentieth century appears to have ushered in a new geographical order in which traditional, metric conceptions of distance are increasingly inadequate.[6] Places and the individuals in them are increasingly less determined by their geographical location and more determined by their location in a global web created by space-shaping technologies.

The aim of this paper is to show how the development of various space-shaping technologies yields a geographical disembedding of place. I will have little to say as to what is causing these technologies to be developed, and hence what motivates connectivity development. I have suggested that this development may be due to a general drive of human beings to overcome the limitations of their physical environment and have access to more goods. Indeed, many authors, from seventeenth-century philosopher Francis Bacon to twentieth-century media prophet Marshall McLuhan, have interpreted technology as a means to satisfy the human drive for greater power and control over the environment. Any such general explanation of the space-shaping dynamic will probably have to be supplemented by more detailed explanations that relate this dynamic to more specific historical constructs, like the institutional structure of modernity and the inherent dynamics of capitalist economies.[7]

Time-Space Compression and the Shrinking World

It is already a cliché to say that our world is becoming smaller. Many have claimed that we live in a "shrinking world," in which distances are increasingly meaningless, and space and time are being progressively conquered. This phenomenon has been described alternatively as the "shrinking of space and time," "time-space convergence," and "time-space compression," the term that is adopted in this essay.[8] Marshall McLuhan even went as far as to suggest that we are now living in a "global village," a world whose inhabitants have abolished distance.[9] In most discussions, the notion of a shrinking world is used as an intuitive concept to capture felt experiences of dissolving boundaries between places and the increasing meaningless of distance. I will now investigate whether and how this intuitive concept can be provided with a more rigorous foundation.

One of the first authors to analyze the intuitive notion of a shrinking world was the geographer Donald Janelle, who in the late sixties introduced the influential notion of *time-space convergence*.[10] Janelle introduced this notion as a way to measure the notion of a shrinking world. Time-space convergence is the process of places moving closer together (or sometimes farther apart) in travel and communication time. The *travel time* between two places is the amount of time needed to travel from one place to another using the fastest available mode of transportation. The *communication time* between two places is the amount of time needed to exchange information between two places using the fastest communication medium available. As the travel and communication times between places shrink, they may be said to move closer to each other in *time-space*, a theoretical construct in which distances between places are not defined as metric distances, but as *time-distances*. The time-distance between two places is the time needed to cross the physical distance between them.

With these notions, it can be shown that although the absolute, metric distance between places is fixed, the time-distance between many places in the world, particularly in the West, has been shrinking steadily over the past two centuries. The distance of 210 miles between New York and Boston, for example, took 4,700 minutes to cross in 1800 (by stagecoach), but only 300 minutes in 1965 (by automobile). Nowadays, the cities are even nearer in time-space because of regular air service between them. Likewise, the communication distance between New York and San Francisco has been decreasing because of the introduction of faster communication technologies. In particular, the *telephone distance* between them (the time needed to place a call from one city to the other) was reduced from fourteen minutes in 1920 to less than thirty seconds. There has hence been a quantifiable time-space convergence between major cities like these, in that they have been moving closer to each other in time-space in several respects.[11]

The notion of time-distance can be used as a measure to give quantitative content to the notion of a shrinking world. It is, however, only one measure, as reductions in travel and communication time may not be the only factors that occasion the experience of a world becoming smaller. Janelle suggests *cost distance* as a second relevant measure. This is the distance between two places defined in terms of the cost of crossing the physical distance between them. The cost distance between many places is also shrinking, and consequently there is a *cost-space convergence* between them. For example, the cost of telephone calls between distant places has been decreasing steadily over time, and progressive decreases in the cost of air travel have been working to decrease cost, along with time, as a barrier for travel to distant places.

Janelle's analyses show that two of the main barriers that create a sense of distance between places, time and cost, are being eroded more and more. Indeed, I want to suggest that the notion of eroding barriers between places may be the key behind the concept of the shrinking world. *Barriers* between places may be defined as factors that help maintain relative distances between places. Relative distances relate to the ease by which places and goods in them can be made accessible. There appear to be several types of accessibility relations between places. The two discussed by Janelle may be called *travel accessibility*, which is the ease by which one can move from one place to another, and *communications accessibility*, the ease by which communication links can be established between places. Other relevant accessibility types may include *informational accessibility* (the accessibility of relevant information about other places), and *visual accessibility* (the ease by which one can find out about other places through recent visual footage). These are different ways in which the perceptual, informational and use availability of goods in places is enhanced.

I also want to suggest that there are barriers other than time and cost barriers that limit place accessibility. The most important one is *effort*: People are not only kept from traveling to distant places or placing calls to people in distant places because it requires a lot of time and money but also because it requires too much effort. Travel, for example, may requires intensive physical effort (e.g., lifting heavy luggage) and cognitive effort (e.g., planning a trip and making arrangements). Effort barriers between places have been reduced over time along with time and cost barriers, through efficiency measures and improvements in service. The shrinking world may consequently be analyzed as a world in which many places are moving nearer to each other in time-, cost-, and effort-distance relating to travel, communication, perception, and informational access.[12]

Janelle attributes the occurrence of time-space and cost-space compression processes to *space-adjusting technologies*: technologies that adjust the time- and cost-distance between places. These include transportation and communication technologies generally, insofar as they work to speed up travel and mediated communication and decrease their cost. Ever faster and cheaper transportation and communication technologies are hence the immediate cause of time-space compression. It should hence be clear how space-adjusting technologies contribute to the geographical disembedding of places. They decrease the amount of time, cost and effort it takes to travel to, communicate with, see, or be informed about (goods in) other places, thereby decreasing the importance of geographical distance as a determinant of the relative distance between places.[13]

Time-Space Distanciation and Global Interdependence

The notion of time-space compression is sometimes confused with the notion of *time-space distanciation* that was introduced in social theory by Anthony Giddens.[14] This is however a quite different process. It does not apply so much to places as it does to social relations and the social systems that contain them. It can be defined as the *stretching* of social systems (like societies and organizations) and social relations (like employer-employee and manufacturer-client relations) across time and space. Social systems and relations are *distanciated* in space and time as a result, which also implies a new type of interaction: *distanciated social interaction*, in which the interacting parties are removed from each other in space and often in time as well. A company, for example, may issue an order in New York that is received and acted on days later in a manufacturing plant in Malaysia. A consumer may order a book over the Internet, which may result in the processing of her order somewhere else days later, which may result weeks later in her receiving a package in her mailbox.[15] Distanciated social interaction stands in contrast to ordinary face-to-face social interaction, in which parties are present in the same space-time frame.

Giddens argues that modern societies are marked by their high level of time-space distanciation. He goes on to identify two conditions that are satisfied in modern societies but not in premodern societies that have made this distanciation process possible. The first condition is the *separation of time and space*. In modern societies, time and space have been disentangled from both each other and the contextual features of local places to which they were tied, to become separate, "empty" parameters that can be used as structuring principles for large-scale social and technical systems. This separation process was effectuated by the introduction of the mechanical clock in the fourteenth century, fixed-viewpoint perspectival maps and global maps in the fifteenth century, and the establishment of analytic geometry in the seventeenth century, and has been continuing since then, with the introduction and further dissemination of still better and more universal time-keeping systems (e.g., universal time zones) and mapping systems.

As Giddens explains, time and space in premodern societies were still linked to both each other and to place. Local places, in which social life was conducted on a face-to-face basis, gave content to the then prevailing notions of time and space. Time was marked by reference to places and the social interactions and events taking place in them, although regular natural occurrences like sunrise also constituted reference points. To refer to a particular time, for example, one referred to "when the last dinner was finished" (or "when the sun came up"). Space was similarly marked in terms of place. Distance was measured by reference to distance between familiar places, and maps were not attempts to locate places in an independently existing space, but to locate them relative to each other.[16]

Giddens claims that the mechanical clock introduced an "empty" dimension of time that was independent of place, and that global maps consecutively introduced a similar "empty" dimension of space, in which there was no privileged viewpoint and places were mere locations in an independently existing space. This "emptying out" of time and space separated these dimensions both from each other and from the contingencies of places. Giddens emphasizes that this separation allowed time and space, as "empty" parameters, to be recombined in ways that coordinate social activities in large-scale forms of organization. Such organization, however, still relied on a second precondition of time-space distanciation: The lifting out of local contexts of social relations and institutions by *disembedding mechanisms*, which are media such as money, time-tables, organization charts, and systems of expert knowledge. Disembedding mechanisms define social relations and guide social interactions without reference to the peculiarities of place. Their combination with time measurement and geographical mapping systems that rely on "empty" conceptions of space and time makes possible the precise coordination of actions of physically remote human beings that is found in distanciated social systems.

Whereas time-space compression implies places moving closer to each other, time-space distanciation gives rise to a different phenomenon that Giddens calls "place as phantasmagoric." This is "the process by which local characteristics of place are thoroughly invaded by, and reorganized in terms of, distanciated social relations." The globalization of social activity through time-space distanciation leads to an "interlacing of social events and social relations 'at distance' with local contextualities." This produces a "dialectic of the local and global" in which "events at one pole of a distanciated relation often produce divergent and even contrary occurrences in another."[17] This dialectic has consequences for individual places, in which no longer just local interactions and events determine their characteristics, but "absent" distanciated social relations and events become equally important. Decisions made in financial markets in New York and Tokyo may cause unemployment hikes in Dublin, Ireland, and the development of downtown shopping areas may be as much determined by distanciated social relations with national chain stores as it is by local governance.[18]

How, finally, is time-space distanciation a factor in the geographical disembedding of place? Time-space distanciation is a process by which more enduring forms of social connectivity between places are established. Through it, human activity in one place can constrain and be constrained by human activity in other places, which may result in places being profoundly changed because of their distanciated social relations with other places. Not all these changes necessarily imply geographical disembedding, however. A distanciated social relation of a city council in a place with a contractor elsewhere may result in a well or office building being built in this place, which changes its identity, but does not change its relative location with respect to other places.

There are two ways, however, in which time-space distanciation does contribute to geographical disembedding. First, distanciated social relations constitute a necessary condition for the maintenance of the space-adjusting technologies discussed in section 3, and hence for the geographical disembedding these instigate. Second, time-space distanciation makes human activity less constrained by the *local social-geographical features* of places, that is, the ecology of social relations that exist within a place, as distanciated social relations may often impose more important social constraints. What Giddens calls "disembedding mechanisms" hence contribute to the geographical disembedding of places because they disembed some of their social-geographical features. Taking these two aspects together, I claim that time-space distanciation is a means to establish and coordinate (unilateral and bilateral) relations of use availability between individuals or organizations. A distanciated employer-employee relationship, for example, makes the labor power of the employee available to the employer in spite of the distance between them.

This is a way of overcoming some of the limitations on use availability that space-adjusting technologies cannot take away: space-adjusting technologies can enhance the perceptual and informational availability of goods in other places, and can facilitate their use ability through travel and transportation, but (barring certain systems that enable tele-operation) they cannot make goods in one place available for use to one while one is located in another. Time-space distanciation makes distanciated people available for use, through the manufacture of social relations that, as Giddens emphasizes, rely on trust as a binding element (e.g., trust that others in remote places are cooperating with one on a project, or trust that money in one's possession will be accepted in remote places). The use availability of people made possible by distanciated social relations often functions as a condition of the facilitation of the availability of goods in the remote places where these people operate. For example, if you want bananas from Brazil without going there, distanciated social relations that ultimately link local growers with your local supermarket work to guarantee their use availability in your place.

Space Blending and Electric Media: The Fusion of Places in the Global Village

In the analysis of time-space compression in section 3, this phenomenon was identified as due to space-adjusting technologies that "shrink" space and so bring places closer together. I will now argue that a large subclass of space-adjusting technologies, consisting of technologies that rely on electric modes of transmission of information, do not just "shrink" the distance between places, but actually work to *blend* places and spaces together. Electric media *abolish* some of the time-space barriers between places that could only be made smaller by other space-adjusting technologies (transportation technologies and non-electric media like the printing press, the postal service system, and photography). These latter technologies may be called *space-compressing technologies* as they compress, but do not abolish distance between places. With them, distant places still remain relatively separate spheres of action. Electric media, however, are capable of bringing two places into actual contact with one another.

Electric media make it possible to be physically located in one place while simultaneously perceiving aspects of other places. In this way, they enable a *partial permeation* of places by each other, in that features in one place are made available as objects of perception (and sometimes even use) in another place. This partial permeation can occur in one or in two directions. Television is a one-way medium, as it blends perceptual and auditory features of one place into other places to become part of their environment. Telephone is a two-way medium, as it blends two places into each other by making their auditory features mutually available.

One of the first scholars to observe this phenomenon of space blending was Marshall McLuhan. His *Understanding Media* can be read as an extended case for the fundamental difference between electric media and the "mechanical" technologies, as he called them, that preceded them. As McLuhan noted, electric media do not just shrink space and time, as some of these older technologies do, they go on to abolish it. As he put it,

> After three thousand years of explosion, by means of fragmentary and mechanical technologies, the Western World is imploding. During the mechanical ages we had extended our bodies in space. Today, after more than a century of electric technology, we have extended our central nervous system itself in a global embrace, abolishing both space and time as far as our planet is concerned.[19]

McLuhan claimed that electric media contract what was first expanded through other technologies. As he puts it, "The stepping-up of speed from the mechanical to the instant electric form reverses explosion into implosion."[20] McLuhan's position can be clarified by reference to Giddens's notion of time-space distanciation. Previous, "mechanical" technologies have helped to create large-scale, distanciated social systems, and have thereby moved attention away from local place to disclose a world of interdependent yet fundamentally dissociated places. With the emergence and widespread use of electric media, these dissociated places are suddenly all drawn together, in an "implosion" that blends them together and makes them even much more interdependent.

The result of this implosion is what McLuhan calls a "global village." The label "global village" appears to be apt in at least three ways. First, electric media enable its inhabitants to find out about or even witness global events instantaneously. This is like life in a local village, in which events of interest to the community are usually local events and are either experienced directly or are found out about quickly. Second, electronic communications media allow for instantaneous communication with remote individuals. This is like the instantaneous communication in villages, in which most anyone can be contacted fast for face-to-face consultation. Third, electric media make a direct and interactive coordination of social activities over remote distances possible, just like local coordination of such activities in villages. For example, a police force may pursue a criminal over an area of hundreds of square miles through a coordinated chase using mobile telephones. Distanciated social interactions hence take on a new dimension with electric media, that of instantaneity. Together, these three properties of electric media sometimes make living in a global society seem like living in a global village.

Lacking in McLuhan's account, however, is a detailed analysis of how electric media fuse places together. Fortunately, this topic is taken up by Joshua Meyrowitz, in a study of how electric media transform places and social situations.[21] Meyrowitz claims that electric media create new *social situations* or *social settings*, that are social environments or "contexts" in which certain types of behaviors are socially expected and exhibited. Examples of social settings are concerts, marriage ceremonies, counseling sessions, hospitals, public squares on Sundays, and restaurants during dinner time. Social settings are defined by various factors, including social custom and legal and cultural codes. Most important, however, is *the pattern of information flow*, which is the pattern of access to *social information* by various actors in the social setting. Social information is "all that people are capable of knowing about the behavior and actions of themselves and others," including "words, gestures, vocalizations, posture, dress, and pace of activity." Meyrowitz explains: "When we find ourselves in a given setting we often unconsciously ask, 'Who can see me, who can hear me?' 'Who can I see, who can I hear?' The answers to these questions help us decide how to behave."[22] These questions are answered by analyzing social settings as *information-systems*, as given patterns of access to the behavior of other people.

Before the advent of electric media, the pattern of information flow in social situations was largely determined by the physical environment in which the social setting was established. Social situations were place-bound. Structures like buildings, walls and windows determined who could see and hear whom, and helped create various social settings for human activity. One could usually find out the kind of information-system one was in by observing one's physical environment. Nowadays, one also has to take into account the presence of electric media, that may make others visible or audible to one, or may make one visible or audible to others. Electric media hence change social settings through their transformation of existing information-systems. A medium like television helps create one-way "windows" between distant places, and telephony may even create a "private chat-room" that blends (part of) the two spaces in which the callers are located.

Meyrowitz's theory provides insight into the process of space blending by analyzing it as the establishment by electric media of patterns of information flow between previously separated information systems (i.e., spatially separate places). There are limitations to his theory, however, as a general account of space blending, as it only considers social information flow. Certainly, space blending also occurs when someone's social situation is not modified, for example if someone in Boston watches a news report showing live footage of an oil spill in the Pacific, which does not show humans behaving. Meyrowitz's theory can be easily modified, however, by redefining information-systems as systems of access to *any* kind of perceptual information, rather than just social information. Space blending is then the process by which electric media blend information systems contained in separate places by establishing perceptual information links or "windows" between them.

Let me now relate the process of space blending more explicitly to the processes of time-space compression and time-space distanciation. Space blending can be analyzed as a special type of time-space compression, in which some aspects of the informational and communicative distance between places are not just shrunk, but actually abolished, and places come to informationally permeate each other. Electric media can moreover be used to help maintain and coordinate distanciated social relations and interactions. Especially the telephone is used in this way, although news and information broadcasts on television and radio may also serve this function. Distanciated social interactions through electric media differ from other distanciated social interactions, because of their immediacy and their greater resemblance to face-to-face interactions.

How, finally, do electric media geographically disembed place? Since they are space-adjusting technologies, the general way they do this was already discussed in section 3. What is distinctive about electric media, however, is the *intensity* with which they geographically disembed places. By allowing places to partially blend together, they manage to abolish geographical distance between places as a factor in determining their perceptual (and sometimes even their use) availability.

The New Geographies of Cyberspace

Computer Media and the Nature of Cyberspace

In the previous section, I analyzed electric media as technologies capable of blending distant physical spaces. I will now argue that *computer media*, especially computer networks, constitute a special type of electric medium that requires special consideration. I define computer media as computer-based information and communication systems, such as desktop computers, computer networks, and virtual reality systems, that communicate with users through a digital interface, usually involving a screen and a keyboard or other input device. Computer media, I claim, have unique capacities of *representation* and *simulation* that allow them to *generate* new spaces, rather than just blend existing spaces together. They are hence *space-generating technologies*. The new spaces they generate have no identifiable location in physical space, and may therefore be called *virtual spaces*. The capacity to generate virtual spaces is most evident in virtual reality systems, which simulate immersive, interactive virtual environments that have no systematic relation to physical space. I will argue, however, that similar generative abilities can also be demonstrated in other computer media. This will then lead me to consider ways in which computer media are geographically disembedding physical places and are generating new, virtual geographies.

The idea that computer media create new, virtual spaces and places is certainly not new. Since the late 1980s, the term "cyberspace" has been used as a term to denote such virtual spaces. Mostly, this term is used to denote the total set of interactive environments generated by computer networks in general, and the Internet in particular. In most discussions, however, the status of this term remains unclear. Is "cyberspace" a metaphorical term, in the way that the expression "surfing the Internet" is mere metaphor, or can it be defended that virtual spaces, although not physically realized, should qualify as genuine spaces that are essentially analogous to physical spaces? To answer this question, more precise definitions of cyberspace are needed first. The term "cyberspace" is ambiguous, as it is used to denote computer environments ranging from a plain MS-DOS operating system to hypothetical future mergers of the Internet with virtual reality technology. I will here adopt a helpful distinction made by Featherstone and Burrows between three varieties of cyberspace:[23]

Barlovian Cyberspace: This is the set of virtual, interactive environments generated by the existing international network of computers. Named after Internet pioneer John Barlow, it is a virtual space nowadays used by some 40 million people. Barlovian cyberspace shows up as a mostly two-dimensional environment on the screen and is largely text-based, although it also includes images and video and audio functions. The ordinary working environment of personal computers may also be defined as Barlovian cyberspace.

Virtual Reality (VR): This is a computer-generated immersive, three-dimensional, interactive environment that is accessed and manipulated using stereo headphones, head-mounted stereo television goggles, data-gloves that allow for touching and grabbing virtual objects, and computerized clothing that senses the relative position of body parts. The simulated environment is constantly being reconfigured in response to bodily movements.

Gibsonian Cyberspace: This is the original concept of cyberspace, first used by William Gibson in his science fiction novel *Neuromancer*.[24] It can be interpreted as an imagined future merger between the Internet and VR systems, in which users put on headsets and other VR equipment to access global databases through three-dimensional graphic interfaces, and to interact with other users in simulated environments.[25]

Clearly, VR environments and Gibsonian cyberspace qualify as genuine virtual spaces, as they are both immersive, interactive, three-dimensional environments in which people can act and interact. The current international network of computers, however, only contains Barlovian cyberspace. To what extent can this network be interpreted as creating new spaces and places?

Space and Place in Contemporary Cyberspace

What appears to speak against a conception of international computer networks as containing virtual spaces and places is that most of the networks software does not simulate interactive, three-dimensional environments. Most of what is represented is flat text, and *prima facie* it seems inappropriate to describe text pages or documents such as those found on the World Wide Web (WWW) as "spaces" or "places" or even "environments." Still, I will argue, there is a clear sense in which computer networks, and even ordinary personal computers, do contain virtual spaces and places.

To have this case made, it is necessary to consider the way computer media function. It is an essential property of computer media that they are devices that manipulate *symbolical representations*, or symbol structures, or symbols in short. Many such symbols remain invisible to users, as they are "machine code" that is interpreted by the machine. Larger symbolical structures that rely on these lower-level symbols may, however, be made accessible to users as objects that they can manipulate. They are usually made visible on the screen, where they are represented by an icon (e.g., one that depicts a folder) or a symbol string (e.g., "msdos.exe" representing a program). Such symbolical structures I will call *virtual objects*. They are virtual rather than real objects because they do not have a physical form or location, although they may be represented on computer screens by icons that do have shape and location.

Consider, by illustration, the virtual working environment created by a modern operating system, like Microsoft Windows or Macintosh OS.

Its virtual "desktop" will normally show various virtual objects, such as files, folders, a trash bin, program icons, open windows, and a pointer. A page on the WWW can also be considered a virtual object, that will moreover contain various virtual objects itself, such as words, hyperlinks, and buttons. Even the old, pre-Windows operating system MS-DOS contains virtual objects. It can only display linguistic and numeric symbols, but these symbols still refer to manipulable virtual objects in the computer, such as files, directories, and numbers.

The notion of virtual object allows us to make sense of the notions of place and space in contemporary computer media. First, a *place* in contemporary, Barlovian cyberspace is a virtual object that is able to *contain* other virtual objects and so may come to function as an *environment* in which other virtual objects may be encountered and activities may take place. This definition of place fits my original definition in section 2 of place as an area or space that is perceived or used as a site of human activity. Windows, desktops and folders constitute places in this sense, as do structures on the Internet like web-pages, web-sites, virtual chat-rooms, multi-user domains (MUDs), and newsgroups.

Second, contemporary cyberspace constitutes a *space* because it consists of a system of *topological relations* between virtual objects. This space is a *topological space*, rather than a geometric space, because the relations between virtual objects in contemporary cyberspace are not, or not primarily, defined in terms of geometric distance. The notion of a topological space has been rigorously defined in mathematical topology. Roughly, a topological space is an abstract space in which objects are subjected to abstract ordering principles, that define connections and trajectories between objects even though these objects have no location in geometric space. In MS-DOS, for example, files and programs may be contained "in" directories, even though none of these objects have geometric shapes. *Web-space*, as another example, is the topological space generated by the system of hyperlinks between pages on the WWW. As one finds oneself at a particular place "in" Web-space, one can "move" to or "visit" another location, or "return" to a previous one, even though Web-pages maintain no (real or virtual) geometric spacings. Contemporary cyberspace hence contains what may be called a *virtual geography*, a topological structure defined over virtual objects.

Activities performed in cyberspace may be called *virtual activities*, as they consist in the manipulation or perception of virtual objects. Examples of virtual activities include deleting a file, posting an e-mail message, making a move in computer chess, reading a Web-page, painting with software, completing a virtual order form, and chatting with a friend in a virtual chat-room. These virtual activities take place in virtual places, as defined earlier. They also partially take place in the real world, however, as they originate in a user who is sitting in front of a monitor, while typing on the keyboard or moving the mouse. Virtual activity takes place, one may say, in a blended environment of virtual and physical space. Virtual and physical spaces may permeate each other in two directions. The display makes virtual objects and places part of the perceptual environment of the physical space in which the user is located, and the keyboard and mouse extend one's hands into virtual space to manipulate these objects. Virtual spaces may moreover blend with more than one physical space at once, as in MUDs, chat-rooms, and networked computer games, to become shared spaces. Such virtual spaces indirectly blend physical places that may be thousands of miles apart.

The Flight to Cyberspace

Human activities in contemporary cyberspace are naturally more limited than those possible in more Gibsonian forms of cyberspace. It turns out, nevertheless, that many important human activities do not require three-dimensional, immersive virtual environments. Contemporary cyberspace is a terrain that has the potential to become a site where a significant proportion of human conduct takes place. Certainly, this has already happened with the individual cyberspaces found in personal computers, and it is happening with cyberspace in computer networks. For some individuals, life in cyberspace is already more engrossing than life in physical space, as for the college graduate interviewed in Sherry Turkle's *Life on the Screen*, who claims: "I feel that I have more stuff on the MUD than off it."[26] I will argue that we are currently witnessing a *flight to cyberspace*, in which the physical, geographical terrain as a site of human activity is being partially replaced by the virtual terrain of cyberspace, as more and more human activities are being relocated to cyberspace. As contemporary cyberspace is getting bigger, faster, and more sophisticated, this flight can only be expected to intensify.

To be replicable in cyberspace, a human activity must be analyzable as, or reducible to, an *information processing task*. Part of the reason is, of course, that computer media are by definition information-processing devices. Notice, however, that virtual human activity is not only sustained by the information-processing capacities of computer media, but also by the information-processing capacities of their users: their abilities to think, perceive information on the display, and issue commands to the computer. It is therefore not just the computer, but the computer in cooperation with the user that is doing information processing. Computers and users team up to constitute *hybrid information-processing systems*, where both units process information internally and exchange information to each other. The question is now what human activities in physical space can be replicated by the information-processing activities of human-computer tandems.

I claim that at least four important classes of human activity can be, and are being, replicated in this way. First, there are what I call *experiential activities*: activities that have as their primary aim to have certain perceptual experiences or to absorb certain types of information. These include activities like reading, watching pictures, and viewing landscapes. The objects of normal experiential activity, such as books, magazines, letters, art collections, photographs, and videos, can be transformed into digital format to be displayed on computer screens, thereby making experiential activities possible. Second, many *creative activities*, activities that are intended to produce new products and forms, can also be virtualized. A condition is that the intended product can be reduced to a digitally coded form. Computers can be used, for example, to create texts, drawings, edited video films, music scores, computer programs, new data that are the outcome of simulations, and design blueprints. Third, *verbal communication* can take place in cyberspace, both in delayed form (e-mail, electronic bulletin boards, newsgroups) and in real time (Internet Relay Chat, MUDs).

The fourth class includes *institutional activities*, which are activities the character of which is constituted by socially sanctioned interpretations of them. Take for instance the activity of paying off a debt to someone by handing them a twenty dollar bill. Now, it is essentially arbitrary that giving someone a green piece of paper would count as paying off a debt. It is only because this type of piece of paper has a sanctioned interpretation, that it is a valuable object that can be used to pay off debts. This interpretation of it is dependent on it being part of an established social institution, the institution of money. Many activities and objects are similarly dependent for their meaning on social institutions, such as activities of buying, selling, marrying, signing legislation, and making a move in chess. These activities depend on social institutions like money, property, marriage, law, and chess, that issue interpretive rules concerning the meaning of certain classes of objects and activities. Now, most such activities can be transferred to cyberspace by devising new rules that are applied to virtual objects and activities. Indeed, many such institutional activities already take place in cyberspace, including ordering, selling, banking, voting, gambling, stealing, trespassing, taking a test, joining a club, and even marrying ("Please press 'yes' or 'no'!").

The reproducibility of such a large part of human activity in cyberspace makes it possible for cyberspace to function as a place that we do not just occasionally visit but that we also come to *inhabit*. Indeed, in *City of Bits* William Mitchell argues that we are building a virtual geography that could best be likened to a city.[27] This "city of bits," in many ways similar to cities made of atoms, has the potential to take over many functions traditionally served by cities. Mitchell points out the many analogies between cyberspace and cities: They are both artificial infrastructures, they both contain places that function as sites of human activity and that are linked to each other by a topography, places in them can be public or private, and both are governed by regulatory systems that organize and control access to places. Looking with more detail, one finds many places in cyberspace that are also found in cities. One finds stores ("netstores"), malls ("cybermalls"), virtual museums, peepshows, virtual schools and universities, electronic trading systems, virtual banking chambers, electronic work floors, electronic sidewalk cafes, electronic game parlors, electronic churches, virtual assembly rooms, electronic town halls, and so on. Many of these structures help define *virtual communities* of individuals who maintain social ties in cyberspace.[28]

Mitchell predicts that the current flight to cyberspace will intensify, and that much of the economic, social, political and cultural action found in geographical, physical cities will shift into cyberspace. This includes the replacement of many public places found in cities by "virtual agoras." He predicts that as a result, geographical cities will be radically transformed. A large part of their infrastructure will become obsolete and will gradually be downsized and transformed. Many public places will disappear, along with a large part of the tertiary sector. Naturally, this will also have implications for the secondary sector: as physical spaces and objects are replaced by virtual ones, the demand for construction and industrial production may be expected to decrease. Physical places, especially homes, will become more malleable and multifunctional, as computer media in them make it possible for them to be used for many different purposes.

How Cyberspace Geographically Disembeds Place

The flight to cyberspace may well turn out to be less dramatic than Mitchell expects. Even as many human activities are replicated in cyberspace, their physical counterparts may well continue to exist. The telephone may have diminished the frequency of face-to-face conversations somewhat, but it has not replaced them. Likewise, I think we can expect that many physical places, and the physical objects and human activities they hold, will end up existing next to their virtual counterparts (e.g., paper journals next to electronic journals, real cafes next to cybercafes, etc.). Even so, there clearly is a flight to cyberspace taking place right now, and cities and the various places they contain are already being transformed as a result. In what way does this "change from atoms to bits"[29] constitute a geographical disembedding of place?

It does so by enabling individuals to transcend the geographical limitations imposed by their physical location, this time not by reducing its relative distance to other physical places, nor through its local development, but by allowing one to access completely artificial virtual places from it, that have no location in physical space, and are hence not constrained by distance relations of the sort that separates physical places. Notice that the construction of virtual places by space-generating technologies has an important advantage over the adjustment of relative distances between physical places by space-adjusting technologies. Space-adjusting technologies, electronic media specifically, make it possible to overcome the perceptual and informational distance between physical places, but cannot overcome the use distance between them; this distance can only be made smaller through faster transportation technologies. Space-generating technologies, however, open up access to places in a way that guarantees the immediate and complete use availability of the goods they contain. These goods, virtual objects, admittedly lack some of the possibilities of their physical counterparts, but nevertheless allow for many useful applications.[30]

Conclusion

In the preceding sections, various conceptions of space have been discussed, like time space, cost space, and virtual space, that do not reduce to some measure of physical, metric space. Apparently, physical space is only one of several types of space relevant to human location and orientation. Geographer Peter Gould accounts for this fact as follows:

> [M]any spaces of great interest to human geographers are not strictly metric at all. . . . In fact, for many spaces of great geographic importance the very notion of metricity may not be pertinent. What may be much more important is the simple fact of how people and things are connected together. It is the sheer *connectivity* of things that creates many spaces of interest to a geographer, spaces that a mathematician would call topological spaces.[31]

I have suggested earlier that the notion of connectivity relevant to an understanding of the places and spaces inhabited by human beings is a *pragmatic* notion, according to which mappable connections between places are defined in terms of various sorts of availability relations between places and their goods, relations that are ultimately defined in terms of human interests in having fast, inexpensive, and easy access to goods.

As noted by Abler et al., geography before 1950 was preoccupied with absolute, metric notions of distance and location, but geography after

1950 has become increasingly involved with mappings that employ relative notions.[32] This novel interest is perhaps not coincidental in light of the great flight that space-shaping technologies have been taking in especially the past sixty or seventy years. New space-shaping technologies have been posing new challenges to geographers, the most recent challenge being posed by the new geographies of cyberspace.

A pragmatic conception of space and place makes it possible to understand the historical evolution of the various space-shaping processes and technologies discussed in this essay, and to understand how these have been changing the identity of places. Place identity has been transformed, first, by the drastic changes in the relative location of places brought about by space-shaping technologies. However, places are also being materially and socially transformed themselves. Connectivity relations between places may cause local development as well as decay and destruction, and may cause massive in- and outfluxes of goods (e.g., local economic growth or decline because of distanciated social relations, or flights to cyberspace). This is also eroding the distinctiveness of places. Places can be distinctive because of the presence of certain goods (e.g., buildings, local foods), as well as through the absence of certain goods (e.g., the absence of modern conveniences in places in the Sahara). Space-shaping technologies, however, often ensure perceptual or use availability of special goods in other places, and help introduce goods into places previously made special through the absence of these goods, thereby reducing their specialty and making places across the globe more homogeneous.

Along with changes in place identity, people's sense of place is changing as well. An individual's sense of place is often defined as his identification with a place that he inhabits, if only temporarily. David Canter has argued that places with which a person maintains a sense of place are thought of by that person as closely related to activities that are so closely tied up to her self-identity that she wants to maintain close control over their availability.[33] However, swift changes in the identity of places brought about by space-shaping technologies and the increased mobility of individuals have made it more difficult to maintain a sense of place. On the other hand, electric media have also worked to make goods from distant places part of one's home environment, thus allowing them to become included in one's "sense of place": movie characters, distant friends on the telephone, and places and things in cyberspace can become familiar goods to which one may grow attached.[34]

It is important to realize, moreover, that different social groups will be subjected to different impacts from space-shaping technologies, and may consequently end up with different senses of place. A major reason why space shaping affects different social groups differently is that access to space-shaping technologies is unequal between social groups. An individual's opportunity to make use of a space-shaping technology like a computer network, a telephone, or an airplane strongly depends on that person's social and economic position, and increasingly also in his or her technological competences and skills. For the average Western business executive, space-shaping technologies have truly turned the world into a global village. For the African peasant who has no access to advanced space-shaping technologies, however, geographically distant places may be just as far away as they were for his forefathers two hundred years ago, and his sense of place may remain relatively unaffected. For the African peasant who gets to watch television every night in the village square, but who is unable to make a telephone call or an airplane flight, things are different again. Television allows her to become an observer of all kinds of places besides her own village, thus affecting her sense of place, but these places will never get the status of places that can be visited or contacted. Her lifeworld remains confined to her village, and the neighboring places to which she has access.

Finally, the geographical disembedding of places has led to changes in our very conception of what a place is. In our contemporary conception of place, places are no longer just understood as inhabitable physical locations, but as any relatively stable environment that holds certain immediately available goods. Next to physical places, such places include places that emerge out of the blending of different physical places by electric media, and nowadays even software constructions in cyberspace.

Notes

1. D. Seamon, *A Geography of the Lifeworld* (London: Croom Helm, 1979).
2. Y. Tuan, *Space and Place. The Perspective of Experience* (London: Edward Arnold, 1977), pages 179, 6.
3. D. Canter, *The Psychology of Place* (New York: St. Martin's Press, 1977).
4. This concept is intended as an extension of the concept of space-adjusting technologies introduced by D. Janelle, "Central Place Development in a Time-Space Framework," *Professional Geographer* 20 (1968): 5–10. Cf. section 3.
5. For example, A. Gatrell, *Distance and Space. A Geographical Perspective* (Oxford: Clarendon Press, 1983).
6. See S. Brunn and T. Leinbach, "Introduction," in *Collapsing Space and Time: Geographic Aspects of Communications and Information*, ed. S. Brunn and T. Leinbach (London: Harper Collins, 1991), xc–xxvi; D. Janelle, "Global Interdependence and Its Consequences," in *Collapsing Space and Time*, 49–81; S. Sassen, *Cities in a World Economy* (Thousand Oaks, Calif.: Pine Forge/Sage Press, 1994).
7. Modernity is singled out by A. Giddens, *The Consequences of Modernity* (Cambridge: Polity Press, 1990), and B. Latour, *We Have Never Been Modern*,

trans. C. Porter (Cambridge, Mass.: Harvard University Press, 1993); capitalism is pointed to by D. Harvey, *The Condition of Postmodernity* (Oxford: Basil Black-well, 1989), and J. Beniger, *The Control Revolution: Technological and Economic Origins of the Information Society* (Cambridge, Mass.: Harvard University Press, 1986).

8. Named, respectively, by Brunn and Leinbach, "Introduction"; Janelle, "Central Place Development in a Time-Space Framework"; and Harvey, *The Condition of Postmodernity.*

9. M. McLuhan, *Understanding Media: The Extensions of Man* (New York: McGraw-Hill, 1964).

10. See Janelle, "Central Place Development in a Time-Space Framework"; "Spatial Reorganization: A Model and a Concept," *Annals of the Association of American Geographers* 59 (1969): 348–364; and Janelle, "Global Interdependence and Its Consequences." See also R. Abler, "Effects of Space-Adjusting Technolo-gies on the Human Geography of the Future," in *Human Geography in a Shrink-ing World*, ed. R. Abler, D. Janelle, A. Philbrick, and J. Sommer (North Scituate, Mass.: Duxbury Press, 1975), 35–66.

11. Janelle, "Global Interdependence and Its Consequences," 49–51.

12. An extensive historical account of time-space compression in which various historical stages are distinguished is found in Harvey, *The Condition of Postmo-dernity*. Harvey moreover extensively analyzes what he construes as the more fundamental cause of this phenomenon: the inherent tendency of capitalism to expand its production system and its markets over space and time in order to speed up the turnover time of capital so as to limit overaccumulation, a fact that has lead to the emergence of a vast network of transportation and communication technologies. Harvey also discusses the perception of space-time compression processes in the arts and human sciences.

13. It should be noted that there are also technologies that may be called space-adjusting technologies that seek to *increase* rather than reduce relative distance between places, by creating new barriers between places. Walls, locks, and v-chips (computerized chips capable of detecting program ratings and blocking adversely rated programs from view) are examples of technologies that are designed to make it more difficult to access (goods in) one place from another place.

Moreover, as has been noted by D. Harvey and M. Ferguson, reductions in relative distance between places brought about by space-adjusting technologies have not necessarily made distances between places less *important* to individuals and organizations. In an increasingly competitive economy, small differences in the relative distance between places, as measured in time and money, may some-times even be *more* important as a factor in human decision-making than larger differences were in the past. See Harvey, *The Condition of Postmodernity*, 293–296, and M. Ferguson, "Electronic Media and the Redefining of Time and Space," in *Public Communication: The New Imperatives*, ed. M. Ferguson (London: Sage, 1990), 152–172.

14. A. Giddens, *The Constitution of Society* (Cambridge: Polity Press, 1984); *The Consequences of Modernity*; *Modernity and Self-Identity* (Cambridge: Polity Press, 1991).

15. Perhaps "socio-technical interaction" would be a better name, as distanci-ated interactions are sometimes wholly technical (e.g., a computer that automati-cally sells stock to other taking computers when it drops below a certain price).

16. See also Harvey, *The Condition of Postmodernity*, 240–243.

17. Giddens, *Modernity and Self-Identity*, 244, 21, 22.

18. That time-space distanciation is a process that is logically distinct from time-space is shown by the fact that there have been highly distanciated social systems, like the Roman Empire, in which transportation and communication systems were nevertheless relatively slow. Conversely, a world can be imagined in which fast and cheap transportation and communication links between places exist, but which nevertheless contains communities that operate relatively inde-pendently from each other and maintain few distanciated social relations. In con-temporary societies, distanciation and compression processes have been taking place in tandem, in a process of mutual enhancement.

19. McLuhan, *Understanding Media*, 3.

20. McLuhan, *Understanding Media*, 35.

21. J. Meyrowitz, *No Sense of Place: The Impact of Electronic Media on Social Behavior* (New York: Oxford University Press, 1985).

22. Meyrowitz, *No Sense of Place*, 37, 39.

23. M. Featherstone and R. Burrows, "Cultures of Technological Embodiment: An Introduction, " in *Cyberspace/Cyberbodies/Cyberpunk: Cultures of Techno-logical Embodiment*, ed. M. Featherstone and R. Burrows (London: Sage, 1995), 1–19.

24. W. Gibson, *Neuromancer* (London: Harper Collins, 1984).

25. An excellent description of such an environment is provided in Neal Ste-phenson's novel *Snow Crash* (New York: Bantam Books, 1992).

26. S. Turkle, *Life on the Screen: Identity in the Age of the Internet* (New York: Simon & Schuster, 1995), 240.

27. W. Mitchell, *City of Bits: Space, Place, and the Infobahn* (Cambridge, Mass.: MIT Press, 1995).

28. See H. Rheingold, *The Virtual Community: Homesteading on the Elec-tronic Frontier* (Reading, Mass.: Addison-Wesley, 1993).

29. N. Negroponte, *Being Digital* (New York: Knopf, 1995).

30. For those who remain unconvinced that the spatial metaphor of cyberspace (the "consensual hallucination," as Gibson has called it) can be taken literally, I will also suggest a different perspective on computer media. Contemporary cyberspace is essentially of two kinds. The first consists of virtual spaces generated locally by one's personal computer. The acquisition of this computer can also be identified as a species of local development (section 2), as one is modifying one's local environment to create added goods. The second kind consists of virtual spaces that are the joint product of one's computer and distant computers to which it is connected. One can also think of this interaction between computers as a type of connectivity development between two physical places, in which goods (software and information) are exchanged.

31. P. Gould, "Dynamic Structures of Geographic Space," in *Collapsing Space and Time*, 3–30, 10.

32. R. Abler, J. Adams, and P. Gould, *Spatial Organization: The Geographer's View of the World* (Englewood Cliffs, N.J.: Prentice-Hall, 1971).

33. Canter, *The Psychology of Place*, 179.

34. See also Giddens, *Modernity and Self-Identity*, 146–7.

Something Wild? Deleuze and Guattari and the Impossibility of Wilderness

Jonathan Maskit

In Jane Austen's *Mansfield Park*, a group of wealthy young people, suitably chaperoned of course, sets off in search of amusement in a tour of Sotherton, a local estate. After touring the house itself, the party takes in the grounds. Having taken several turns around the terrace, they arrive again at "the door . . . which opened to the wilderness." Finding the door unlocked

> they were all agreed in turning joyfully through it, and leaving the unmitigated glare of day behind. A considerable flight of steps landed them in the wilderness, which was a planted wood of about two acres, and though chiefly of larch and laurel, and beech cut down, and though laid out with too much regularity, was darkness and shade, and natural beauty, compared with the bowling-green and the terrace.[1]

The wilderness, as trope of the English garden, is ground which is planted and then left to take its own course. This particular wilderness comes in for criticism from Austen: the trees are wrong, perhaps not impressive enough; it is "laid out with too much regularity." Nevertheless, she praises its "natural beauty," although not without the caveat that this is only in comparison with the lawns. But, we are liable to offer other criticisms of this picture. We might object that, having been planned and planted, this is no wilderness at all. This is an illusion; part of a planned garden offering itself as the image of that which is unplanned, and, in this case, failing to pull off the trick. But having recognized this description as being of something other than wilderness, does this mean that we have an articulable concept here? Perhaps. But, perhaps not.

Wilderness, it sometimes seems, is like right action or pornography: we may have difficulty in defining it, but we think we know it when we see it. We know, upon reading Austen's description, that while this may have qualified as wilderness for her (and even that is unclear), it will not do for us. For a place to qualify as wilderness, it must have a certain purity to it—the word *pristine* is often used. It often must have a certain remoteness to it. It should show no (or few) visible signs of civilization—roads, houses, power lines, and the like are all things that make a place less wild.

While the discussion below will be couched in terms of space, an abstraction, concern for wilderness begins not as one for the abstract but for the concrete. We do not encounter and come to care about wilderness in the abstract but about particular places. Something about them strikes us, or some of us at least, as important and worth being preserved. One of the implications of this paper is that the very possibility of a place being wild will be called into question. For to be a place is to be located (or at least locatable), named, known. The characteristics to which I will point as those which are of concern in discussions of wilderness are those which, were they all present, would make of any wilderness no place at all. In other words, to the degree to which we can term a wilderness a place, it fails to be wild; and insofar as it is wild, it is no-place. Our failure to find places that live up to these standards will mean that (1) we will need to reconsider what we mean by wilderness and (2) that anything we call wilderness (despite its prior cultural shapings) will, because of those cultural shapings and despite its wildness, turn out to be a place.

In what follows I will argue that our reaction to the traditional view of wilderness is not so easy as it seems. What I would like to do is to pose *the* metaphysical question: what is wilderness? The investigation which follows we might term, after Heidegger, ontogeography or, if one prefers, geoontology. I begin by discussing the links between *wilderness* and *wildness* through an etymological investigation. I then turn to some views on wilderness as found in the ecophilosophical literature and suggest that we find a set of positions there beset with metaphysical problems. In section three, I introduce several of the notions from Gilles Deleuze and Félix Guattari's *A Thousand Plateaus*, primarily those of smooth and striated space, and use them to discuss the distinction between wilderness and wildness. In the fourth section, I suggest that "wilderness" is an example of striated rather than smooth space and that our politics should focus on the broader idea of wildness rather than narrowly on wilderness. Finally, I suggest a new way of thinking about wilderness which seeks to overcome many of the problems found in other conceptions.

"Where the Wild Things Are"

The importance of wilderness as both a philosophical and a cultural concept is not at all new.[2] The Jews wandered for forty years in the wilderness before being allowed to enter Palestine. Kant links wilderness, under the name *rohe Natur* [raw nature], with the sublime and thus with morality (albeit through a circuitous path).[3] Roderick Nash, although a bit optimistic in his conclusions, did groundbreaking work tracing the development of the concept of wilderness in American thought.[4] My discussion of wilderness is not rooted in the historical manifestations of this term in thought. It rests instead in a tension in both contemporary and historical usage of the word. Wilderness, it seems clear, carries with it connotations of wildness. It suggests a nature untrammeled by humanity: pristine, apart, uncultured and uncivilized. Crops do not grow in the wilderness; production for human purposes forms no part of what it is all about. Wilderness, in this sense, functions as the other of culture. It is a place that we can visit, but we do not belong there. It is dangerous and unpredictable. With only a touch of irony, one might remark: unlike in our cities, bastions of security, one could get hurt in the wilderness.

The word *wilderness* is not at all new in English. And, it can be found in recognizable forms in multiple precursors of our modern tongue. For example, the Middle Low German and Middle Dutch *wildernesse* or the (conjectured) Old English *wild(d)éornes*. The *Oxford English Dictionary* (OED) offers two possible etymologies. One of them traces "wilderness" to *wilder* or *wil(d)déor*—wild deer. The other, more probable one, traces it to *wilddéoren*—wildern.[5] What is clear in both cases is that the word goes back to *wild*.[6] *Wild* itself has a long history in many Teutonic languages. In both Dutch and German, *wild* means, amongst other things, "game" as in "wild game." While most of the roots of *wild* had essentially the same meaning as the modern word—the Old English, Old Frisian, and Middle Dutch *wilde*, the Old High German *wildi*—some of them are a bit different. The Old Norse *villr* meant "bewildered, astray." The modern Norwegian *vill* means "wild" as in "wild child"; the Swedish *vill*, "confused" or "giddy." But, the OED is cautious with *wild*, noting that "the problem of the ulterior relations of this word is complicated by uncertainty as to its primary meaning."[7] We cannot know whether it is first and foremost an adjective or a noun. I hope we can agree that in the case of wilderness, the essential meaning of *wild* is that of wild nature, where wild means untrammeled, uncultivated, uncivilized, raw, perhaps, free. Wilderness is certainly not someplace bewildered or confused (although it can have that *effect*).

If this is what we mean by wilderness today, then we both appeal to and re-instantiate, in our usage, the dualist distinctions between culture and nature or, if one prefers, "man" (human) and nature.[8] We introduce a rift between a wild person and a wild place, and insist that the place has a certain purity to it—as they used to say in advertising, "untouched by human hands." In order to see this more clearly, we need to leave the field

of etymology behind and turn to some of the contemporary ecophilosophical literature on wilderness.

Differing Viewpoints

The literature on wilderness usually does not bother with questions of
etymology. In fact, most of the literature on the topic does not even grapple with the most basic of questions: what is wilderness? The metaphysical question *par excellence* is one we either do not address because we are
doing ethics, or it is one that we see no need for.[9] I ask here after wilderness, and its connection with wildness, because I believe that wilderness
presents a very serious problem for us today. The point, I take it, of writing about wilderness is often to offer resources for conservation. Wilderness is threatened and is in need of being protected. If we are to protect
it, we must be able to offer reasons why. These reasons usually take one
of two forms: either wilderness is worthy of protection because of something inherent to it (intrinsic value arguments) or it is worthy of protection because it offers a way to attain things which are themselves worthwhile and could not be attained without it (instrumental value
arguments). While both sides have their proponents, my sense of the literature is that it is generally agreed upon that intrinsic value arguments
would be stronger or more convincing. Such arguments, if successful,
might necessitate, for example, the granting of rights (perhaps to self-
determination or to life) to wilderness. But even those who believe that
what is needed is an argument for intrinsic value will often be willing to
offer instrumental value arguments with the acknowledgment that such
are likely to hold more sway in the realm of contemporary politics.[10]

Now, these two positions vis-à-vis wilderness preservation tend to line
up with two metaphysical positions concerning wilderness. One of these
sticks closely by the etymology of the word (usually without invoking it)
and insists that wilderness is the other of culture, a sphere apart. Wilderness, for these thinkers, has a certain ontological solidity: it was before
we were, it will be after we are gone. Its essence is wildness, and wildness
means self-subsistence and independence. To bring laws and rules and all
the other trappings of civilization to wilderness is to tame it and, in effect,
to destroy it. In part because of its ontological stature, wilderness, for
these thinkers, carries with it an intrinsic value. Independent and self-
directed, it should be treated as, to borrow Kant's phrase, an end-in-itself.
These authors, amongst whom I include Thomas Birch, Eric Katz, Peter
Reed, Holmes Rolston III, and Alan Shields, I call the "wilderness ontologists."[11]

The other camp—"wilderness constructivists"—follows Kant's epistemological vision more closely. Wilderness, for writers such as Robert W. Loftin, Bill McKibben, Philip M. Smith and Richard A. Watson, David M. Graber, and Steve Vogel, is not something independent and free. Rather, it is a human construct. Wilderness is not the other of culture, but a "product" of culture. This production of wilderness happens at two levels. The first is that of language: we name something "wilderness," because it is someplace other than where we live and work. Wilderness is a place which is not ours, to which we do not belong. We thus linguistically produce wilderness as that which seems not to have been produced. But, at the same time, wilderness is produced in a second way: geographically. We draw lines on maps, we designate some spaces as wilderness and not others. Of course, it is not planned as extensively as Central Park or the *Tuileries*. But, nevertheless, it is a human production. For those authors who hold that wilderness is an artifact, the grounds to be offered for its preservation are often similar to those we might give for great works of art. At other times, it is argued that wilderness is important as a "playground" or for the survival or leadership skills it can teach. But, in all cases, the arguments proffered treat wilderness as an instrumental good.[12]

The first camp, the wilderness ontologists, run into certain problems: some of a metaphysical nature, others practical. The metaphysical problem is that this position requires a pre-Kantian metaphysics. It is no wonder that the figure in the history of philosophy most often cited with praise by deep ecologists and other wilderness ontologists is Spinoza. But, if one accepts the Kantian turn against substantialist metaphysics—as almost all of post-Kantian philosophy does—then a position which holds that wilderness is tenable as both an ontological and a value category is going to need argumentation. Unfortunately, such argument is more often than not lacking or unconvincing. The practical problem for the wilderness ontologists is that wilderness as they understand it is either rapidly disappearing or gone already.[13] If there is no such thing as wilderness so understood, then arguing for its value or preservation makes little sense. In order to address this difficulty, some wilderness ontologists appeal to the connection between wilderness and wildness and suggest that protection of wildness simply *is* protection of wilderness. But, this solution is not without problems of its own. I will return to this in my final section.

The wilderness constructivists are also not without their problems. And again, these problems are both metaphysical and practical. The metaphysical aspect of the problem arises from the difficulty in saying what constitutes an artifact with value. Why is this area, and not that one, worthy of preservation? Most of the wilderness constructivists beg this question entirely either by beginning with the assumption that there is such a thing as wilderness or, more problematically, making appeals to some kind of clear value in wilderness, a value which, by their own theories could not be there. The practical problem of this view is straightforward. Humanity, as a series of cultures, has shown little skill in preserving that which was valued by previous cultures. Only if something could be picked up and transposed into a new symbolic order was it worthy of being saved. Haggia Sophia has seen life as both a church and a mosque and has, for this reason, been preserved for centuries. The temples of Rome have not fared so well. And the Parthenon's stint as a fifteenth-century munitions depot has scarred it to this day. If we have come to value these things today, this does not mean that they will continue to hold such a position. And if wilderness matters to some of us now, we have a difficult task ahead of us to pass on that sense of value to those who are to come.

In order to try to help move the discussion forward, I would like now to appeal to the work of two thinkers whose names do not often come up in discussions of ecophilosophy: Deleuze and Guattari.

Deleuze and Guattari: The Smooth and the Striated

Strictly speaking it is not quite right to say that Deleuze and Guattari never come up. Even if mentioned only sporadically in English-language discussions, their work is, nevertheless, often ecologically motivated. Guattari was, at the time of his death, attempting to bridge the ideological differences between France's two ecologically oriented political parties: the right greens and the left greens. However, the notion of wilderness does not appear in their work. What does appear, and what plays a central role, are the notions of *space* and *territory.* In their last co-authored book, *What is philosophy?*, they describe the process of philosophy itself as a transformation of earth (*terre*) into territory (*territoire*). Such a process, described already in *A Thousand Plateaus,* goes by the name *territorialization.* But, like Heidegger's play of revealing and concealing, there can be no pure territorialization. Rather, any territorialization is always a re-territorialization. And, conversely, there is always also deterritorialization. The two occur together: "There are two components, the territory and the earth, with two zones of indiscernability, the deterritorialization (from territory to earth) and the reterritorialization (from earth to territory). It is impossible to say which is primary."[14] We can use this structure of de/re-territorialization to grasp the ways in which the human understanding of wilderness has come into being. But, in order to do so, it will be helpful to introduce another set of terms that Deleuze and Guattari use in the description of space: smooth and striated. To give a full explication of what any of these terms means would require a detailed exegesis of some very dense texts. They are linked with an entire complex of concepts which serve to open up not merely possibilities for thinking but new ways of living as well.[15] I cannot undertake such an exegesis here and seek, instead, to treat Deleuze and Guattari's thought the way Foucault, a great admirer of Deleuze, wished his own work to be treated: as a toolbox. I borrow here several screwdrivers and files; and, as anyone who has worked with their hands knows, sometimes a tool can be put to uses other than those for which it was designed.

In brief, smooth space is space which allows movement in a multiplicity of directions without impediments. The image Deleuze and Guattari offer of smooth space is usually the desert (the biblical wilderness) or the sea. However, it will soon become clear that neither of these spaces is as smooth as they may at first appear. Striated space is that which has been codified, gridded, subjected to concepts. The possibilities for movement within striated space are limited, sometimes severely. If one wants to travel by car, one must follow the roads. Trains only travel on tracks.[16] And airplanes, moving through the apparently smooth space of the ether, follow strictly regulated flight paths.

Like material correlates (although this understanding twists Deleuze and Guattari's text somewhat) of de- or re-territorialization, smooth and striated space do not exist in pure form. Space is always in a state of becoming. Old striations are replaced with new, what was severely striated becomes smoother, what was smooth becomes striated. If we wished, we could line up smooth space with the earth and striated with territory, but always only with the understanding that there is no pure earth, no territory that is not also earth, and no space which is not smooth, striated, and in transition. This is a system not of being but becoming: a Nietzschean or Heraclitean world.

Before returning to the question of wilderness, which I shall do by linking the concept of smooth space as developed by Deleuze and Guattari with the idea of wildness we find in the ecophilosophical literature, I should like to say a bit more about these notions of smoothness and striation—do a little philosophical geography.

What is at issue in Deleuze and Guattari's work is the task of thinking in a way which is as non-metaphysical as possible. This means that the basic oppositions which we accept all-too-easily are questioned from the outset. The distinctions between thought and action, space and time, culture and nature, mind and body, etc. are all put in play here. So, in the course of a discussion which concerns itself explicitly with the notion of *space*, we find discussions not only of "physical" space (the seas, the deserts) and of "theoretical" space (geographical space, geometrical space), but also of musical space (Pierre Boulez), technological space (different varieties of cloth-making), and aesthetic space (different types of vision).

I cannot treat all these aspects here and, at the risk of subjecting Deleuze and Guattari's text to an interpretation which forces it back within the sphere of metaphysical dichotomies—but also with the awareness that what I am doing here is an appropriation for specific purposes—I will focus primarily on their discussions of what we might term physical space.

In their discussion of the difference between smooth and striated space, Deleuze and Guattari offer several different ways of contrasting them. The first, and most thorough, I take the liberty of quoting at length:

> Smooth space is filled by events or haecceities, far more than by formed and perceived things. It is a space of affects, more than one of properties. It is *haptic* rather than optical perception. Whereas in the striated forms organize a matter, in the smooth materials signal forces and serve as symptoms for them. It is an intensive rather than extensive space, one of distances, not of measures and properties. . . . A Body without Organs instead of an organism and organization. Perception in it is based on symptoms and evaluations rather than measures and properties. That is why smooth space is occupied by intensities, wind and noise, forces, and sonorous and tactile qualities, as in the desert, steppe, or ice. The creaking of ice and the song of the sands. Striated space, on the contrary, is canopied by the sky as measure and by the measurable visual qualities deriving from it.[17]

The striated: capturable, describable, reducible to language, measurable, constraining movement. The smooth: explosive, aesthetic (in the Greek sense of *aesthesis*), expressive itself (but perhaps not capturable in other expressions), a space of happenings and becomings rather than of Being. Striated space is the space of the State. It is the space of laws and principles, of maps and roads. Smooth space, for Deleuze and Guattari, is the space of the nomad—those who live outside the State. It is the space in which movement is not channeled and directed or subjected to the strictures of instrumental reason, which brings us to geometry:

> The smooth and the striated are distinguished first of all by an inverse relation between the point and the line (in the case of the striated, the line is between two points, while in the smooth, the point is between two lines); and second, by the nature of the line (smooth—directional, open intervals; striated—dimensional, closed intervals). Finally, there is a third difference, concerning the surface or space. In striated space, one closes off a surface and "allocates" it according to determinate intervals, assigned breaks; in the smooth, one "distributes" oneself in an open space, according to frequencies and in the course of one's crossings. (MP, 600/480–1)

Here the difference becomes clearer. Striated space is *Newtonian* or *Cartesian:* an infinite array of points awaiting the plotting of lines. The point always pre-exists the line. So, to move in such space is to travel from one preexistent point to another. Striated space's array of points and linkage of directions of movements define the surface of the space "in advance" of any movement. The movement itself is only "necessary" insofar as it serves to bridge the space between the two points. This is why speed is so important in travel: the faster you go, the "shorter" the line.[18] In smooth space, the speed of travel is not so important. And, maybe where you are going isn't even that important either. You head this way or that, with no particular destination whatsoever. Because, if one could find oneself in a pure smooth space, there would be no destinations preexistent to one's arrival. The points are "determined" by the lines. Movement in this direction and then that creates a point where the direction of motion changes: a linkage of rays. The partitions of smooth space follow upon motion, and then erase themselves. The water does not show the path of a boat for too many minutes; the desert sands cover one's tracks with the wind.

Although quite insistent that there is no such thing as smooth space or striated space—these are concepts—there are several examples that Deleuze and Guattari refer to repeatedly: the desert, the steppes, the ice (of the Eskimos), and the seas.[19] It is the last of these which comes in for the most extended discussion. At first thought, the open sea presents us with a wonderful example of smooth space: motion is possible in any direction, points of reference are non-existent; wherever one chooses to go, one leaves no tracks; directionality is all-important for there are no points. As Deleuze and Guattari put it, "the sea is a smooth space par excellence, and yet," they continue, "[it] was the first to encounter the demands of increasingly strict striation" (MP, 598/479). The sea, while apparently a smooth space, is actually gridded and plotted, charted and divided. Because of the absence of natural "landmarks," the sea requires the imposition of a grid from outside. There is no pretense here that the striations of the sea follow natural patterns or express what was already there. This transformation from smooth to striated is necessitated because of the sea's very smoothness: it is the problems of navigation in open water that motivated the development of better maps and means of navigation.[20]

Now, this striation of the sea, like any striation, is never complete and always gives rise to new smooth spaces. We can imagine the sort of "primordial" smoothness of the sea arising once more for those lost in lifeboats with neither maps nor navigational aids. Tossed on the waves, they can move in whatever direction they like. But, without knowing what would be the best way to go, there is almost no point in moving at all. But striated space can give rise to new smooth spaces in other ways as well. The channeling of shipping into routes and lanes opens up avenues for pirates who will cross those lanes and sail where they will. But it also allows the possibility for groups like Greenpeace or the Sea Shepherd Society to play against those striations (as well as whole other sets of striations) and produce a form of movement which does not fit in with the patterns the striations should allow. "Nothing is ever done with: smooth space allows itself to be striated, and striated space re-imparts a smooth space, with potentially very different values, scope, and signs" (MP, 607/486).

What I would like to suggest here is that this notion of smooth space seems to have a certain element of *wildness* about it. It is a space of openness and freedom, unconstrained by laws and regulations. And part of why I think that this idea of smooth space can be helpful here is that, if it is not clear already, Deleuze and Guattari much prefer smooth space to striated. Part of the goal of their philosophical enterprise is to find ways to smooth out spaces which are now striated. But it remains to be seen where wilderness fits in to this picture.

The Impossibility of Wilderness

One thing is clear from Deleuze and Guattari's text: one never finds a pure space. All space "in the world" is an admixture of smooth and striated. And, the mixture is always unstable and changing. Space that is more smooth than striated can change: maps are drawn, roads are built, trees are cut. But, the transformation can work in the other direction as well: demonstrations clog the streets, buildings crumble, new trees sprout, new possibilities arise within (and against) the striations. It is this alloyed character of these spaces which blocks this from being just another metaphysical dualism. The smooth and the striated are not nature and culture. The concept of smooth space is intended to capture simultaneously the understanding of wildness which is traditional to the West, as well as the understanding of space which is traditional to nomadic cultures.

What the analysis of space presented by Deleuze and Guattari allows us to understand are the ways in which, even within striation, smoothness re-erupts. Thus, where there have been planned spaces, wild ones can reappear. In other words, no smoothing is ever final. City dwellers and suburbanites know this all too well. The smooth space of manicured lawn is rudely interrupted by patches of dandelions; the order and cleanliness of the home is shattered by roaches and mildew. Or perhaps one finds rabbits and deer eating in the garden. But, we must be careful here. For, wildness is not the same as wilderness; there never was an originary smooth space and resmoothed space certainly doesn't qualify. The etymological link between wilderness and wildness often allows us not to consider the difference between originary smooth space and re-smoothed space. But, etymology is not destiny. And the etymological confusion leads to a notion of *purity* at the core of the entire discussion of wilderness in ecophilosophy. Now, purity is one thing if it concerns concepts. But it is quite another when what is at issue is space. When we strive to protect wilderness, it is not only because it is wild, or, in Deleuze and Guattari's terms, smooth. Not at all. What we strive to protect is *both* the wildness and the purity. We resist notions of multiple use, we resist road-building, we may even resist trail-construction. We seek to have a wilderness whose wildness is of a character other-than-human. But how do we go about this?

We pass laws. We fight for stricter and stricter controls on what can, and cannot, be done in the wilderness. We fight to keep out the RV's and the mountainbikes, the pack-animals and the snowmobiles. We cultivate a wilderness ethic and are quick to chastise those who do not abide by its rules of conduct. Of course. We must do these things to preserve the wilderness. For the wilderness is the space of the other-than-human and, as such, must be protected from the ravages we are likely to inflict on it. But, in this process of drawing boundaries and passing laws, of controlling conduct and making maps, of cutting trails and providing rescues, we change something important. Let us assume that the space in question is, before we begin, more smooth than striated. In the process of making it into a wilderness—and let us be clear that this is what is going on here—we are striating this space. We are making it less wild. If what we mean by wilderness is wild space, and if, in turn, that means smooth space, then the one way we are not going to achieve this is through the processes we have followed for wilderness protection.[21]

Wilderness cannot be brought about by processes of striation. Fair enough. So, what is needed are processes of smoothing. But, processes of smoothing do not produce wilderness. They produce wildness. Like a dialectic with neither guiding principles nor *telos,* the interplay of smoothing and striating can never give rise to spaces with the purity we would like to see in our wilderness.

In what I consider to be the best piece yet in the literature on wilderness, Thomas Birch argues for the importance of protecting wilderness through processes of striation because what is needed is the preservation of possibilities of wildness which can take hold against the imperium or the State. But the wildness which is at stake here is not of a piece with wilderness as pure space of becoming outside the control of humanity. The wildness is, on the one hand, that of anarchist politics and, on the other, the space of a wild becoming in which nature re-erupts where it had been suppressed. But, is the re-eruption of nature along abandoned railway lines wilderness? Are the grasses insistently poking through the sidewalks and shattering their coherence wilderness? Birch seems to think so, and Eric Katz cites him approvingly on just this point: "Birch thus recommends that we view wilderness, wherever it can be found, as a 'sacred space' acting as 'an implacable counterforce to the momentum of totalizing power.' Wilderness appears anywhere: 'old roadbeds, wild plots in suburban yards, flower boxes in urban windows, cracks in the pavement. . . .' And it appears, in my life, in the presence of the white-tailed deer of Fire Island."[22] This entire passage depends on a failure to distinguish between wilderness and wildness. Just four pages before this passage, Katz, this time citing Eugene Hargrove, praises the notions of authenticity and continuity with its past which distinguishes wild nature from restored nature. But if wild nature—wilderness—depends on a continuity and authenticity, and this continuity cannot contain acts by humanity, then we are not apt to find wilderness in old roadbeds or backyards. Wildness, yes, wilderness, never. These are striated spaces in the process of becoming smooth. But, they are not the smooth spaces that were there before striation. And they certainly don't have any sort of purity or authenticity about them.

None of this means that we cannot have spaces that are more or less wild. But even for those spaces where no one ever goes, there exist maps. And, of course, satellite location devices. Let me repeat, there can be, for us, no truly smooth space.[23] Now, I agree wholeheartedly that it is a worthwhile project to try to smooth out some of the spaces that we do have. And I agree as well that we should resist further striations in spaces which are now relatively smooth. But I am also in agreement with Birch here in my skepticism that the State—*the* greatest force of striation we have—is the place to look for smoothing.

If we are interested in smoothing out space, what this calls for is a politics: a politics of smooth space, what Deleuze and Guattari might term nomad politics. Such a nomad politics not only plays off the smoothnesses opened up in striated space—Tiananmen Square in 1989, Greenpeace, 1968, Earth First!—it creates (or may create) new smooth spaces as it goes. But, these smooth spaces may also be re-striated. And, of course, they will have neither purity nor authenticity to them. Pure wilderness, I am afraid, is not a possibility.

The Smooth and the Wild

In this final section I would like to suggest a way of thinking about wilderness which might move us beyond some of the problems discussed above. This will require a mediation of the two camps (wilderness ontology and constructivism) currently engaged in the debate. This mediation will depend on a reformulation of the notion of wilderness in the wake of the Deleuzo-Guattarian analysis offered here. I will also add a further element to the mixture in order to give a normative ground which some may find lacking in Deleuze and Guattari's distinction.

First, a non-metaphysical notion of wilderness.[24] We might call it smooth wilderness, but I prefer historically smooth space.[25] Not all smooth spaces qualify as historically smooth space. Birch's old roadbeds and cracked pavement may well be smooth spaces. But, I would hesitate to call them historically smooth space just as others would hesitate to call them wilderness. But in order to be able to make this distinction on more solid ground than mere intuition, what is needed is an introduction of a notion of history or temporality. Deleuze and Guattari's distinction between smooth and striated is useful because it shows the fruitlessness of many discussions about wilderness. But, without the addition of this second axis of analysis, it does not yield normative grounds for preferring one smooth space over another. The notion of historically smooth space is designed to do just that. Deleuze and Guattari maintain that there are no pure spaces, neither smooth nor striated. But even if there are no purely smooth spaces (wilderness in the metaphysical sense), there are surely different degrees of striation. If, having grasped that the distinction is drawn along a spatial continuum, we then fail to see that the *processes* of smoothing and striation happen along a temporal continuum, we then risk lapsing back into the sort of thinking that we were trying to avoid. We can't get back to some preconceptual Eden, but, we might ask ourselves, aren't there some places more Edenic than others? Aren't there some places that have historically been less striated? Surely the answer to this question must be yes. While we might be interested in smooth spaces in general, the notion of historically smooth space seeks to distinguish those spaces which have been severely striated and then resmoothed from those which have seen no such striation.[26] For something to be historically smooth space, it must have some sort of historical continuity to it. For example, a clearcut and replanted "forest" cannot qualify as historically smooth space; a selectively logged and "naturally" regenerated forest might. Because there can be no pure notion of historically smooth space, discussions as to what constitutes such space are problematic. However, even if we (and who this "we" is remains to be decided) were to decide that a particular "restored" place did not constitute historically smooth space, it might still be valued as a resmoothed space.

In addition, we need to take account of the fact that not all human actions are interchangeable or equivalent. If we accept Deleuze and Guattari's distinction between nomadic (organized but non-Statist) and State action and politics, we might be able to see many places as historically smooth space even though they have been lived in and manipulated by human beings over the course of time. We gain a further advantage from this distinction as well: we can see these places as lived in and changed while still maintaining the character of historically smooth space *without* lapsing into a naturalization of the "noble savage" so common in the eighteenth century.

What should be clear by now is that this notion of historically smooth space, which makes no appeals to purity, is a far more unwieldy concept than other notions of wilderness; it cannot allow us to draw the clear and sharp lines we might like. But if such a concept is less clear-cut than we might like, it is not without its usefulness. For starters, such a concept accords better with the world we live in. Recent evidence is quite clear that many of the places taken as archetypal wildernesses show signs of human alteration.[27] These signs may not be dramatic. The events which caused them may have happened a long time ago. But if we insist that wilderness is a space free of human action, then such spaces must be disqualified.[28] But, if what we mean by wilderness is historically smooth space, then we are not necessarily constrained in this way. The problem remains of *how* and *where* we draw the lines between that which constitutes historically smooth space and that which does not. If an inability to clarify where these lines are to be drawn at a theoretical level appears as a shortcoming, it is worth remembering that no previously offered "definition" of wilderness has shown itself to be acceptable, and thus offering a more fluid way of looking at these issues may not be such a bad option after all. As a preliminary formulation, let me suggest that no space which has undergone severe striation in the recent past qualifies, and only those that have been re-smoothed a long time ago—e.g., the Mayan jungles *before* the restoration of the ruins *qua* ruins—could. It is not the presence, either currently or historically, of humans which "taints" a space; it is the processes of striation which matter. And, since no striation is permanent, even those places which have been severely striated can be smoothed again. The concept of historically smooth space serves only to delimit those spaces which have either never undergone severe striation or which did so such a long time ago that processes of re-smoothing have had sufficient time to re-work the space. The relevant question is whether a space is smooth enough (and the specification of this "enough" I leave open).

Second, the notion of historically smooth space allows us better to take account of restoration ecology than other notions of wilderness might. Seen from a Deleuzo-Guattarian perspective, restoration ecology is not about putting things back the way they were. There is no recoverable "way they were." Instead, the best to be hoped for is that we can find spaces which have not been striated too much and can endeavor to re-smooth them. The space "restored" in this way is thus not the same as the space that was "there" precedent to the striation. But this brings me to the greatest problem of all, and returns us to the link between wilderness and wildness with which this paper began.

What is needed at this point is thoughtful reflection on what forms of wildness or smoothness are of value. I have suggested that the link between wilderness and wildness is problematic at best, and that a better way to think of wilderness issues is using Deleuze and Guattari's distinction between smooth and striated space. However, if we accept this distinction as merely a spatial one, without the addition of an element of temporality or historicity, then we risk losing all grounds for distinguishing one kind of smooth space from another. In order to overcome this difficulty, I have suggested historicizing the notion of smooth space into historically smooth space. This addition can help us to take account of degrees and shadings of wildness or smoothness. However, I would like to conclude this paper with two problems that are in need of further work. The first is more theoretical, the second more practical.

The first hinges on the traditional distinction between nature and culture. If the notion of smooth space seemed to make this distinction no longer valid in these discussions, the notion of historically smooth space seems to bring it back with a vengeance. This worries me. Traditionally from the standpoint of the West, the activities of aboriginal peoples (read non-Westerners) were often perceived as "natural." The peoples of Africa, the Americas, Australia, and the South Pacific in particular were taken as "not there," i.e., part of the landscape. For discussions about wilderness, the valid questions remain *who* (or *what* in the case of institutions) was doing *what* to *which* landscapes for *how long* (and *how long ago*) and *why*. Coming up with answers to these questions is a tall order indeed. What seems clear at this point are two things: (1) the world of nature is not at all a static one and (2) wherever people have been, they have changed that place. The first of these means that there is no stable nature we can preserve or leave alone. The second means that we have to draw finer distinctions between sorts of actions. Perhaps, and this is only a suggestion, the distinction between smooth and striated might again be helpful here in assessing actions. Some actions are smoothing (or re-smoothing), others are striating. An area which has seen primarily smoothing actions historically could qualify as historically smooth space, one which had seen severe striation followed by resmoothing might only be newly smooth space (and not historically smooth space), etc.

Ancillary to this, and still in need of argumentation, is the preference for smooth over striated space (or historically smooth space over other sorts of space). If my preference is clear enough to me, that does not mean that it is clearly articulated enough to convince others that they ought to share it. And even if others are convinced of the value of smooth space, there still remains the question of the distinction between historically smooth spaces and other smooth spaces and why one ought to prefer one rather than the other. A humanist, anarchist, nomad politics could well opt for smooth spaces in urban areas and care not a wit for historically smooth spaces. If, however, the value of smooth space remains to be demonstrated, the converse also remains the case: striated space is also in need of justification by its apologists (the State, industry, etc.). If rather than justification we have had, up until now, the unstoppable march of "progress" (i.e., striation) backed up by force, that is not, in and of itself, satisfactory justification for the status quo.

The second problem is the more vexing of the two. If at the level of discussions about wilderness, ecology, and environmental issues in general there has been much progress (or at least much said), at the level of practice we are often lacking in concrete ideas. The analysis of smooth and striated space offered here only complicates matters. If earlier voices (e.g., John Muir) could suggest State action as the appropriate means for wilderness protection, it is no longer so clear that this avenue is open to proponents of either smooth space *or* historically smooth space. One of the central points in Deleuze and Guattari's analysis, and one with which I tend to agree, is that the State is primarily a force of striation. As such, proponents of the State as a force for smoothing find themselves in a paradoxical position. Birch has suggested this already, but the problem is even worse than he acknowledges. Wilderness areas are not simply prisons in which wildness is incarcerated. Like good modern prisons, which do not simply throw walls (whether physical or otherwise) around a region and then allow unrestricted movement within it, wilderness areas are striated within. Some species are kept out, others controlled. Human activities and motions are channeled. One need only look at what has become of Yosemite Valley, Yellowstone, and the Grand Canyon for evidence of State striation in the name of protection. Given this, the question is: can the State be a force for smoothing? If the answer to this is yes, some account needs to be given of how this can be the case. If, however, the conclusion we reach is that the State cannot be a force for smoothing, then a rethinking of political practice is in order. Although Deleuze and Guattari hint broadly in the direction of a nomad politics, much work still needs to be done in this area in particular in order to see what such a politics would look like and how it would work.

Notes

This paper was originally written under the financial auspices of the *Belgian American Educational Foundation*. An earlier version was read at the *Society for Philosophy and Geography* meetings in New York City, December 1995. The paper has been greatly improved thanks to the helpful suggestions from Noam Cook, Barbara Fultner, Katrina Korfmacher, Andrew Light, Ulrich Melle, Dan Smith, Rudi Visker, Steve Vogel, Michael Zimmerman, and two anonymous reviewers.

1. Jane Austen, *Mansfield Park* in *The Novels of Jane Austen, Vol. III* (London: Oxford University Press, 1960), 91.

2. The title of this section is borrowed, of course, from Maurice Sendak's wonderful children's book, which I loved so much as a child.

3. Eliane Escoubas discusses *rohe Natur* as the showing of nature without concepts in her "Kant or the Simplicity of the Sublime" in Jean-François Courtine et al., *Of the Sublime: Presence in Question*, trans. Jeffrey S. Librett (Albany: SUNY Press, 1993), 55–70.

4. Roderick Nash, *Wilderness and the American Mind* (New Haven: Yale University Press, 1973).

5. *Oxford English Dictionary*, 2nd. ed., s.v. "wilderness."

6. Jay Hansford C. Vest argues that *wilderness* is rooted in an early notion of "will-of-the-land" and already contains within it a notion of agency. See his "Will-of-the-Land," *Environmental Review* 9 (1985): 323–29 as well as his "The Philosophical Significance of Wilderness Solitude," *Environmental Ethics* 9 (1987): 303–30.

7. *Oxford English Dictionary*, 2nd. ed., s.v. "wild."

8. I acknowledge, but will not address here, the ecofeminist criticisms of the conflation between man and human.

9. There are also those who offer what we might term a phenomenology of wilderness and thus, following the dictates of pre-Heideggerean phenomenology, do not see the need to ask ontological questions. For example: Philip M. Smith and Richard A. Watson assert that "wilderness is not a simple geographic concept" (61) and depends upon experience ("New Wilderness Boundaries," *Environmental Ethics* 1 (1979): 61–64).

10. The clearest case of this is William Godfrey-Smith, "The Value of Wilderness," *Environmental Ethics* 1 (1979): 309–319.

11. See Thomas H. Birch, "The Incarceration of Wildness: Wilderness Areas as Prisons," *Environmental Ethics* 12 (1990): 3–26. Eric Katz, "The Call of the Wild: The Struggle against Domination and the Technological Fix of Nature," *Environmental Ethics* 14 (1992): 265–74. Peter Reed, "Man Apart: An Alternative to the Self-Realization Approach," *Environmental Ethics* 11 (1989): 53–69. Holmes Rolston, III "Values Gone Wild," *Inquiry* 26 (1983): 181–207 and "Valuing Wildlands," *Environmental Ethics* 7 (1985): 23–48. Allan Shields, "Wilderness, Its Meaning and Value," *Southern Journal of Philosophy* 11 (1973): 240–53.

12. See Robert W. Loftin, "Psychical Distance and the Aesthetic Appreciation of Wilderness," *International Journal of Applied Philosophy* 3 (1986): 15–19. Bill McKibben, *The End of Nature* (New York: Random House, 1989). Philip M. Smith and Richard A. Watson, "New Wilderness Boundaries," *Environmental Ethics* 1 (1979): 61–64. David M. Graber, "Resolute Biocentrism: The Dilemma of Wilderness in National Parks" in *Reinventing Nature? Responses to Postmodern Deconstruction*, eds. Michael E. Soulé and Gary Lease (Washington, D.C.: Island

Press, 1995), 123–36. Steve Vogel, *Against Nature* (Albany: SUNY Press, 1996) and "Habermas and the Ethics of Nature" in *The Ecological Community*, ed. Roger Gottlieb (New York: Routledge), 175–92.

13. McKibben and Vogel both argue this point as concerns *nature*. But, if there is no nature, then, ipso facto, there can be no wilderness (as a category of that nature).

14. Gilles Deleuze and Félix Guattari, *Qu'est-ce que La Philosophie?* (Paris: Les Éditions de Minuit, 1991), 82.

15. There is already a large body of literature on Deleuze and Guattari. For example, Ronald Bogue, *Deleuze and Guattari* (London: Routledge, 1989); Constantin V. Boundas and Dorothea Olkowski, ed., *Gilles Deleuze and the Theater of Philosophy* (New York: Routledge, 1994); Michael Hardt, *Gilles Deleuze: An Apprenticeship in Philosophy* (Minneapolis: University of Minnesota Press, 1993); Brian Massumi, *A User's Guide to Capitalism and Schizophrenia: Deviations from Deleuze and Guattari* (Cambridge, Mass.: MIT Press, 1992). *Gilles Deleuze and the Theater of Philosophy* contains an extensive bibliography of both the literature on Deleuze as well as that on Deleuze and Guattari.

16. I write these words in a hotel room in Strasbourg. The space of France, striated in the extreme, is, at this moment, disrupted by a general strike. Train travel is utterly impossible in all of France. The strike disrupts the possibilities for movement allowed by the striations and thus brings motion to a halt. At the same time, new possibilities are opened up in the space where trains might ordinarily be.

17. Gilles Deleuze and Félix Guattari, *Mille plateaux: Capitalisme et schizophrénie 2* (Paris: Les Éditions de Minuit, 1980), 598 [*A Thousand Plateaus: Capitalism and Schizophrenia*, trans. Brian Massumi (Minneapolis: University of Minnesota Press, 1987), 479]. All further references to be given within the text as *MP* with the paginations to the French first and the English after a solidus.

18. Paul Virilio has written extensively on the idea of speed. See, for example, his *Vitesse et Politique* (Paris: Éditions Galilée, 1977) [*Speed and Politics: An Essay on Dromology*, trans. Mark Polizzotti (New York: Semiotext(e), 1986)] and *Défense populaire et Luttes écologiques* (Paris: Éditions Galilée, 1978) [*Popular Defense and Ecological Struggles*, trans. Mark Polizzotti (New York: Semiotext(e), 1990]. This obliteration of space through speed finds its conclusion in that perennial love of the science fiction author: the transporter chamber.

19. Deleuze and Guattari's understanding of the links between space, concepts, and thinking is rather complex. Thus, while their notions of space are clearly conceptual, their notions of conceptuality are themselves spatial. In a section entitled "Geophilosophy," they write: "Absolute deterritorialization is not without reterritorialization. Philosophy reterritorializes itself through the concept. The concept is not an object, but a territory. It has no Object, but a territory" (*Qu'est-ce que La Philosophie?*, 97).

20. While Deleuze and Guattari offer the open ocean as a smooth space, it is no doubt true that there are certain regularities, such as currents, that make it more prone to some striations than others. Currents and prevailing wind patterns serve, just as mountains and rivers do, as either facilitators or inhibitors of motion

in certain directions. Nevertheless, until the maps are drawn, establishing shipping lanes and bringing nautical hazards within the sphere of human knowledge, the seas remain, from the standpoint of politics and trade, a space which is without striations.

21. Thomas Birch's "The Incarceration of Wildness: Wilderness Areas as Prisons" makes a similar argument, although in different terms. I agree with Birch's analysis of wilderness areas. It is his mildly optimistic conclusions I take issue with (see below).

22. Eric Katz, "The Call of the Wild: The Struggle against Domination and the Technological Fix of Nature," *Environmental Ethics* 14 (1992): 273.

23. A completely smooth space would be one that had never been mapped, traversed, named, transformed, or brought within the sphere of state power in any way. There may someday be smooth spaces again. But such a radical re-smoothing would (1) require a break in the continuity of civilization (and perhaps the disappearance of humanity) and (2) would still fail to re-instantiate the smooth spaces we insist on thinking wildernesses should be.

24. This suggestion was made by Noam Cook in an e-mail to the author of 2 February 1996.

25. John O'Neill argues persuasively for taking time and history seriously in environmental debates in "Time, Narrative, and Environmental Politics" in Gottlieb, 22–38.

26. Such re-smoothing could happen in a number of ways. Whenever striation stops, spaces "naturally" re-smooth themselves. Jan E. Dizard discusses a reservoir as, in my terms, a striated space that has re-smoothed itself in some ways, but not others (see "Going Wild: The Contested Terrain of Nature," in *In the Nature of Things: Language, Politics, and the Environment*, ed. Jane Bennett and William Chaloupka [Minneapolis: University of Minnesota Press, 1993], 111–35). But, there are also, as discussed above, cultural processes of re-smoothing. Perhaps the strongest forms of these are connected with warfare. War severely restriates space in some ways, but also smoothes it as well (destruction of lines of communication and transportation, for example). In its most extreme form, thermonuclear war is an almost purely smoothing process. However, I would hesitate to equate space smoothed in this way, wild as it might be, with wilderness.

27. See Gary Paul Nabhan, "Cultural Parallax in Viewing North American Habitats," in *Reinventing Nature? Responses to Postmodern Deconstruction*, ed. Michael E. Soulé and Gary Lease (Washington, D.C.: Island Press, 1995), 87–102.

28. Part of the problem here is that for Deleuze and Guattari not all human actions are striating. Actions by the state are almost always striating, actions by others may be smoothing. For a recent discussion of ecological restoration, an issue not unrelated to wilderness preservation, which justifies restoration by an appeal to the value of the outcome of natural processes *without* appealing to those processes themselves see William Throop, "The Rationale for Environmental Restoration" in Gottlieb, 39–55.

Down to Earth:
Persons in Place
in Natural History

Holmes Rolston III

The Storied Place

Earth is a storied place. On other planets, so far as we know, there is little story, although they too have their astronomical records—events in their physics, chemistries, geomorphologies, meteorologies. Earth adds biology and natural history; there is a cumulative historical evolution, coded in genes, lived out in each new generation, with novel mutants, varied genotypes becoming new phenotypes, and producing new chapters in the history. Genes remember, research, and recompound discoveries; and the storied achievements, the values achieved, rise, over several billion years, to spectacular levels of attainment and power. Past achievements are recapitulated in each present generation, with variations; and these results get tested in that generation and then folded into the future, resetting the initial conditions with new possibility spaces for development.

Beyond natural history, Earth adds humans in their cultures, persons in their biographies, and now the story is stored in cumulative transmissible cultures, lived out in each present generation, as persons choose their careers and have their adventures, form their nations and ideologies, and write new chapters in the story. Persons in their developing cultures are even more historical than the plants and animals in their evolutionary natural histories. The pace of change and the possibilities of innovation are accelerated by several orders of magnitude.

Earth is the only place we know in which any living thing has a home territory. The logic of life is both biography and geography. The etymology of "bio-graphy" is to graph a life; the etymology of "geo-graphy" is to graph that life on Earth. "Biology" is the logic of life, but there is no logic of life that is not historical; and, in that sense, the idea of "graphing," of drawing out a world line, biography, is more historical, better catching the logic of biology. Life is not a timeless syllogism; human life has to be distributed on Earth. Biology requires geography, graphing a world line, and biology plus geography yields history. Life is always taking a journey through time and place.

Here we want to put persons in their places, in cultural history and, even more, in natural history. This emphasis is not because the latter is more important, but because it has been more neglected. Man is, Aristotle said, the political animal, the animal that builds a city. Yes, but humans are first and always earthlings too. We remain territorial animals. In finding our place in the built environment, we have tended to get displaced from our natural environment. We ought to live in storied residence on landscapes. The logic of that home, the ecology, is finally narrative, and the human career is not a disembodied reason but a person organic in history. Character always takes narrative form; history is required to form character. The only history we humans know is as flesh and blood moves through time and space. So we cannot know *who* we are; we cannot know *what* is going on, until we know *where* life is taking place. Behind ethics is *ethos*, in the Greek, an accustomed mode of habitation.

Natural History

Nature generates; that is the root meaning of "nature," "to give birth." On Earth, nature launches life, located in cells, always embodied in individuals who are embedded in ecologies, and these ecologies undergo evolutionary history. Storied residence does not begin with humans. Prehuman nature is already historical. At long ranges, evolutionary ecosystems have been spinning stories on Earth that are never twice the same. Only in a short-range perception is there seasonal recurrence, recycling, homeostasis, dependable patterns, repeated order. Words such as "homeostasis," "conservation," "preservation," "stability," or even "species" and "ecosystem" are only penultimate in a metaphysics and an ethics of nature, although they are the words with which environmental philosophy was launched. The ultimate word is "history."

Humans awaken to their historical subjectivity in an already historically objective world. The genome is a historical genetic set, though without historical awareness. Plants and animals are historical beings objectively, although they do not know this subjectively. They do not know their own larger stories. Some animals have memories, precursors of historical consciousness. But animals make no considered reflection on the historical character of their own natures, much less of nature, or culture. Humans are the only species that can become historians, or biologists, or geographers, who can reflect over the history of life and its distribution over places over times. Humans have the opportunity to decipher natural history, as well as to remember their own cultural heritages.

The story of applied science has been one of learning to remake the world in human interests, to use it resourcefully; but the story of pure science has been one of discovering the nature of nature, learning the natural history of sources we inherit. Early science thought this nature to be lawlike and repetitive, but recent science has learned the evolutionary Earth history. And life is still arriving. Earth is not so much a syllogism with premises and conclusions as a text to be interpreted. Like the books in our libraries, the landscapes are to be read, palimpsests of the past. Deep time and deep history lie behind and around us. Biological science has cleverly detected much of the past; it reads the story out of the historically produced landscapes, as well as the records left in the biomolecular genetic coding. Bioscience understands what is going on at present in terms of that past.

But bioscience can present little theoretical argument explaining this history—little logic (tracking causes) by which there came to be a primeval Earth, Precambrian protozoans, Cambrian trilobites, Triassic dinosaurs, Eocene mammals, Pliocene primates, and Pleistocene *Homo sapiens*. No theory exists, with initial conditions, from which these events follow as conclusions. And bioscience can predict little of future natural history. To the contrary, evolutionary theory neither predicts outcomes nor, looking back after the outcomes are known, retrodicts why this course of events occurred rather than thousands of others equally consistent with the theory.

Whatever their repetitions, each locality, each ecosystem is unique. No two waterfalls, mountains, beaches, bays, creeks, or maple trees are identical. Sometimes the differences are trivial and, even when notable, we may want to abstract out covering laws or general trends. Sometimes we think that the idiographic elements, punctuating the nomothetic elements, are noise in the system. But they are not really noise, they are news, good news—because this historical and topographic variation elevates nature into a territory for storied residence.

Likewise, passing from science to ethics, philosophy can present no argument why these stories ought to have taken place. The best that I can give you is good stories, and hope that you can accept them for that. We may even come to love the epic, and prefer narrative over argument, over some theory by which natural history would follow as an inevitable conclusion, or even a statistically probable one. In that sense, neither science nor philosophy can present an argument that either necessitates or justifies the existence of each (or any!) of the five million species with which we coinhabit Earth. But we can begin to sketch nesting sets of marvelous tales. There is no logic with which to defend the existence of elephants or lotus flowers, squids or lemurs; but each enriches Earth's story. That alone is enough to justify their existence.

Persons in Cultural History

Natural history is necessary but not sufficient for cultural history; in non-human nature there are no persons. Persons live in cultural history, in which our humanity is constituted. Unlike coyotes or bats, humans are not just what they are by nature; they come into the world by nature quite unfinished and become what they become by culture. Being human is more than biochemistry, physiology, or ecology. Humans superimpose cultures on the wild nature out of which they once emerged. There is no greater drama than this long struggle (late in the evolutionary story) of the climb to humanity. If ever visitors from space were to file a report about Earth, volume one might cover the geological and biological phenomena, volume two the anthropological and sociological events.

Cultural history brings radical innovations. Information in wild nature travels intergenerationally on genes; information in culture travels neurally as persons are educated into transmissible cultures. The higher animals can learn limited behaviors from parents and conspecifics (as when birds, genetically disposed to migrate, imprint specific routes by following the flock). Still, animals do not form cumulative transmissible cultures. In nature, the coping skills are coded on chromosomes. In animals these may be expressed in the learning experiences of the phenotype. Offspring may model behavior after parents. But there are no longstanding and accumulating educational traditions, deliberately teaching the future generations. In culture, the skills are coded in craftsman's traditions, religious rituals, or technology manuals. Information acquired during an organism's lifetime is not transmitted genetically; the essence of culture is acquired information transmitted to the next generation.

Information transfer in culture can be several orders of magnitude faster and overleap genetic lines. A typical couple in the modern world may have only two or three children, who inherit their genetic information. But those children are educated by learning from dozens of friends and teachers, by reading hundreds of books, even, if they take a higher education, using libraries with tens of thousands of books, written by authors to whom they are genetically quite unrelated, who may have been dead for centuries. The children learn from newspapers and television programs with information coming from all over the world.

A human being develops typically in some one of ten thousand cultures, inheriting a heritage that is historically conditioned, perpetuated by language, conventionally established, using symbols with locally effective meanings. Cultures exchange ideas; sometimes people are reared at the crossroads of cultures; well-educated persons choose and criticize their cultures. Animals are what they are genetically, instinctively, environmentally, with few or no options in what they shall be at all, even if they do make some limited choices. They do not choose their careers, nor do they evaluate and espouse worldviews. Humans have myriads of lifestyle options, evidenced by their cultures; and each human makes daily decisions that affect his or her character.

Natural selection pressures are relaxed in culture; humans help each other out compassionately with charity; they insist on human rights. They study medicine to cure their diseases. The determinants of animal and plant behavior are never anthropological, political, economic, technological, scientific, philosophical, ethical, or religious. Animals do not hold elections and plan their environmental affairs; they do not make bulldozers to cut down tropical rainforests. They do not fund development projects through the World Bank, or contribute to funds to save the whales. They do not teach their religion to their children. They do not read or write articles wondering about their sense of place.

Humans evolved out of nature, and that can confuse people into saying that humans are just natural, since their origins were natural. But that is to fall into a "nothing but" fallacy (the genetic fallacy), which confuses what a thing now essentially is with what its historical origins once were. This fallacy cannot take emergence seriously. We are animals, but with culture, and that gives us an exodus from mere nature. Humans are not like beasts immersed in a niche. In a sense modern humans have no ordinary ecological niche at all. The average bite of food eaten in the United States has travelled over 1,200 miles, for instance. The energy warming one's home may be from coal, and from sunshine hundreds of millions of years ago, or from nuclear power, splitting atoms fused in ancient stars.

We could say that culture is the human niche, provided that we realize that the architectures of wild nature and of human culture are different. We face a dialectical truth; the thesis is nature, the antithesis is culture, and the synthesis is culture situated in nature, the two forming a home, a *domicile* (Greek: *oikos*, the root of ecology). That is our home territory.

With culture now, as before with nature, I cannot give a scientific argument explaining how humans arrived, some logic by which the Earth story eventuates in *Homo sapiens*. No theory exists from which we follow as conclusions. And, passing again to ethics, I can give no argument why humans ought to be here. But I can invite you to appreciate the story that lies in, with, and under the Earth we inhabit, to enrich the story by telling it. Perhaps you may even come to prefer that role to a lesser one by which humans are empirically necessary as outcomes of a determined process, or statistically probable as outcomes of stochastic process.

The mission of historians is to tell these stories of peoples on their landscapes. That will be volume two in the Earth story. But humans are also the only species who can tell the natural history, volume one. A narrative role might make the story, and the human role in it, seem meaningful, despite the lack of sufficient logical premises or theory with which to reach the human presence as a conclusion.

Persons in Natural History

Animals are wholly absorbed into their niches, but humans can stand apart from the world and consider themselves in relation to it. Humans are, in this sense, eccentric to the world. Humans are only part of the world in biological and ecological senses, but they are the only part of the world that can orient themselves with respect to a critical theory of it. Humans can begin to comprehend what comprehends them; in this lies their paradox and responsibility. They have a distinct metaphysical status because only they can do metaphysics. The metaphysics humans do may lead them to experiences of unity with nature, to responsible care for other species, but such unity paradoxically puts humans beyond the rest of nature, where nothing else is capable of such philosophical experience and ethical caring. When humans assert the value of the global Earth and its creatures they exceed the animal scope of value. Thus the human capacity for a transcending overview of the whole imposes strange duties.

Humans had relatively little biological role in naturally evolving ecosystems, nor have they today such roles, in the sense that were they subtracted from ancient African savannas or present Appalachian forests, those ecosystems would not be negatively affected. They are not some capstone species, pivotal in the ecosystems they inhabit. Humans are not important as predators or prey; they play little role in food chains or in regulating life cycles. They are a late add-on to the system; and, when they come, modify and disrupt their landscapes though they may, they hardly have an adapted fit analogously to the other species. Still, humans have a kind of eminence.

Humans reach vast ranges of valuational experience unshared with the animals. If I am hiking with my dog and come to an overlook, we may both pause and enjoy the rest, but I can look at the scenery. He can look, but not at the view. Perhaps he smells what escapes my detection. But the human considers the canine perception, although not undergoing it, enjoys the exercise, rest, and also the aesthetic experience, all in the midst of a worldview that sets a context of explanation for events in the view. The animal has only its own horizon; the human can have multiple horizons, even a global horizon. In that sense, animals have a habitat; but humans have a world. The human has only a limited understanding of what is going on, but this is less limited than that of the dog and that establishes an advanced value richness.

Humans should not "look down on" the "lower" orders of life, but humans alone can "look out over" or "look out for" other orders of life. They try to see where and who humans are, and comprehensively what others are. They have increasingly seen more of what there is to see, through the unfolding of art, literature, philosophy, natural history, science. In this looking out, humans are the form of life in which valuational capacities are most (but not exclusively) developed. This is advanced capacity based on accident of birth. Humans drew human genes; monkeys got monkey genes. But this is also a kind of superiority based on evolutionary achievement for which humans have to be grateful. It is no mark of intelligence or morality to refuse a value endowment.

Humans ought to be moral overseers. Humans have oversight; they are worldviewers—today more than they have ever been before. Mind forms an intelligible view of the whole and defends the stories of life in all their forms. Interhuman ethics has spent the last two millennia waking up to human dignity. As we turn to a new millennium, environmental ethics invites awakening to the greater story of which humans are a consummate part. From this, morality follows as a corollary—more than before. This takes humans past *resource* use to *residence* and constrains their policy, economics, science, technology. Such dwelling takes us past questions of management of places we own to moral questions about well-placed goodness in communities we inhabit, both biotic and cultural.

Humans can get "let in on" more value than any other kind of life. They can share the values of others and in this way be altruists. Animals have the capacity to see only from their niche; they have mere immanence. Humans can have a view from no niche, transcendence in immanence. Skeptics and relativists may say that humans just see from another niche, and it is certainly true that when humans appraise soil or timber as resources, they see from within their niche. But humans also see other niches and the ecosystems that sustain niches; they study warblers or see Earth from space. Humans are, if we may play on words, spectacular because they emerge to see the spectacle they are in. Humans ought to be spirit incarnate in place.

These cultural and moral options introduce the possibility of going astray, of making mistakes, of falling into tragedy. Humans make their own history, beyond biology, but this is not always to praise humans and belittle beasts. Humans have a superiority of opportunity, capacities unattained in animal life. Alas, however, the human capacity is forever unattained, brokenly attained. Much of the history that humans have made is sordid enough. There are good moments, noble achievements; but all too often humans stand condemned because they could and ought to have made for themselves better history than they did. If humans were biologically constrained in their history, if they could not do otherwise by nature, then they ought not be so censured. But humans are the beasts made to image God and fallen into sin—so the classical monotheist view of ourselves put it.

That sin is pride, and here we can enlarge the insight of the classical theologians. Traditional, anthropocentric ethics has tried to make humans the sole loci of value, transcending the otherwise valueless world. But this stunts humanity because it does not know genuine human transcendence—a transcending overview caring for the others. Humans, with their intrinsic worth, which features moral agency, double back on the world out of which they have emerged. Humans use their excellent rationality as a survival tool for defending the human form of life; they build culture, for better or for worse. But rationality, conscience, and emotions can do more than give integrity, excellence, self-esteem, and satisfaction, the various "virtues" we seek in our personal lives. These gifts ought to lead to a further transcendence that defends life in all its forms, to a stewardship over creation.

The Home Planet

This is the home planet. Views of Earth from space have given us an emerging vision of Earth and the place of human life on it. Leaving home, we discover how precious this Earth place is. The distance lends enchantment, brings us home again. The distance helps us to get real. We get put in our place. A virtually unanimous experience of the hundred or more astronauts, from many countries and cultures, is the awe experienced at the first sight of the whole Earth—its beauty, fertility, smallness in the abyss of space, light and warmth under the sun in surrounding darkness. The astronauts are earthstruck.

They are struck not only with the beauty and fertility of this, their home place, but with its fragility. The late-coming, moral species, *Homo sapiens*, has still more lately gained startling powers for the rebuilding and modification, including the degradation, of this home territory. Perhaps the four most critical issues that humans currently face are peace, population, development, and environment. Earth is the only planet with an ecology, the only planet that is a home; and, on Earth, home to several million species, humans are the only species of moral agents. Ethics has been almost entirely interhuman ethics, persons finding a way to relate morally to other persons. But ethics too is now troubled, anxious about the troubled planet.

We worried throughout most of this century, the first century of great world wars, that humans would destroy themselves in interhuman conflict. Fortunately, that fear has subsided. Unfortunately, it is rapidly being replaced by a new one. The worry for the next century is that humans may destroy their planet and themselves with it. We are turning a millennium. The challenge of the next millennium is to contain those cultures within the carrying capacity of the larger community of life in our biosphere. To continue the development pace of the last century for another millennium will produce sure disaster. If we humans are true to our species epithet, "the wise species" needs an Earth ethics, one that discovers a global sense of obligation to this whole inhabited planet.

We need to lift our horizons from living politically to living ecologically. Once the mark of an educated person could be summed up as *civitas*, the privileges, rights, responsibilities of citizenship. People ought to be good citizens, productive in their communities, leaders in business, the professions, government, church, education. That appropriated, and appropriately transmitted and developed, one's historical cultural lineage. But the mark of an educated person is today something more. It is not enough to be a good "citizen." It is not enough even to be "international" because neither of those terms have enough "nature" or "earthiness" in them. "Citizen" is only half the truth; the other half is that we are "residents" dwelling on landscapes. We are natives on Earth. Our responsibility to Earth might be thought the most remote of our responsibilities; it seems so grandiose and vague beside our concrete responsibilities to our children or next door neighbors. But not so: the other way round, it is the most fundamental, the most comprehensive of our responsibilities. We can hardly be responsible to anything more cosmic—unless perhaps to the divine Ground of Being.

An ethics about dirt? That is sometimes taken to be the ultimate *reductio ad absurdum* in environmental ethics. Put like that, we have to agree. A clod of dirt, just some earth (spelled with the lower case "e") has little or no intrinsic value, nor do we have duties to it. But when we go from earth to Earth, from dirt to the prolific planetary system of which it is part, perspectives change. Earth is Mother Earth, the womb out of which we come and which we never really leave. Dealing with an acre or two of real estate, perhaps even with hundreds or thousands of acres, we can think that this earth belongs to us. But on the global scale, Earth is not something we own. Earth does not belong to us; rather we belong to it. We belong on it. The question is not of property, but of community. The vision of human life we ought to seek is not that of maximum exploitation of Earth as a big property resource; it is that of valued residence in a created community of life. In that sense, an Earth ethics is not the *reductio ad absurdum* of silly and peripheral concern about squirrels and flowers, extrapolated to rocks and dirt. To the contrary, it is an urgent world vision. It is ultimate concern about our home territory.

When we say that Earth is *valuable* in a humanistic perspective, we mean that it is a resource for people who are *able* to *value* it instrumentally in myriads of ways. Earth is so valuable that humans have a right to an environment with integrity. But when we say that Earth is *valuable* in an ecological perspective, we mean that Earth is a place *able* to produce *value*, and has long been doing so as an evolutionary ecosystem. A late though remarkable product of the place-process is humans, who are also valuable—of value in an advanced way. When humans come, they find Earth often *valuable*, able to satisfy preferences, *able* to produce *valued experiences*. The subjective value events are a subset—perhaps a capstone subset but still a superposed subset—of the larger, objective production and support of natural values. Our responsibility is to find our role both benefiting from and conserving this community of life. Earth is indeed a storied place.

Home Places

Creating a global ethic, and epic, of place may seem to require too advanced an appreciation of natural history, too much scientific education, skills well past the capacities of most of Earth's residents. Only a minority of humans have had, or can have, such a global overview; most persons in their built environments live most of the time with little sense of evolutionary time, hardly even with a sense of ecological time over the decades of succession and change on landscapes. Most persons are not world travelers, not cosmopolitan citizens. Can we bring the sense of global residence, needed on planetary scales, also into focus at native range? What is the logic of residence in a more local territory?

Even though we think globally, we have to live locally. Residence in a local environment senses the recurrent universals particularly displayed in that place—the seasons, the soil, the wind, the rain, the sun, the biological powers regenerating the landscape, the native fauna and flora, the proportions of time and place. One enjoys these perennial givens exemplified in local areas. A person in his or her biography—as much as a scientist collecting herbarium specimens or peering through a microscope—is a detection device for catching something of the richness and integrity of what is taking place on the landscape he or she moves through. In this sense, every person can and ought to live geographically, optimizing one's experience of place.

An environmental philosophy does not want merely to abstract out laws and universals, if such there are, from all this drama of life, formulating some set of duties applicable across the whole. True, an environmental ethics demands a theory of the whole, an overview of Earth, but not a unity that destroys plurality. We also want an ethic colored by the agent's own history, cultural identification, personal experiences, and choices. The moral point of view must belong to a proper-named person who lives in a particular place. An ethic has to be instantiated in individuals, who live biographies, each with their local geography. Here, finally, intensely, intimately, we want to continue the logic of storied residence.

Ethics must be written in theory with universal intent, but the theory must permit and require ethics to be lived in practice in the first person singular. The logic of the home, the ecology, is finally narrative, and human life will not be a disembodied reason but a person organic in history in some particular time and place. In dialectic with what was claimed before, now we specify an ideal of humans inseparably entwined with particular times and places. If a holistic ethic is really to incorporate the whole story, it must systematically embed itself in historical eventfulness.

No two human careers are identical because over historical time cultures change and because genetic sets, choices, circumstances, and contingencies differ. Endlessly singular human subjects confront an endlessly singular environment. The practical, applied character of environmental ethics will have to recognize this singularity if it is to do justice to the form of the world and of human life in it. These story lines are not simply found; they must also be constructed. Humans want a storied residence in nature where the passage of time integrates past, present, and future in a meaningful career. This does not make nature mere instrument in a human story, any more than it makes the fellow persons in our drama merely tools. Rather, we have reached the richest possible concept of life in community, where all the actors contribute to storied residence.

Complementing now the global oversight considered earlier, we seek a local view, living participant stories in time and place. We must complement transcendence with immanence. Humans are not to be free from their environment but to be free in their environment. An environmental ethic needs roots in locality and in specific appreciation of natural kinds—not always rooted in a single place, but moving through particular regions and tracks of nature so as to make a narrative career. Life will include its adventures in natural history. Our role is to live out a space time, place time ethic, interpreting our landscapes and choosing our loves within those landscapes. We endorse the world with our signatures. This is, ultimately, what the evolutionary epic has been about, now consummated in environmental ethics, an adventure in the love of life and in increasing freedom in one's environment, entwined in biotic community.

Living Stories in Place

An ethic in the sense we are developing it is a creative act, not simply the discovery and following of rules and duties. It is writing an appropriate part of an ongoing story. In this dimension, your career is one of environmental interpretation. Life has, and ought to have, other dimensions: a family ethic, a business ethic, a community ethic; but the moral life is not complete without a sensitive approach to one's place—to the fauna, the flora, the geomorphology surrounding one's life. A person's role is to enrich his or her environment by appreciating it. A person's role is to be a moral geographer. Persons are consciousness *in place*; they always have a location. Persons are place become conscious of itself. In that sense, biography that is lived as historical geography is the only possible argument for life.

Note

This is an *apologia*; I am taking up a view of the world, and inviting others to share it. The style and format embody the argument, as existential as it is academic. I am searching for a sense of place. An ethic must be lived; humans are persons incarnate in the world; they are who they are where they are. The challenge in environmental philosophy, and the opportunity in relating philosophy to geography, is to get persons intelligently both naturalized and socialized. Only then will we realize the distinctive human genius, the promise and the power of the human spirit on Earth.

Index

A "n" after a number indicates that the reference occurs in a note.

About the Editors and Contributors

The Editors

Andrew Light is assistant professor of philosophy and environmental studies at the State University of New York at Binghamton.

Jonathan M. Smith is associate professor of geography at Texas A & M University, College Station.

The Contributors

Philip Brey is assistant professor in the department of philosophy at Twente University, Enschede, The Netherlands.

Lea Caragata is assistant professor in community development for the Faculty of Social Work at Wilfrid Laurier University, Canada.

James Dickinson is professor of sociology at Rider University.

David Glidden is professor of philosophy at the University of California at Riverside.

Sara Gottlieb is a faculty research assistant in the Maryland Sea Grant Extension program, University of Maryland, College Park.

Bruce Hannon is jubilee professor of the liberal arts and sciences at the University of Illinois, Urbana.

Ian Howard received his doctorate in philosophy from the University of Guelph, Ontario, and now lives in British Columbia, Canada.

Jeff Malpas is chair of the department of philosophy at Murdoch University, Perth, Western Australia and a Humboldt Research Fellow for the Philosophisches Seminar at Universität Heidelberg, Germany.

Katya Mandoki is professor of aesthetics and theory of design for the Division of Sciences and Arts for Design at Autonomous Metropolitan University, Xochimilco, Mexico.

Jonathan Maskit is visiting assistant professor of philosophy at Denison University, Ohio.

Bryan Norton is professor of public policy at the Georgia Institute of Technology, Atlanta.

David Roberts is a Ph.D. student in the department of philosophy at the University of Alberta, Edmonton, Canada.

Holmes Rolston III is university distinguished professor of philosophy at Colorado State University, Fort Collins.

Izhak Schnell is a lecturer in the geography department at Tel Aviv University, Israel.

David Wasserman is a research scholar at the Institute for Philosophy and Public Policy, School of Public Affairs, University of Maryland, College Park.

Mick Womersley is a trainee with Maryland Sea Grant, University of Maryland, College Park.

Style and Submission Guide
Philosophy and Geography

Philosophy and Geography is a peer reviewed annual with each volume focusing on a specific theme. Each issue addresses a topic of mutual interest to philosophers and geographers. The annual is edited by Andrew Light and Jonathan M. Smith, in consultation with the editorial board, and published by Rowman & Littlefield Publishers Inc. All material submitted to the editors is subjected to peer review by members of the editorial board, Associate Editors of the journal, or others, serving at the behest of the editors. (Themes and deadlines for upcoming issues are listed at the front of this volume.)

Length

Authors should aim for manuscripts of about 10,000 words, including the notes. If you are using a type size and font similar to the one in this letter, this will yield a double spaced manuscript of about thirty pages. Shorter and longer manuscripts will be considered, but only extraordinary circumstances will justify acceptance of manuscripts of less than 6,000 or more than 12,000 words. As this length includes the notes, authors are urged to limit notes to citation of works directly relevant to your argument.

Submission

Authors should send three copies of their manuscript to:

Andrew Light, Co-Editor
Philosophy and Geography
Department of Philosophy
SUNY Binghatmon
P.O. Box 6000
Binghamton, NY 13902-6000

Each copy must be single-sided, double-spaced, in a large type size, with wide margins (one inch margins preferred). Illustrations submitted with the final draft of accepted manuscripts must be camera ready. Please do not send bound manuscripts. Once an article has been accepted authors must submit a disk copy of their manuscript.

Notation Style

Authors should follow the *Chicago Manual of Style* and use American spelling. Notes will be printed as endnotes, and should be used judiciously. Do not use more than one note in a single sentence, and whenever possible group all of the citations and asides from an entire paragraph in a single note. Here are examples of some common citations:

Book: Clarence J. Glacken, *Traces on the Rhodian Shore* (Berkeley and Los Angeles: University of California Press, 1967), xiii.

Volume Chapter: Roger J. H. King, "Relativism and Moral Critique," in *The American Constitutional Experiment*, ed. David M. Speak and Creighton Peden (Lewiston, N. Y.: The Edwin Mellen Press, 1991), 145–64.

Journal: Eric Katz, "The Call of the Wild: The Struggle Against Domination and the Technological Fix," *Environmental Ethics*, 14, no. 3 (1992): 271.

Newspaper: Timothy Egan, "Unlikely Alliances Attack Property Rights Measures," *New York Times*, 15 May, 1995, A1.

The full citation should be given only in the first note in which a work is cited. A short form should be used in all subsequent notes. Short forms of the works cited above might appear as follows:

Book: Glacken, *Traces on the Rhodian Shore*, 372.

Volume Chapter: King, "Relativism and Moral Critique," 146.

Journal: Katz, "The Call of the Wild," 272

Newspaper: Egan, "Unlikely Alliances."

Originality

Authors are asked to submit a letter with their manuscript stating that the material in the manuscript has not been published elsewhere, that it is not presently under consideration by another publication, and that it will not be submitted for consideration by another publication until the author has been notified of the final decision of the editors of *Philosophy and Geography*. Upon publication, Rowman & Littlefield will possess the copyright.

Editorial Policy

Philosophy and Geography is on an accelerated production schedule. Papers accepted in February appear in print in the Fall of the same year (paperback in October, hard cover in November), and the editorial work occurs in a much shorter period. It may not be possible to return either the final copy-edited manuscript or the page proofs to the authors for approval. The editors will contact an author if there appears to be a need for an extensive, significant, or objectionable change to his or her manuscript, but they will not seek an author's consent to make minor alterations, additions, or deletions. These decisions are made at the editor's discretion.